ESSAYS ON RICARDIAN LITERATURE

J. A. BURROW

Essays on Ricardian Literature

In Honour of J. A. Burrow

EDITED BY
A. J. MINNIS
CHARLOTTE C. MORSE
THORLAC TURVILLE-PETRE

CLARENDON PRESS · OXFORD
1997

Oxford University Press, Great Clarendon Street, Oxford OX2 6DP
Oxford New York
Athens Auckland Bangkok Bogota Bombay
Buenos Aires Calcutta Cape Town Dar es Salaam
Delhi Florence Hong Kong Istanbul Karachi
Kuala Lumpur Madras Madrid Melbourne
Mexico City Nairobi Paris Singapore
Taipei Tokyo Toronto Warsaw
and associated companies in
Berlin Ibadan

Oxford is a trade mark of Oxford University Press

Published in the United States by
Oxford University Press Inc., New York

British Library Cataloguing in Publication Data
Data available

Library of Congress Cataloging in Publication Data
Data available

ISBN 0–19–818282–1

1 3 5 7 9 10 8 6 4 2

Typeset by
Pure Tech India Ltd, Pondicherry
Printed in Great Britain by
on acid-free paper by
Bookcraft Ltd,
Midsomer Norton, Somerset

Preface

THE title of this collection of essays by John Burrow's friends, colleagues, and former students echoes the title of a book which he published in 1971, *Ricardian Poetry*. That after nearly thirty years we should be going back to this classic account of four major writers of the later fourteenth century to re-examine many of the issues it raises (and, inevitably, to append some of our own) is sufficient indication of its central position within the history of the study of medieval English literature. If we could be said to have widened its parameters, it should at once be admitted that such amplification is fully in accord with the distinctive spirit of John Burrow's criticism—a generously inclusive spirit, which while ardently championing the special achievements of English texts is fully conscious of the trilingual culture in which they were produced, the Continental genres and conventions without which they would have been unthinkable, and the intellectual contexts to which they owe so much.

John Burrow's first book was *A Reading of 'Sir Gawain and the Green Knight'*, published in 1965 and still recommended to each new generation of students as the fundamental study of the poem. It is probably impossible for its first-time readers of today to appreciate how ground-breaking it was in its time. What a breath of fresh air it was to those of us who were students in the early 1960s, for whom medieval English studies seemed more preoccupied with the developments of $æ_1$ and $æ_2$ than with sensitive attention to the nuances of such an exotically crafted work. So quietly impeccable was Burrow's scholarship and his style so lucid (thanks to an art which hides art) that *Sir Gawain* was opened up, rendered accessible, in a way which never compromised its enticing complexity. We were stimulated to try out such reading methods on other works that had previously been seen as fit only for linguistic dissection.

Also published in 1965 was 'The Action of Langland's Second Vision', an article in which Burrow applied his formidable talents to an analysis of the work of that other great alliterative poet of the Ricardian Age. Again, this study is still essential reading for anyone who wishes to trace the complex contours of the structure of *Piers Plowman*. In fact, Burrow's study of Langland had begun some years previously, in 1957, with a paper on 'The Audience of *Piers Plowman*'. He has been heard to express some scepticism regarding the now-fashionable enthusiasm for studies of text-reception, and yet this early article is the very model of such an approach, in that it learnedly assesses the limited evidence available with discernment and caution. In his continuing studies of *Piers* he has concentrated on its shifting meaning and diverse poetic strategies, an emphasis that is quite marked in the four linked lectures that constitute *Langland's Fictions* (1993). Here is Burrow at his best, writing with that understated intensity which sets him apart.

Yet another study of *Piers*, 'Langland *Nel Mezzo del Cammin*' (1981), shows the importance of the tradition of 'the ages of man' for an understanding of the Dreamer's progress. This was followed by an analysis of Chaucer's dependence on the same tradition, published in Burrow's collection *Essays on Medieval Literature* (1984). These individual accounts presaged a book which appeared two years later, *The Ages of Man: A Study in Medieval Writing and Thought*. In it the different methods of dividing and distinguishing the crucial stages of human life are pursued, from their origins in classical writers to their widespread manifestations in medieval literature, both Latin and vernacular. Perhaps more than any other of Burrow's books, this monograph demonstrates how well his scholarship encapsulates the principle which Harry Bailly recommended to the Parson: *Beth fructuous, and that in litel space.*

Here as elsewhere Burrow writes as one who seeks to profess literature to the widest possible public, as a thorough professional who has no truck with the narrow professionalization which our trade has undergone in the past twenty years or so. He would *gladly teche* anyone who has the desire to learn, and will not use *o word* of coterie discourse *moore than was neede*, to borrow some terms from Chaucer's praise of the Clerk of Oxenford. These gifts make Burrow an obvious choice as an author of introductory guides and presenter of selected texts. In fewer than 150 pages, his 1982 book *Medieval Writers and their Work*—Burrow was ever one for the modest title—magisterially reviews a stunning array of literary genres, styles, and subject-matters, conveying a sense of their fascination instead of their difficulties. *English Verse 1300–1500* (1977) and *A Book of Middle English* (1992 and 1996) present collections of texts and discussions of language that well demonstrate his unerring instinct for the revealing extract, the definitive illustration, the telling phrase, the *mot juste*.... Here economy and insight pull together rather than apart. Little wonder that these anthologies have become standard course-books throughout the world.

In recent years Burrow's ability to arouse interest in neglected writers has been turned to excellent effect in a series of studies on Thomas Hoccleve. Beginning with his Gollancz lecture (delivered to the British Academy in 1982), Burrow has set about revealing Hoccleve as a poet of unusual significance both in the detail of his 'autobiographical' revelations and in the survival of major poems in holograph copies. The 1994 booklet on Hoccleve in the series 'Authors of the Middle Ages' cogently assembles the facts about his career, while a forthcoming edition of the *Complaint* and *Dialogue with a Friend* will show how the holograph sections of Hoccleve's *Series* may be used as a basis for restoring those parts of the text that survive only in the hands of other scribes.

John Burrow's work has had a deep and wholly beneficial influence on Middle English studies. He has taught us (*inter alia*) to appreciate the characteristics of medieval English style, and to respect the talent of certain writers who manipulated a comic view of human nature and self-depreciating attitudes to themselves as artists. He has also tried to teach us—a lesson we have learnt less well—that the profoundest insights can be expressed in a language that makes the argument abundantly clear and available to a wide and varied audience. The contributors offer this volume to a man who has embodied the very best in the English liberal humanist tradition—and who, despite the vagaries of *newefangelnesse*, continues to do so with that unassuming brilliance which is the hallmark of his words and works. We dedicate it with admiration and affection to the finest of teachers, the most supportive of colleagues, and the truest of friends.

Contents

List of Abbreviations

ANTS	Anglo-Norman Text Society
ChauR	*Chaucer Review*
CL	*Comparative Literature*
EETS ES, SS	Early English Text Society, Extra Series, Supplementary Series
ELH	*Journal of English Literary History*
ELN	*English Language Notes*
ES	*English Studies*
JEGP	*Journal of English and Germanic Philology*
LSE NS	*Leeds Studies in English*, New Series
MÆ	*Medium Ævum*
M&H	*Medievalia et Humanistica: Studies in Medieval and Renaissance Culture*
MED	*Middle English Dictionary*
MLN	*Modern Language Notes*
MLR	*Modern Language Review*
MP	*Modern Philology*
N&Q	*Notes and Queries*
NM	*Neuphilologische Mitteilungen*
OED	*Oxford English Dictionary*
PBA	*Proceedings of the British Academy*
PL	*Patrologia Latina*, ed. J.-P. Migne
PMLA	*Publications of the Modern Language Association of America*
RES NS	*Review of English Studies*, New Series
SAC	*Studies in the Age of Chaucer*
SATF	Société des anciens textes français
VQR	*Virginia Quarterly Review*
YLS	*Yearbook of Langland Studies*

Unless otherwise stated, references to the works of the Ricardian poets are to the following editions:

Geoffrey Chaucer: *The Riverside Chaucer*, gen. ed. Larry D. Benson (Boston, 1987; Oxford, 1988)

John Gower: *The Works of John Gower*, ed. G. C. Macaulay, 4 vols. (Oxford, 1899–1902)

William Langland: '*Piers Plowman*': *The A Version*, ed. George Kane (London, 1960); *The Vision of Piers Plowman: A Critical Edition of the B-Text*, ed. A. V. C. Schmidt, 2nd edn. (London, 1995); '*Piers Plowman' by William Langland: An Edition of the C-Text*, ed. Derek Pearsall (London, 1978)

The *Pearl/Gawain*-poet: *Cleanness*, ed. J. J. Anderson (Manchester, 1977); *Patience*, ed. J. J. Anderson (Manchester, 1969); *Pearl*, ed E. V. Gordon (Oxford, 1953); *Sir Gawain and the Green Knight*, ed. J. R. R. Tolkien and E. V. Gordon, 2nd edn. rev. N. Davis (Oxford, 1967)

Contributors

Colin Burrow is a Fellow of Gonville and Caius College and a University Lecturer in the English Faculty of the University of Cambridge. His publications include *Epic Romance: Homer to Milton* (1993) and *Edmund Spenser* (1996). He is currently editing Shakespeare's *Poems and Sonnets* for the Oxford Shakespeare.

Ardis Butterfield is a Lecturer in English at University College, London. She has published on Chaucer, Machaut, Froissart, the *Roman de Fauvel*, *Aucassin et Nicolette*, and on French motets and refrains, in journals such as *Studies in the Age of Chaucer, Medium Ævum, The Huntington Library Quarterly*, and *Plainsong and Medieval Music*. Her book, *Script and Performance: Poetry and Music in France 1200–1400*, is forthcoming with Cambridge University Press.

Richard Firth Green is a Professor in the English Department of the University of Western Ontario in Canada. He is the author of *Poets and Princepleasers: Literature and the English Court in the Later Middle Ages* (1980) and of numerous articles in such journals as *Speculum, Medium Ævum, Chaucer Review*, and *Studies in the Age of Chaucer*. He has recently completed work on a major study of literature and law in fourteenth-century England.

Nicholas R. Havely is a Senior Lecturer in the Department of English and Related Literature at the University of York. His publications include *Chaucer's Boccaccio* (1980), editions of *The House of Fame* (1994) and Chaucer's Dream Poems (1997, forthcoming), and articles and essays on Dante, Boccaccio, and Chaucer.

Nicolas Jacobs is a Fellow of Jesus College, Oxford. His publications include *Medieval English Romances* (with A. V. C. Schmidt, 1980), *The Later Versions of 'Sir Degarre'* (1995), and a variety of articles on Old and Middle English literature and the theory and practice of textual criticism. He now works chiefly on medieval Welsh Literature.

Carol M. Meale is Reader in Medieval Studies at the University of Bristol. She is editor of *Readings in Medieval English Romance* (1994), *Women and Literature in Britain, 1150–1500* (2nd edn., 1996), and, with Maldwyn Mills and Jennifer Fellows, *Romance in Medieval England* (1991); moreover, she has written a series of articles on late-medieval book production, patronage and reception.

Stephen Medcalf is Reader in English in the School of European Studies at the University of Sussex. He has written on Thomas Usk in *The Later Middle Ages* (1981), which he edited, and elsewhere. Outside the Middle Ages, his interests are in the nature and changes of consciousness, and parts of his work on T. S. Eliot's poetry as an anatomy of consciousness have already been published.

A. J. Minnis is Professor of Medieval Literature and Head of the Department of English and Related Literature at the University of York. His publications include *Medieval Theory of Authorship* (2nd edn., 1988), *Medieval Literary Theory and Criticism c.1100–c.1375: The Commentary Tradition* (with A.B. Scott, revised edn., 1991), *Chaucer's 'Boece' and the Medieval Tradition of Boethius* (1993), and *Oxford Guides to Chaucer: The Shorter Poems* (1995).

Gerald Morgan, formerly a Meyricke Exhibitioner at Jesus College, Oxford, is now a Senior Lecturer and Fellow of Trinity College, Dublin. He is the editor of *Chaucer's Franklin's Tale* (1980, reprinted 1992) and the author of *'Sir Gawain and the Green Knight' and the Idea of Righteousness* (1991).

Charlotte C. Morse is a Professor of English at Virginia Commonwealth University. Her publications include *The Pattern of Judgment in the 'Queste' and 'Cleanness'* (1976) and articles on Chaucer's Clerk's Tale and the story of Griselda. She is editing the Clerk's Tale for the Variorum Chaucer and has co-edited a memorial volume for Judson Boyce Allen, *The Uses of Manuscripts in Literary Studies* (1992).

Derek Pearsall became Gurney Professor of English at Harvard University in 1985 after teaching for twenty years at the University of York. Published work includes *John Lydgate* (1970), *Old English and Middle English Poetry* (1977), *'Piers Plowman': An Edition of the C-Text* (1978), a critical study of *The Canterbury Tales* (1985), and *The Life of Geoffrey Chaucer: A Critical Biography* (1992).

A.G. Rigg is a Professor at the Centre for Medieval Studies in the University of Toronto. His publications are principally on Medieval Latin—including *The Poems of Walter of Wimborne* (1978), *Gawain on Marriage: The 'De coniuge non ducenda'* (1986), and *A History of Anglo-Latin Literature 1066–1422* (1992) — but also on *Piers Plowman* (the Z-version) and Thomas Hoccleve.

John Scattergood is Professor of Medieval and Renaissance English at Trinity College, Dublin. His most recent book is *Reading the Past: Essays on Medieval and Renaissance Literature* (1996). A revised edition of his *John Skelton: The Complete English Poems* is due to appear soon.

A.C. Spearing is William R. Kenan Professor of English at the University of Virginia and a Fellow of Queen's College, Cambridge. His publications include *Medieval to Renaissance in English Poetry* (1985), *Readings in Medieval Poetry* (1987), and *The Medieval Poet as Voyeur: Looking and Listening in Medieval Love-Narratives* (1993).

Thorlac Turville-Petre is Professor of Medieval English Literature at the University of Nottingham. His publications include *England the Nation: Language, Literature and National Identity 1290–1340* (1996) and (with J. A. Burrow) *A Book of Middle English* (rev. edn., 1996).

A Ricardian 'I': The Narrator of 'Troilus and Criseyde'

A. C. SPEARING

It seems scarcely believable that *Troilus and Criseyde* could once have been discussed without reference to 'the narrator', yet this now indispensable figure was invented less than fifty years ago.[1] In 1915 Kittredge, identifying in *The Book of the Duchess* a fictional narrator who 'is not Geoffrey Chaucer', nevertheless continued to refer to the 'I' of *Troilus* simply as 'Chaucer'. That practice was followed in other standard studies. Root wrote of 'Chaucer's assumed ignorance' and of how the poet, like Troilus, was 'captivated' by Criseyde's 'loveliness and charm'. Lowes declared that 'Criseyde, though frail, is dear' to Chaucer and that the poem ends with an unparalleled 'access of personal feeling'—the poet's own. Lewis wrote an influential chapter on *Troilus* without once mentioning the narrator, who is equally absent from a chapter by Coghill.[2] All this changed in the 1950s. In 1954 E. Talbot Donaldson published his elegant paper arguing that the 'I' of the General Prologue is a fictional persona who is 'the victim of the poet's pervasive—not merely sporadic—irony'.[3] This insight was soon applied to the 'I' of *Troilus*. In a series of further publications,

---

[1] The one exception, Henry Lüdeke, *Die Funktionen des Erzählers in Chaucers epischer Dichtung* (Halle, 1928), had no immediate influence in the English-speaking world.

[2] George Lyman Kittredge, *Chaucer and his Poetry* (Cambridge, Mass., 1915), 50; Robert Kilburn Root, *The Poetry of Chaucer* (Cambridge, Mass., 1922), 111–12; John Livingston Lowes, *Geoffrey Chaucer* (Oxford, 1934), 140, 152–3; C. S. Lewis, *The Allegory of Love* (Oxford, 1936), ch. 4; Nevill Coghill, *The Poet Chaucer* (London, 1949), ch. 6.

[3] 'Chaucer the Pilgrim', *PMLA* 69 (1954), 928–36, here quoted from Donaldson's *Speaking of Chaucer* (London, 1970), 3. Ralph Baldwin, *The Unity of the 'Canterbury Tales'* (Copenhagen, 1955), distinguished between Chaucer the Pilgrim with his 'bias and inadequacies' and Chaucer the Poet with his 'unlimited knowledge' (p. 68); but his study had far less impact than Donaldson's.

Donaldson himself made this fallible persona responsible for many of the features that earlier critics had attributed to the poet—the captivation with Criseyde's 'loveliness and charm' and the 'nervous breakdown in poetry' manifested in what Lowes had called 'the tumultuous hitherings and thitherings' of the conclusion.[4] Other critics, many to become leading figures in Chaucer studies, were working along similar lines. In 1957 Morton W. Bloomfield, noting a debt to Donaldson, wrote that 'Chaucer takes pains to create himself as a character in his poem and also to dissociate this character continually from his story',[5] and Charles Muscatine, while not centrally concerned with the narrator, gave him a capital 'N', saw him as descended from 'the first person Narrators of the dream visions', and referred to his 'apparent obtuseness'.[6] The following year brought the first systematic unfolding of the implications of Donaldson's theory for *Troilus*: Robert M. Jordan, arguing that Bloomfield understressed 'the distinction between the narrator's point of view and that of the poet', claimed that 'The character through whose consciousness we witness the events of *Troilus and Criseyde* is more elusive but no less palpable than the characters he tells about', and even proposed that 'the real subject of the poem is not Troilus but the narrator'.[7]

Thus a theory already widespread in the criticism of more recent literature, that of the unreliable narratorial persona through whose words the author's concealed meaning must be discerned,[8] came to play the central part in *Troilus* interpretation that it has held ever since, especially in North America. Some critics indeed continued to refer to the poem's 'I' as 'Chaucer' or 'the poet': among these, to mention three of otherwise strikingly dissimilar views, are P. M.

---

[4] *Chaucer's Poetry*, ed. E. T. Donaldson, 2nd edn. (New York, 1975), 1129–44 (1st pub. 1958); 'The Ending of Chaucer's *Troilus*', in Arthur Brown and Peter Foote (eds.), *Early English and Norse Studies Presented to Hugh Smith* (London, 1963), 26–45; 'Criseide and her Narrator', in *Speaking of Chaucer*, 65–83. Donaldson quotation from *Speaking of Chaucer*, 91; Lowes quotation from *Geoffrey Chaucer*, 153.

[5] 'Distance and Predestination in *Troilus and Criseyde*', PMLA 72 (1957), 14–26 (pp. 14 n. 1 and 21–2).

[6] *Chaucer and the French Tradition* (Berkeley and Los Angeles, 1957), 135–6.

[7] 'The Narrator in Chaucer's *Troilus*', ELH 25 (1958), 237–57 (pp. 237–8, 249). In *Chaucer and the Shape of Creation* (Cambridge, Mass., 1967), ch. 4, Jordan, influenced by Bronson (see n. 18 below), modified this view of the narrator.

[8] See e.g. Wayne C. Booth, *The Rhetoric of Fiction* (Chicago, 1961), ch. 12; Robert C. Elliott, *The Literary Persona* (Chicago, 1982).

Kean, Stephen Knight, and D. W. Robertson.[9] Others adopted the term 'narrator' to refer not to a fictional being but to the poet, at least in the sense of 'the author thought of as internal to the work'.[10] But by 1970 it could be written of Donaldson's 'Chaucer the Pilgrim' that 'The concept of the Chaucerian *persona* developed in this seminal essay is second nature to many Chaucerian scholars today';[11] and most subsequent criticism has simply taken for granted that in *Troilus* 'I' refers to a fictive individual clearly separable from the poet and variously characterized as 'naïve', 'glib', 'obtuse', 'imperceptive', 'fallible', 'self-deceived', 'unreliable', and 'wayward'. A recent 39-page chapter on *Troilus* contains over 130 references to 'the narrator', occasionally in forms such as 'our naïve narrator', 'the detached narrator', 'Our "objective" narrator', the 'earnest but erring narrator', and 'our self-styled objective narrator'; and the wretched fellow is denounced as 'deluded', 'confused', 'foolish', 'presumptuous', 'condescending', 'superior', 'blithely unaware', 'frantic', and 'blind'.[12]

My first encounter with the persona theory of *Troilus* was as a student in the 1950s; in which version I no longer recall. Like others I had found Chaucer's poem enthralling while being baffled by its seeming uncertainties of tone and viewpoint; and the persona theory promised immediate clarification. Now I could see how to position myself as reader, enjoying the poet's irony at the expense of his narrator's misunderstandings; and some years later I was writing confidently of how 'The idiot-dreamer of *The Book of the Duchess* develops into the idiot-historian of *Troilus and Criseyde*'.[13] In time, though, I became increasingly dissatisfied with this bold resolution of the poem's difficulties. Few would deny that

[9] P. M. Kean, *Chaucer and the Making of English Poetry*, vol. i (London, 1972), ch. 4; Stephen Knight, *Geoffrey Chaucer* (Oxford, 1986), ch. 2; D. W. Robertson, *A Preface to Chaucer* (Princeton, 1963), 472–502.

[10] E.g. John F. Ganim, *Style and Consciousness in Middle English Narrative* (Princeton, 1983), ch. 3; Dieter Mehl, *Geoffrey Chaucer: An Introduction to his Narrative Poetry* (Cambridge, 1986), ch. 6. Quotation from Robert M. Durling, *The Figure of the Poet in Renaissance Epic* (Cambridge, Mass., 1965), 3.

[11] Ann Chalmers Watts, 'Chaucerian Selves—Especially Two Serious Ones', *ChauR* 4 (1969–70), 229–41 (p. 229 n. 3).

[12] I refer to Lisa J. Kiser, *Truth and Textuality in Chaucer's Poetry* (Hanover, NH, 1991), borrowing from my review in *M&H* NS 20 (1994), 228–33. The epithets in the previous sentence come from a variety of sources.

[13] Maurice Hussey, A. C. Spearing, and James Winny, *An Introduction to Chaucer* (Cambridge, 1965), 121.

Troilus has an engagingly human mode of story-telling, yet the theory that converts this vague effect into a single unreliable narrator has in practice been used to simplify the poem—to resolve ambiguity, to stabilize what in reading feels mobile, to claim knowability for what feels obscure, and often to reduce a work that in his Retraction Chaucer listed first among those requiring forgiveness to rigid orthodoxy and ungenerous antifeminism. One critic writes that 'It is to the narrator that we must turn...if we are to understand the poem's ambiguous evaluation of the nature, function, and worth of poetry'; another that 'the narrator plays a role of major importance in providing the clue to the significance of the ambiguities of its surface structure'; a third that 'At the end, Chaucer as narrator arrives at Augustine's position about the tears he had shed over Dido, and attains the wisdom of Peter of Blois.'[14] Carolyn Dinshaw shows how the 'concept of an omniscient poet' in Troilus, equally present in Robertson's alleged historicism and in Donaldson's apparently opposing formalism, underpins a 'concern to authorize, legitimate, and, finally, delimit meanings'.[15] Yet she too takes for granted the concept of 'the narrator', one which surely belongs to the very project she diagnoses; for 'omniscient poet' and 'unreliable narrator' form an interdependent pair, functioning as an interpretative mechanism to produce univalent meaning; only by dissolving that binary could Dinshaw truly escape from what she calls 'reading like a man'.

Underlying many readings of Troilus in these terms is a wish not just to delimit meaning but to safeguard the poem's perfection by shifting apparent faults to a narrator whose unreliability is part of the omniscient—and omnipotent—poet's fully achieved plan. This emerges clearly from one of the most carefully argued persona readings, by Monica E. McAlpine. She warns against the 'disdainful superiority' towards the narrator exemplified in the epithets quoted above; for her his 'most significant deficiency' is 'the

[14] Donald E. Rowe, O Love O Charite! Contraries Harmonized in Chaucer's 'Troilus' (Carbondale, Ill., 1976), 153; Bernard F. Huppé, 'The Unlikely Narrator: The Narrative Strategy of the Troilus', in John P. Hermann and John J. Burke (eds.), Signs and Symbols in Chaucer's Poetry (University, Ala., 1981), 179–94 (p. 194); Thomas H. Bestul, 'Chaucer's Troilus and Criseyde: The Passionate Epic and its Narrator', ChauR 14 (1979–80), 366–78 (p. 375). Cf. Mehl, Geoffrey Chaucer, 83: 'Many studies of the poem only express the understandable desire of readers and critics for a simple reading that resolves all the contradictory elements.'
[15] Chaucer's Sexual Poetics (Madison, 1989), 37.

absence of a unifying vision', and she adds that 'A narrator who goes through a process of development is necessarily a fallible narrator; a capacity for change is also...a capacity for imperfection'.[16] The unspoken implication, that the poet and his poem are free of this fallibility and capacity for imperfection, has only to be stated for its dubiousness to be apparent. The greatest poets are fallible, and some of the greatest works lay no claim to perfection. Dante and Racine, perhaps, seek and achieve the nearest to a perfect art that lies within human reach, but would it make sense to judge *King Lear* in these term—a poetic drama whose greatness depends on its very imperfection, if assessed by normal moral and aesthetic standards? *Troilus* is a genuinely exploratory poem, one in which Chaucer had to struggle to find ways to give sufficient value to a merely human and ultimately betrayed love; and even after revision that struggle remained real, not a mere fiction enacted by a fallible narrator. Elizabeth Salter suggests that 'the very magnitude of what Chaucer attempted to do in *Troilus* was the guarantee of some measure of failure';[17] if so, he resembles some of the greatest poets of his own and other ages.

I am not of course the first to feel dissatisfied with the consequences of an approach that initially seemed so promising. As early as 1960, Bertrand H. Bronson, deploring the 'rash of talk about Chaucer's *persona*', saw his poetic self-representation as more like the 'self-mockery' found in friendly conversation.[18] In 1966 Salter interpreted *Troilus*' first-person discourse as a record of Chaucer's own 'conflicting purposes, unresolved difficulties' in responding to Boccaccio's *Filostrato*. She was later to mount an explicit critique of the persona theory for its neglect of *Troilus*' concern with 'the pressing problems of the poet himself'; in 1966, in her intense engagement with a 'poem which forbids the easy use of terms such as "unity", "consistency"', that theory was simply swept aside.[19] Dieter Mehl emphasizes the variety of the poem's

---

[16] *The Genre of 'Troilus and Criseyde'* (Ithaca, NY, 1978), 133, 41, 124.

[17] 'Troilus and Criseyde: A Reconsideration' (first pub. 1966), here quoted from her *English and International*, ed. Derek Pearsall and Nicolette Zeeman (Cambridge, 1988), 215–30 (p. 216).

[18] *In Search of Chaucer* (Toronto, 1960), 26, 30.

[19] 'Troilus and Criseyde: A Reconsideration' and 'Troilus and Criseyde: Poet and Narrator' (first pub. 1982), quoted from *English and International*, 231–8; quotations from 216, 230, 233.

narrative stances and that variety's value in inciting sympathetic participation and individual response among its audience.[20] Derek Brewer associates the variety with the multiple, often inconsistent viewpoints of oral poetry and Gothic painting, and suggests that the 'multiplicity of narrative points of view almost becomes...a multiplicity of narrators'.[21] More theoretically developed interrogations of the persona theory have come from David Lawton and Robert Edwards, who both propose that 'the narrator is not an object of imitation, much like the story he tells, but part of the narrative code'.[22] There have been other sceptics, too, and Donaldson himself came to question the constrictive consequences of his liberating insight, and to believe that 'many of us, myself included, have been too anxious to separate the narrator from the poet Chaucer'.[23]

Why then resurrect a question that forty years of criticism would seem to have buried? One reason is the absence of dialogue from much existing discussion. Whether the 'I' of *Troilus* is or is not thought to label an unreliable narrator must substantially affect one's understanding of the whole poem; yet studies questioning the validity of the persona theory have largely fallen on deaf ears, and what might be called 'normal' Chaucer criticism (on the analogy of Kuhn's 'normal science') has proceeded as if it were an unshakable axiom. At the same time, some of the most perceptive developments of this theory have also been disregarded and had virtually no influence on discussion. Among these I include Geoffrey Shepherd's account of Chaucerian story-telling as a stylization of 'the ephemeralness of a living entertainment and the mobility of actual delivery',[24] and John Lawlor's reading of the narrator's 'growing and involuntary involvement' in a story that deflects him from his 'initial poise' as testimony to the unbearable yet unalterable pain-

---

[20] 'The Audience of Chaucer's *Troilus and Criseyde*', in Beryl Rowland (ed.), *Chaucer and Middle English Studies in Honour of Rossell Hope Robbins* (London, 1974), 173–89, and Mehl's *Geoffrey Chaucer*, ch. 6.

[21] 'The Reconstruction of Chaucer', *SAC Proceedings*, No. 1, 1984 (1985), 3–19 (p. 14).

[22] David Lawton, *Chaucer's Narrators* (Cambridge, 1985); quotation from Robert R. Edwards, *The Dream of Chaucer* (Durham, NC, 1989), 43; note also the implications of Lawton's 'The Subject of *Piers Plowman*', *YLS 1* (1987), 1–30.

[23] *The Swan at the Well* (New Haven, 1985), 128.

[24] 'Troilus and Criseyde', in D. S. Brewer (ed.), *Chaucer and Chaucerians* (London, 1966), 65–87 (p. 72).

fulness of Chaucer's story.[25] Literary interpretation is not a science, and we cannot hope for the collaborative progress that comes from testing hypotheses, discarding those proved false, and developing those with strongest explanatory power; but it is hard to survey discussion of the 'I' of *Troilus* since the 1950s without feeling that we could collectively have done a better job in thinking about this issue. Hence my reconsideration of the first person in Chaucer's greatest poem: a reconsideration aimed not at a wholly new reading but, in part, at recovering and reassessing what others have written.[26] 'Tempest thee noght al croked to redresse' is sound Chaucerian advice, and so is 'Be war, and keep thy nekke-boon from iren!'; but I may at least be a stone for others to sharpen their carving instruments.

There can be small need by now to argue for the importance of narratorial discourse in *Troilus* or to call attention to apparent indications of its unreliability. Taking these as given, I begin by examining two other aspects of the poem: one that makes it hard to see 'the narrator' as unreliable and another that complicates the possibility of distinguishing a narratorial element at all. I start with the former. Most critics interested in the narrator have focused on his alleged deficiencies in sensibility and in wisdom, seeing him as naïvely idealistic in responding to the characters' emotions and foolish in failing to relate those emotions to a larger philosophical scheme. 'Narrator' draws its meaning from opposition to 'poet' or 'author'; this may be why less attention has been given to the places, including the proems to Books I–IV, the quasi-proem to Book V, and passages such as II. 50–5 and III. 1807–13, where 'I' presents himself as author, and indeed specifically as poet—not a mere entertainer or 'maker', but the vessel of a higher inspiration. This conception of the vernacular poet was new in fourteenth-century England: Chaucer himself was the first English writer to adopt an idea already emergent in Italian and French—that a vernacular writer could be a modern classic, the exponent of a poetic vocation comparable to that of the great masters of antiquity.[27] Near the end of *Troilus* this idea is explicitly formulated,

[25] *Chaucer* (London, 1968), 64–5.

[26] Space forbids a comprehensive survey of existing criticism; in particular I omit consideration of the relation of the 'I' of Chaucer's writing to the living Chaucer's social and political situation.

[27] See e.g. Glending Olson, 'Making and Poetry in the Age of Chaucer', *CL* 31 (1979), 272–90, and Kevin Brownlee, *Poetic Identity in Guillaume de Machaut*

when the 'I' addresses not the sources of inspiration but the book
which is their product, urging it,

> no makyng thow n'envie,
> But subgit be to alle poesye;
> And kis the steppes where as thow seest pace
> Virgile, Ovide, Omer, Lucan, and Stace. (V. 1789–92)

Chaucer, temperamentally closer to Machaut than to Dante, could
never commit himself completely to an Italian exaltation of the
vernacular poet, and so pride and humility coincide, as do inspiration and imitation: the book is to vie proudly with no *makyng*, no
mere vernacular entertainment, but to subject itself humbly to
poesye, the body of lasting classical achievement. To claim inspiration is to follow those who have done so in the past and to declare
inability to match one's subject-matter without such assistance:

> Thesiphone, *thow help me* for t'endite
> Thise woful vers, that wepen as I write....
> To the clepe I, thow goddesse of torment,
> Thow cruwel Furie, sorwynge evere in peyne,
> *Help me.* (I. 6–10)

Whatever Chaucer's misgivings, the style of such self-presenta-
tions—elevated, learnedly allusive, elaborately figured, difficult
and yet mellifluous, with words and word-order divergent from
those native to English—seems designed precisely to authenticate
the poetic vocation they assert.

How can the 'I' of such passages be thought to refer to an
unreliable narrator? Adherents of the persona theory generally
disregard them altogether or attribute them arbitrarily to 'poet'
rather than 'narrator';[28] and the few brave attempts to do otherwise are instructive in their very implausibility. McAlpine, recognizing the need to apply to the whole poem her view of it as 'an
extended speech by the [unreliable] narrator', claims that Book II's
opening lines 'dramatize the narrator's lack of feeling as he
describes Troilus' sorrow in tired Petrarchan conceits and then

(Madison, 1984), ch. 1. On the conspicuous absence of any such conception of the
'I' as poet, or even as writer, from the works of a major Ricardian contemporary, see
A. C. Spearing, 'Poetic Identity', in Derek Brewer and Jonathan Gibson (eds.), *A
Companion to the Gawain-Poet* (Cambridge, 1997), 31–51.

[28] Jordan even states that the narrator is 'emphatically *not* an "auctour" or poet'
('The Narrator in Chaucer's *Troilus*', 238).

flatly explicates his own metaphors'[29] but it is hard to see how the images of the boat as the poet's skill and the sea as 'the tempestous matere | Of disespeir' (II. 5–6) could have been perceived as 'tired Petrarchan conceits' when they had never before been used in English and there is no evidence that any Englishman other than Chaucer knew Petrarch's poetry. Donald W. Rowe similarly regards the proem to Book III, where Chaucer's poetic style reaches its height in a magnificently sustained apostrophe to Venus, as indicating 'the narrator's confusion and lack of control'; and he considers the epilogue to reveal the narrator's 'inadequate, ambiguous, and often comic' efforts 'to deal with the poem he has created'.[30] Even critics unimpressed by the verbal grandeur of places where the 'I' of *Troilus* figures as a poet need to acknowledge that they represent a claim to inspiration and a correspondingly elevated style hitherto unknown in English, except in a few passages by Chaucer himself. Could he possibly have expected them to be understood as revealing a narrator's incompetence and confusion? The elevated 'poetic' style may occasionally be touched with a playfulness reflecting Chaucer's reservations about its absolute validity:

> The dayes honour, and the hevenes yë,
> The nyghtes foo—al this clepe I the sonne. (II. 904–5)

Even in such moments, though, he must also have felt the need to explicate a metaphorical richness unfamiliar to his audience. The logical conclusion of attempts to read the poem's most exalted poetry as the product of an unreliable narrator is that the text we have is a *Thopas*-like travesty produced by a fictional parody of a poet, and that Chaucer's real *Troilus* exists only in the minds of enlightened twentieth-century readers.[31]

Not all the passages where 'I' features as the poem's composer involve these high claims to inspiration. In many he is no more than an unobtrusive compiler or organizer of existing material, as

[29] *Genre*, 36, 126. Winthrop Wetherbee, *Chaucer and the Poets* (Ithaca, NY, 1984), 147–8, reads the same lines as revealing the narrator's 'lack of control' and 'utter confusion'.

[30] *O Love O Charite!*, 159, 164.

[31] Cf. Derek Pearsall, *The Life of Geoffrey Chaucer* (Oxford, 1992), 86: 'The cult of the persona has . . . become a technique for systematically ironizing the text and appropriating it to the service of particular kinds of programmatic interpretation.'

in first-person clauses like these from Book IV: 'as I shal yow devyse' (238, 735); 'which that I yow devyse' (259); 'and seyde as I shall telle' (686); 'I shal yow tellen soone' (1127); 'As I seyde erst' (1134). Such clauses clarify narrative structure without evoking either an inspired poet or an unreliable narrator. They often give the second person equal emphasis to the first, summoning us into the poem's fictional space to attend to its events. Perhaps such phrases do not relate to the 'I' *as poet* at all; yet they merge readily into longer metanarrative passages in which the first person discusses problems of poetic composition. In Book I after a four-stanza digression concerning love's power comes a stanza recalling the poet's obligation to keep to the point, and using the technical terms *collateral* and *matere*:

> But for to tellen forth in special
> Of this kynges sone of which I tolde,
> And leten other thing collateral,
> Of hym thenke I my tale forth to holde,
> Both of his joie and of his cares colde;
> And al his werk, as touching this matere,
> For I it gan, I wol therto refere. (I. 260–6)

A little later, introducing Troilus' song, allegedly translated from 'myn auctour called Lollius' (I. 394), 'I' mentions the two traditional modes of translation, by *sentence* and by *word*, and ends with an expanded 'managerial' locution referring specifically to his verse medium: 'and whoso list it here, I Loo, next this vers he may it fynden here' (398–9). Similar expansions defining the 'I' not just as story-teller but specifically as writer occur elsewhere:

> And what she thoughte somwhat shal I write,
> As to myn auctour listeth for t'endite (II. 699–700)

or

> His resons, as I may my rymes holde,
> I yow wol telle, as techen bokes olde. (III. 90–1)

First-person passages of this kind, far from claiming inspiration, may disclaim it, as in elaborations of the inexpressibility-topos like this:

> Who koude telle aright or ful discryve
> His wo, his pleynt, his langour, and his pyne?
> Naught alle the men that han or ben on lyve.

Thow, redere, maist thiself ful wel devyne
That swich a wo my wit kan nat diffyne;
On ydel for to write it sholde I swynke,
Whan that my wit is wery it to thynke. (V. 267–73)

Do we come closer here to an unreliable narratorial persona? So it might seem, yet the next stanza beautifully displays Chaucer's elevated style in a *chronographia*:

On hevene yet the sterres weren seene,
Although ful pale ywoxen was the moone,
And whiten gan the orisonte shene. (V. 274–6)

Read separately, the two stanzas seem expressions of two different first persons; put together, the first becomes rhetorical self-depre-ciation designed not to reveal an incompetent narrator but to emphasize the intensity of Troilus' suffering and invite readers to share in imagining it.

As these examples illustrate, passages where 'I' is the poem's writer tend to introduce concepts from medieval *ars poetica*. When John Burrow remarks how few 'fragments of technical literary vocabulary' occur in Ricardian poetry, he perhaps exaggerates where Chaucer is concerned; *Troilus* surely includes terminology adequate to analyse most of its own poetic technique. But Burrow valuably proceeds to explain one such technical term used by Chaucer: *poynte*, meaning describe in detail.[32] It would be 'a long thyng for to here', 'I' observes, if he were to *poynte* 'every word, or soonde, or look, or cheere' of someone in Troilus' dis-tracted condition (III. 491–7). The extraordinary detail in which Chaucer recounts the development of the love affair is, as Burrow observes, quite uncharacteristic of earlier English romances. The detail expands in Books II and III, and it seems likely that this intensified 'pointing' in the representation of the lovers' private behaviour and inner lives arose from Chaucer's imaginative engagement with Boccaccio's story as he retold it, not necessarily from any preconceived plan. He was proud of this technical inno-vation and eager to call attention to it—

I have naught herd it don er this
In story non, ne no man here, I wene (III. 498–9)

---

[32] *Ricardian Poetry* (London, 1971), 69 and 69–72.

—but he could well have been worried by the amplified scale of the resultant scenes and concerned to reassure his audience that he had not forgotten the main narrative outline. Many passages of poetic self-presentation, easily taken to indicate the naïve enthusiasm or incompetence of a fallible narrator, are probably better understood in this light. The second half of Book II is especially full of first-person refusals to describe, promises of brevity, and summaries of what will not be 'pointed':

> What sholde I lenger sermoun of it holde?
> As ye han herd byfore, al he hym tolde (965–6)
>
> Of which to telle in short is myn entente
> Th'effect, as fer as I kan understonde (1219–20)
>
> What sholde I make of this a long sermoun? (1299)
>
> And al this thyng he tolde hym, word and ende (1495)

or simply 'To telle in short...' (1266, 1493). At 1541 begins a whole stanza of *occupatio*—'What nedeth yow to tellen...'—soon followed by an emphatic promise of brevity, including another technical term:

> But fle we now prolixitee best is,
> For love of God, and lat us faste go
> Right to th'effect, withouten tales mo. (1564–6)

Book III contains similar first-person intrusions.

This large metanarrative element might be expected to have a distancing effect, deflecting attention from the love-story to its teller's self-consciousness; but in practice this is not so. In Book II, where Chaucer diverges from Boccaccio by entering more deeply into Criseyde's inner life, the difficulty and interest of imagining and of representation seem scarcely distinguishable, and the third-person treatment of that life is deeply intertwined ('plited ...in many fold') with first-person references to the compositional process:

> And, Lord! So she gan in hire thought argue
> In this matere of which I have yow told,
> And what to doone best were, and what eschue,
> That plited she ful ofte in many fold.
> Now was hire herte warm, now was it cold;
> And what she thoughte somwhat shal I write,
> As to myn auctour listeth for t'endite. (II. 694–700)

Later the same applies to Troilus' feelings. Sympathy with the bashfulness that deprives him of words merges into engagement in the task of finding words, one that is the poet's as well as the protagonist's:

> But Lord, so he wex sodeynliche red,
> And sire, his lessoun, that he wende konne
> To preyen hire, is thorugh his wit ironne...

> But whan his shame gan somwhat to passe,
> His resons, as I may my rymes holde,
> I yow wol telle, as techen bokes olde. (III. 82–4, 89–91)

The task is ours too. 'I' and 'yow' are constantly juxtaposed, and many critics, whatever their view of 'the narrator', have noted the narratorial method's effectiveness in making us sympathetic participants in the story and contributors to its meaning.[33]

On numerous much-discussed occasions the poem's 'I' conveys ignorance or uncertainty, usually about Criseyde:

> Nought list myn auctour fully to declare
> What that she thoughte whan he seyde so. (III. 575–6)

> Kan I naught seyn, for she bad hym nought rise,
> If sorwe it putte out of hire remembraunce,
> Or elles that she took it in the wise
> Of dewete, as for his observaunce. (III. 967–70)

> But trewely, I kan nat telle hire age. (V. 826)

> Men seyn—I not—that she yaf hym hire herte. (V. 1050)

Whatever, if anything, we may feel about the narrator on such occasions, they summon our imaginations to fill the gaps thereby created in the narrative. Sometimes the summons is explicit, as with Troilus' bashful silence, when the final line of Book II invites us, as 'ye loveres that ben here', to consider, 'O myghty God, what shal he seye?' (II. 1751, 1757). The question seems gleeful, and to focus on 'the narrator' and his inadequacies is to disregard the imaginative pleasure revealed in the innumerable first-person references to the compositional process. Here too the invitation to share in that process is occasionally explicit, as when Pandarus'

---

[33] E.g. Ida L. Gordon, *The Double Sorrow of Troilus* (Oxford, 1970), 90; Bestul, 'Chaucer's *Troilus*', 373; Mehl, *Geoffrey Chaucer*, 75.

planning for the affair's consummation approaches its climax, and the past tense is suddenly replaced by the present and 'I' by a 'we' incorporating the audience:[34]

> Now al is wel, for al the world is blynd
> In this matere, bothe fremde and tame.
> This tymbur is al redy up to frame;
> Us lakketh nought but that we witen wolde
> A certeyn houre, in which she comen sholde. (III. 528–32)

House-building, a metaphor for planning a love affair, becomes one for planning the poem itself—a reversal of an earlier development, Pandarus' analogy between planning an affair and planning a house (I. 1065–71), which originated in a passage about planning poems from Geoffrey of Vinsauf's *Poetria nova*. Parallels between the crafts of love and of poetry were familiar to Chaucer, as the opening of *The Parliament of Fowls* witnesses; in *Troilus* such parallels are always near the surface, holding narrative and metanarrative together even as they threaten to diverge.

These first-person admissions of ignorance and uncertainty are doubtless the seed of the conception of an 'unreliable narrator' through whose consciousness the whole story is told; and yet, as we see, they coexist within the poem's first-person discourse with claims to the proud status of modern classic, along with various other kinds of self-presentation. A second barrier to any clear-cut interpretation of the poem's 'I' lies in the indefiniteness of the boundary to the poem's first-person discourse, and to this I now turn.

How can we decide what should be attributed to 'the narrator'? In theory we might hope to apply some principle such as Käte Hamburger's 'Within the fiction sentences of pure narration cannot be false; they can only contribute to the "facts" of a story.'[35] In practice, however, *Troilus*' recurrent emphasis on the origin of 'pure narration' in individual understanding of documents of uncertain authority—'Take every man now to his bokes heede' (V. 1089)—undermines the very category of 'fact'. Karla Taylor, holding that 'the work is not simply a history of things past, but

---

[34] Cf. Evan Carton, 'Complicity and Responsibility in Pandarus' Bed and Chaucer's Art', *PMLA* 94 (1979), 47–61 (p. 55), and Richard Waswo, 'The Narrator of *Troilus and Criseyde*', *ELH* 50 (1983), 1–25 (p. 10).

[35] *The Logic of Literature* (Bloomington, Ind., 1973), 136.

also an account of the narrator's experience in reading about them', nevertheless argues that 'it is nearly always possible to tell the difference between the "world of the story" and the "world of the commentary"'.[36] Yet, if the poem has a single narrator, that narrator must surely be held responsible for everything in it, even 'factual' elements such as the many quoted speeches attributed (by him—who else?) to the poem's characters. The 'world of the commentary' foregrounds an 'I' gathering material from written sources; if he is unreliable how can we know that in doing so he transmits the 'world of the story' without distortion? To avoid being deluded, we need to doubt everything: interpretation of anything but 'the narrator' himself becomes impossible, and *Troilus* must be read as one of those 'long speeches expressing, directly or indirectly, the [speakers'] characters' that Kittredge found in *The Canterbury Tales*.[37]

Few would go so far; but if many accounts of 'the narrator' are arbitrary in deciding which 'I's count as characterizing him, nearly all fail to observe that narratorial agency is manifested in many 'I'-less passages. To illustrate this, we need to examine a narrative sequence closely; I choose the earliest relevant example. After the expansively first-personal proem to Book I comes a markedly concise passage of historical scene-setting. This is formally impersonal ('Yt is wel wist...') and we might apply Benveniste's words that 'there is no longer a "narrator"...The events seem to tell themselves';[38] yet we must surely sense some efficient summarizing agency at work to produce the very conciseness. A narrator controlling the story and us as audience is implied by the *Now* of stanza-openings at lines 92 and 113, a deictic that must have the story-teller rather than the characters as its focus. Even quite neutral conjunctions such as *For* (78, 97), *And* (127, 155, 162), *But* (141, 148, 152), also frequently heading stanzas, still more formulas such as 'And so bifel' (155), cannot help conveying the existence of narratorial agency at the level of basic articulation. Other examples of deixis implying a narrator (or perhaps narrator and audience) as focus are phrases such as 'this lady' (99, 106),

---

[36] *Chaucer Reads 'The Divine Comedy'* (Stanford, Calif., 1989), 128, 17.
[37] *Chaucer and his Poetry*, 155.
[38] Emile Benveniste, *Problems in General Linguistics* (Coral Gables, Fla., 1971), 208.

'thise othere folk' (169), 'this Troilus' (183). A narrator surfaces explicitly in 'As to my doom' (100), but his organizing power has been implicit throughout, especially in the narrative's frequent hypotaxis. He surfaces again in a whole stanza at lines 141–7, now manifesting the organizational power (shown especially in selection and omission) latent in the very structure of the poem's sentences, and the corresponding grasp of rhetorical concepts such as *matere* and *digression*; and at the same time making explicit the interpellation of his public as impatient listeners ('it were … yow to long to dwelle') or diligent readers ('Whoso that kan may rede hem') that, as we have seen, so frequently accompanies narratorial appearances. Narratorial agency is implied even in asseverations like 'out of doute' (152): *someone* is assuring us (assuring *us*) that what is stated is true. Burrow notes the persistence in 'literary' Middle English narratives of 'a minstrel manner, full of tags and formulas, appeals to the audience and heavily marked narrative transitions';[39] in *Troilus* such effects contribute to a general personalization of story-telling.

Again, consider the remark that in the Trojan–Greek conflict 'The thynges fellen, as they don of werre' (134). It exemplifies what Barthes calls the 'cultural codes',[40] areas of tacit agreement supplied by a shared culture to which narratives appeal for support; and the reference to this agreed truth existing outside the *énoncé* has to be made by someone ('the narrator') for someone's benefit (ours). When we are told that Criseyde was first in beauty 'Right as oure firste lettre is now an A' (171), the deictics *oure* and *now* allude more precisely to knowledge shared by story-teller and audience. So too with 'And yet as proud a pekok kan he pulle' (210): the deictic *yet* refers to a time that has narrator and audience jointly as its focal point, and asserts a quasi-proverbial truth about love to which assent is assumed. Such cases must imply narratorial agency and audience response, yet 'the narrator' evoked is elusive: he is no particular person, neither the inspired creator of *poesye* nor the 'self-styled objective' (but perhaps really 'deluded') compiler of historical material, but simply the mouth-piece of 'a collective and anonymous voice originating in traditional human experience'.[41] The analysis might be continued, but I

---

[39] *Ricardian Poetry*, 14.   [40] Roland Barthes, *S/Z* (New York, 1974), 18.
[41] Ibid.

hope my point has already emerged. Middle English narrative is often warmly personal, offering and demanding emotional response to the events and feelings recounted. Chaucerian narrative continues this tradition; it also incorporates more complex effects such as skilful summary and ironic exaggeration, but these too in their different ways create a diffused personalization quite opposite to any notion of objective neutrality. Yet this pervasive and flexible personalizing does not necessarily imply impersonation of a narrator. Doubtless Chaucer was more interested than most Middle English poets in the ways that any narrative *énonciation* may be relatable to its utterer (revealing, unrevealing, surprising, predictable...), and this interest culminates in *The Canterbury Tales*; yet there is often no reason to attribute the *énonciation* to any identifiable individual.

The specific case can be set in a more general context. A pioneering study states that 'By definition narrative art requires a story and a story-teller'; more recent narratology has tended to encourage this assumption that a narrative must have a 'person who utters it', and most *Troilus* critics evidently take for granted the communication model stated by one of them, that 'in all utterances, someone says something to someone else for a purpose'.[42] Belief in the need to read any narrative as the utterance of a story-teller is one factor that has led critics to understand inconsistencies within the poem's first-person discourse as symptoms of the story-teller's fallibility. A study of gesture in *Troilus* remarks, 'It is this wayward narrator, differing significantly from himself at various points in the poem, who causes the gestures of his characters to take on such undeniable importance';[43] but if he differs significantly from himself, ought we not to question whether he has (or is) a self at all? The assumption that narrative must have *a* narrator, even if 'wayward', may seem beyond question when the model is oral story-telling, with a teller physically present to

[42] Robert Scholes and Robert Kellogg, *The Nature of Narrative* (New York, 1966), 240; Gérard Genette, *Narrative Discourse*, trans. Jane E. Lewin (Ithaca, NY, 1980), 212; Taylor, *Chaucer Reads 'The Divine Comedy'*, 7. For questioning of the communication paradigm for narrative, see Ann Banfield, *Unspeakable Sentences* (Boston, 1982).

[43] John P. Hermann, 'Gesture and Seduction in *Troilus and Criseyde*' (originally pub. 1985), here quoted from R. A. Shoaf (ed.), *Chaucer's 'Troilus and Criseyde': 'Subgit to alle Poesye'* (Binghamton, NY, 1992), 139–60 (p. 143).

listeners; but narrative can exist in other forms (pictorial, musical, choreographic, cinematic) lacking such presence. The narrative of *Troilus* exists as a written text frequently mimetic of oral story-telling. It seems likely that it was intended for delivery to listeners and, if so, that will doubtless have affected its design; but it remains a written text. Derrida, in his critique of Saussurean linguistics, has famously questioned the 'metaphysical presupposition about the relationship between speech and writing' that casts writing as mere 'representation of the self-present voice',[44] yet in general narratology has retained this presupposition: it is still assumed that even a written story must have a teller, envisaged as a fictive human person, a textual representation of the speaker of an oral narrative. Manifestly, however, once a narrative is written, this ceases to be necessary. If we must posit a *Troilus* 'narrator', a textually impersonated human source of the words constituting the poem, then Brewer is surely right that we need to imagine not one wayward narrator but 'a multiplicity of narrators'—as would not be true of a poem such as *Winner and Waster*, with its consistent mimesis of minstrel delivery at a feast. Given the reciprocal relation noted by Mehl and others between the first and second persons of the narrative, it is hard to see why *Troilus*' first person should refer more definitely to a unitary individual than its second, which (apostrophized deities aside) shifts rapidly among 'ye loveres that ben here' (II. 1751), 'Thow redere' (V. 270), 'litel bok' (V. 1786), 'yonge, fresshe folkes, he or she' (V. 1835), 'the and . . . the' (V. 1857: Gower and Strode), and other addressees, no more literally present than the 'I'. And the multiplicity will involve self-contradiction, for at the very least, in a narrative of such explicit textuality, we must construct the first person as existing both inside and outside 'Thise woful vers, that wepen as I write' (I. 7).

In spoken narrative, as in speech generally, the first person is anchored materially to the body from which the speaking voice issues, and continuity of reference for first-person pronouns is guaranteed by the reciter's physical presence. But even could we enter into the illusion that a written text exactly reproduced this situation, we would still need to allow for the nature of perfor-

---

[44] Jacques Derrida, *Of Grammatology*, tr. Gayatri Spivak (Baltimore, 1976), 28, 30.

mance, to which critics such as Shepherd and Lawlor have called attention. Live performance does not necessarily constitute utterance in which 'someone says something to someone else' in any normal sense of those words. The stand-up comedian or the talkshow host utters words spoken inconsistently from a wide variety of imaginary positions; they issue from a single mouth, but not from a single identity or even from a single fixed persona. Shepherd, emphasizing the 'mobility' of performing art, alludes tellingly to the *Troilus* epilogue: 'How often does an entertainer at the end of his piece add, "But all you people here, seriously now, I want to say a few special words in conclusion..."'[45] Much criticism has disregarded this mobility of the performing 'I', the rapid movement among roles and the porosity of their borders, treating the first person legalistically and asking in effect, 'Are you Geoffrey Chaucer?', 'How do you know what you tell me?', 'Why should I believe what you say?' Such questions are still less appropriate when addressed not to a real performer but to the ghostly textual 'I' that marks his final elusion: ''Tis here!' ''Tis here!' ''Tis gone!'

These considerations might be thought peculiar to the age of television and deconstruction, but in the Middle Ages too it could be understood that a textual 'I' need not correspond to a unitary person. Much medieval narrative is largely narratorless: on the rare occasions when 'I' occurs in a romance such as *King Horn*, it is in forms belonging to the rhetoric of story-telling—'A sang ihc schal you singe', 'Also ihc you telle may'—without reference to any characterizable story-teller.[46] In medieval *ars poetica*, the question of impersonation arises not on the level of narratorial style but on that of recitation, and here there is clear awareness of multiplicity or mobility of voicing. Geoffrey of Vinsauf, in the *Poetria nova* known to Chaucer, envisages recitation first of an angry man's speech, then of a rustic's:

If you act the part of this man, what, as reciter, will you do? Imitate genuine fury, but do not be furious. Be affected in part as he is, but not deeply so.... yet suggest, as is fitting, the emotion itself. You can represent (*praesentare*) the manner of a rustic and still be graceful: let your voice

[45] 'Troilus and Criseyde', 72, 85.
[46] *King Horn*, ed. Rosamund Allen (New York, 1984), ll. 3, 30.

represent (*figuret*) his voice; your facial expression, his own; and your gesture his gesture—by recognizable signs (*per notulas*).[47]

Such advice openly warns against the sort of total impersonation implied by 'unreliable narrator' theories. More telling, perhaps (since Geoffrey still envisages a *kind* of impersonation, even though oblique, *per notulas*, and with anger or rusticity qualified by the poet's gracefulness), is the type of analysis of the first person found in a long tradition of academic commentaries. Barbara Nolan has recently discussed the likely debt of Benoît de Sainte-Maure's 'multiform authorial presence' in the *Roman de Troie* to commentaries such as those of Servius on Virgil and Conrad of Hirsau on Boethius.[48] The issue was especially pressing in regard to the human authors of biblical texts, and A. J. Minnis notes Bonaventure's recognition, in a widely-read prologue to Ecclesiastes, that the 'I' of this book cannot be understood to refer solely to Solomon, or to any single individual. In it, rather, Solomon 'proceeds like an arranger (*concionator*), setting forth the opinions of various people—at one point that of a wise man, at another that of a foolish man—so that out of these many opinions one clear vision of the truth may dawn in the minds of his hearers'. The parallel with *Troilus* is incomplete, for the ultimate author of Ecclesiastes is God, and Bonaventure assumes that, provided 'attention is paid to its totality', the book's various human voices can be read as forming a kind of disputation, whose various teachings resolve into a single truth.[49] But commentators long before Chaucer had clearly grasped that the 'I' of a single text need not refer to a single narratorial persona.

Borrowing from John Burrow the concept that has changed our way of thinking about the poetry of Chaucer's age, I call the narratorial subject of *Troilus* 'a Ricardian "I"'. I do so because, as I see it, this unstable first person, which recent criticism has valiantly attempted to turn into a stable persona, belongs to the Ricardian Age, not just to Chaucer. To argue this case would take

---

[47] *The Poetria nova of Geoffrey of Vinsauf*, tr. Margaret F. Nims (Toronto, 1967), ll. 2047–54; Latin from *Les Arts poétiques du XIIe et du XIIIe siècle*, ed. Edmond Faral (Paris, 1926), 260.

[48] *Chaucer and the Tradition of the 'Roman Antique'* (Cambridge, 1992), 44–6.

[49] *Medieval Literary Theory and Criticism c.1100–c.1375*, ed. A. J. Minnis and A. B. Scott (Oxford, 1988), 231–2; discussed by A. J. Minnis, *Medieval Theory of Authorship*, 2nd edn. (Philadelphia, 1988), 110–12.

a book, but I want to conclude with a rough sketch of how the argument might run. My view can best be defined by contrast with that expressed in the *Troilus* chapter of Durling's *The Figure of the Poet in Renaissance Epic*:[50]

The fullest understanding of the statement of the poem is possible only in retrospect. In this respect there is an important kinship between *Troilus and Criseyde* and the other chief poetic monument of the fourteenth century, the *Divina Commedia*. The Narrator of the *Commedia*—Dante looking back over the journey as a whole—cannot in his commentary at the beginning of the poem convey the full measure of his understanding. By definition, that understanding can only come through the experience itself.... The *Commedia*, like *Troilus and Criseyde*, leads the reader through sympathetic participation in the protagonist's experience to a perspective that transforms and transcends the nature of each step along the way. Both as a whole and in its parts, the *Commedia* proceeds by a process of retrospective illumination.... Like the *Commedia*, then, *Troilus and Criseyde* ... rests upon the Christian conception of the ascent in truth through experience. (The description applies equally well, of course, to such other fourteenth-century works as *Piers Plowman* and *The Pearl*.)

One reason why the parallel suggested here will not work is that the two poems belong to fundamentally different genres: the *Commedia* is a visionary narrative, with the first person's 'ascent... through experience' as the central motive, while *Troilus* is a romance, the story of Troilus' double sorrow where it is he who finally rises through the heavenly spheres. *Troilus* hesitates on the brink of being the story of Criseyde's experience too, but the experience of 'the narrator', amounting at most to an intermittent commentary on 'historical' sources, can only be peripheral. (Is it possible to imagine the *Commedia* ever being read as Chaucer's poem was for over five centuries—without anyone noticing that it had a narrator at all?) A more important reason why the parallel is invalid is that Chaucer is a different kind of poet from Dante.[51] As suggested above, Chaucer is an exploratory poet; for that very reason he is a poet of the unfinished, not one like Dante whose goal is an art in which 'casüal punto non puote aver sito' (*Paradiso*, xxxii. 54). *Troilus*, unlike many of Chaucer's works, is complete, but bears marked traces of the difficulty of completion; and in this, I believe, the poem, like its poet, is characteristically

---

[50] Durling, *Figure of the Poet*, 65–6.
[51] Cf. Taylor, *Chaucer Reads 'The Divine Comedy'*, e.g. 3–5.

Ricardian. Movement towards 'a perspective that transforms and transcends the nature of each step along the way' may represent a Ricardian aspiration, but it is one that major Ricardian poems rarely achieve. *Pearl,* on its smaller scale, is perhaps an exception; *Piers Plowman* is not, nor is Gower's *Confessio Amantis.*

Chaucer, Langland, and Gower are writers whose greatest works record a struggle to find ways of saying things for which their culture provided no ready formulations or artistic forms: things that if understood would transform their readers' understanding of life, and thus transform the culture itself. One crucial element common to *Troilus, Piers,* and the *Confessio* is the coexistence, in dynamic and unstable equilibrium, of opposing frames of reference—ideological systems and literary structures. This view of *Piers Plowman* might be acceptable to many Langland scholars; most Gower scholars, subordinating his English text to the moralizing Latin commentary that defines its 'I' as a unitary fictional persona, would probably dissent from such a view of *Confessio Amantis.*[52] In each case the work's greatness is associated precisely with the absence or failure of a 'unifying vision'; and the first-person subject, to the degree of its importance, is the focus of instability and conflicting allegiance: a fragmented 'I' gives access to fragments of a merely putative unitary truth. Chaucer is the only one of the three to move beyond unstable equilibrium (barely sustained in *Troilus* by application of the age's most powerful closural system) to an acceptance of fragmentation, pluralism, and relativism, the 'Diverse folk diversely they seyde' of the *Tales.* Whereas in the *Commedia* the growth of understanding is dramatized systematically and consistently, in *Troilus, Piers,* and the *Confessio* this is not so. The Ricardian 'I' never achieves the final position or wholeness of Dante the pilgrim, from which reality can be seen in a single perspective. What he encounters on his journey will not fit into such a single view, however strongly the poets and their readers may wish that it could; and our attempts to make it do so, by defining the 'I' as unitary and unreliable, involve impoverishing distortion of the poets' real achievements.

[52] But cf. Paul Strohm, 'A Note on Gower's Persona', in Mary J. Carruthers and Elizabeth D. Kirk (eds.), *Acts of Interpretation* (Norman, Okla., 1982), 293–8. In '*Canace and Machaire*', *Mediaevalia,* 16 (1993 for 1990), 211–21, I try to show how Gower adapts Ovid to produce effects contrary to 'the purpose that medieval commentators attributed to the *Heroides* in their attempt to control Ovid's unruly narratives' (p. 219).

2

Pre-empting Closure in 'The Canterbury Tales': Old Endings, New Beginnings

DEREK PEARSALL

The subject-matter of this essay, as will be evident from its title, has a certain appropriateness in a volume of tribute to a scholar at an important turning-point in his long and distinguished career; it also takes up an issue which Professor Burrow has discussed in a characteristically incisive, erudite, and level-headed way, in his 'Poems without Endings', though without mentioning the 'ending-lessness' of the well-known Ricardian poem that I want to talk about.[1] Professor Burrow's essay, remembered particularly as a wonderfully urbane and informative lecture at the New Chaucer Society congress at Canterbury in 1990, is concerned chiefly with *The House of Fame, The Legend of Good Women*, the Cook's Tale and the Squire's Tale, and the questions that arise from their unfinished state: whether they were left incomplete by Chaucer, whether they were completed by Chaucer but are now incomplete through accidental loss of manuscript leaf or leaves, or whether they transcend, in their apparent incompleteness, the petty bounds of our notions of completeness and aspire to represent the grand inconclusiveness and indeterminacy of all things. Professor Burrow is not keen on this last idea, preferring 'that the accidental option should be kept open' against the pressures of 'undiscriminating over-interpretation' (p. 37). I shall try not to disagree with him, and, if the idea of 'accident' is part of the conceptual world that includes also the idea of 'authorial intention', as I believe it must be, then I am not in danger of doing so, for the view I shall put

[1] John Burrow, 'Poems without Endings', the Biennial Chaucer Lecture (1990), *SAC* 13 (1991), 17–37.

forward here is that Chaucer, having written the tale designed to stand at the end of *The Canterbury Tales* and having nearly completed the whole work as first planned, deliberately devised a new plan for the poem in which the existing ending was superseded. The accident of mortality was in a way 'planned into' this new design; it is incompleteness of a very high order.

I

The Canterbury Tales are customarily presented to us in a critical edition that uses the Ellesmere manuscript as its base-manuscript, and follows the order of the tales in that manuscript.[2] The authority of the modern edition, and the book in which it is contained, is such that the order of the *Tales* in Ellesmere has come to be thought of as the order that Chaucer intended, even as the order in which Chaucer wrote the tales.[3] Yet there is strong evidence that the Ellesmere text is inferior to the text of the *Tales* contained in a slightly earlier manuscript, the Hengwrt manuscript, and strong evidence too that the order in which the tales or fragments are placed in Ellesmere is editorial not authorial.[4] Even those editions

[2] I refer to Larry D. Benson (ed.), *The Riverside Chaucer*, now used in virtually all scholarly reference to Chaucer's poem.

[3] That Chaucer wrote the *Tales* in the order in which the critic is discussing them, that is, in the order in which they appear in the Ellesmere manuscript, is an assumption of much writing on the *Tales*, for example Alfred David's *The Strumpet Muse: Art and Morals in Chaucer's Poetry* (Bloomington, Ind., 1976), where it structures David's narrative of Chaucer's later artistic career.

[4] For a summary of the debate concerning the relation between Hengwrt (Aberystwyth, National Library of Wales, MS Peniarth 392D) and Ellesmere (San Marino, Huntington Library MS El.26.C.9), henceforth Hg and El, see Derek Pearsall, *The Canterbury Tales* (London, 1985), 8–23. It has been generally accepted, since the publication of John Matthews Manly and Edith M. Rickert (eds.), *The Text of the 'Canterbury Tales'*, 8 vols. (Chicago, 1940), that Hg contains the best text of the *Tales*. Even George Kane, who is scathing about the methods and most of the conclusions of Manly and Rickert in his essay on 'John M. Manly and Edith Rickert', in Paul G. Ruggiers (ed.), *Editing Chaucer: The Great Tradition* (Norman, Okla., 1984), 207–29, and who suggests that the treatment of Ellesmere in Manly–Rickert was 'emotionally based, as if the editors were under some compulsion to discredit the manuscript which clouded their judgment' (p. 220), does not argue that El contains a better text than Hg. Likewise, Ralph Hanna III, in his sceptical scrutiny of the 'Hengwrtization' of the *Tales*, 'Problems of "Best Text" Editing and the Hengwrt Manuscript of *The Canterbury Tales*', in Derek Pearsall (ed.), *Manuscripts and Texts: Editorial Problems in Later Middle English Literature* (Cambridge, 1987), 87–94, accepts that Hg is 'probably marginally superior to El'

that drift towards Hengwrt in their choice of readings, such as those of Manly–Rickert and Donaldson, will still follow the tale-order of Ellesmere, with or (mostly nowadays) without 'the Bradshaw shift' (the movement of Ellesmere Fragment VII to follow Fragment II so that references to places on the way to Canterbury are in the right geographical order).[5] In other words, a manuscript has been promoted to a position of unique authority which represents merely the best efforts of Chaucer's first editors to present *The Canterbury Tales* as a complete work, as 'the book of the tales of Caunterbury', which is what the scribe of Ellesmere calls it in his final colophon (Chaucer, in his Retraction, refers only to 'the tales of Caunterbury').[6] This is quite different from the situation with the older and more authentic Hengwrt manuscript, which presents the tales in an unordered state. I say unordered, rather

(p. 92). As to the order of the *Tales*, the most vigorous defence of the Ellesmere order has been mounted by Larry D. Benson, 'The Order of *The Canterbury Tales*', *SAC* 3 (1981), 77–120; he argues that the Ellesmere order and another order, slightly different and inferior, are the source of all other manuscript orderings, including that of Hg, and that the Ellesmere order is Chaucer's. His arguments are countered by N. F. Blake, *The Textual Tradition of 'The Canterbury Tales'* (London, 1985), 41, 173–4, 187–8, and by Charles A. Owen, *The Manuscripts of the 'Canterbury Tales'* (Cambridge, 1991), 3–4. It is very hard, for instance, for Benson to explain how Hg comes to have what he accepts to be the best text and yet such an inferior tale-order, except by suggesting that the scribe or director of Hg got his text from one source and his order, including the necessary links, from another (p. 104); this seems an unlikely, indeed inexplicable circumstance. Benson is also mistaken, I think, in claiming that the Ellesmere tale-order must be Chaucer's because it is so good; he tells us how impossible it was that there was 'an unknown literary prodigy who has left no other traces of his genius' and who 'had a sophisticated literary sense that enabled him to get the right order' (p. 111). Everyone agrees that El is the best order available, but I don't think it needed a genius to arrive at it: juggling with the order of the fragments of *The Canterbury Tales* is a five-finger exercise, which is perhaps why Chaucer left it to others.

[5] See Manly and Rickert, *The Text of the 'Canterbury Tales'*, i. 276; E. Talbot Donaldson (ed.), *Chaucer's Poetry: An Anthology for the Modern Reader* (New York, 1958; 2nd edn. 1975). The only edition that uses the Hengwrt manuscript consistently for both text and tale-order is that of N. F. Blake, *The Canterbury Tales*, York Medieval Texts, 2nd series (London, 1980); the edition, since it presents the tales in an apparently haphazard order, has not caught on.

[6] Donald R. Howard, *The Idea of the 'Canterbury Tales'* (Berkeley and Los Angeles, 1976), acknowledges that the colophon is 'scribal and likely did not come from Chaucer's pen; the scribes who copied the work might have thought it a book though its author did not' (p. 56), but goes on, 'Yet it seems to me out of the question that Chaucer did not think of *The Canterbury Tales* as a "book"' (p. 57). He continues with further discussion of this 'book' (pp. 57–67) in which it imperceptibly becomes the reality that is desired rather than a hypothesis that requires the ordinary weighing of evidence.

than disordered, because the evidence is so strong that this was the state in which the *Tales* came to Chaucer's first editors.[7] In other words, there is no authorized order: but editors have to print the tales in some order, because of the nature of the codex, in which page inexorably follows page, and the order they print them in comes to have a specially privileged status as the order that the author intended.

What the evidence of the manuscripts demands that we recognize, though, is that *The Canterbury Tales* are unfinished—never released or even prepared for publication, and with the stages of revision and recomposition manifest in the surviving manuscripts. Publishers have not traditionally been much interested in preserving the traces of such unfinished composition, and editors have generally conspired with them in obscuring or erasing the evidence of authorial variants in the manuscripts. The usual editorial procedure is to print everything that is plausibly Chaucerian, and to collapse the processes of textual evolution into a single textual moment. At most, as in *The Riverside Chaucer*, there are small square brackets around passages such as the Man of Law's Epilogue and the Nun's Priest's Epilogue to indicate that they appear only in the alpha group of manuscripts and were therefore presumably 'cancelled' by Chaucer and superseded in revision.[8] This has the consequence that critics will collate for the purposes of interpretation passages from the poem that belong to different stages of its existence. They will also tend to treat the text as if it were what Chaucer intended to stand as final, and evolve more or

---

[7] The most compelling evidence of the piecemeal and unordered manner in which the fragments came to Chaucer's first editors is in the meticulous palaeographical introduction by A. I. Doyle and M. B. Parkes to Paul G. Ruggiers (ed.), *'The Canterbury Tales': A Facsimile and Transcription of the Hengwrt Manuscript, with Variants from the Ellesmere Manuscript* (Norman, Okla., 1979), pp. xix–xlix. It is difficult to believe that the same scribe (Hg and El are almost universally accepted to be the work of the same scribe) had at an earlier stage copied the beautifully ordered Ellesmere manuscript.

[8] For the alpha group of manuscripts and their evidence of authorial 'first shots', see Manly and Rickert, *The Text of the 'Canterbury Tales'*, ii. 421–3, ii. 480, iv. 517; for the Man of Law's Epilogue, see Benson, 'The Order of *The Canterbury Tales*', 100 n. 14. Other passages that carry the traces of the evolutionary processes I have spoken about include the Nun's Priest's Prologue, the link between the Clerk's Tale and the Merchant's Tale, the Wife of Bath's Prologue, and the Physician–Pardoner link. For further examples, see Benson, 'The Order of *The Canterbury Tales*', 99, 115.

less elaborate schemes to explain or celebrate a tale-order that in fact derives from editorial decisions alone.

Two of the most important and influential recent commentators on the poem, for instance, show little hesitation in assuming as fact that the Man of Law's Introduction, Prologue, and Tale were intended by Chaucer to follow the unfinished Cook's Tale. V. A. Kolve, in *Chaucer and the Imagery of Narrative*, argues that the Man of Law's Introduction and Tale follow Fragment I in 'all the best manuscripts', adding in a footnote 'with the notable exception of Hengwrt', whose ordering of the tales, says Kolve, 'carries no authority'.[9] (No ordering of the tales, it has to be reiterated, 'carries authority'.) Kolve concludes: 'I would consign to critical oblivion the convention—necessary and appropriate to editors only—of dividing Chaucer's opening text into Fragments I and II' (p. 284). As for the Hengwrt scribe, who writes, in the blank space below the unfinished Cook's Tale, 'Of this Cokes tale maked Chaucer na moore',[10] Kolve has this to say: 'We may properly doubt that Chaucer intended him to preserve it in this fashion, or (if so preserved) that Chaucer would have wished us to grant it the formal status it has assumed' (p. 284). Doubt about the manner in which Chaucer's intentions and wishes have been communicated accepts, of course, that it is those intentions and wishes that we seek to understand and define: I am not sure why the activities of editors and those of critics are thought of, in this respect, as separate, or why critics can afford to ignore what editors feel obliged to draw to their attention.

Lee Patterson, in *Chaucer and the Subject of History*, says pretty uncontroversially that the Ellesmere order 'represents a plausible and intelligent hypothesis about Chaucer's intention', and concludes, after some discussion, 'To read the *Tales* as the Ellesmere manuscript recommends, then, seems a thoroughly appropriate enterprise.'[11] This seems entirely reasonable: the making and testing of hypotheses is the normal business of literary scholarship, and Patterson makes quite clear what he is doing. There are two problems, however, with his argument. The first is that a

---

[9] V. A. Kolve, *Chaucer and the Imagery of Narrative: The First Five 'Canterbury Tales'* (London, 1984), 257, 462.
[10] Ibid., pl. 131.
[11] Lee Patterson, *Chaucer and the Subject of History* (Madison, 1991), 43, 45.

'hypothesis about Chaucer's intention', as it may be represented in Ellesmere, would already have built into it a mistaken premiss, namely, that there was an 'intention', a single resolved purpose, albeit unfulfilled, that could be invoked to regulate the working of the hypothesis. The suppressions and elisions of material in Ellesmere, however, are evidence that any hypothesis has to be a hypothesis about Chaucer's intentions, plural, contradictory, and unresolved, not intention, single and unfulfilled. The second problem is that the testing of the hypothesis is not carried out on the same evidential basis as the statement of the reason for putting it forward. Patterson advances a massively cogent historical theory of *The Canterbury Tales* which will have a permanent influence on the reading of the poem: its strength is in the subtlety and power with which it makes evident the larger historical, political, and social structures of which the poem is part; its weakness is in its attachment to the 'hypothesis of intention', which is activated but not tested or strengthened by these independently derived hypotheses of the historical process and Chaucer's function within it. Ellesmere's 'plausible and intelligent hypothesis about Chaucer's intention' remains just that, and is a precarious base on which to build further hypotheses of a different kind; as a hypothesis it has the same status in relation to Chaucer's 'intention' as a proffered completion of *The Mystery of Edwin Drood*, plausible and intelligent to the highest degree, has to the intention of Charles Dickens.[12]

Patterson's reading of *The Canterbury Tales* requires not only that the Man of Law should follow the Cook but also that the Wife of Bath's Prologue should follow the Man of Law's Epilogue.

---

[12] This is not a very good analogy, as Professor Patterson has pointed out to me, since the question in the case of *The Canterbury Tales* has to do with the ordering of elements in an uncompleted and unordered compilation and not, as in *Edwin Drood*, with the completion of an uncompleted narrative. Another analogy for *The Canterbury Tales*, hardly less unsatisfactory, would be with the 'collected works' of individual poets and the question of the order in which editors are to place them in the printed book. Chronological order, if it could be known for certain, would be at least incontrovertible, but it can rarely be known for certain, and is disturbed by revision and other activities in which authors legitimately indulge; all other orders, in the absence of explicit directives from the author, are open to objection, and necessarily unsatisfactory. For discussion of the question, see Ian Jack, 'A Choice of Orders', in Jerome J. McGann (ed.), *Textual Criticism and Literary Interpretation* (Chicago, 1985), 127–43. Of course, *The Canterbury Tales* differ obviously from the collected poems of Herbert, Herrick, or Housman in having a framing narrative and a partial programme of links.

In Ellesmere, the fragment beginning with the Wife of Bath's Prologue follows the fragment containing the Man of Law's Tale, and this is the order we are used to in the standard editions. The Man of Law's Epilogue, however, does not appear in Ellesmere, in the very manuscript, that is, whose order is declared to be authoritative, and has no place in the ordering of the tales there represented. The reason for this is that the tale it was designed to introduce, presumably the tale first assigned to the Wife of Bath, was reallocated in revision and the Man of Law's Epilogue left functionless, 'a mere vestigial organ, a sort of literary vermiform appendix'.[13] The situation is a simple one, but it cannot be accurately represented in a printed edition, with its insistence on progressive linear sequence. It may be that in any case the matter was placed beyond the reach of rational discussion by Talbot Donaldson, who set the Wife of Bath's Prologue after the Man of Law's Epilogue, exactly as Patterson and others would argue was Chaucer's intention, and also emended the disputed reading of II (B¹) 1179 (*Sompnour/Squyer/Shipman*) to *Wif of Bathe*, a reading which appears in no manuscript and which, given the uncompleted processes of composition and revision, could have existed in no copy deriving from Chaucer. Donaldson explained his procedure thus: 'This gives coherence to the chosen order, though it probably does not represent Chaucer's final intention—assuming that he had one.'[14] There is an irresistible mischievousness and a very Chaucerian irresponsibility about this, as well as an admirable frankness about the impossibility of presenting an 'edition' of a work still in process of being composed, but the effect, on the printed page of Donaldson's edition, is to 'authorize' an order that is accepted, in the notes, to have no authority. In a later essay, where on the whole he supports the Ellesmere order, Donaldson returns to the question of the Man of Law's Epilogue (or endlink) and suggests that in 'a critical edition' various expedients might be employed to show that the Man of Law's endlink is 'genuinely Chaucerian, but not placeable'.[15] 'In a less austere edition', he continues, 'I should do what I have already done.' A 'less austere edition' is evidently

---

[13] Manly and Rickert, *The Text of the 'Canterbury Tales'*, ii. 190.

[14] Donaldson (ed.), *Chaucer's Poetry*, 913.

[15] E. T. Donaldson, 'The Ordering of the *Canterbury Tales*', in Jerome Mandel and Bruce A. Rosenberg (eds.), *Medieval Literature and Folklore Studies: Essays in Honor of Francis Lee Utley* (New Brunswick, NJ, 1970), 193–204 (p. 202).

one that ignores the complex historical facts in the interests of providing an easier read (and one more productive of 'interpretations').

I have examined the statements of Kolve, Patterson, and Donaldson in detail, since they know and make very clear what they are about and since they speak explicitly about Chaucer's intentions. It is appropriate to point out that another influential commentator on the *Tales*, Carolyn Dinshaw, in *Chaucer's Sexual Poetics*, makes similar assumptions about the Ellesmere sequence, but always in terms of the reader's experience, and never and most scrupulously never in terms of the author's intentions.[16] Her presentation of her opinions is thus inaccessible to the kind of argument I wish to make; for her, the order of the *Tales* is a matter for the reader to decide, not because there is no other way of deciding but because the author's intentions concerning that order (if he had any, and if they were known) are irrelevant.

On the basis of assumptions about the Ellesmere order, scholars have thus drawn conclusions that have important consequences for their interpretation of the *Tales*. Yet, as I argue, it is the illusion alone of 'the textual moment' fostered by the modern critical edition and the book that contains it that allows such assumptions to carry weight. There is also the problem of the vulnerability of the author to posthumous ideas of betterment. 'Be kind to my remains', said Dryden to Congreve, his literary executor, and that is what all authors wish to say to those who assume the responsibility of publishing their works after their death. It means, 'Change nothing'. It is what Chaucer says at the close of *Troilus and Criseyde* (V. 1795). But the Ellesmere editor of *The Canterbury Tales* was not content to be kind: the remains were in an unsatisfactory state and there were opportunities for improvement that needed to be taken. This is not what authors want:[17] 'Change

---

[16] Carolyn Dinshaw, *Chaucer's Sexual Poetics* (Madison, 1989). See e.g. 88, 112–13.

[17] Ian Hamilton, in an essay in the *Observer* for 19 Mar. 1995 entitled 'Haunted by Ghost Writers' (where I found the Dryden quotation), tells how editors at Scribners of New York carved a series of 'novels' out of Hemingway's posthumous remains, one of which, *The Garden of Eden*, finally earned him the accolade of having learnt 'the rudiments of feminist perspective'. 'Well thanks', Hamilton imagines Hemingway saying, and I imagine Chaucer responding similarly to the Ellesmere order and the determination of modern critics to find in

nothing' means 'Change nothing', and it is always worth reminding ourselves, therefore, that for *The Canterbury Tales* Chaucer
left only a half-assembled kit with few directions; ideally, the work
should be edited partly as a bound book, with the first (though not
the last) fragment fixed, and partly as a set of fragments in folders,
with the incomplete information as to their nature and possible
placement fully displayed. I made this suggestion some years ago,
in my book on *The Canterbury Tales* (p. 23), but, regrettably, it
has not yet been taken up by any publisher.[18]

II

Against the background of this general argument concerning the
order of the *Tales*, it is to the last fragment, containing the Parson's
Prologue and Tale and Retraction, that I now want to turn. The
Host announces his plan for the tale-telling competition at the end
of the General Prologue, and there are further references, mostly in
Fragment I, to a competition or at least to a competitive element in
the tale-telling, often in terms of 'quiting' or getting one's own
back.[19] But there are no further references to a four-tale two-way
plan. Indeed there are several references that seem to suggest an
unawareness of the existence of the four-tale plan. The Friar and
the Summoner, in their acrimonious exchange at the end of the
Wife of Bath's Prologue, speak of telling a tale or two, or two or
three, against each other, but this is more in the nature of vitriolic
excess than a plan to use up a set proportion of their allocation in
abusing each other. The Host, speaking to the Franklin, says:

> What, Frankeleyn! Pardee, sire, wel thou woost
> That each of yow moot tellen atte leste
> A tale or two, or breken his biheste. (V (F) 696–8)

that order the lineaments of the grand design that he spent some effort trying to
keep clear of.

[18] Thorlac Turville-Petre has reminded me of a novel by Bryan Stanley Johnson,
The Unfortunates, published in London by Panther Books in 1969 with the first and
last sections fixed and the rest loose. He thinks it was not a great success. One
reason is that it was not a proper 'book': the Widener Library at Harvard University
has all of Johnson's other novels, but not this one.

[19] See e.g. I (A) 3119, 3127, 3864, 3916, 4324, 4362; III (D) 1292.

He does not say that everyone was supposed to tell four tales but that the plan has now been modified, under pressure of unforeseen circumstance, so that everyone has to tell at least one or two, whatever at least one or two might mean. Likewise, when the Host offers Chaucer and the Monk, on different occasions, the option of telling an alternative tale, after their first has been interrupted, the implication is not that this is the second tale of their four, but that telling this second tale will simply enable everyone to forget the unpleasant experience of the first. Finally, when the Host addresses the Parson, he says quite clearly,

> Be what thou be, ne breke thou nat oure pley;
> For every man, save thou, hath toold his tale. (X (I) 24–5)

He does not say, Everyone has told their four tales but you have not told any, nor does he say, Everyone has told their four tales and you have only told three of your four, nor does he say, Everyone but you has told his one tale, according to the revised scheme of a one-tale-per-pilgrim competition which I have decided on without telling any of you anything about it.

Those who are determined to have the *Tales* complete are undeterred by this apparently major discrepancy in the framing narrative. The work is thought incomplete, says Donald Howard, because it is so far from fulfilling the four-tale plan. 'And yet', he goes on, 'this is not Chaucer's statement; it is the Host's, as reported by the narrator. It may or may not at some point have been Chaucer's idea—we do not know.' Plans are always going awry, anyway. So Howard proposes to read 'the book as it is, not as we think it might have been . . . and to argue *that it is unfinished but complete*'.[20] Later, addressing the problem of the Host's remarks to the Franklin and the Parson, Howard says: 'This is generally taken to mean that Chaucer changed his idea of the plan; yet it is the Host whose idea changes. What Chaucer's idea was *at first* we cannot know. Perhaps he meant to identify it with the Host's suggested plan in the General Prologue; if so, he ended up revealing a grandiose plan unfulfilled and his own control unsustained, which could be Chaucerian self-humor' (p. 28). All this

---

[20] Howard, *Idea of the 'Canterbury Tales'*, 1 (author's italics). For the distinction between 'unfinished' and 'uncompleted', Howard cites Northrop Frye, *The Structure of Imagery in 'The Faerie Queene': Studies in Poetic Mythology* (New York, 1963), 69–87.

seems extraordinarily casual in its approach to the evidence and at the same time absolutely determined to have everything fit in with the 'idea' of the completed *Canterbury Tales*. The attempt to make the discrepancy between the plan announced in the General Prologue and the competition as it is spoken about in other parts of *The Canterbury Tales* into a drama of gradually changed minds and grand ideas frustrated by circumstance is a prize example of the linear compulsions exerted by the edited book-text of *The Canterbury Tales*, as well as an example of the resistance to what Donald Howard calls, contemptuously, 'the workroom theory of the *Canterbury Tales*'.[21] The evidence seems, though, to speak simply of conflicting authorial intentions surviving side by side in an uncompleted series of drafts—not discrepancies within an over-all plan but plain contradictions, explicable otherwise only in terms of some quite gratuitous neglect of what is set forth as an important element in the frame narrative.

The Host's four-tale, two-way plan stands further in direct contradiction with the existing 'ending' of *The Canterbury Tales*: the whole of the Parson's Prologue and most specifically the words of the Parson himself clearly imply a pilgrimage now ending at its destination, that is, at Canterbury, the place of pilgrimage.

> And therfore, if yow list—I wol nat glose—
> I wol yow telle a myrie tale in prose
> To knytte up al this feeste and make an ende.
> And Jhesu, for his grace, wit me sende,
> To shewe yow the wey, in this viage,
> Of thilke parfit glorious pilgrymage
> That highte Jerusalem celestial. (X (I) 45–51)

When one speaks of a pilgrimage as an allegory of the journey of human life, from the earthly city to the heavenly city, one does not speak or think of the going home that follows the pilgrimage. This would in every respect unmake the allegory, and assert a priority and propriety to worldly life quite inappropriate to the circumstances. Pilgrims did of course go home when they had finished their pilgrimage, unless they were exceptionally devout, like Galahad, or fortunate enough to die at the place of pilgrimage, but going home was not part of the spiritually significant or allegorizable part of the journey. Howard, in the context of his own

---

[21] Howard, *Idea of the 'Canterbury Tales'*, 6.

argument, is particularly firm on this point: 'The custom', he says, 'was to declare the Jerusalem pilgrimage finished at its destination'; the pilgrimage of human life, as 'a conventional metaphor and topos', had no return journey.[22]

There is no doubt about the finality of the Parson's Tale, as it is introduced in the Parson's Prologue, and I assume that it is the Parson's Tale that is introduced in the Parson's Prologue. The finality of the Parson's Tale is the finality of a terminal illness: you are going into a hospital where you will die; various things will be done to you; you will never come out.[23] There is no doubt either about the finality of the Retraction. It is the final act of *The Canterbury Tales*, the act of contrition which answers the urgent call for penitence at the end of the Parson's Tale, and it is ostensibly the final act of Chaucer's poetic career, in which, symbolically, he unwrites those of his writings that have to do with sin, that is, with earthly matters and desires. It is not just the closure of a fiction, but the denial of fiction and of any non-doctrinal value that might be attached to it, and the exit from the world of fiction-making.[24]

I take it that Fragment X was once the conclusion to an almost-completed *Canterbury Tales*, in which pilgrims were to tell one tale on a one-way journey, whether or not in some form of competition. Somewhat later in the history of the evolution of the *Tales*, perhaps when the crisis that brought on the Retraction was passed, Chaucer evolved a new and impossibly grandiose scheme for the *Tales* in which the ending he had already written became the ending of a poem that no longer existed.[25] The appar-

---

[22] Howard, *Idea of the 'Canterbury Tales'*, 30, 28.

[23] I owe this metaphor to John Norton-Smith, *Geoffrey Chaucer* (London, 1974): 'The experience of reading the tale suggests admission into a large hospital where one is obliged to accommodate mentally to the regimen, to the rules of the establishment, and where every mental adjustment raises a growing suspicion that one is never going to come out' (p. 157).

[24] Patterson has written particularly well on the 'terminal' nature of the Parson's Tale: see Lee W. Patterson, 'The "Parson's Tale" and the Quitting of the "Canterbury Tales"', *Traditio*, 34 (1978), 331–80 (p. 380).

[25] The absence of any manuscript evidence for the change of plan needs a little special pleading, but since the survival of *any* evidence of the processes of recomposition and revision is such a matter of chance, it is not difficult to believe that the evidence of some of those processes has been lost. The General Prologue is the very likeliest site of all for extensive revising activity, especially late in the development of the *Tales*.

ent finality of the Parson's Tale and Retraction seems to me no objection at all to this hypothesis. 'We have Chaucer's own word', says Benson, 'in the Retraction, that, unfinished as *The Canterbury Tales* obviously was, he was finished with it...We have the work in what Chaucer regarded as its final state.'[26] But this view seems as sentimental and unfounded as the older idea that the Parson's Tale and Retraction were written on Chaucer's death-bed. Everyone has their bad moments. I agree, therefore, almost entirely, with what Charles Owen has said over many years on the matter, most recently in his essay on '*The Canterbury Tales*: Beginnings (3) and Endings (2+1)'.[27] The Parson's Tale and Retraction are not an 'effort to bring to an end a patched up *Canterbury Tales*, but rather an early ending associated with the Man of Law's Prologue, superseded when Chaucer thought up the contest as the context for the storytelling' (p. 206).

III

There are a number of things that I find agreeable about the hypothesis of the superseded ending. One is that it demonstrates Chaucer's determination to live for ever and to have a plan for *The Canterbury Tales* so capacious that it could accommodate everything that he had no chance or intention of writing. It is

[26] Benson, 'The Order of *The Canterbury Tales*', 80–1; Donaldson agrees that the Parson's Tale and Retraction show that the work was finished ('The Ordering of the *Canterbury Tales*', 198).

[27] *Chaucer Yearbook*, 1 (1992), 189–212. For Owen's earlier discussion of the 'ending' of *The Canterbury Tales*, see e.g. *Pilgrimage and Storytelling in the 'Canterbury Tales': The Dialectic of 'Ernest' and 'Game'* (Norman, Okla., 1977), 31. Some of the other views that Owen has put forward, in association with his hypothesis concerning the ending, are a great deal less persuasive, and have probably done something to help people avoid accepting the obvious point about the ending: the evidence, for instance, that Chaucer ever did anything to set in motion the return journey involved in his new plan seems extremely flimsy, while arguments questioning the authenticity of the Parson's Tale and Retraction are unlikely to make much headway. It is very pleasing to see Charles Owen, in his most recent essay on the subject, quietly shelving the question of the authenticity of the Parson's Tale and Retraction, whilst showing clearly the 'undercurrent of discomfort' concerning them that runs through the manuscripts and presenting a strong case that they were never attached by Chaucer to the Parson's Prologue: see Charles A. Owen Jr., 'What the Manuscripts Tell us about the Parson's Tale', *MÆ* 63 (1994), 239–49 (quotation at p. 244).

almost as if the impending completion of the original scheme of *The Canterbury Tales* would have signalled the approach of death, and so Chaucer evolved a new scheme that held closure at bay almost indefinitely, much as we might fancy Mahler and Bruckner hesitating before committing themselves to a *ninth* symphony. I am reluctant to make anything of it, since making anything of it would sound pretty silly, but I cannot help remembering the inexplicable circumstances in which Chaucer took a fifty-three-year lease on the house in the Westminster Abbey precinct that he rented in December 1399. There is no explanation that I know of, or that anyone has come up with, for the peculiar terms of the lease, which would have taken Chaucer to the age of 110 at least.[28]

I also find it agreeable that the new scheme involves such a healthily unspiritual view of pilgrimages—not only recognizing the need to while away the time with tale-telling and talk of competitions to avoid the boredom inherent in pilgrimages, but also to be thinking already of coming back and having prizes and celebration dinners. It also means that Chaucer spent his last years or months, not working on the Parson's Tale and writing the Retraction, but revising and writing Fragment I, and may even have spent his last days on the unfinished Cook's Tale.

Finally, it seems to me that the view of the so-called ending of *The Canterbury Tales* as itself superseded by subsequent unfinished planning is very apt to Chaucerian practice. *The House of Fame, The Legend of Good Women*, and *Anelida*, as well as a number of the *Canterbury Tales* themselves, are all apparently unfinished, *The Parliament of Fowls* ends with a postponement and a beginning, and *Troilus and Criseyde* ends with a conclusion so ruthlessly conclusive as to disturb rather than satisfy our desire for resolution. To deduce from this a principle of 'inconclusiveness' in Chaucer's narrative poems, through which they 'repeatedly express conflicting perceptions and beliefs that are left unresolved',[29] would be to claim for Chaucer a role as a practitioner of a kind of pre-emptive deconstruction, as well as making for a

[28] See Martin M. Crow and Clair C. Olson (eds.), *Chaucer Life-Records* (Oxford, 1966), 535–40.
[29] Larry Sklute, *Virtue of Necessity: Inconclusiveness and Narrative Form in Chaucer's Poetry* (Columbus, Oh., 1984), 5.

certain monotony of frustrated expectation. But I have no interest in claiming Chaucer for the modern or the post-modern: it is simply that he seems, rather deliberately, to have made his poem unavailable for the kind of systematic interpretation, whether theocentric or anthropocentric, that his readers seem always to have wanted to make.

The concludedness of *The Canterbury Tales* has in the printed editions been so prominently advertised that the idea of the super-seded ending may come as something salutary in the way of a shock. It is a falsification of expectations so unusual, so far beyond the usual crises of representation, or what Kermode calls 'the tension or dissonance between paradigmatic form and contingent reality',[30] as to be unable to be borne. 'We cannot, of course, be denied an end', says Kermode; 'it is one of the great charms of books that they have to end' (p. 23). But it is Chaucer's readers who have devised an end for his collection of poems, for his own revised scheme made *The Canterbury Tales* into a 'book' that does not 'have to end': the new beginning undoes the old ending.

A literary parallel is hard to find, as I have said. Keats's *Hyperion* was rebegun in 1819 and left unfinished, as *The Fall of Hyperion: A Dream*, but the situation is quite different, since the first version was itself left unfinished, and expressly designated *A Fragment*. Balzac devised a new plan for *La Comédie humaine* in his 'Catalogue' of 1845, increasing the number of novels from 120 to 137, written or projected, and proposing a new and different order, but since all the novels are 'scenes from French life', and allow for infinite extension and insertion, there can be no 'ending' to be superseded.[31] A more useful analogy may be drawn from architecture, not so much with the 'inconclusiveness' of Gothic buildings of which Arnold Hauser speaks,[32] as with the 'uncon-cludedness' of those many Gothic churches where a massive rebuilding in a new style has been begun but has progressed only as far as the provision of a new chancel or a new nave or a new west front. For many years, during Chaucer's lifetime and well on into the fifteenth century, Westminster Abbey presented just such

---

[30] Frank Kermode, *The Sense of an Ending: Studies in the Theory of Fiction* (Oxford, 1967), 133.

[31] See Marcel Bouteron (ed.), *La Comédie humaine*, i (Paris 1951), pp. ix–xxi.

[32] Arnold Hauser is cited from A. C. Spearing in Burrow, 'Poems without Endings', 35.

an aspect, as the rebuilding of the old nave on the scale of Henry III's choir proceeded by fits and starts. Henry III's vast rebuilding of the Norman church of Westminster Abbey had been left unfinished, at his death, at the fifth bay of the nave from the transept, which was connected by a temporary porch to the western Norman bays of the Confessor's church.[33] Building was recommenced by Richard II, but ceased with his death, and had to be taken up again by Henry V. The building had been 'finished', but had become incomplete because of the introduction of a new and grander design; so with the cathedrals of Beauvais and Le Mans. Of course, cathedrals cannot be left yawning to the skies, for the rain to fall on their altars, and they are always completed after some fashion that is regarded as satisfactorily timeless if not authored. In *The Canterbury Tales*, the undisguised collision of the different elements is not productive of an experience of mysteriously transhistorical and impersonal unity but part of the experience of high artistic endeavour inextricably entangled in the contingencies of history.

---

[33] See Christopher Wilson, 'The Gothic Abbey Church', in Christopher Wilson, Pamela Tudor-Craig, John Physick and Richard Gem, *Westminster Abbey* (London, 1986), 22–69 (pp. 31–4). As Wilson says, 'The contrast between the old and new parts of the nave must have been stark indeed' (p. 31).

3

Women's Piety and Women's Power: Chaucer's Prioress Reconsidered

CAROL M. MEALE

Readings of the persona of Chaucer's Prioress, as she is described in the General Prologue, have long been influential in generating opposing interpretations of the Tale which is assigned to her in the Canterbury sequence. The Tale itself, as a consequence of the divergence of critical opinion concerning the virtues and short-comings of the teller, has become the site of conflicting ideological discourses, which have ranged from defences of her religious prac-tices and sensibility and her Mariolatry, to condemnations of the crude anti-Semitism embodied in the miracle which she recounts.[1] It is this latter aspect of her story-telling which, above all, has occasioned the greatest unease amongst modern readers, many of whom have been reluctant to accept that Chaucer himself could have subscribed to the particular brand of religious and racial bigotry given expression here.[2] But by seeking to shift the respon-sibility for the narrative bias from author to fictional speaker such

[1] See the summaries of views given in Florence H. Ridley, *The Prioress and the Critics*, University of California Publications, English Studies 30 (Berkeley and Los Angeles, 1965); and in *A Variorum Edition of the Works of Geoffrey Chaucer*, ii: *The Canterbury Tales*, pt. 20, *The Prioress's Tale*, ed. Beverly Boyd (Norman, Okla. 1987), 27–60. For an extensive critique of previous scholarship see Louise O. Fradenburg, 'Criticism, Anti-Semitism, and the Prioress's Tale', *Exemplaria*, 1/1 (1989), 69–115.

[2] For an early expression of this view see Richard J. Schoek, 'Chaucer's Prioress: Mercy and Tender Heart', in *Chaucer Criticism*, 2 vols. (Notre Dame, Ind., 1960–1), ii: *The Canterbury Tales*, 245–58; and, more recently, Gloria Cigman, 'Piety and Prejudice', in André Crépin (ed.), *The Medieval Imagination. L'Imagination médiévale: Chaucer et ses contemporains*, Publications de l'Association des Médiévistes Anglicistes de l'Enseignement Supérieur (Paris, 1991), 133–47. Cf. Edward I. Condren, 'The Prioress: A Legend of Spirit, a Life of Flesh', *ChauR* 23 (1989), 192–218, who characterizes the Tale as not 'especially anti-Semitic' (p. 192).

critics are, it may be argued, using the figure of the Prioress to make the process of reading more comfortable: by avoiding addressing the question of the author's responsibility for his fiction—by attempting to displace that responsibility—we are provided with a means by which the Chaucer we have chosen to create out of our own biases and preconceptions may be exonerated, placed outside a system of beliefs which we, in the late twentieth century, find alien.[3]

Interpretations of the Tale and its teller are rendered even more problematic when the issue of gender is taken into account. The Prioress is one of only three women listed by Chaucer as being amongst the group of thirty-two pilgrims,[4] and her Tale therefore assumes an additional weight and significance amongst those which Chaucer completed, in that it seems to offer a rare opportunity within the narrative framework to hear a female 'voice' unmediated by a male pilgrim narrator. But implicit in the act of literary construction in which Chaucer is engaged is an element of ventriloquism, and his assumption of a female/feminine voice is precisely that—loath as some commentators have been to recognize this fact, preferring instead to pursue a reading in which the fictional representation of a woman is granted an autonomy of speech and action, and hence a psychological stature, independent of the author.[5] Yet it is important to realize that the image we are given of this nun, as of the Wife of Bath, is refracted through a

---

[3] See Emmy Stark Zitter, 'Anti-Semitism in Chaucer's *Prioress's Tale, ChauR* 25 (1991), 277–84, for an account which acknowledges the Tale's bias, but attempts to reconcile the opposing views by placing the Prioress at a distance from Chaucer, whilst contextualizing Chaucer's own 'misinterpretation of the Judaic tradition' (p. 282). Steven F. Kruger, 'The Bodies of Jews in the Late Middle Ages', in James M. Dean and Christian K. Zacher (eds.), *The Idea of Medieval Literature: New Essays on Chaucer and Medieval Culture in Honor of Donald R. Howard* (London, 1992), 301–23, compares the anti-Semitism here with that of the later Croxton *Play of the Sacrament*. For a forceful argument against critical 'neutrality' on the question, see Philip S. Alexander, 'Madame Eglentyne, Geoffrey Chaucer and the Problem of Medieval Anti-Semitism', *Bulletin of the John Rylands Library*, 74 (1992), 109–20.

[4] Chaucer the narrator numbers the pilgrims as twenty-nine (General Prologue 24); the number I give includes the figure of Chaucer as pilgrim. For discussion of this discrepancy see *The Riverside Chaucer*, 806, note to General Prologue, 1(A) 164.

[5] See e.g. Condren, 'The Prioress: A Legend of Spirit', 193: 'We...wonder whether [the Prioress] understands her tale', and cf. his comments justifying this approach, based on the theory of the self-construction of characters within texts, pp. 195 and 217 n. 30.

masculine lens.[6] The critical methodology employed by some of those who would champion the womanliness of Dame Eglentyne's patterns of thought and behaviour (a methodology which on occasion leans towards a simplified essentialism)[7] is thus to some extent convergent, perhaps paradoxically, and certainly unexpectedly, with that of the defenders of Chaucer's presumed political correctness in relation to the question of the Jews. Extreme proponents of either view appear unwilling to admit of the historical distance, and hence difference, which separates the fourteenth century from the twentieth. Whilst in the course of this chapter I shall, inevitably, have occasion to re-engage with the critical issues which I have outlined briefly, my primary aim is to suggest the necessity for just such a historicized reading of Chaucer's text, one which, whilst alive to its status as fiction, seeks to situate it within the particular cultural formations of the late Middle Ages.

The most valuable attempts to initiate the process of historicization of *The Canterbury Tales*, and specifically of the Prioress, date back to the 1920s. This decade witnessed, on the one hand, J. M. Manly's tracing of correspondences between various of the pilgrims and actual historical personages; and on the other, Eileen Power's conclusions as to the veracity of the implied criticisms of the Prioress's religiosity, or lack of it, when compared with the recorded abuses of those in the enclosed orders as detailed in

[6] This is a question not adequately addressed in many studies, including recent ones: see e.g. H. Marshall Leicester, Jr., *The Disenchanted Self: Representing the Subject in the 'Canterbury Tales'* (Berkeley and Los Angeles, 1990), ch. 8, 'The "Feminine" Imagination and *Jouissance*', esp. 211–13. Compare with this analysis John Ganim's comments on the Wife of Bath, 'The Literary Uses of the New History', in Dean and Zacher (eds.), *The Idea of Medieval Literature*, 209–26 (pp. 221–2).

[7] See e.g. Eileen Power, *Medieval People* (London, 1924), ch. 3, 'Madame Eglentyne: Chaucer's Prioress in Real Life', 75: 'Nuns, after all, were but women, and they had the amiable vanities of their sex.' Also Hardy Long Frank, 'Chaucer's Prioress and the Blessed Virgin', *ChauR* 13 (1978–9), 346–62 (p. 359): 'both Mistress [the Virgin] and handmaiden [the Prioress], Chaucer saw, were stereotypically feminine—whimsical, capricious, emotional, irrational, unconventional.' It is odd that the Prioress has received little attention in feminist readings of Chaucer: she is conspicuous by her absence in e.g. Carolyn Dinshaw, *Chaucer's Sexual Poetics* (Madison, 1989); Jill Mann, *Geoffrey Chaucer* (Hemel Hempstead, 1991); and Elaine Tuttle Hansen, *Chaucer and the Fictions of Gender* (Berkeley and Los Angeles, 1992).

contemporary accounts of bishops' visitations.[8] Manly, for example, cited the resemblance between the name of Chaucer's nun
and the 'do*mi*ne Argentyn' who was residing at the priory of St
Leonard's, Stratford at Bow, at the time of the death of Elizabeth
of Hainault, the sister of Queen Philippa, in 1375: this nun was the
recipient of two bequests from Elizabeth.[9] He later established the
identity of the prioress of Stratford during the early 1380s as Mary
Syward, and the source of his information—a lawsuit on the part
of this prioress against a London goldsmith, which involved the
sale of a cage 'and a bird called "thrusshe"'—offered a nicely
substantiating touch to Chaucer's portrait of a woman who,
against the rules of her enclosure, kept 'smale houndes' (VII. 146)
as pets.[10] Chaucer's apparent critique of the worldliness of
'madame Eglentyne', in her fondness for fine clothing, her discreet
table manners, and her undertaking of a pilgrimage (popes and
bishops alike made numerous attempts during the medieval period
to regulate movements of both men and women outside the cloister),[11] was seen to be apposite when set against the historical
documentation of the falling-off in piety amongst women religious.

The picture of such women which emerges from these archives
has for many critics been fortuitously coincident with that which
arises from a study of comparable literary materials, not only from
the Continental poems singled out by Jill Mann in her contextual-
ization of the Prioress within a tradition of estates satire,[12] but
also from English poems of the time, such as *Piers Plowman*, in
which Langland places Wrath within the backbiting and gossiping

[8] J. M. Manly, *Some New Light on Chaucer* (1926; repr. Gloucester, Mass.,
1959), 202–20; Eileen Power, *Medieval English Nunneries c.1275 to 1535*
(Cambridge, 1922), and 'Madame Eglentyne'. A more recent attempt to place the
Tale by itself within a historical context, Sumner Ferris, 'Chaucer at Lincoln (1387):
The *Prioress's Tale* as a Political Poem', *ChauR* 15 (1981), 295–321, has not
commanded much support amongst critics.

[9] Manly gives a translation of the will in *New Light*, 206–8; I have used the
transcription of the original in [Samuel Bentley], *Excerpta historica* (London, 1831),
24–5. The identification which Manly offers of 'domine Argentyn' strikes an odd
note: he records a family with the name Argentine (pp. 211–12), but I am not aware
that it was common for a nun to be distinguished in this way.

[10] J. M. Manly, 'A Prioress of Stratford', *Times Literary Supplement*, 10 Nov.
1927, p. 817.

[11] Power, *Medieval English Nunneries*, 69–73, 341–93.

[12] Jill Mann, *Chaucer and Medieval Estates Satire: The Literature of Social
Classes and the General Prologue to the 'Canterbury Tales'* (Cambridge, 1973),
128–37.

locale of a convent governed by his aunt (B V. 151–66). Wrath's rumour-mongering and stirring-up of trouble—neatly encapsulated by Langland both literally and metaphorically in his depiction of Wrath's activities as cook—engendered accusations of lack of chastity, illegitimate births, and physical violence amongst the inmates of the nunnery, all of which may be paralleled within the records of visitation.[13]

Dame Eglentyne sits easily amidst this emerging view of the lack of commitment amongst many women to the religious life. Whilst some of the criticisms which have been levelled against her in the past, such as her 'symple and coy' 'smylyng' (119), and her manner of singing the divine service 'Ful weel...Entuned in her nose' (122–3), may have more recently been qualified by lexical study and investigations into differing practices of communal chanting of the divine office,[14] the overall slipperiness of tone of Chaucer's description of her continues to elicit unease. His repeated insistence, for example, on the correctness and seemliness with which she conducts herself, whether in the choir, or at meat, combined with her evident concern for her outward appearance, and the compassion which she is said to express towards dumb animals, rather than the human needy, all contribute to an impression of a woman who aspires to gentility, and public recognition of her standing: 'she was...ful plesaunt, and amyable of port, | And peyned hire to countrefete cheere | Of court, and to ben estatlich of manere, | And to ben holden digne of reverence' (137–41). Although the presumed full satirical charge of Chaucer's comment on her speech, that 'Frenssh she spak ful faire and fetisly, | After the scole of Stratford atte Bowe, | For Frenssh of Parys was to hire unknowe' (124–6), has been defused by a demonstration of the extent to which the vocabulary of Chaucer himself is permeated by Anglo-Norman, rather than Parisian, coinages (perhaps as a consequence of his professional life in England, in which he was

---

[13] Cf. Power, *Medieval English Nunneries*, esp. 284–5 and app. II, 634–69; and the printed editions of archiepiscopal and episcopal registers listed in her bibliography, 694–7.

[14] See the *Middle English Dictionary*, gen. ed. Hans Kurath, pt. C. 3 (Ann Arbor, 1959), 369: *coi* (a): 'Quiet, modest, demure; reserved, reticent, discreet'. And on chanting, *The Riverside Chaucer*, 804, note to l. 123, and bibliography cited there. The particular manner of singing which Chaucer is apparently describing was first commented on by Manly, *New Light*, 217.

surrounded by documents in the former language),[15] the adverbial and adjectival stress placed on her *manner* of speaking ('ful faire and fetisly') retains its potentially subversive ambivalence. And, whilst Chaucer's description of the fastidiousness of her conduct at table may have been interpreted and reused with complete seriousness in the fifteenth century by the author of the courtesy book known from its published form as 'Lytel Iohn',[16] the closeness with which this portion of the General Prologue corresponds with La Vieille's discourse to Bel Acueill as to how young women ensnare men, from *Le Roman de la Rose*, serves to undermine its surface decorum.[17]

These features of Chaucer's descriptive technique fit tidily with the evidence of literary analogues and historical records I have referred to so far, and the comparisons are powerful to the extent that they establish some of the parameters within which he was writing. But I would argue that Chaucer's depiction of female piety and devotional practice is a partial one, the result of a process of conscious selection of detail, and that recognition of the absences which characterize his text is crucial to a reading of both the Prioress and her Tale. A significant opposition to Chaucer's (however gentle) satirical treatment of a late fourteenth-century nun[18] is provided by recent investigations into the devotional lives of medieval women, investigations which extend beyond the recording of their shortcomings and failures. The biographies of a number of enclosed women contemporary with Chaucer, for instance, pieced

[15] W. Rothwell, 'Chaucer and Stratford atte Bow', *Bulletin of the John Rylands Library*, 74 (1992), 3–28.
[16] *Caxton's Book of Curtesye*, ed. F. J. Furnivall, EETS ES 3 (London, 1868); the text in Oxford, Oriel College, MS 79, is the best: see esp. 18, 20, ll. 176–89. The invocation to Chaucer, ll. 330–50 (p. 34) is suggestive of this poet's indebtedness to him.
[17] See *Le Roman de la Rose*, ed. Félix Lecoy (Paris, 1985), ll. 13355 ff.; or *The Romance of the Rose*, tr. Frances Horgan (Oxford, 1994), 206–7. Colin Wilcockson, 'A Note on Chaucer's Prioress and her Literary Kinship with the Wife of Bath', *MÆ* 61 (1992), 92–6, associates the two female pilgrims through Chaucer's use of the *Roman* as a common source: he therefore describes them as being 'bonded in ironic literary sisterhood' (p. 95). Douglas Loney, 'Chaucer's Prioress and Agur's "Adulterous Woman"', *ChauR* 27 (1992), 107–8, detects a complementary scriptural allusion underlying the Prioress's wiping of her upper lip.
[18] See e.g., *The Works of Geoffrey Chaucer*, ed. F. N. Robinson, 2nd edn. (London, 1957), 653: Chaucer's 'satire—if it can be called satire at all—is of the gentlest and most sympathetic sort'. Cf. Loney, 'Chaucer's Prioress and Agur's "Adulterous Woman"', 108.

together from a variety of sources, show them to have been resourceful and independent, with a strongly developed interest in books and learning, and a determination to direct their own religious lives and provide spiritual enrichment for those for whom they were responsible. For the purposes of this present essay I shall confine my discussion to those resident in two houses of Benedictine nuns in close proximity to each other, as well as to London, both of which houses Chaucer apparently knew: the priory of St Leonard's at Stratford at Bow, in Middlesex, which is invoked in the description of the Prioress; and the abbey of Barking in Essex, which bore a joint dedication to St Ethelburga (sister of the reputed founder, St Erkenwald) and the Virgin.[19]

Chaucer's semi-humorous reference in the Invocation to *The House of Fame*, in which the narrator claims that he was too tired to undertake the 'pilgrymage myles two | To the corseynt Leonard' (116–17), suggests acquaintance with the priory (the actual distance to which from his London home tallies with this particularity of detail). Since as a young man he was for a time in the service of Elizabeth of Ulster, wife of Lionel, duke of Clarence, he may well have been in her retinue when she visited Lionel's aunt Elizabeth of Hainault in the priory in 1356; and the duchess's daughter Philippa seems to have spent some time in residence there.[20] The evidence for Chaucer's acquaintance with Barking derives from his relationship with his later patron, Lionel of Clarence's elder brother John of Gaunt. In 1381 Gaunt authorized the substantial payment of £51 8s. 2d. when one Elizabeth Chaucy—surmised to have been either the sister or the daughter of the poet—was admitted as a nun to the house.[21] Gaunt's patronage of the foundation is further suggested by the election of Margaret Swynford to the office of abbess in 1419: she had been admitted as a nun in 1377, and it has been suggested, with some plausibility, that she was the daughter of Gaunt's mistress and third wife Katherine (sister of Chaucer's own wife) by her first

---

[19] For St Leonard's see *The Victoria County History* (hereafter cited as *VCH*), *Middlesex*, i (Oxford, 1969), 156–9; and for Barking, *VCH: Essex*, ii (London, 1907), 115–22.

[20] *VCH: Middlesex*, i. 157.

[21] *Chaucer Life-Records*, ed. Martin M. Crow and Clair C. Olson (Oxford, 1966), 546; *John of Gaunt's Register, 1379–1383*, 2 vols., ed. Eleanor C. Lodge and Robert Somerville, Camden Society, 3rd ser. 56 and 57 (1937), i. 169, entry no. 524.

husband: hence, she would have been the poet's niece by mar-riage.[22]

Of the two foundations Barking was the older, and the wealth-ier. (At the dissolution it was recorded as being the third wealth-iest female house.) It enjoyed royal patronage throughout the nearly 900 years of its existence; its abbess took precedence over all others in the kingdom; and it had a well-established reputation for learning. Of the three Anglo-Norman saints' lives to which a fairly reliable attribution of female authorship may be given, Bark-ing can lay claim to two: *The Life of St Catherine* by the late twelfth-century nun Clemence; and the contemporary *Vie d'Édouard le confesseur*.[23] And in the present context it may not be insignificant to note that the second version of the earliest translation of a Latin *mariale*, or collection of miracles of the Virgin, into the vernacular, by William Adgar, was dedicated to an abbess of Barking—Maud, natural daughter of Henry II.[24] A substantial number of books belonging to the abbey are still in existence, and in the *Ordinale* drawn up for Abbess Sybil de Felton in 1404 (Oxford, University College, MS 169) reference is made to a librarian, one of whose duties was to organize the annual dis-tribution of books amongst the resident nuns after Terce on the first Monday of Lent.[25] During Chaucer's lifetime Katherine de Sutton (abbess between 1358 and 1377) and Sybil de Felton (1393–1419) made quite substantial contributions to the cultural life of the abbey. Katherine, for example, initiated the rewriting of part of the Easter liturgy: the *Elevatio Hostiae* was moved from its traditional position before Matins, to follow the third response in

[22] *VCH: Essex*, ii. 121.
[23] See *The Life of St Catherine by Clemence of Barking*, ed. W. McBain, ANTS 18 (1964); *La Vie d'Édouard le confesseur, poème anglo-normand du XIIe siècle*, ed. Ö Södergaard (Uppsala, 1948); M. Dominica Legge, *Anglo-Norman Literature and its Background* (Oxford, 1963), esp. 66–72, 60–6; Jocelyn Wogan-Browne, '"Clerc u Lai, Muïne u Dame": Women and Anglo-Norman Hagiography in the Twelfth and Thirteenth Centuries', in C. Meale (ed.), *Women and Literature in Britain 1150–1500* 2nd. edn. (Cambridge, 1996), 61–85, esp. 67–74.
[24] Legge, *Anglo-Norman Literature*, 187–91, and bibliography cited there.
[25] *The Ordinale and Customary of the Benedictine Nuns of Barking Abbey*, ed. J. B. L. Tolhurst, 2 vols., Henry Bradshaw Society 65 and 66 (London, 1927–8), i. 67; the distribution of books is commented upon by A. I. Doyle, 'Books Connected with the Vere Family and Barking Abbey', *Transactions of the Essex Archaeological Society*, 25 (1958), 222–43 (p. 240). For extant books see N. R. Ker, *Medieval Libraries of Great Britain: A List of Surviving Books*, 2nd edn. (London, 1964), 6; and the *Supplement* to this, ed. Andrew G. Watson (London, 1987), 2.

this service, combining it with the *Visitatio Sepulchri*, to produce a quasi-dramatic performance. The status of liturgical celebration as drama remains disputed, but the ceremony as carried out at Barking certainly contains elements of the mimetic, in addition to the ritual or cultic.[26] Especially striking is the inclusion of the nuns as active participants. The entire convent, together with several priests, processed to the Chapel of Mary Magdalene, in symbolic representation of the souls of the patriarchs descending to hell prior to Christ's releasing of them following the resurrection. The patriarchs' liberation from spiritual imprisonment was enacted by three blows being administered to the door of the chapel by another priest, on the last of which the nuns and their accompanying priests emerged in triumph. The following *Visitatio* is significant in relation to women's active demonstration of piety in that, contrary to usual practice, three nuns represented the three Marys; the abbess herself arranged white veils upon their heads. That this was no private celebration, intended for the members of the convent alone, is indicated by the displaying by the officiating priest of the Host, contained within a crystal monstrance, to the laity present (*ad populum*), after the release of the patriarchs; and by the explanation of Katherine's rationale in reforming the service and encouraging spiritual observance and enthusiasm, as given in the *Ordinale*:

Quoniam populorum concursus temporibis illis videbatur deuocione frigessere, et torpor humanus maxime accrescens, venerabilis Domina Katerina de Suttone, tunc pastoralis cure gerens vicem, desiderans dictum torporem penitus extirpare et fidelium deuocionem ...excitare, vnanimi consororum consensu instituit ut statim post tertium responsorium Matutinarum die Pasche fieret Dominice Resurexionis celebracio.

[26] The text is printed in *The Ordinale and Customary... of Barking Abbey*, ed. Tolhurst, i. 100, 107–9; and in Karl Young, *The Drama of the Medieval Church*, 2 vols. (Oxford, 1933), i. 164–77, 381–5 and pl. 10; see also Pamela Sheingorn, *The Easter Sepulchre in England* (Kalamazoo, Mich., 1987), 29–30, 131–7, and pls. 10–17. For discussion see Nancy Cotton, 'Katherine of Sutton: The First English Woman Playwright', *Educational Theatre Journal*, 30 (1978), 475–81; William Tydeman, 'An Introduction to Medieval English Theatre', in Richard Beadle (ed.), *The Cambridge Companion to Medieval English Theatre* (Cambridge, 1994), 1–36 (p. 8). Liturgical 'drama' is usefully and interestingly discussed by Hans-Jürgen Diller, *The Middle English Mystery Play: A Study in Dramatic Speech and Form* (Cambridge, 1992), 9–68; and cf. R. N. Swanson, 'Medieval Liturgy as Theatre: The Props', in Diana Wood (ed.), *The Church and the Arts* (Oxford, 1992), 239–53.

(Since the assembly of people seemed to grow cold in their devotion at this time, with human apathy greatly increasing, the venerable Lady Katherine of Sutton, being then in her post of pastoral care, desiring to root out the said apathy entirely, and to stimulate more the devotion of the faithful . . . - laid down with the unanimous agreement of the sisterhood that immediately after the third Respond of Matins on Easter Day a celebration of the Lord's Resurrection should be performed.)[27]

There is an intriguing hint that dramatic enactment of some sort may have been established at Barking at an earlier period in the visitation record of 1279: Archbishop Peckham, following the report given to him by the bishop of London, instructed that nuns, rather than children, should be involved in the devotional rites held on Holy Innocents' Day; this prohibition may indicate that the participation of boys in the revels associated with the so-called 'Boy Bishop' had become customary within the house.[28]

Sybil de Felton's concerns seem to have centred more on the acquisition of books for the abbey, and her ownership inscriptions survive in several manuscripts. On fo. 4v of the Foyle copy of Nicholas Love's *Myrrour of the Blessed Lyf of Jesu Christ*, for example, are written the words 'Iste liber constat domine Sibille de ffelton abbatisse de Berkyng', and this volume remained at the foundation until the dissolution, when it was given by a former nun, Margaret Scrope, to another woman.[29] Oxford, Bodleian Library, MS Bodley 923, a copy of *The Clensyng of Mannes Sowle*, bears a similarly worded *ex libris* on fo. 153v, and the reference within the text to an earlier work written for enclosed religious women, *The Chastisyng of Goddis Children*, a treatise upon which the *Clensyng* is partly dependent, has led to the

---

[27] The Latin quotation is taken from Young, *The Drama of the Medieval Church*, ii. 411; and the translation from William Tydeman, *The Theatre in the Middle Ages: Western European Stage Conditions c.800–1576* (Cambridge, 1978), 223.

[28] *Registrum epistolarum Fratris Johannis Peckham Archiepiscopi Cantuariensis (1272–92)*, ed. C. Trice Martin, 3 vols, Rolls Series 77 (London, 1882–5), i. 82–3; *VCH: Essex*, ii. 117. Young, *The Drama of the Medieval Church*, i. 105–10, discusses the phenomenon.

[29] *Nicholas Love's Mirror of the Blessed Life of Jesus Christ*, ed. Michael G. Sargent (New York, 1992), pp. lxxviii–lxix; Doyle, 'Books Connected with the Vere Family', 240–1. I discuss this manuscript further in my paper ' "Oft sipis with grete deuotion I þought what I miȝt do plesyng to god": The Early Ownership and Readership of Love's *Myrrour*, with Special Reference to its Female Audience', in S. Ogura, R. Beadle and M. G. Sargent (eds.), *Nicholas Love at Waseda* (Cambridge: forthcoming).

suggestion that the *Chastisyng*, too, was intended for the readership of Barking nuns, though the case for this remains possible
rather than proven.[30] The inscription in another volume, a copy of
the French *Vies des saints Pères*, now Paris, Bibliothèque Nationale, MS fr. 1038, indicates that Sibyl was active in hunting out
suitable reading material whenever opportunity offered itself. A
note records that 'cest livere achàta dame sibilla de feltonne
abbesse de berkyng de les executurs de dame philippe coucy duch-
esse d'Ireland et contesse d'oxenford'. Philippa, who died in 1411,
was the daughter of Enguerrand de Coucy, and wife of Robert de
Vere, 9th earl of Oxford and duke of Ireland (d. 1392).[31] A
number of other Barking books are extant from the fifteenth
century, which lends weight to the argument that there was a
continuing tradition of reading and learning at the abbey.[32]

By comparison, the cultural evidence relating to the house at
Stratford, founded in 1122, is scanty. Elizabeth of Hainault, however, bequeathed 'unum psalterum' to the Dame Argentyn mentioned above, and a primer covered in red to her servant Sarah,
although it is not clear whether this latter was a religious or a
secular, and whether she remained at the priory after Elizabeth's
death. Aside from this there is a possibility that a fifteenth-century
volume described as a commonplace book, copied on parchment,
and with miscellaneous contents in Latin and English—amongst
them medical and other recipes and charms, prognostications, and
tables of weights and measures—may have belonged to Stratford,
although the evidence for this is equivocal: the codex only came to
light when it came onto the commercial book-market some thirty-
odd years ago.[33] One explanation for this paucity of material

[30] *The Chastising of God's Children and the Treatise of Perfection of the Sons of
God*, ed. Joyce Bazire and Eric Colledge (Oxford, 1957), 36–7.

[31] Léopold Delisle, *Les Cabinets des manuscrits de la Bibliothèque Impérial*, 3
vols. (Paris, 1868–81), i. 109–10; Doyle, 'Books Connected with the Vere Family',
241, who notes that the manuscript later entered the library of Charles d'Orléans. I
am grateful to Julia Boffey for supplying me with the full details of the inscription.

[32] Doyle, 'Books Connected with the Vere Family', 241–3.

[33] See *Excerpta historica*, 25, for Elizabeth of Hainault's bequest. For a
description of the so-called 'commonplace book' see Sotheby's Sale Catalogue, 15
June 1959, lot 204 (p. 57); the volume was bought by a private buyer, J. S. Cox,
listed in Watson's *Supplement* to Ker's *Medieval Libraries* as being of St Peter Port,
Guernsey. The ascription to Stratford rests on an inscription in a hand of *c*.1500
which refers to 'Robert Suffyngton of Stratforde the Dowe [door] porte of the
Nonery there', and was evidently not regarded as being sufficient evidence of

evidence may lie in Stratford's relative smallness and poverty. In common with many female houses, Stratford frequently pleaded lack of funds. By 1380–1, for example, according to the poll-tax return, there were only fourteen resident nuns, including the prioress and subprioress: this compares with a total of thirty nuns recorded in 1354.[34] Nevertheless, the house was popular throughout the later Middle Ages amongst the bourgeoisie and clerics of London. Citizens and priests not only made bequests to the house (including rents of named properties within the city, which were essential to the maintenance of the convent's income) and to individual members within it, but several wills enrolled in the Court of Husting from the late thirteenth century onwards testify to the fact that the daughters of Londoners were placed there as professed religious, amongst them Juliana, daughter of John de Evere, in 1277/8; Isabella, daughter of the merchant Robert le Bret, in 1293/4; and Leticia, daughter of John Briklesworth, who held extensive properties in the city, in 1368; whilst in 1477 Elizabeth, daughter of John Gayton, steward to the convent and subsequently prioress, was left a small pension by her father.[35] The lack of hard evidence of literacy and book-learning amongst the nuns at Stratford compared with those of Barking should not, however, be taken to indicate a high level of ignorance and/or a deficiency in piety at the former house: account must be taken of the vagaries of manuscript survival, certainly prior to the fifteenth century, and of the general lack of wealth amongst female, as opposed to male, foundations, where the existence of extensive libraries is more frequently recorded.[36] The increasing amount of attention which is being directed towards the reading of women

ownership by the priory by either Ker or Watson, since they do not include it in their catalogues. I am indebted to A. S. G. Edwards for bringing the sale entry to my attention, and to Christopher de Hamel for supplying me with further information.

[34] *VCH: Middlesex*, i. 158.

[35] Ibid. 157 and references cited there. The examples I quote are taken from the *Calendar of Wills Proved and Enrolled in the Court of Husting, London*, ed. Reginald R. Sharpe, 2 vols. (London, 1889–90), i. 34, 110–11; ii. 119–20; *VCH: Middlesex*, ii. 157 (quoting from Guildhall MS 9171/6, fos. 234^v–36^v).

[36] For a comparison between the book-holdings of male and female houses see Ker (ed.), *Medieval Libraries*, and the *Supplement*, ed. Watson. On the poverty of female foundations see Power, *Medieval English Nunneries*, 161–228; and especially on the poverty of post-Conquest houses, Sally Thompson, *Women Religious: The Founding of English Nunneries after the Norman Conquest* (Oxford, 1991), *passim* (for Stratford see p. 12).

religious is unsettling the long-standing consensus as to their lack of learning, and recent studies of book acquisition and care at the house of Clares (better known as the Minoresses) at Aldgate in London, at Henry V's foundation of Syon in Middlesex, and of more provincial communities such as those of the Dominicans at Dartford in Kent and of Franciscan nuns at Denny in Cambridgeshire, should caution against unquestioned assumptions as to the level of devotion at any one institution.[37]

Having argued the case for Chaucer's acquaintance with a different model of female piety from that he chose to represent fictionally, the question remains: why did he choose to portray a Prioress who conformed to a stereotype familiar from a well-defined and essentially satirical literary tradition, a stereotype which may be substantiated only through the partial evidence of one particular kind of historical record? To begin with, it is worth

---

[37] Much of the evidence—documentary and codicological—again dates from after Chaucer's lifetime, but this is also true where secular readers are concerned. On the Minoresses see in particular Julia Boffey, 'Some London Women Readers and a Text of *The Three Kings of Cologne*', *The Ricardian*, 10/132 (1996), 387–96. On Syon see Mary Carpenter Erler, 'Syon Abbey's Care for Books: Its Sacristan's Account Rolls 1506/7–1535/6', *Scriptorium*, 39 (1985), 293–307, and Ann M. Hutchison, 'Devotional Reading in the Monastery and in the Late Medieval Household', in Michael G. Sargent (ed.), *De cella in speculum: Religion and Secular Life and Devotion in Late Medieval England* (Cambridge, 1989), 215–27; on Dartford, Doyle, 'Some Books Connected with the Vere Family', esp. 228–9, 233–5. It was apparently for the nuns of Denny that the sole surviving complete manuscript of Osbern Bokenham's *Legendys of Hooly Wummen* was made: see the edition by Mary J. Serjeantson, EETS OS 206 (London, 1938), and A. S. G. Edwards, 'The Transmission and Audience of Osbern Bokenham's *Legendys of Hooly Wummen*', in A. J. Minnis (ed.), *Late-Medieval Religious Texts and their Transmission* (Cambridge, 1993), 157–67. See also David N. Bell, *What Nuns Read: Books and Libraries in Medieval English Nunneries*, Cistercian Publications, 158 (Kalamazoo, Mich., 1995). The unpublished letter to 'Welbiloued susturs in our lord ihesu crist' in Durham, University Library, Cosin MS V.III.16, dating from c.1500, which invokes earlier women religious as examples to be followed by contemporary nuns, is important for the stress it places on learning: 'Women in the olde tyme of | high degree as quenes & princesses come to religion to leue | ther pleasure & ther own [will] & to lyue in grete penaunce & to | kepe the seid vertues streitly . In so much that mony holy | bisshopps & other seynts toke her lernyng of nonnes tho | dayes by ther holy conuersacion . Then women of religioun | vsed contynuelly devoute [preier] & contemplacion . wacch & grete | abstynence with other...vertues afore rehersid . neuer vnoccupied . as in redyng . studiyng . writyng . suying . wasshyng | delfyng or herbys settyng or sowyng with other....' Dr Ian Doyle has commented in conversation that the letter may well have been intended for the nuns of Syon. It is, whoever its intended recipients were, a significant indicator as to the expectations placed upon professed women.

emphasizing that, with relatively little adjustment, the behavioural traits through which the persona of Dame Eglentyne is defined could be presented in a positive light. The heads of religious households had, of necessity, to be acquainted with the world: the similarities between the organization and running of secular and religious households were numerous, and an abbess or prioress was, through the necessity placed upon her to welcome guests, inevitably going to come into frequent contact with seculars.[38] Indeed, many women of noble or gentle birth chose to live out their lives within the confines of a convent. Some of them apparently did so out of a genuine sense of piety—like Elizabeth of Hainault and Elizabeth de Vere, wife of the 12th earl of Oxford, who, like her earlier namesake, died at Stratford; others may have been encouraged, if not forced, into such confinement due to changing political circumstances (such as Elizabeth Wydville).[39] Elizabeth of Hainault's bequest of expensive items of clothing and of jewellery to the convent of Stratford would, no doubt, have been welcome: to the prioress, Mary Syward, she left a gold ring embellished with a ruby and an emerald; to the Mary chapel her best mantle and surcoat, and her best veil, together with a fillet of pearls; whilst to the main altar of the house she bequeathed her

[38] Power, *Medieval English Nunneries*, 131–60, and 563–8 for an account of the *Charthe longynge to the Office of the Celeresse of the Monasterye of Barkinge* (London, British Library, MS Cotton Julius D. VIII, fos. 40ʳ–47ᵛ) which illustrates the complexity of monastic household management (cf. Doyle's comments, 'Books Connected with the Vere Family', 240). See the early 15th-cent. Middle English prose version of the *Rule of St Benet*, in BL Lansdowne MS 378, which shows signs of adaptation for female readers, and the contemporary metrical version, in BL MS Cotton Vespasian A.25, in which all the pronouns are feminine, for the standards of hospitality expected of abbesses and prioresses of the Benedictine order: *Three Middle-English Versions of the Rule of St Benet*, ed. Ernst A. Kock, EETS OS 120 (1902), 35–6, 102–3. The Prioress's 'professional role' is considered briefly by Hardy Long Frank, 'Seeing the Prioress Whole', *ChauR* 25 (1991), 229–37, but little is offered by way of historical documentation.

[39] It has often been assumed that Elizabeth of Hainault was a nun (e.g. in *Excerpta historica*, 24), but I can see no incontrovertible evidence that this was the case. On Elizabeth de Vere who, whilst dying at Stratford, gave a book of French devotional treatises to Barking, see Doyle, 'Books Connected with the Vere Family', 235; and on the dispute over the reasons for the enclosure of Edward IV's widow Elizabeth Wydville at the Cluniac abbey of Bermondsey, David MacGibbon, *Elizabeth Woodville 1437–1492: Her Life and Times* (London, 1938), 190–1, 197, 198–200; S. B. Chrimes, *Henry VII* (London, 1972), 76; and Anne F. Sutton and Livia Visser-Fuchs, 'A "Most Benevolent Queen": Queen Elizabeth Woodville's Reputation, her Piety and her Books', *The Ricardian*, 10 (1995), 214–45 (p. 234).

second-best mantle furred with 'gris', a matching surcoat, and her second-best veil. On one level such legacies may be seen as an intrusion of worldly values into the conventual life, but numerous collections of wills, and complaints recorded in bishops' visitations as to the insufficiency of clothing for nuns in many areas of the country, make it clear that for financial reasons uniformity and austerity in dress were ideals imperfectly realized for many enclosed religious.[40] Equally, as has been pointed out by Jonathan Nicholls, notions of courtesy and good behaviour were advocated for nuns and monks alike: it was not only in secular households that regard was taken of the niceties of communal living.[41]

That Chaucer chose not to emphasize these realities of female monastic existence, but instead represented his Prioress with an ironic humour, must, I think, be related to the ideological strategies he deployed in the General Prologue as a whole, as well as to the tradition of estates satire which he utilized for many of the pilgrims' portraits. This is clearly too large a topic to be explored in any detail within the present discussion, but I suspect that the target for much of Chaucer's satire against the Prioress was class-, rather than gender-, specific. It is in this respect that his reference to Stratford at Bow takes on significance for, whilst it has been taken as an indication that the Prioress was a resident of this house (and, therefore, a Benedictine), Chaucer himself, in his role as pilgrim narrator, makes no such identification. His glancing comment serves instead to place the nun socially: it is her provincialism, and, as I have already observed, her pretensions towards a

[40] *Excerpta historica*, 24; and for legacies of clothing see e.g. the bequest made by Agnes Stapilton of Carlton, Yorkshire, of 'unam flammiolam de lawne, unam de Raynes, et duas de smal barbes, et unum anulum de auro cum ymagine Trinitatis' to 'Domine Elizabethe Maudesley' in 1448: *North Country Wills... 1383–1558*, ed. J. W. Clay, Surtees Society 116 (London, 1908), 49. Cf. the volumes of *Testamenta Eboracensia*, ed. James Raines, Surtees Society 4, 30, 45, 53 (London, 1836, 1855, 1865, 1869), *passim*. For the regulations relating to dress for the Benedictines see *The Rule of St Benedict*, tr. Justin McCann, with commentary by Paul Delatte (London, 1921), 346–57; and *Three Middle-English Versions of the Rule of St Benet*, ed. Kock, 36, 104–5.

[41] Jonathan Nicholls, *The Matter of Courtesy: Medieval Courtesy Books and the Gawain-Poet* (Cambridge, 1985), 22–44. He suggests (p. 25) that the Prioress's 'knowledge of good courtesy could have come from the customary of her nunnery at Stratford atte Bow'. His discussion of the Syon customary, finished by the early 1430s, is especially relevant to this issue; see for the text the appendix, 'Additions to the Rules', in George J. Aungier, *The History and Antiquities of Syon Monastery, the Parish of Isleworth, and the Chapelry of Hounslow* (London, 1840).

gentility which is in some measure foreign to her, which he seems to find amusing. The findings of a recent investigation into the social composition of the office-holders amongst East Anglian female religious, which demonstrate that the majority were drawn from the ranks of the lower gentry, rather than from those of the upper gentry and the nobility, would offer support for this interpretation.[42] For Chaucer's primary audience, composed in all probability of professional men like himself, there may have been a pointedness in the reference to Stratford and, by extension, to its popularity in the later fourteenth century amongst the citizenry, as opposed to the more élite members of the gentry and upper bourgeoisie, which has been lost to later generations of readers.[43]

A similar condescension, and social critique, may be traced in the depiction in the General Prologue of the five guildsmen—'An Haberdasshere and a Carpenter, | A Webbe, a Dyere, and a Tapycere', and their association with 'a great fraternitee' (361–2, 364). From the variety of crafts which they practise, and the comparative lowliness of their standing within the merchant class as a whole (the more prestigious of the mercantile companies are not represented), it is evident that the guild to which they belong is not craft-based, but is instead likely to have been a religious guild based within a particular parish—and not necessarily, it may be remarked, one within London.[44] Chaucer's swiftly drawn sketch of the guildsmen's self-importance, and that of their wives who, the narrator naïvely comments, gloried in their claims for social precedence and in their right to be addressed as 'madame' (a title open

---

[42] See Marilyn Oliva, 'Aristocracy or Meritocracy? Office-Holding Patterns in Late Medieval English Nunneries', in W. J. Sheils and Diana Wood (eds.), *Women in the Church* (Oxford, 1990), 197–208. The assumption that Chaucer's Prioress is of noble birth has been held to with some tenacity, underlying such arguments as that by Joseph A. Dane, 'The Prioress and her *Romanzen*', *ChauR* 24 (1990), 219–22.

[43] On Chaucer's primary audience see Paul Strohm, *Social Chaucer* (Cambridge, Mass., 1989), 24–83, and additional bibliography cited there.

[44] See George Unwin, *The Gilds and Companies of London* (London, 1908), 110–26; Sylvia L. Thrupp, *The Merchant Class of Medieval London [1300–1500]* (1948; repr. Ann Arbor, 1962), *passim*; Caroline M. Barron, 'The Parish Fraternities of Medieval London', in Caroline M. Barron and Christopher Harper-Bill (eds.), *The Church in Pre-Reformation Society* (Woodbridge, 1985), 13–37 (see p. 30 and n. 73 for her observation, supported by quotation from the General Prologue, that 'What seems clear is that the parish fraternity movement was, predominantly, a "middle class" artisan movement and to such men the parish fraternity was often the centre of their social and spiritual world'). For a wider geographical survey see F. H. Westlake, *The Parish Gilds of Medieval England* (London, 1919).

to the wives of the individuals who became aldermen of parish guilds or fraternities) and who 'goon to vigilies al bifore' with mantles 'roialliche ybore' (374–8),[45] places them securely in the same category as Dame Eglentyne—that of the aspirant lower middle class. No modern historian or literary historian of the period has, to my knowledge, chosen Chaucer's portrayal of these individuals as the basis for an assessment of the values and shortcomings of parish guilds in the fourteenth and fifteenth centuries—but then, if he had got round to assigning tales to them, they might well have been a subject of greater interest to both. It is unfortunate that the eminence accorded the Prioress in literary studies—partly through a sustained interest over the course of the centuries in anticlerical satire, and partly through what may be characterized as the equivocal power of her Tale—has exerted such an influence over historical studies of women religious.[46]

This leads me on to the consideration of the relationship between the Prioress and the Tale which she recounts. There is not, I believe, a necessary and inevitable relationship between the two, and I find attempts to account for the Tale's supposed sentimentality or its affective lyricism (depending on the individual critic's standpoint) by reference to either the frustrated sexuality, the frustrated maternal feelings, or the genuine spiritual impulse of a devotee of the Virgin, deeply unconvincing.[47] Piero Boitani's tracing to Dante of the motif of the religious supplicant comparing her-himself to an infant, for example, offers sufficient evidence to suggest that Chaucer was not making a statement specific to, or critical of, the Prioress when, in the Prologue to the Tale, she

[45] On the question of hierarchy and precedence within congregations see Margaret Aston, 'Segregation in Church', in Sheils and Wood (eds.), *Women in the Church*, 237–94.

[46] Again, I come back in particular to the work of Eileen Power, in her 'Madame Eglentyne', and in *Medieval English Nunneries*, e.g. 94–5; and cf. appendices I and J, pp. 604–26, on the representation of nuns in literary sources other than Chaucer.

[47] For representative examples of these interpretations see Hope Phyllis Weissman, 'Antifeminism and Chaucer's Characterizations of Women', in George D. Economou (ed.), *Geoffrey Chaucer: A Collection of Original Articles* (New York, 1975), 104; Condren, 'The Prioress: A Legend of Spirit'; Winthrop Wetherbee, *Geoffrey Chaucer: 'The Canterbury Tales'* (Cambridge, 1989), 97–9; Frank, 'Chaucer's Prioress and the Blessed Virgin'. I am more in sympathy with the position taken by Derek Pearsall, *The Canterbury Tales* (London, 1985), 43, 247, 250, and by Carolyn P. Collette, who explores the Tale in the context of late medieval affective devotion in 'Sense and Sensibility in the *Prioress's Tale'*, *ChauR* 15 (1980), 138–50.

declares her inability to do justice to her subject-matter (481–5). Any psychological interpretation which would take this passage as an expression of her emotional and/or intellectual immaturity is inappropriate.[48] Whilst authorial interjections within the narrative confirm that the Tale has been adapted, if not originally written for, the Prioress[49] (for instance the distancing 'quod she' of l. 454 of the Prologue; the implied criticism of monks, ll. 643–4; and the fervent celebration of the murdered child's virginity, ll. 579–81, a state of being in which the Prioress obviously has a personal and professional investment), the Tale stands by itself as a self-contained and at times movingly written profession of faith in the mercy of Christ's mother. Profoundly repellent though the entrenched anti-Semitism is, it is essential to acknowledge that Chaucer, as so often, is exploring the limits of a particular literary genre and, in so doing, reproduces it with a skill which far outpasses that of his predecessors.[50] Anti-Semitism, as has often been noted, is a common feature of Marian miracles, but in many of the tales the Jews, either collectively or singly, are converted. In the closest surviving vernacular analogue to the Prioress's Tale, 'Hou þe Iewes in despit of vre lady þrewe a chyld in a gonge', the second legend in the miracle sequence preserved in the Vernon manuscript (Oxford, Bodleian Library, MS Eng. poet. A. 1), the punishment accorded the murderer of the innocent is noted but not dwelt upon, the author commenting that 'þe Ieuh was Iugget for þat Morþere' (114). Chaucer, however, both heightens the association of the Jews with Satan (558–64) and emphasizes the guilt of the Jews as a race, not simply the individual guilt of the murderer, in his description of the judgment meted out to the community of the ghetto by the Provost—the officer of a government which, it is relevant to stress, has actively encouraged the presence of the Jews within the country as money-lenders (628–34; 488–91).[51]

[48] Piero Boitani, *The Tragic and the Sublime in Medieval Literature* (Cambridge, 1989), 211–13.

[49] Helen Cooper, *The Canterbury Tales*, Oxford Guides to Chaucer (Oxford, 1989), 287.

[50] Cf. C. David Benson, *Chaucer's Drama of Style* (Chapel Hill, NC, 1986), 131–46.

[51] For texts to compare with Chaucer's see Carleton Brown, 'Chaucer's *Prioress's Tale* and its Analogues', *PMLA* 21 (1906), 486–518, and *A Study of the Miracle of Our Lady Told by Chaucer's Prioress*, Chaucer Society, 2nd ser. 45 (London, 1910);

But the implicit (and on occasions, explicit) anti-Semitism of Chaucer's sources is not the only aspect of the genre which Chaucer has elaborated upon. His depiction of the child's mother, of the agony of her search for him (586–606), is deeply compassionate and more convincingly rendered than, for example, in the Vernon legend.[52] That Chaucer himself took this piece of writing seriously, that he was not using it as a means of revealing the psychological shortcomings of its imagined narrator, is, by and large, a conclusion unpalatable to modern readers. But the facts that he chose to compose it in his most elevated rhyme-scheme, rhyme royal, and that he interwove echoes of liturgical offices into its Prologue, demonstrates the extent to which he had assimilated the purposes and techniques inherent in antecedent examples.[53] If its spirituality (as distinct from its theology), finally, has to be judged as wanting, the judgement should be applied to the genre, and not to the author, or to the fictional narrator. Within the framework of the *Tales* as a whole the Prioress's contribution acts as a sobering influence on the assembled pilgrims (691–2), and there is every indication that Chaucer's secondary audiences in the fifteenth century were neither critical nor sceptical, as to the Tale's import. Its inclusion—separated from the framework of the pilgrimage—in six manuscripts, in several of which, such as London, British

the Vernon miracles are edited by C. Horstmann, *The Minor Poems of the Vernon MS*, i, EETS OS 98 (London, 1892), 138–67. On one level the anti-Semitism in the Tale serves explicitly Christian ends, hence the reference to Herod and the invocation of the massacre of the Innocents (l.574, and cf. n. 53 below). The murder of the boy is, simultaneously, a re-enactment of the Jews' killing of Christ, hence the child's mother is a figure of Mary; and the Virgin herself is prefigured in the Old Testament story of Rachel, referred to by Chaucer in his characterization of the mother as 'this newe Rachel' (l. 627). Useful discussions of this layering of scriptural allusion are J. A. Burrow, *Medieval Writers and their Work: Middle English Literature and its Background 1100–1500* (Oxford, 1982), 102; and Roger Ellis, *Patterns of Religious Narrative in the 'Canterbury Tales'* (London, 1986), 69–81. Acknowledgement of this scheme of reference does not render the heightening of anti-Semitism any more acceptable: cf. Alexander, 'Madame Eglentyne, Geoffrey Chaucer and the Problem of Medieval Anti-Semitism' (cit n. 3 above).

[52] Compare Chaucer, ll. 583–606, with *Minor Poems of the Vernon MS*, i, ed. Horstmann, 142–3, ll. 54–88. For Derek Pearsall Chaucer's Tale involves 'a woman speaking of a woman, and of children': see *The Life of Geoffrey Chaucer* (Oxford, 1992), 265.

[53] For discussion of liturgical allusions, particularly to the Little Office of the Virgin and the Mass of Holy Innocents' Day (Childermas), see *The Prioress's Tale*, ed. Boyd, 4–8.

Library, MSS Harley 1704 and 2382, it occurs in the context of saints' lives and other devotional writings, testifies to its place within the tradition of popular piety.[54]

There is, though, one final question to be addressed. If the issue of the inscribing of the Prioress's 'character' within the Tale may be placed to one side, how appropriate within the scheme of *The Canterbury Tales* as a whole is the assigning of a miracle of the Virgin to a female religious? Whilst some misgivings have been voiced on the historical credibility of members of the religious orders being readers of vernacular miracles,[55] there is evidence enough from the period in which Chaucer was writing to suggest that women—religious and secular—took an especial interest in miracles of the type represented by the Tale. Wealthy laywomen commissioned manuscripts in which visual depictions of the legends associated with the Virgin formed an integral part of programmes of illustration, and the dedication of a *mariale* translated into the vernacular in the late twelfth century to an abbess of Barking, mentioned above, is suggestive of the receptivity to this kind of devotional material on the part of enclosed religious.[56] Furthermore, the Vernon manuscript which, as also noted, contains the closest extant contemporary analogue to the Prioress's Tale, and which was produced at around the time that Chaucer was working on his compilation, was in all likelihood intended for a female community, whether of professed nuns or of laywomen attached to a convent.[57] Theories as to the appeal to women of the cult of the Virgin may abound, and at different periods different

[54] The Prioress's Tale, along with the Clerk's, is the one most frequently anthologized in the 15th cent: see John M. Manly and Edith Rickert, *The Text of the 'Canterbury Tales'*, i (Chicago, 1940), 82–4 (Manchester, Chetham's Library, MS 6709); 238–40 (London, British Library, MS Harley 1704); 241–4 (BL MS Harley 2251); 245–8 (BL MS Harley 2382); 302–3 (Cambridge, University Library, MS Kk. 1. 30); 472–5 (Oxford, Bodleian Library, MS Rawlinson C.86; on which see also Julia Boffey and Carol M. Meale, 'Selecting the Text: Rawlinson C.86 and Some Other Books for London Readers', in Felicity Riddy (ed.), *Regionalism in Late Medieval Manuscripts and Texts* (Cambridge, 1991), 143–69).

[55] E.g. by Strohm, *Social Chaucer*, 70.

[56] See Carol M. Meale, 'The Miracles of Our Lady: Context and Interpretation', in Derek Pearsall (ed.), *Studies in the Vernon Manuscript* (Cambridge, 1990), 115–36.

[57] See e.g. A. I. Doyle, introd. to *The Vernon Manuscript: A Facsimile of Bodleian Library, Oxford, MS Eng.Poet.a. 1* (Cambridge, 1987), 14–15; and N. F. Blake, 'The Vernon Manuscript: Contents and Organisation', in Pearsall (ed.), *Studies in the Vernon MS*, 45–59 (p. 58).

explanations may be offered. But it is beyond contention that representations of Mary formed a vital part of the iconography adopted by female religious foundations. A study of the seals associated with nunneries, for example, has shown that over half depict incidents relating to the life of the Virgin, and that amongst this group the majority are of the type known as the 'Throne of Wisdom', in which Mary is shown crowned and seated, with the infant Christ on her knee.[58] The deployment of this iconic image, which simultaneously emphasizes Mary's maternity and her regality—the singularity, that is, of her position in relation to that of other women—has considerable relevance both to an understanding of women's religious vocation, and to readings of the miracles associated with her name. Where the Prioress's Tale is concerned, the Prologue establishes her role as 'blisful Queene' (481), and her uniqueness as a virgin mother, whilst in the Tale itself she is shown as manifesting a tenderness towards the dead child which is recognizably maternal: as he reports, she has told him, her 'litel child', that when the grain is removed from his tongue she will 'fecche' him; and her final words, 'Be nat agast; I wol thee nat forsake' (669), offer a comfort which can extend beyond their immediate fictional recipient, to all those in the Tale's audience who dedicate themselves to her. It is with a certain wryness that I offer the observations that Barking was one of the foundations to replicate the 'Throne of Wisdom' on its seal (though given the joint dedication to the Virgin, this is perhaps not surprising); and that the second, and later, of the seals associated with the priory of St Leonard's at Stratford at Bow shows the Virgin holding Christ on her right arm, with a figure, perhaps that of a nun, kneeling in prayer before her.[59] Whether Chaucer knew of this, or whether the seal was even in use in his lifetime, can only be a matter for speculation.

I would suggest, then, that Chaucer articulates a spirituality in the Tale which was especially apt for women, and specifically for women religious.[60] But this very aptness, and the lyrical and

---

[58] Roberta Gilchrist, *Gender and Material Culture: The Archàeology of Religious Women* (London, 1994), 143–8.

[59] Gilchrist, ibid., does not list the seal from Stratford, for a description of which see *VCH: Middlesex*, i. 159.

[60] Cf. Elizabeth Robertson, 'Aspects of Female Piety in the *Prioress's Tale*', in C. David Benson and Elizabeth Robertson (eds.), *Chaucer's Religious Tales*

narrative skills which are deployed in its telling, are opposed to the satirical method adopted in the construction of the Tale's narrator. In authorizing what can be seen as a distinctively female form of piety, the Tale in effect works against the depiction of the Prioress in the General Prologue. The resulting tension between the two texts, and the destabilizing influence the one exerts on the other, may offer one explanation for the differing responses each has evoked. Whether this disjunction was intentional on Chaucer's part is impossible to determine, and largely irrelevant to the exercise of critical judgement. Recognition of the discontinuities, however, serves a wider purpose for readers of *The Canterbury Tales* as a whole, in that it should alert us to the sometimes haphazard, and certainly piecemeal, process of compilation; and lead us to question Chaucer's stance and status, as author, in relation to his historical moment.[61]

(Cambridge, 1990), 145–60. Study of the manuscript contexts of the excerpted Tale (n. 54 above) may well reveal a 'female' bias in the choice of contents, and hence offer suggestions as to intended audiences: see, in particular, BL MS Harley 2382.

[61] Cf. the approaches taken by the contributors to Barbara Hanawalt (ed.), *Chaucer's England: Literature in Historical Context* (Minneapolis, 1992); and by Lee Patterson, *Chaucer and the Subject of History* (Madison, 1991). For judicious criticism of Patterson's notion of 'historical' positioning, see the review by J. A. Burrow, *MÆ* 62 (1993), 131–3.

4

Muses and Blacksmiths: Italian Trecento Poetics and the Reception of Dante in 'The House of Fame'

N. R. HAVELY

Chaucer's *House of Fame* is the first known work in English to mention and appropriate Dante, and the seriousness with which it does so has, over the last ten years or so, been subject to varying degrees of emphasis. One critic finds the poem taking from the *Commedia* 'nothing less than an assurance that the "art poetical" was its own justification'; another sees Chaucer here recognizing 'full well his limitations as a poet because he has grasped what Dante is doing with *his* poetry and his "art poetical"'; whilst another more cautiously concedes that the two poets do 'have several interests in common and that Chaucer does [in *The House of Fame*] sustain an ironic counterpoint to Dante's poem'.[1] Most readers find here, in Chaucer's first articulated response to Dante, a mixture, in varying proportions, of ambition and scepticism. The scepticism of *The House of Fame* towards the Dantean enterprise has been stressed in several of the more recent interpretations, and Chaucer's poem has even been seen as 'launching a...specific critique...that strikes at the very heart of Dante's self-characterization as both historian and prophet of judgment in the *Commedia*'.[2]

---

[1] J. A. W. Bennett, 'Chaucer, Dante and Boccaccio', in P. Boitani (ed.), *Chaucer and the Italian Trecento* (Cambridge, 1983), 89–113 (p. 107); P. Boitani, 'What Dante Meant to Chaucer', ibid. 115–39 (p. 120); J. M. Fyler, headnote in *The Riverside Chaucer*, 348.

[2] L. J. Kiser, *Truth and Textuality in Chaucer's Poetry* (Hanover, NH, 1991), 40. For comparable views see also S. Ellis, 'Chaucer, Dante and Damnation', *ChauR.* 22 (1988), 282–94, and K. Taylor, *Chaucer Reads 'The Divine Comedy'* (Stanford, Calif., 1989), ch. 1.

The House of Fame is, however, an extremely eclectic poem, even by Chaucerian standards, and its response to Dante cannot be considered in isolation. This response is, it will be argued, partly determined by other Italian writing on the status of poetry, and by the reputation of Dante as vernacular author in the culture of late fourteenth-century Florence—a culture that is known to have been encountered by Chaucer in 1373, near the start of a decade that saw the last of Petrarch and Boccaccio and the genesis of *The House of Fame*.[3]

Debates and assertions about the status of poetry in the fourteenth century and earlier frequently involved the invocation or interpretation of the Muses.[4] The opening of *The House of Fame*'s second book invokes both the Goddess Venus (whose temple has been the setting of the first Book) and the nine Muses:

> Now faire blisfull, O Cipris,
> So be my favor at this tyme,
> And ye, me to endite and ryme
> Helpeth that on Parnaso dwelle
> Be Elicon, the clere welle. (518–20)[5]

This passage is claimed by J. A. W. Bennett, and more recently the note to *The Riverside Chaucer* edition, to be 'the first appearance of the Muses in English poetry'.[6] Towards the end of his study of the poem, Boitani asserts that 'Chaucer is the first English poet to invoke the Muses, here in the *House of Fame*'.[7] The point is a significant one, but such assertions distort its significance. As a first acknowledgement of the intertextual complexities here, Boitani's statement should be emended to read 'the first English

---

[3] On the evidence about Chaucer's visit to Genoa and Florence in 1372–3, see *Chaucer Life-Records*, ed. M. M. Crow and C. C. Olson (Oxford, 1966), 32–40. On the problems of dating *The House of Fame* see H. H. Schless, *Chaucer and Dante: A Revaluation* (Norman, Okla. 1984), 39–41, and *Chaucer: 'The House of Fame'*, ed. N. R. Havely (Durham, 1994), 9–10.

[4] See E. R. Curtius, *European Literature and the Latin Middle Ages*, tr. W. R. Trask (London, 1953), ch. 13. For more recent discussion, see P. Hardman, 'Chaucer's Muses and his "Art Poetical"', *RES* NS 37 (1986), 478–94, and P. B. Taylor and S. Bordier, 'Chaucer and the Latin Muses', *Traditio*, 47 (1992), 215–32.

[5] All quotations from *The House of Fame* follow the text in my edition of the poem (cited n. 3 above).

[6] Bennett, 'Chaucer, Dante and Boccaccio', 108, and *The Riverside Chaucer*, 982 (n. on *The House of Fame*, 520–6). The claim is reiterated in Taylor and Bordier, 'Chaucer and the Latin Muses', 219.

[7] P. Boitani, *Chaucer and the Imaginary World of Fame* (Cambridge, 1984), 203.

vernacular poet', since the tradition of English writers invoking and alluding to the Muses in Latin verse goes back at least as far as Joseph of Exeter's twelfth-century *Iliad*—a work which Chaucer of course knew.[8]

It is indeed probable that, when Chaucer invokes the Muses for the first time in *The House of Fame*, he is following 'the example of Dante and Boccaccio'.[9] Yet a further gloss is also needed here, and a further acknowledgement has to be made regarding the mixed parentage of Chaucer's Muses. The subsequent passage about 'Thought' (*House of Fame*, 523–8) is surely modelled on Dante's invocation to the Muses at the opening of *Inferno*, ii (7–9). On the other hand the appeal to those 'that on Parnaso dwelle | Be Elicon the clere welle' appears to be confusing Helicon (the Muses' mountain) with Hippocrene (the Muses' actual well)—and there are possible sources for that confusion not only in Italian but also in French and Anglo-Latin.[10]

It must none the less be recognized that the whole pattern of Chaucer's invocations in *The House of Fame* is increasingly Dantean. The invocation to Book III—the *lytel laste boke* of the poem—is obviously a more sustained imitation of a passage in the *Commedia* than is the passage invoking 'Thought' in Book II, whatever mixture of ambition and scepticism there may be behind that imitation. There is also undoubtedly a tendency for Chaucer's poems of the late 1370s or early 1380s to locate invocations to the Muses in a Dantean context. The *Anelida and Arcite* (which may have been the next poetic venture after *The House of Fame*) opens with the combination of an appeal to the Muse Polyhymnia, and the topos of writing as voyaging—a combination that also occurs

---

[8] Joseph of Exeter invokes a sombre Muse at the opening of his description of the death of Priam in VI. 784–6 of his *Frigii Daretis Iliados* (*c.*1185), and he refers to Muses (including Clio) on several occasions in Book II (98, 450, 483); see *Joseph Iscanus: Briefe und Werke*, ed. L. Gompf (Leiden, 1970). Yet further back, in the 8th cent., Alcuin had allowed the Muses a place in secular verse; see Curtius, *European Literature*, 237. For other invocations of the Muses in English (Anglo-Latin) poetry before Chaucer, see A. G. Rigg, *A History of Anglo-Latin Literature, 1066–1422* (Cambridge, 1992), 22–3, 25, 27, 28, 173, 230.

[9] Boitani, *Imaginary World of Fame*, 203–4.

[10] See e.g. Boccaccio, *Teseida*, xi. 63; Deschamps, *Œuvres*, ed. le marquis de Queux de Saint-Hilaire and G. Raynaud, SATF, 11 vols. (Paris, 1878–1903), i, no. 124 and ii, no. 285; J. A. Wimsatt (ed.), *Chaucer and the Poems of 'Ch'* (Cambridge, 1982), 20–1, 52–5, 60; Walter Map, *De nugis curialium*, dist. iv, c. 2.

in *Paradiso*, xxiii. 55–69. In the next dream-poem, *The Parliament of Fowls*, the nearest approach to an invocation is the stanza appealing to Venus as if she were a Muse (113–19). This appeal occurs at the opening of the actual vision in the *Parliament*—a stage of the poem which is also punctuated by allusions to the beginning of Dante's pilgrimage in *Inferno* ii and iii (*Parliament of Fowls*, 85–6, 123–40). And in the proem to Book II of *Troilus and Criseyde* (1–4) the consciousness of the writer's enterprise as a voyage and the invocation of another Muse (Clio) are linked to Dante through Chaucer's unmistakable reworking of the exordium to *Purgatorio*, i.

Dante himself had adapted and developed the classical practice of invoking the Muses at important turning-points: at or near the beginning of each of the *Commedia*'s three *cantiche* and towards the end of the *Inferno* and the *Purgatorio*.[11] We should be cautious about claiming 'firsts' too readily, but it seems probable, on the available recorded evidence, that Dante and Chaucer were the first poets in their respective vernaculars to invoke the Muses.[12] Whether Chaucer was conscious of following Dante's precedent here can never be known, but *The House of Fame* appears to register a strong if uneasy response to this feature of the *Commedia*'s discourse. Such a response could perhaps be construed as part of a poetic agenda in process of definition from *The House of Fame* through to *Troilus*: an agenda that involved coming to terms with Dante as *auctor*, the only vernacular writer (apart from Petrarch) to whom Chaucer was to give the title of *poete*.[13]

Most of the Dantean invocatory passages mentioned so far signal new beginnings in the Chaucerian texts: Books II and III of *The House of Fame*, the beginning of the actual dream in the

---

[11] *Inferno*, xxxii. 10–12 and *Purgatorio*, xxix. 37–42. See also Curtius, *European Literature*, 239.

[12] For the evidence of Dante's usage, see the *Grande dizionario della lingua italiana* (Turin, 1961–), s.v. *Musa*[1] (sf.), senses 1, 3, and 4. For Chaucer's, see MED, s.v. *Muse* n., senses (a) to (d). The earliest recorded uses of the word in English are probably in *House of Fame*, 1399, and in Book I of the *Boece*, metrum 1. 4, prosa 1. 78, and prosa 5. 72.

[13] Chaucer gives this title to Dante in the Monk's Tale (VII (B²) 2460–1) and in the Wife of Bath's Tale (III (D) 1125–6), and his reference to Petrarch as *poete* is in the Clerk's Prologue (IV (E) 31). On the application of the term to vernacular writers at this time, see K. Brownlee, *Poetic Identity in Guillaume de Machaut* (Madison, 1984), 7–8, 220–1 (n. 11); and G. Olson, 'Making and Poetry in the Age of Chaucer', *CL* 31 (1979), 272–90.

Parliament, and the movement out of 'despair' in Book II of *Troilus*. *The House of Fame*, too, is itself largely a tissue of beginnings. The moment at which it makes its first references to both Dante and the Muses is at the end of Book I and the opening of Book II—where one journey (Aeneas') is coming to a close and another (the dreamer's) is just beginning. It is during the final summary of Virgil's *Aeneid* that Chaucer's poem makes its first mention of Dante, and during the hundred lines or so that span the end of Book I and the beginning of Book II the Italian poet's presence is registered in three distinct ways. Initially he is mentioned (after Virgil and Claudian) in a position that reflects his status as *auctor*. Secondly, the *Commedia* provides a source for Chaucer's narrative to transform into further comedy: the dream-Eagle that sweeps the pilgrim up to the sphere of fire in *Purgatorio*, ix is a fiction within a fiction—but in *The House of Fame* he becomes Chaucer's dreamer's *grym* reality, with 'paws', 'nails', and 'claws'. And thirdly, the appeal to 'Thought' that, in *The House of Fame* (523–8), follows the invocation to Venus and the Muses contains specific verbal echoes from *Inferno*, ii and *Paradiso*, i.

But whilst Dante as vernacular author is a major item in *The House of Fame*'s poetic agenda and a significant source for its invocatory language, the *Commedia* is by no means the only influence upon its representation of Muses or its concern about the status of poetry. In his discussion of 'Chaucerian authorities' in *The House of Fame*, Christopher Baswell points out that 'beyond Virgil and Ovid only Boethius is openly named then quoted in the poem'.[14] That there should be a Boethian as well as Dantean context for Chaucer's Muses need not be surprising. 'Boece' is mentioned by name and *De consolatione philosophiae* is directly quoted in Book II of the *House of Fame*, as well as being appropriated for ideas about fame and glory and the figure of Fame herself.[15] And if the current dating of *Boece* as a work of the late 1370s or early 1380s is accepted, then Chaucer could well have

---

[14] Christopher Baswell, *Virgil in Medieval England: Figuring the 'Aeneid', from the Twelfth Century to Chaucer* (Cambridge, 1995), 224. On Boethius in *The House of Fame* see 237–40.

[15] *The House of Fame*, 973–8, quotes from Book IV, metrum 1 of *De consolatione philosophiae*. See also, for instance, the description of the smallness

been actively engaged in the translation of Boethius whilst composing *The House of Fame*.[16]

The Invocation to Book II of *The House of Fame* thus locates the Muses in a Dantean context. They actually appear on the scene before the throne in Fame's hall in the early stages of Book III:

> And, lord, the hevenyssh melodye
> Of songes ful of armonye
> I herd aboute her trone y-songe,
> That al the paleys walles ronge.
> So songe the myghty Muse, she
> That cleped ys Calliope,
> And hir eighte sustren eke
> That in her face semen meke.
> And ever mo, eternally,
> They synge of Fame, as thoo herd y:
> 'Heryed be thou and thy name,
> Goddesse of renoun or of Fame!' (1395–406)

Fame's own appearance on her throne just before this passage draws together material from the Bible and Virgil, as well as parodying the appearance of Lady Philosophy in Boethius.[17] About her throne is heard—as from the Muses of Macrobius and Martianus—the 'melody and song' that is led by Calliope, the 'mighty muse'—the *bona vox* of the etymologizers and commentators.[18] But is the song itself somewhat suspect? Critical opinion seems widely divided here—as is so often the case with specific readings of this poem's tone and personifications. B. G. Koonce, for instance, insists that we have here not only a parody of the songs of praise before the throne of the Lamb (Rev. 5 and 7) but

of the earth in *The House of Fame*, 906–7, against Chaucer's *Boece*, II, prosa 7. 25–7 (and context).

[16] A number of resemblances reinforce this impression; see Havely edn., 10 (n. 44) and 16 (n. 81).

[17] Cf. Rev. 4: 6 and 8 (the beasts 'full of eyes'); *Aeneid*, 4. 181–3 (Rumour's eyes, ears, and tongues); and *De consolatione philosophiae*, I, prosa 1. 8–13 (Philosophy's stature; the line references are to the edition of Boethius by H. F. Stewart, E. K. Rand, and S. J. Tester (Cambridge, Mass., 1973)).

[18] Macrobius, for instance, identifies Calliope as the 'best voice' (*Commentary on the Dream of Scipio*, ii. 3); cf. the etymology in Balbus' *Catholicon* (completed 1287). Fulgentius associates her with the completion of the process of expression (*Mythologiae*, i. 15); cf. Boccaccio, *Genealogia*, xi. 2. See also Hardman, 'Chaucer's Muses and his "Art Poetical"', 481–3, and Taylor and Bordier, 'Chaucer and the Latin Muses', 221.

also a representation of the 'siren-like' poetical Muses of the *Consolatio philosophiae*, Book I, prosa 1: the *scenicas meretriculas* or 'commune strompettis' (to use Chaucer's phrase) that Lady Philosophy banishes from Boethius' bedside.[19] On the other hand, J. A. W. Bennett finds no such sinister intention here: the Muses' scriptural postures, he argues, 'are simply a means of hypostatizing that appearance of glory which Chaucer here, and only here unqualifiedly, concedes to Fame'.[20] Boitani takes this view yet further, claiming that the Muses are here 'depicted in the attitude of the angelic choirs of the *Praefatio* and the *Sanctus*' as, 'precisely, the *angheloi*, harbingers of fame'.[21]

The song of the Muses here may indeed initially seem to affirm the value of Fame, and its *armonye* certainly contrasts with the noises that recurrently break out in the final book of *The House of Fame*. Yet there remains something problematic about the 'meek-seeming' faces of these Muses and the somewhat banal words of their song. There is no need to go (with Koonce) to the extreme of identifying them with the Boethian 'strompettis' whose sweet flatteries destroy the 'fruytes of resoun'.[22] They can, instead, be seen as neither strumpets nor angels, but rather as manifestations of a double vision that at this stage of the poem encompasses not only the shrinking/expanding, Virgilian/Boethian goddess of Fame but also the illustrious writers who subsequently appear on their columns like rooks nesting on trees (1516). This doubleness can in turn be seen as a reflection in Chaucer's text of a debate about fame and poetry that goes back at least as far as *De consolatione philosophiae*, where Boethius represents himself as the lifelong companion of the Muses (I, metrum 1), and where the poetical Muses are soon banished from his company by Lady Philosophy as *scenicas meretriculas* ('histrionic harlots'; I, prosa 1).

The debates about the value of poetry in the Italian trecento show a more explicit awareness of the problematic nature of Boethius' Muses. Boccaccio responded at length to the problem

[19] B. G. Koonce, *Chaucer and the Tradition of Fame: Symbolism in 'The House of Fame'* (Princeton, 1966), 213 and n. 79.
[20] J. A. W. Bennett, *Chaucer's Book of Fame: An Exposition of the 'House of Fame'* (Oxford, 1968), 132.
[21] Boitani, *Imaginary World of Fame*, 15.
[22] Koonce, *Tradition of Fame*, 213 n. 78.

in the last two books of *De genealogia deorum gentilium*[23]. The significance of the argument for Chaucer has been noted before, but Boccaccio's development of it into an extensive gloss on the Boethian passage deserves some closer attention. In *Genealogia*, xiv, ch. 20, Boccaccio distinguishes at some length between the solitary, contemplative Muse of the Neoplatonic tradition and, on the other hand, the kind of performer who (in C. G. Osgood's inimitable rendering) 'is seduced by disreputable comic poets to mount the stage, pre-empt theatres and street-corners: and there for a fee she calmly exhibits herself to loungers in low compositions'.[24] He concludes that when Boethius called the Muses *scenicas meretriculas* he was, literally, 'thinking only of theatrical muses' (*de theatrali Musarum specie intellexisse*).[25] This distinction mattered so much to Boccaccio that he repeated it in the vernacular at an early stage of his last major work: the *Esposizioni sopra la Commedia di Dante* (1373–4). Here Virgil's statement of poetic identity in *Inferno*, i. 73 (*poeta fui*) becomes Boccaccio's cue for an extensive defence of poetry which has been described as 'a lively contribution to a debate aroused by early Italian humanism', and which also includes some observations about the kind of theatrical performance that Plato, Boethius, and others are supposed to have condemned.[26]

During this decade of the 1370s, therefore, Boccaccio, towards the close of his career, and Chaucer, near the beginning of his, were addressing the question of the status of poetry with some awareness of both Boethius and Dante. In their different ways they were each confronting the problem of the Muses in Book I of Boethius' *Consolatio*, and both were putting their own glosses on the lines through which Dante initially mobilizes his poetic resources in the second canto of the *Inferno*:

[23] The complete edition of the *Genealogia* is by V. Romano (Bari, 1951). There is a more recent edition of the penultimate book (xiv) by J. Reedy, *Boccaccio: In Defence of Poetry* (Toronto, 1978), and C. G. Osgood's *Boccaccio on Poetry* (Princeton, 1930; repr. Indianapolis, 1956) translates Books xiv and xv.

[24] Boccaccio, *Genealogia*, xiv. 20 (ed. Reedy, 84; tr. Osgood, 95–6).

[25] *Genealogia*, ed. Reedy, 84 (ll. 57–8); tr. Osgood, 96.

[26] Boccaccio, *Esposizioni sopra la Comedia di Dante*, ed. G. Padoan (Milan, 1965; vol. vi of *Tutte le opere di Giovanni Boccaccio*, ed. V. Branca), 33–43. Padoan's comment (which I translate here) is on p. 780 (n. 67), and Boccaccio's description of Greek and Roman comic performers, influenced (according to Padoan, n. 85) by Trevet's commentary on Seneca's *Thyestes*, is on pp. 37–8 (paras. 84–8).

O muse, o alto ingegno, or m'aiutate
o mente che scrivesti ciò ch'io vidi
qui si parrà la tua nobilitate. (7–9)

(O Muses, lofty invention, now come to my aid; Memory which recorded
what I saw, here let it be seen what you are worth.)

In order to locate *The House of Fame* in this kind of context, it
is not necessary to suppose that Chaucer had direct access to
Boccaccio's arguments. For, despite assertions to the contrary, it
cannot be positively demonstrated that Chaucer is, here or elsewhere, specifically indebted to the *Genealogia*.[27] It is, however,
possible that he could, at some point in the 1370s or later, have
come across one of the unauthorized copies about which Boccaccio had complained in 1372.[28] His interest in Boccaccio's approach
to the Muses is, in any case, likely to have been stimulated by some
of the Italian writer's vernacular works of which he must have
gained some direct knowledge during the 1370s: the *Filostrato*
(which alludes to the Muses at the start of the narrative) and the
Teseida, where there are a number of invocations and references to
them.[29]

Boccaccio's work was not, however, the only Italian source from
which arguments about the Muses might in this period have been
derived. The debate about the value and status of poetry had, of
course, been going on for some time and the issues involved had

[27] The parallels suggested by Bennett and Godman (in Boitani, *Chaucer and the
Italian Trecento*, 108 and 290) are of a very general sort, and the evidence adduced
by C. G. Child in 'Chaucer's *Legend of Good Women* and Boccaccio's *De
genealogia deorum*', *MLN* 11 (1896), 476–90, is based on a later Italian translation
and is hardly conclusive. The *Genealogia* seems, however, to have been well known
in England, at least from the early 15th cent. onwards; see H. G. Wright, *Boccaccio
in England from Chaucer to Tennyson* (London, 1957), 3 (nn. 1 and 2) and 36, and
E. Reiss, 'Boccaccio in English Culture of the Fourteenth and Fifteenth Centuries',
in G. Galigani (ed.), *Boccaccio nella cultura inglese e anglo-americana* (Florence,
1974), 15–26 (see p. 24, on Humphrey of Gloucester, Lydgate, and John
Whethamstede).
[28] On the manuscript tradition of these copies (the 'vulgate' tradition) see P. G.
Ricci, 'Contributi per un' edizione critica della *Genealogia deorum gentilium*',
Rinascimento, 2 (1951), 99–144 (esp. p. 125), and G. Billanovich, 'Pietro Piccolo
da Monteforte tra il Petrarca e il Boccaccio', in C. Antoni (ed.), *Medioevo e
Rinascimento: Studi in onore di Bruno Nardi*, 2 vols. (Florence, 1955), i. 37–40.
Boccaccio's complaint about the unauthorized copying is in a letter of 5 Apr. 1372
to Pietro Piccolo da Monteforte; see Billanovich, 'Pietro Piccolo da Monteforte',
61–2.
[29] See *Filostrato*, i. 1 and *Teseida*, i. 1; viii. 2; xi. 63; xii. 52 and the final sonnet.

been well worked over by the Fathers and the schoolmen long before the fourteenth century.[30] It appears, however, to have intensified during the Italian trecento, partly because of the expansion of vernacular literacy and partly because of the advance of Latin humanism. Hence we find enlisted among the 'defenders of poetry' several Italian humanists whose primary commitment was to Latin—such as Albertino Mussato at the beginning of the century and Coluccio Salutati at the end—as well as authors like Boccaccio and Petrarch whose work was in both Latin and the vernacular.[31] Mussato had glossed the Boethian passage about the Muses in a letter some time before 1309, where he made high claims for the 'fictions of poets' whilst condemning their theatrical counterparts (*fictiones scenice*).[32] And it is known that Boccaccio himself, in his various glosses on Boethius, is responding to and drawing upon the contributions of others—notably Petrarch, in the *Invective contra medicum*, and the Neapolitan Pietro Piccolo da Monteforte, in a letter of 1372.[33]

Awareness of such trecento controversies—along with Chaucer's own reading and 'translation' of Boethius and Dante—can be seen reflected in *The House of Fame*'s representation of the Muses before Fame's throne and the implied poetics of Book III. This awareness makes Chaucer less straightforwardly Boethian in his poetic self-fashioning than is his English contemporary John

[30] For a brief account of the debate, from antiquity to the 14th cent., see R. G. Witt, 'Coluccio Salutati and the Conception of the *Poeta Theologus* in the Fourteenth Century', *Renaissance Quarterly*, 30 (1977), 539–40. For examples of scholastic attitudes on the subject, see A. J. Minnis and A. B. Scott (eds.), *Medieval Literary Theory and Criticism c.1100–c.1375: The Commentary Tradition* (Oxford, 1991), 9–10, 122.

[31] On Mussato's debate about poetry with the Dominican Giovannino of Mantua in 1316 see Witt, 'Conception of the *Poeta Theologus*', 540–1; C. C. Greenfield, *Humanist and Scholastic Poetics 1250–1500* (London, 1981), 80–5 and 87–9; and M. Dazzi, *Il Mussato preumanista (1261–1329): L'ambiente e l'opera* (Vicenza, 1964), 110–15, 191–5.

[32] Mussato, *Epistola* VII (to Giovanni of Vigonza); for a summary and an Italian translation see Dazzi, *Il Mussato preumanista*, 108–9, 181–3.

[33] For Petrarch's treatment of the Boethian Muses in the *Invective*, see *Francesco Petrarca: Prose*, ed. G. Martellotti et al. (Milan, 1955), 658–61. For Pietro da Monteforte's letter (2 Feb. 1372) and Boccaccio's borrowings from it in Books xiv and xv of the *Genealogia*, see Billanovich, 'Pietro Piccolo da Monteforte', esp. 35–6, 44–58. One of such borrowings is the distinction about 'theatrical Muses' in *Genealogia*, xiv. 20 (cf. the edition by Reedy, 55, ll. 239–46). On the knowledge of Mussato's opinions about poetry in the later 14th cent., see Witt, 'Conception of the *Poeta Theologus*', 542 and n. 12.

Gower. Gower was also aware of the two kinds of Muses in Boethius—but the duality seems not to have troubled and fascinated him to the same extent. At the end of the *Confessio Amantis* (in two versions written some ten years or so later than *The House of Fame*), Gower acknowledges the direction of his Muse in the following terms:

> But now that I am feble and old,
> And to the worschipe of mi king
> In love above alle other thing
> That I this bok have mad and write,
> Mi muse doth me forto wite
> That it is to me for the beste
> Fro this day forth to take reste,
> That I no more of love make.
>   (VIII. 3070–7; 1390 version)

Gower here seems content to resolve the question in terms of reason succeeding passion, perhaps along the lines suggested by Nicholas Trevet in his gloss on the Muses in Boethius.[34] Thus, as his dreamer bids farewell to Venus and love, the writer accepts the advice of a Muse who has nothing in common with Boethius' sweetly destructive 'sirens', but is, rather, to be identified with the upright characters (*meis... Musis*) in Lady Philosophy's nursing team. Chaucer, on the other hand, like Boccaccio, seems to have been continually exercised by the question of poetic identity that derives from the Boethian scenario: the question of whether the poet is 'a dispenser of "sweet venom" or of the wholesome remedies by which Philosophy seeks to restore Boethius to spiritual health'.[35]

Yet, although the Muses in *The House of Fame* are not straightforwardly Boethian (or Gowerian), they do not, on the other hand, simply derive from Italian poetics. There are some obvious and pronounced differences between the defence of poetry in trecento polemic and the oblique approaches to the subject of writing and performance in Chaucer's dream-poem. These differences are reflected, for instance, in *The House of Fame*'s manner of appropriating Dante at the opening of Book III:

---

[34] Trevet's commentary on *De consolatione philosophiae*, in the unpublished edition by the late E. T. Silk (copy provided by A. J. Minnis).
[35] A. David, *The Strumpet Muse: Art and Morals in Chaucer's Poetry* (Bloomington, Ind., 1976), 3. Hardman, 'Chaucer's Muses and his "Art Poetical"', 491–3, discusses the Boethian Muses in relation to Chaucer's *Troilus*.

O god of science and of lyght—
Appollo, thurgh thy grete myght
This lytel laste boke thou gye!
Nat that I wilne for maistrye
Here art poetical be shewed—
But, for the ryme ys lyght and lewed,
Yit make hyt sumwhat agreable,
Though some vers fayle in a syllable—
And that I do no diligence
To shew craft, but o sentence.
And yif, devyne vertu, thow
Wilt helpe to shewe now
That in myn hede y-marked ys—
Loo, that is for to menen this,
The Hous of Fame for to discryve—
Thou shalt se me go as blyve
Unto the next laure y see
And kysse yt, for hyt is thy tree.
Now entreth in my brest anoon! (1091–109)

In invoking Apollo, the patron of the Muses, Chaucer is clearly, like Dante in *Paradiso*, i. 13–36, acknowledging the connection between poetry and the 'god of science and of lyght'. But there is in this invocation also a certain subversion of the exalted Dantean enterprise. Along with the appeal to Apollo's *devyne vertu* (a verbal echo of *Paradiso*, i. 22) there are, as in the proem to Book II of *Troilus*, recurrent disclaimers, references to the insignificance of the 'light and lewed' rhyme—as well as the sturdy avowal that 'I do no diligence | To shew *craft* but o sentence'. As this passage suggests, there are a number of ways in which Chaucer, at this juncture of the poem— the opening of the 'lytel laste bok'— could have made a bid for high ethical and illustrious status had he so wished. The august figure of Orpheus appears on the façade of the castle of Fame shortly after this:

Ther herd I pleyen upon an harpe
That sowned bothe wel and sharpe,
Orpheus, ful craftely. (1201–3)

But Chaucer's Orpheus is not, as in Book xiv of Boccaccio's *Genealogia*, the 'earliest of the theologians...prompted by the Divine mind', or one of the 'holy men who have sung divine mysteries in exalted notes'.[36] Instead, Chaucer's Orpheus is a *performer*, whose presence could indeed be an oblique tribute to the romance tradition that includes the English *Sir Orfeo*. In Book III of *The House of Fame* he heads a line, not of pagan theologians, but of minstrels, entertainers, and *jugelours*; and he is linked to them by the use of the words *craftely* and *craft* (1203, 1213), which in the opening lines of Book III cover a wide semantic field, from high skill to low cunning.[37]

The invocation to Apollo and the appropriation of Dante's *Paradiso* at this stage of *The House of Fame* thus seem to be determined not so much by a view of poetry as theology or 'divine mysteries' as by a recognition of its associations with various kinds of performance. This view of poetry in practice is vividly conveyed by the motley crew of classical, Welsh, Dutch(?), Spanish, and English minstrels and *jugelours* attendant upon Orpheus (1201–81); but it could also have been informed by awareness, on Chaucer's part, of how another illustrious poet, Dante, was being performed in the fourteenth century.

Dante's *Commedia* in this period was not only seen as a book embellished by the commentary tradition, but was also heard, as a work that could be and was performed. Indeed, by the time Chaucer visited Florence in 1373, the questions of Dante's 'popularity' and the appropriation of his poem by an oral as well as literary culture had themselves become issues for comment and debate.

The implications of oral performance and common currency are already apparent in certain features of the *Commedia*'s own text and context.[38] Dante's very choice of title for his poem was (it has been argued), at least in part, a humility topos, underlining his difference from Virgil, linking the poem with satire, and associating it with the middle and humble vernacular.[39] A recent survey of early trecento reception of the *Commedia* notes the description of

---

[36] *Genealogia*, xiv. 8 (ed. Reedy, 38, ll. 69–70 and 39, ll. 89–90; tr. Osgood, 44–5); and xiv. 16 (ed. Reedy, 66, ll. 16–21; tr. Osgood, 76).

[37] See *MED*, s.v. *craft* n. (1), senses 2, 3, 5, and 8; and *craftili* adv., senses *a–c*.

[38] The evidence is reviewed by P. Armour, 'Comedy and the Origins of Italian Theatre around the Time of Dante', in J. R. Dashwood and J. E. Everson (eds.), *Writers and Performers in Italian Drama from the Time of Dante to Pirandello* (Lewiston, NY, 1991), 1–31 (esp. pp. 19–21).

[39] These are some of the reasons suggested by Armour, 'Comedy and the Origins of Italian Theatre', 25 n. 15 (quoting Z. Baranski).

performances by Lombard comedians (found in the Latin translation of Jacopo della Lana's *Commento* by Alberigo da Rosciate)
and suggests that if 'serious comedians' existed, their art may have
'played a role in Dante's choice of a title for his work'.[40]

Whether Dante knew of such comedians or not, it seems likely
that the *Commedia* has some connections with Italian vernacular
theatre, as well as with more illustrious traditions. There is evidence in the poem of the influence of the dramatic *laude* and
contrasti, as well as of civic spectacle.[41] Much of the discussion
of the *Commedia*'s theatricality centres upon the *nuovo ludo* of the
Malebranche cantos (*Inferno*, xxi–xxiii), but there are other
exchanges and episodes in it that are more than vaguely theatrical,
and Dante appears to have envisaged the poem as both book to be
read and work to be performed—perhaps recited formally at the
court of one of his patrons.[42]

Oral performance of the *Commedia* at a less exalted level was
already a cause for anxiety in at least one of Dante's contemporaries. The scholar Giovanni del Virgilio (in a letter to Dante)
envisaged the poem being 'sounded tritely on the lips of women'
or 'croaked forth, all undigested, at street corners by some buffoon
with a comic actor's shock of hair' (*comicomus nebulo*), all for the
benefit of the *vulgo* or *gens idiota*.[43] Giovanni's argument was
later given a more personal inflection by Petrarch in his letter to
Boccaccio about Dante in 1359 (*Familiares*, xxi. 15). Petrarch's
reservations about Dante as a poet 'popular in style' are intensified
by his sense of how the illustrious poet's reputation has been
'disturbed and afflicted' by 'the windy applause of the masses'
(*ventosis . . . vulgi plausibus*).[44] That Petrarch is projecting a recur-

[40] H. A. Kelly, *Tragedy and Comedy from Dante to Pseudo-Dante* (Berkeley and
Los Angeles, 1989), 32–3.

[41] See Armour, 'Comedy and the Origins of Italian Theatre', 9–12, and U. Bosco,
'Dante e il teatro medievale', in G. Varanini and P. Pinagli (eds.), *Studi filologici,
letterari e storici in memoria di Guido Favati*, 2 vols. (Padua, 1977), i. 135–47 (esp.
pp. 135, 140, 147).

[42] See Armour, 'Comedy and the Origins of Italian Theatre', 20, and J. Ahern,
'Singing the Book: Orality in the Reception of Dante's *Comedy*', *Annals of
Scholarship*, 2/4 (1981), 17–40 (esp. pp. 30–3).

[43] Ahern, 'Singing the Book', 18–19. For the correspondence between the two
writers, see P. H. Wicksteed and E. G. Gardner, *Dante and Giovanni del Virgilio*
(London, 1902), 146–73.

[44] Petrarch, *Familiares*, xxi. 15, in *Petrarca: Prose*, ed. Martellotti, 1002; tr. in
M. Bishop, *Letters from Petrarch* (Bloomington Ind., 1966), 177.

rent anxiety about losing his identity in the city and becoming the property of the masses becomes clearer later on in the letter when he describes his dismay at hearing his own vernacular poems being 'continually mangled by the tongues of the vulgar' (*vulgi linguis assidue laceror*).[45] Petrarch's rhetoric here and his argument about the devaluing of the illustrious poet's reputation by the coarse praise of 'fullers, inn-keepers and cloth-workers' may well have set the tone for later humanistic discourse and debate about Dante's popularity.[46] For, around the turn of the century, both opponents and defenders of Dante's vernacular use a very similar vocabulary to describe the *Commedia*'s popularity, among 'cloth-workers [again], bakers, cobblers, apothecaries and grocers' (*lanarii, pistores, calzolai, speziali, pizzicagnoli*).[47]

The terms (though not the stance) of this argument about Dante and the *vulgo* may also be reflected in the contrasts between illustrious writing and vulgar speech in Book III of *The House of Fame*. They were certainly influential on Petrarch's correspondent Boccaccio. It has recently been suggested that Boccaccio's toning down of his praise for the *Commedia*'s popular appeal in the second revision of his biographical *Trattatello in laude di Dante* (in the early 1360s) may be attributable to the influence of Petrarch's 1359 letter.[48] Indeed, Boccaccio's commitment to the popularization of Dante was beset by misgivings to the last. His final major work, the *Esposizioni sopra la Commedia di Dante* of 1373–4, may be confident enough in its general defence of poetry (cf. p. 68 above), but it is rather less enthusiastic than the first revision of the *Trattatello* about Dante's choice of the *volgare*—

[45] *Petrarca: Prose*, ed. Martellotti, 1008; tr. Bishop, 180.

[46] *Petrarca: Prose*, ed. Martellotti, 1010; tr. Bishop, 181.

[47] For the first two terms, see Leonardo Bruni, *Ad Petrum Paulum Histrum Dialogus* (c.1401–7), in *Prosatori latini del quattrocento*, ed. E. Garin (Milan, 1952), 70; tr. in D. Thompson and A. F. Nagel (eds.), *The Three Crowns of Florence: Humanist Assessments of Dante, Petrarca and Boccaccio* (New York, 1972), 36. On Bruni's ambivalence towards Dante, see M. Caesar (ed.), *Dante: The Critical Heritage* (London, 1989), 189–90. For the other three terms, cited (as slurs of the *literatissimi*) by vernacular defenders of Dante, see the *Invettive* of Cino Rinuccini (d. 1407) and Domenico da Prato (d. after 1425), both in *Il Paradiso degli Alberti: Ritrovi e ragionamenti del 1389*, ed. A. Wesselofsky, 3 vols. (Bologna, 1867), i, pt. 2, pp. 310, 322. On this part of the humanist debate about Dante, see A. Mazzocco, *Linguistic Theories in Dante and the Humanists* (Leiden, 1993), 86–8 (and nn. 18–36).

[48] C. Paolazzi, *Dante e la 'Commedia' nel trecento* (Milan, 1989), 189–94.

even conceding at one point that the *Commedia* would have been
yet more graceful and sublime if it had been written in Latin.[49]
And, if we are to take seriously the evidence of his two sonnets
about the *Esposizioni*, Boccaccio soon came to regret his whole
enterprise of exposing Dante to the *vulgo indegno*.[50]

Yet, if Boccaccio's *lettura* of Dante was in some ways an uncertain performance, it was still undeniably an important public,
indeed civic, occasion. The proposal to appoint 'a worthy and
wise man, learned in the art of poetry...to read the book that is
commonly called *Dante* in the city of Florence to all who wish to
hear' (*ad legendum librum qui vulgariter appellatur* El Dante, *in
civitate Florentie omnibus audire volentibus*) had been put before
the Priors and the Council of Twelve by a number of Florentine
citizens who wished 'to be instructed about the book of Dante on
their own behalf and that of other citizens aspiring to virtue, as
well as for the benefit of their followers and descendants'.[51] It
looks almost as if these seekers for self-improvement were taking
Boccaccio up on his assertion some twenty years earlier (in the first
revision of the *Trattatello*) that Dante had composed the *Commedia* in the *fiorentino idioma* in order 'to make it more generally
useful to his fellow citizens and to other Italians' (*per fare utilità
più commune a' suoi cittadini e agli altri Italiani*).[52] Whether such
citizens felt they had received good value for the Commune's 100
florins is another question—but it is quite clear from the surviving
text of Boccaccio's *Esposizioni* that the author has the needs of his
present listeners in mind, as well as those of his future more erudite
readers, since he addresses both kinds of audience.[53] And among

---

[49] *Esposizioni*, ed. Padoan, 5 (para. 19). Boccaccio's unease about the question is
also reflected at the end of the *accessus*, pp. 17–18 (paras. 74–7). A translation of
the passages (by D. Wallace) is in Minnis and Scott, *Medieval Literary Theory*, 507–
8, 518–19.

[50] Sonnets 122 and 123, in *Giovanni Boccaccio: Opere minori in volgare*, ed. M.
Marti, 4 vols. (Milan, 1972), iv. 134–5.

[51] The petition is printed in I. Del Lungo (ed.), *Dell' esilio di Dante* (Florence
1881), 164–5.

[52] *Trattatello in laude di Dante*, ed. P. G. Ricci, in *Tutte le opere di Giovanni
Boccaccio* (gen. ed. V. Branca), iii (Milan, 1974), first revision, pp. 486–7, paras.
190–2. The second revision, of the early 1360s, omits most of the argument about
usefulness to fellow-citizens and tones down the ensuing reference to the beauty of
the Florentine dialect (pp. 528–9, paras. 128–30), perhaps as a result of Petrarch's
letter of 1359 (see above, n. 48).

[53] The evidence (e.g. use of verbs such as *leggere* and *scrivere* to describe the
lecturer's procedure) is reviewed in G. Padoan, *L'ultima opera di Giovanni*

the citizens who gathered to hear him over the autumn and winter of 1373/4 in the shabby church of Santo Stefano in Badia, even those whose minds began to drift back to their bakeries or groceries when their lecturer reached the profounder levels of his *esposizione allegorica* may perhaps have had their attention recaptured by his reading aloud of copious quotations from *El Dante*.[54]

One of Boccaccio's contemporaries who was both a poet and a civic official had, shortly before this, participated rather more wholeheartedly in the process of bringing Dante back into the Florentine *volgare*. Antonio Pucci (*c*.1310–1388) was for over thirty years an employee of the Commune, as bell-ringer, auditor, and town-crier.[55] He was also a voluminous writer of verse, much of which (his *cantari*) was popular narrative of the kind despised by the likes of Giovanni del Virgilio and Petrarch—and much of which (such as the description of the Mercato Vecchio in *terza rima*) vividly reflects the *campanilismo* of this son of a Florentine bell-founder. His commitment to the popularization of learning is reflected in the range of his vernacular prose work, the *Libro di varie storie*, and his civic patriotism is evident in his versification of Giovanni Villani's chronicle, the *Centiloquio*, which may have been completed in the year that Boccaccio began the *Esposizioni* (1373) and the year that Chaucer visited Florence.[56] In the *Centiloquio*, Pucci's longest elaboration of Villani is his versification of the biography of Dante, which runs to over 300 lines of *terza rima*. Here he emphasizes the entry into common currency of Dante's

---

Boccaccio (Padua, 1959), 6–7. See also *Esposizioni*, e.g. p. 19, para. 1 ('per *leggere* siamo'), p. 57, para. 18 ('come voi potete aver... *udito*'), and p. 92, para. 177 ('basti d'avere *scritto*').

[54] Longer quotations appear to be signalled frequently throughout the text (e.g. at the start of the 'allegorical exposition' of Canto i, the 'literal exposition' of Canto ii, etc.), and it is possible that whole cantos might have been read at some points (which would take about ten minutes in each case). Reading the text before commenting on it was standard academic practice; see H. Rashdall, *The Universities of Europe*, 3 vols. (Oxford, 1936), i. 216–21, and R. S. Rait, *Life in the Medieval University* (Cambridge, 1912), 140–4.

[55] On Pucci's life and works, see *Antonio Pucci: 'Le Noie'*, ed. K. McKenzie (Princeton, 1931), pp. xvi–liv; N. Sapegno, *Pagine di storia letteraria* (Palermo, 1960), 133–81; and K. Speight, '*Vox Populi* in Antonio Pucci', in C. P. Brand *et al.* (eds.), *Italian Studies Presented to E. R. Vincent* (Cambridge, 1962), 76–91.

[56] Manuscript evidence indicates either 1373 or 1376 as the date for the final canto of the *Centiloquio*; see *Pucci: 'Le Noie'*, ed. McKenzie, p. xxvii. The *Libro di varie storie* (*c*.1362?) has been edited by A. Varvaro (Palermo, 1957).

verse, and (following the better-known story in Boccaccio's *Trattatello*) refers to the popular belief of the *gente grossa* that Dante had actually visited the otherworld.[57] *Grosso* ('coarse, ignorant, stupid') is an adjective that recurs several times in the discourse of Florentine appropriators of Dante.[58] In his prologue to the *capitolo* on Dante in the *Centiloquio*, Pucci applies it and the related noun (*grossezza*) twice to his own writing as he tries to deal with the life of the illustrious vernacular author:

> My mind that once was quick to find a way
> Of doing justice to a serious theme,
> Now, tasked with this, is all in disarray.
> The lines of verse that usually I seem
> To summon up with ease are hanging back,
> As if they held themselves in low esteem;
> And, knowing they're the work of such a hack,[59]
> They seem reluctant even to show their faces
> Or face a task that shows how much they lack.
>   Emperors, popes, and others in high places,
> Along with commoners, I have dealt with long,
> Not bothered by my want of finer graces;[60]
> But in this case it would be wholly wrong
> Not to call on my verse's best endeavour,
> As fits the present subject of this song;
> So, though, among the poets, I was ever
> Like some squat thorn-bush by the lofty palms,
> I'll do the best I can, but it won't be clever. (*Centiloquio*, lv. 1–18)[61]

Pucci's description of himself at the end of this passage as (literally) 'among the poets more base than a thorn-bush among the palms' can be seen as a graceful inversion of Brunetto's praise

---

[57] *Centiloquio*, lv. 214–19, in *Poeti minori del trecento*, ed. N. Sapegno (Milan, 1952), 417–18. Cf. Boccaccio, *Trattatello*, ed. Padoan, 465 (para. 113) and 512 (para. 69).

[58] *Grande dizionario della lingua italiana*, s.v. *grosso*[1] (agg.), senses 28 and 30–1. A Florentine grain-merchant, Domenico Lenzi, who alludes to Dante a number of times in his *Specchio umano* (*c*.1340), describes himself at the start of his work as *grosso e ydiota componitore*; see *Il libro del biadaiolo*, ed. G. Pinto (Florence, 1978), 159, and V. Branca, 'Un biadaiuolo lettore di Dante', in E. Paratore (ed.), *Studi in onore di Alfredo Schiaffini*, Rivista di Cultura Classica e Medievale 7 (Rome, 1965), 200–8 (p. 203). See also Sacchetti's use of the same adjective, below, n. 63.

[59] Original: 'perché riconoscendo lor *grossezza*.'

[60] Original: 'sanza curarmi del mio *grosso ingegno*.'

[61] My translation. The original is in *Poeti minori*, ed. Sapegno, 411.

of Dante as a sweet fig among sour sorb-apples in *Inferno*, xv (65–6). In several respects—including its tentativeness with regard to the quality of its rhymes and its lack of aspiration to 'art poetical'—the passage also shows affinities with the 'Dantean' invocation to Book III of *The House of Fame* (composed some seven or eight years later).[62]

A similar mode of discourse characterizes the appropriation of Dante by Pucci's friend and fellow-Florentine Franco Sacchetti. In another prologue (to the *Trecentonovelle*) Sacchetti claims to be following in some respects the example of the *vulgare poeta fiorentino Dante*, whilst in the same breath describing himself as a *fiorentino* who is *discolo e grosso* ('ignorant and coarse').[63] Both Pucci and Sacchetti make frequent allusion to the *Commedia* in their prose and verse—and in the *Trecentonovelle* Dante becomes at times a kind of folk-hero, as well as a source of proverbial wisdom.[64] On occasion quotation from the *Commedia* can be given a raucously coarse application—as in the adaptation of the horrific opening line of *Inferno*, xxxiii ('La bocca sollevò dal fiero pasto') at a crucial moment in Sacchetti's story of the fisherman, his wife, the crab, and the blacksmith (*Trecentonovelle*, no. 208).

Sacchetti is also capable of appropriating Dante as *vulgare poeta fiorentino* in some considerably more sophisticated ways. In his famous story of Dante and the blacksmith (no. 114 in the *Trecentonovelle*), the central Florentine street-scene is described as follows:

he ['Dante', on his way to an appointment with a friend] passed by the Porta San Piero where there was a blacksmith beating a piece of iron on the anvil and belting out Dante's poem like someone singing a street-ballad (*come si canta uno cantare*)—mangling the verses, hacking bits out and tacking bits on—in such a way that Dante felt he was being done considerable injury. He said nothing, but went straight into the workshop where this blacksmith kept the tools of his trade, grabbed the hammer and threw it out into the street, did the same with the tongs and the scales, and likewise flung out a great deal of the ironmongery. The blacksmith, contorted with rage, swung round and said:

---

[62] Pucci's *Libro di varie storie* is also comparable in some ways to Chaucer's project in *The House of Fame*—at least as a vernacular compendium dominated by the figure of Dante. For a list of the quotations from the *Commedia* in Pucci's *Libro*, see Varvaro's ed., 349–50.

[63] Franco Sacchetti, *Il Trecentonovelle*, ed. E. Faccioli (Turin, 1970), 4.

[64] *Trecentonovelle*, nos. 4, 8, 121, and 193. Other references to Dante are in nos. 15, 114, 115, 175, 208, and 210.

'What the hell do you think you're doing? Are you out of your mind?
Dante said: 'And what do you think *you*'re doing?'
'I'm just doing my job' said the blacksmith. 'And you'll ruin my gear—
throwing it out on the street like that.'
Dante answered: 'If you don't want me to ruin your stuff, don't ruin
mine.'
'And what of yours am I ruining?' asked the blacksmith.
Dante replied: 'You're singing my text (*canti il libro*), but not the way I
wrote it. I've got no other job and you're ruining it for me.'
Speechless with rage, the blacksmith picked up his tools and went back
to work. And if, after that, he felt like singing, he sang about Tristan and
Lancelot and left Dante alone.[65]

Sacchetti's story is obviously a fabrication, as any Florentine
familiar with the story of Dante's exile must have known. Its
particular interest, though, lies in the way it confronts 'Dante'
with one version of his afterlife and shows the villain of the piece
(the 'blacksmith') tormenting the *Commedia*'s text like some Male-
branchean demon. The word for 'blacksmith' here is not *manis-
calco*—as in the rather coarser *novella* referred to above (no.
208)—but *fabbro*, which can at this time in Italian run the
gamut of meaning from 'blacksmith' through 'workman' and
'maker' to 'artist' and 'divine creator'.[66] Sacchetti may thus be
entertaining the idea of linking the image of the *fabbro* with the
concept of the *volgare*. This is indeed an association that occurs at
least twice in Dante's own writing—for instance, in the familiar
line from *Purgatorio*, xxvi (117), where Guinizelli describes
Arnaut Daniel as a *fabbro* working on the *parlar materno*, and
in a less well-known passage from *Convivio* where the vernacular
itself is represented as the *fabbro* which has had a hand in shaping
Dante's very being (*Convivio*, I. xiii. 4).
     The *Trecentonovelle* is mainly a work of the 1390s and is thus
probably too late to have been known to Chaucer.[67] But the civic
culture from which its representation of Dante as *vulgare poeta
fiorentino* derives was already well established by the time of
Chaucer's visit to Florence in the spring of 1373.
     Of course, 1373 was also the year in which the Commune
decided to set up Boccaccio's lectureship on Dante and the year

[65] My translation. The original is in *Trecentonovelle*, ed. Faccioli, 299–300.
[66] See *Grande dizionario della lingua italiana*, s.v. *fabbro*[1] (sm.), senses 1–3.
[67] See *Trecentonovelle*, ed. Faccioli, p. xxii.

by which Pucci's *Centiloquio* with its celebration of Dante as *antico cittadino della città di Firenze* may have been completed.[68] There is no need to suppose that Chaucer came back from Florence with a manuscript of the *Centiloquio*—still less that he got any detailed advance notice of Boccaccio's *Esposizioni*. It does, however, seem possible that the concern about the popularity and performance of *El Dante* in the urban culture of late fourteenth-century Florence may offer another context for Chaucer's reception of the *Commedia* and his initial appropriation of it in *The House of Fame*. *The House of Fame* is itself, in ways which writers from the seventeenth century onwards recognized, a markedly urban poem.[69] It is also an essentially hybrid work, incorporating both the learned and the lewd—the silent private reader 'dombe as any stoon' and the avid audience of 'every maner man'—and it is a location in which common performers and tale-bearers mingle with illustrious writers. This very hybridity of Chaucer's poem is in tune with some late fourteenth-century Florentine representations of Dante's *Commedia* as a seriously vulgar work: a work in play between the Muses and the blacksmiths.

[68] But see above, n. 56.
[69] See *The House of* Fame, ed. Havely, 19 and nn. 119–22.

5

French Culture and the Ricardian Court

ARDIS BUTTERFIELD

I

The French thirteenth-century fabliau *La Male Honte* plays on the comic confusion that arises when the English and the French both try to speak the same language. The joke begins with a pun in the title (it can mean both 'foul shame' and the bag ('une male') of a man called Honte) but the fabliau develops into more than merely a chauvinistic gag. Part of its cleverness consists in showing not so much that the English cannot speak French—perhaps the most enduring type of simple mockery between the two cultures—but rather how rampantly misunderstandings can develop when two speakers from different cultural contexts use the same piece of language, each assuming a total cultural possession over its meaning that makes the awareness of a potential ambiguity quite unthinkable. The fabliau writer achieves the difficult dramatic feat of allowing his audience, by listening to a dialogue laden with linguistic misunderstandings, to appreciate both the ambiguity and the confusing and comic consequences of failing to see that ambiguity.[1]

An extra complexity of the tale, itself not above ambiguity, involves the question of its precise cultural location. The two speakers are both English, although one is a king and the other a *vilain*. Given that the author is usually taken to be French, it seems

---

[1] A. E. Cobby, 'Understanding and Misunderstanding in *La Male Honte*', in Gillian Jondorf and D. N. Dumville (eds.), *France and the British Isles in the Middle Ages and Renaissance: Essays in Memory of Ruth Morgan* (Woodbridge, 1991), 155–72. I have consulted the dual-text edition by J. Rychner, *Contribution à l'étude des fabliaux: Variantes, remaniements, dégradations*, 2 vols. (Neuchâtel, 1960), ii. 16–27.

as if he is pointing simultaneously towards two kinds of cultural gap, the French spoken by the English as opposed to the French spoken by the French, and the French spoken by the *courtois* as opposed to the *vilain*.[2] But the very fact that he can run two kinds of argument alongside each other shows that his perception of cultural difference is neither single nor simple, but made up of a complicated and not fully congruent mixture of social and national preoccupations. 'English' and 'French' are categories that are blurred in this fabliau, even while its humour depends on the audience taking these categories for granted.

It is well to be reminded of such culturally delicate moments in thirteenth-century writing when one comes to reflect on the character of Anglo-French relations in the later fourteenth century. It is all too easy to start by assuming a position of cultural difference that bears little resemblance to the fluctuating and convolutedly mutual history of that relationship. Rather than talk of the influence of one—French—upon the other—English—as if one could separate and isolate such influences, it makes more sense of their interwoven political, social, and literary history to try to grasp the ways in which the categories of 'English' and 'French' invite contradiction in the later medieval period. One consequence, for instance, of the prolonged war between England and France seems to have been that the war gradually and fitfully provoked and stimulated a sense of national identity rather than that it arose originally in defence of such an identity. From this point of view, the war looks more like a family quarrel than an expression of hostile difference, where it is often more important to *assert* difference than for the differences themselves to be genuinely experienced as such. Much of the time, indeed, members of the English royalty were keen both to assert and experience what they saw as their indivisibility from French estates, and spent long periods exercising their rule on the French mainland.

John Burrow has always been concerned to give due weight to the importance of French poetry to Ricardian culture: 'Deschamps's description of Chaucer as a "grant translateur", partial though it is, points to a cardinal truth about Middle English

---

[2] It should be pointed out that the tale exists in two versions, by at least two authors (see Rychner, *Contribution*, and Cobby, 'Understanding and Misunderstanding', *passim*).

literature as a whole: its heavy dependence upon French.'[3] At the same time, the principal effort of *Ricardian Poetry* is to assert the distinctively English cultural achievement of the later fourteenth century, sometimes characterized in quite conscious contradistinction to French style. This essay seeks to look again at the question of how fully we can categorize the writing produced in England during this period as 'English', given our awareness of the dominant nature of contemporary European and, especially, French vernacular writing. This is hardly a new topic: it seems as if it has been on or near the surface of modern thinking about the medieval period since the early years of this century. However, we have not always examined our notions of cultural identity from a broad perspective, or even from any perspective apart from our own. The Chaucerian imperative has tended to cast European and, especially, French culture into a shadow of our own making, which is not at all visible from France. It is a harsh truth, from the English point of view, that, looked at from the Continent, the huge, rich vernacular production of medieval France leaves English efforts seeming small, sparse, and only intermittently brilliant.

None the less, my interest is not in weighing up the two cultures in a quasi-competitive spirit but in trying to find better ways of understanding the relations between them. I will be asking questions about the kinds of distinction one might draw between the poetic cultures of France and England in this period, whether the circumstances in which French poetry comes to be written shed any light on the circumstances in England, how comparable the notion of the court is in French and English terms, how far the cultural interchange between the two influenced the kinds of poetic approach taken by their major figures, and how, finally, ideas of cultural difference can be said to arise out of a period of deep cultural interaction. These are the kinds of question that require large answers: here I can do little more than suggest some ways of beginning a reply.

One of the best ways of appreciating the embeddedness of cultural interaction in this period, as the author of *La Male Honte* implies, is to look at language. The more closely medieval vernaculars are studied, the more it appears that they did not

---

[3] J. A. Burrow, *Medieval Writers and their Work* (Oxford, 1982), 7.

separate neatly into discrete, culturally exclusive linguistic groups, but that people often wrote a shifting kind of lingua franca. It is not enough to recognize that England was a trilingual culture—Latin, French, and English—since, in certain contexts, the kind of linguistic barrier implied by these labels was overridden. Business documents are a fascinating source of evidence for the circulation of a kind of mixed language, in some cases a mixture of Latin and English, in others of English and Anglo-Norman or else of Anglo-Norman and Latin. It is partly a matter of semantic infiltration, whereby, as William Rothwell puts it, 'the language appears to be Latin, but the Latin words carry French, not Latin, meanings'.[4] Yet word-order is also affected; more generally, the Latin is used as a kind of grammatical casing for a highly flexible system of vernacular communication.[5] The system of heavy abbreviation in business records further means that 'the semantic core' of a piece of writing stands out in relief. This enables the gist of a document to be read quickly by someone whose knowledge of Latin case-endings is limited. It also gives the language geographical flexibility, since the Latin acts as a grammatical constant to which varying local vernacular words and phrases can be added according to context.[6]

Such an intimate and mobile means of juxtaposing languages is a striking model for the very mixed character of late medieval 'English' literacy. Not all communication, whether spoken or written, was necessarily macaronic, of course, but the language of official records shows that a high proportion of 'English' writing was an intensely composite linguistic process. Many other kinds of instance or historical anecdote can be cited to demonstrate how broad or perhaps how contradictory the notion of Englishness

---

[4] W. Rothwell, 'The Trilingual England of Geoffrey Chaucer', *SAC* 16 (1994), 45–67 (p. 47).

[5] The prepositions, conjunctions, and articles were in a Romance language and the nouns and verb-stems were either Romance or Germanic—that is, the former were in the prestige language (Latin or Anglo-Norman) and the latter in the vernacular (Anglo-Norman or English): see Laura Wright, 'Trade between England and the Low Countries: Evidence from Historical Linguistics', in Caroline Barron and Nigel Saul (eds.), *England and the Low Countries in the Late Middle Ages* (Stroud, 1995), 169–79. For further references to Wright's work, see Rothwell, 'The Trilingual England'.

[6] For examples of the wider European usage of this macaronic style, see Wright, 'Trade between England and the Low Countries'.

appears to be. War naturally produced such cases, where, for instance, towns on French soil were defined as English, and their subjects as owing allegiance to the Black Prince and expected to fight as English against the French. The Savoyard poet-knight Oton de Graunson is an example of a French nobleman who was in the English court for twenty years, in the service of John of Gaunt and the earls of Pembroke and Derby, and who fought for the English on the Continent as the 'home lige de vie et de membres' of the king;[7] conversely the Black Prince himself was—at one stage—a French liege lord. These, amongst others, are thoroughly familiar textbook examples: it perhaps needs stressing, none the less, how often, even how routinely, they confirm the linguistic evidence in showing English and French to be deeply as well as superficially interchangeable cultural positions.

The most prominent French literary figure in the English court was Jean Froissart. As is well known, he spent much of the 1360s in the service of Philippa of Hainault, Edward III's French queen, during which time he composed most of his love *dits*, including those known intimately by Chaucer. I will be returning to these later in the essay: my interest here is in Froissart's cultural status. His period in England seems to have marked out his English preoccupations in a lasting way. For although, after Philippa's death in 1369, he returned to the mainland to work for Wenceslas, duc de Brabant, and later Gui II de Châtillon, his great literary achievement, the *Chroniques*, reveals an open and continuing obsession with English aristocratic politics. More than this, Froissart's huge, often glamorous, mythologizing account is an instance of French historiography that becomes utterly English, not only in the sense that its subject largely focuses on the English, but also because it enters into the English perception of history. In its representation of the English past, and in its function as a means of national identification, the *Chroniques* created history as well as narrated it. This process was entrenched in the sixteenth century through Sir John Berners's translation, assimilated in turn by Shakespeare. Froissart, in this sense, is more than merely a contemporary

---

[7] Haldeen Braddy, *Chaucer and the French Poet Graunson* (Baton Rouge, La. 1947), 40–8. Graunson swore an oath of allegiance to the throne of England on 19 Nov. 1393. See also A. Piaget, *Oton de Grandson: Sa vie et ses poésies* (Lausanne, 1941), 43–4.

French counterpart to Chaucer, but an author whose last great work, notwithstanding its Frenchness, becomes as much of an English cultural icon as Chaucer's poetic *œuvre*.

At the risk of over-emphasizing the mutuality of English and French concerns, a harder look at the character of their interchange would create a more nuanced sense of their relationship. Ideally, one would trace the process back to the thirteenth century, or even earlier, since one of the difficulties involved in assessing the level of French fluency in later medieval England concerns the degree to which shifts occurred in the relative status of English, French, and Latin between the thirteenth and fourteenth centuries. That such shifts occurred is clear; taking account of the multiplicity of factors, such as the social, literary, and scholarly function of each language, the different regional uses, the relationship between lay and ecclesiastical usage, courtly and non-courtly, male and female, is not so easy. The distinction between French and Anglo-Norman itself becomes harder to sustain or perceive by the end of the fourteenth century. Recent accounts have tended to seize on the same anecdotal hints in order to draw very different conclusions as to whether and at what date French in England was widely or narrowly spoken, a genuine vernacular or a language only of record, a native or acquired language.[8]

Rather than rehearse these debates, I want to emphasize the cultural importance in the fourteenth century of instances of long-term naturalization, such as the presence of French poets, like Froissart, living for long periods in the English court. For these provide opportunities for reflecting on how far English patrons—whether aristocratic or mercantile—encouraged an international cultural approach, or conversely how thoroughly 'foreign' writers attempted to participate in an English cultural landscape.

---

[8] See for instance the discussions in E. Salter, 'Conditions and Status', and her 'Chaucer and Internationalism', in *English and International: Studies in the Literature, Art and Patronage of Medieval England*, ed. D. Pearsall and N. Zeeman (Cambridge, 1988), 239–44; R. F. Green, *Poets and Princepleasers: Literature and the English Court in the Late Middle Ages* (Toronto, 1980), 152–55; V. J. Scattergood, 'Literary Culture at the Court of Richard II', in V. J. Scattergood and J. W. Sherborne (eds.), *English Court Culture in the Later Middle Ages* (London, 1983), 29–43. For a view emphasizing Chaucer's native poetic inheritance, see D. S. Brewer, 'The Relationship of Chaucer to the English and European Traditions', in D. S. Brewer (ed.), *Chaucer and Chaucerians: Critical Studies in Middle English Literature* (London, 1966), 1–38.

My starting-point is with an organization rather than an individual: the London *puy*. Although the records of its charter and membership have long been published, they have attracted little attention until recently.[9] The attempts to link Gower and even Chaucer, Froissart, and Oton de Graunson with the *puy*, by postulating its shadowy (and undocumented) existence right through the century, are far-fetched.[10] As Anne Sutton has convincingly shown, it flourished in the last quarter of the thirteenth century but did not survive much beyond 1300.[11] The complaints of extravagance amongst certain members in the second set of statutes give some clue as to the atmosphere which led to its dispersal. The character of the London *puy* draws its inspiration, and probably its origin, from the well-established northern French *puys* and *confréries* of Arras, Lille, Valenciennes, and Abbeville.[12] These were poetic guilds, usually founded from a religious or charitable motive, which met to hold poetic contests. The significance of the London *puy* in the present context is that it represents a cultural import from France, not just of a single work or a single author, but of a complete poetic institution. Its members included mercers, mayors, aldermen, sheriffs, learned clerks, and royal collegiate clergy, some of whom were among the wealthiest merchants in the city. One of the reasons for participating in the *puy* is given in the regulations as 'for the renown of London'; the composition of French chansons, on the model of French *puys*, amongst bourgeois businessmen is seen as a means of enhancing the self-image of England's prime urban centre.[13]

[9] 'Regulations of the Feste de Pui', ed. H. T. Riley, *Munimenta gildhallae Londoniensis*, Rolls Series, 3 vols. (London, 1859–62), II. i: *Liber customarum*, 216–28.

[10] John H. Fisher, *John Gower: Moral Philosopher and Friend of Chaucer* (London, 1965), 78–83, cautiously echoed by James I. Wimsatt, *Chaucer and his French Contemporaries: Natural Music in the Fourteenth Century* (Toronto, 1992), 276 and n. 7.

[11] Anne F. Sutton, 'Merchants, Music and Social Harmony: The London Puy and its French and London Contexts, circa 1300', *The London Journal*, 17 (1992), 1–17, and 'The *Tumbling Bear* and its Patrons: A Venue for the London Puy and Mercery', in Julia Boffey and Pamela King (eds.), *London and Europe in the Later Middle Ages* (London, 1995), 85–110.

[12] Ardis Butterfield, 'Puy', in *Medieval France: An Encyclopaedia*, gen. ed. W. W. Kibler (New York, 1995), 771; Wimsatt, *Chaucer and his French Contemporaries*, 274–81.

[13] Only one *chanson couronnée* appears to have survived in English sources, and even this is not conclusively associated with the London *puy*, since the attributed

It is not entirely clear from the surviving records whether the London *puy* was an expatriate concern, partly run by foreign businessmen in their own cultural style, or an attempt by English merchants to emulate the social activities of their counterparts in northern France. Even this distinction is probably a false one, in that Henry le Waleys, one of the wealthiest members, was a past mayor of Bordeaux as well as of London, and thus can hardly be characterized as having a narrowly English outlook.[14] The point is rather that then, as now, London was run by a large international community, for whom it was natural to turn to French practice for an international model of a literary society. There seems to have been no question of such an organization existing to promote the amateur writing of lyric poetry in English: amateur, vernacular poetry in London at this date was pre-eminently French.

The next period of cultural exchange that I wish to consider centres on the marriage of Edward III and Philippa of Hainault. This was an event that reverberated with its own cross-cultural significance, but it also marked the start of a particularly rich period of mutual acculturation between England and France. Recent archival and codicological research reveals a fuller picture than hitherto of the carefully crafted cultural impact of the union.[15] Isabella, the French queen of Edward II, paid several lengthy diplomatic vists to France during 1325–6 to make the preparatory negotiations for her son's marriage, which took place on 1 November 1327. The records of these numerous diplomatic meetings indicate that the marriage was delicately pitched to set in motion claims by the English to the French throne. Of particular interest is the way in which these claims were articulated through various artistic ploys, encapsulated in the manuscript Edward and Philippa gave to each other on their wedding, now Paris, Bibliothèque Nationale, MS fr. 571. This includes a copy of

author has not been identified in the *puy* records, and the song text does not match the regulations specified for the *puy* competition. On the *cantus coronatus*, see C. Page, *Voices and Instruments of the Middle Ages* (London, 1987), 196–201.

[14] For further references confirming the French connections of several of the merchants named in the London *puy* statute see Sutton, 'The *Tumbling Bear*', esp. 90–3.

[15] See Andrew Wathey, 'The Marriage of Edward III and the Transmission of French Motets to England', *Journal of the American Musicological Society*, 45 (1992), 1–29.

Brunetto Latini's *Livre du trésor*, the *Secreta secretorum* by Pseudo-Aristotle, the *Roman de Fauvain*, and two motets from the Paris, Bibliothèque Nationale, MS fr. 146 version of *Le Roman de Fauvel*. The codex makes an emphatic statement of political union, beginning with an opening picture of a young woman bearing the arms of Hainault, and a young man bearing those of the heir apparent of England. More discreet attempts to show family links with French royalty are made by additional heraldic decoration surrounding this representation of the betrothed couple, showing Philippa's full lineage on both her maternal and paternal side, with further portrayals of arms at the opening of each work, and in the major sections of the *Trésor*. As Andrew Wathey has recently argued, it seems very likely that the two *Fauvel* motets are an additional subtle reference to the French claims of Edward and Philippa in the way that their texts emphasize the couple's common ancestry.

The production of BN fr. 571 turns out to be an intricately mixed cultural enterprise. The decoration, including the heraldic frontispiece, is by English illuminators, drawing heavily on East Anglian models. Yet their materials are of Franco-Flemish origin, implying, as Lucy Freeman Sandler has argued, that the book was finished by English artists working in Hainault for Isabella, who made use of local pigments.[16] Some of the texts were also copied by English scribes: since the *Trésor*, however, was copied by a scribe from Valenciennes, it seems likely that French and English scribes were working alongside one another in Hainault during an earlier stage in the book's assembly. Once completed, the manuscript was taken to England, and perhaps later given to Henry, duke of Lancaster, but its role as a symbol of Anglo-French exchange was mirrored in its return to France where, by 1396, it was in the possession of Louis, duc d'Orléans.

Since we are more familiar with the notion that in general England looked to France for inspiration and practical expertise in the making of manuscripts, it is interesting to find evidence to suggest that English scribes and artists were specially brought over to Hainault to help carry out this important marital commission.

---

[16] Lucy Freeman Sandler, *A Survey of Manuscripts Illuminated in the British Isles, v. Gothic Manuscripts, 1285–1385*, 2 vols. (Oxford, 1986), ii, no. 96, 103–5 (105).

The cultural significance of the occasion radiates in several directions. It shows, once more, how mutual the cultural influence was between England and France, and how this was a natural product of the close familial links between the royal houses. Isabella clearly took cultural advantage of her pivotal role as a Frenchwoman and an English queen to make political and artistic capital of the role of her future daughter-in-law, a second generation Frenchwoman and English queen. This role Philippa appears to have fulfilled enthusiastically: her reign signalled a high degree of contact and exchange between the English and French royal households.

Attention to the behind-scenes official documentary record of such contacts further shows how much communication there was between French and English clerks, of a direct and personal kind, and, moreover, how this ran in parallel with artistic production of all kinds, poetry, painting, and music. Gervès du Bus, for instance, the author of the version of *Le Roman de Fauvel* in BN fr. 146, brilliantly interpolated with 169 musical pieces in Latin and French and a series of remarkable illuminations, was a senior notary at the time of Isabella's negotiations who was specially chosen as senior witness, owing to his 'specialism, built over several years, in the area of Anglo-French affairs and the familiarity with English forms of document that this necessitated.'[17] The celebrated composer Philippe de Vitry was a junior royal notary of Charles IV, from 1323. He likewise, must have had dealings with many English clerks in the series of meetings with English bishops that took place during the 1320s. We know that several motets from *Fauvel* circulated in England: it is not difficult to see, with such evidence of Anglophile leanings among the French clerical community, how such circulation might have taken place. It is frustratingly difficult to find hard evidence of the circulation of any manuscripts of Machaut's poetry in England during the fourteenth century (apart from the single example in the 1390s of Isabella, duchess of York, who left a copy of Machaut's poems to her son, along with a French *Lancelot*),[18] but the bureaucratic route, given its connections with other well-known

---

[17] Wathey, 'The Marriage of Edward III', 9–10.
[18] Salter, 'Conditions and Status', 35. Salter raises the intriguing possibility that the 'large livre de Trese amoireux et moralitez et de carolles frannceis bien esluminez' itemized in Thomas, duke of Gloucester's library could have included poetry by Machaut ('Chaucer and Internationalism', 244).

musicians and poets, is most plausible. It is possible, for instance, that Machaut was present at Edward and Philippa's wedding, since it was attended by his patron John, king of Bohemia, and members of John's domestic household.

Other information about the households of Philippa and Edward in the later part of their reign shows that the level of cultural exchange between England and France continued to be high. The most prominent periods were those in which French royal hostages were kept in England: Jean II of France (Jean le Bon) and, after the Treaty of Brétigny in 1360, his three sons, the dukes of Berry, Burgundy, and Anjou. Philippa is reputed to have played a key role in providing hospitality for the hostages who effectively held their own courts.[19] Records survive of the household chapels in England of all four French princes between 1357 and 1364.[20] Not only did their presence cause an influx of French musicians and poets into England, it also coincided with a rising level of new appointments to the English royal households of French personnel. Certain clerks were poached back and forth between the French and English administrations, such as the min-strel or two hired before 1374 by Louis, duc d'Anjou, younger brother of Charles V, who had formerly worked for Sir John Chandos in England and Aquitaine or, in the reverse direction, the French musician Matheus de Sancto Johanne, who became a chaplain in Philippa's household having earlier worked in the same capacity for the same duc d'Anjou.

One of the major reasons for the increase in movement between the English and French courts was the period of truce between 1360 and 1369. The sudden release of tension seems to have encouraged a greater volume of traffic across the Channel, in both directions, showing how far conditions of war between the

[19] Nigel Wilkins, 'Music and Poetry at Court: England and France in the Late Middle Ages', in Scattergood and Sherborne (eds.), *English Court Culture*, 183–204 (pp. 194–7). On the question of Froissart's status in the households of Jean II and Jean's eldest son Charles, see R. Barber, 'Jean Froissart and Edward the Black Prince', in J. J. N. Palmer (ed.), *Froissart: Historian* (Woodbridge, 1981), 25–35 (pp. 25–6). Froissart comments on his double connection with the English and French royal households as follows: 'de ma jeunesse je fui .v. ans en l'ostel du roy d'Angleterre et de la royne, et si fu bien de l'ostel du roy Jehan de France et du roy Charle son filz.'

[20] A. Wathey, 'The Peace of 1360–1369 and Anglo-French Musical Relations', *Early Music History*, 9 (1990), 129–74 (p. 133).

two countries were in a sense feeding off their mutual intimacy. Froissart's stay was itself a product of the truce. As James Wimsatt has rightly emphasized, Froissart was filling in a role earlier occupied by the poet-musician Jehan de la Mote.[21] Jehan de la Mote, like Gervès du Bus and Philippe de Vitry, was a chancellery clerk: there is a record that he was working in this capacity in Hainault in 1327. His existing connection with Philippa was confirmed and maintained by Edward, who, in 1338, appears to have given the poet an annuity of £20. He was commissioned by Philippa to write an elegy for her father Guillaume, comte de Hainault, in 1339. Further records indicate that he continued to have an association (though not an exclusive one) with the English royal household at least as late as 1343, when he is mentioned as having entertained the king as a minstrel at Eltham.[22] This anticipates Froissart's composition of a *pastourelle* to record a visit paid by Jean II to Eltham in 1364 during his time as hostage.[23] Jehan le Bel, who fought in Edward's service in Scotland in 1327, was another poet-predecessor of Froissart who found patronage in the English court;[24] contemporary with Froissart, though on a different social footing, was Oton de Graunson, who entered Lancastrian service in 1374.[25]

These French poets, over two generations, make up an interesting phenomenon. We may distinguish them from those English

---

[21] Wimsatt, *Chaucer and his French Contemporaries*, 48–9.

[22] Wilkins, 'Music and Poetry at Court', 192.

[23] Jean Froissart, *Œuvres poétiques*, ed. A. Scheler, 3 vols. (Brussels, 1870–2), ii. 308–10; cited with tr. by Kristen Mossler Figg, *The Short Lyric Poems of Jean Froissart: Fixed Forms and the Expression of the Courtly Ideal* (New York 1994), no. 2, pp. 213–16.

[24] Froissart drew heavily on Jehan le Bel's *Vrayes Chroniques* for the first stages of his own *Chroniques* whilst in Philippa's service; see F. S. Shears, *Froissart: Chronicler and Poet* (London, 1930), 75–87. Le Bel was a fellow Hainaulter, closely associated with Jean of Hainault, Philippa's uncle. He also composed songs and virelais, but none has survived. On his fervent support for Edward III over Philippe VI, see J. J. N. Palmer, 'Book I (1323–78) and its Sources', in Palmer (ed.), *Froissart: Historian*, 17.

[25] Florimont, sire de Lesparre, collaborated briefly with Graunson, interpolating some lines into one of Graunson's *complaintes*. After a long association with Pierre of Cyprus (one of Machaut's patrons), Florimont fought with the Black Prince against the Spanish, and received patronage from Edward III and John of Gaunt. By contrast, the more notable poet-chevalier Jehan de Garancières, whose grandfather was a voluntary hostage in Jean le Bon's retinue at the Treaty of Brétigny, fought consistently against rather than for the English (see n. 31 below).

courtiers who wrote French poetry in the English court, such as John Montagu, earl of Salisbury, in that they were not writing as 'native' English speakers but in a semi-naturalized lingua franca.[26] Their role, in English terms, promoted the international character of 'English' writing in a direction that was different from the indigenous French writing. That is, I think it would be misleading to think of them as temporary cultural imports: their settled presence wrought permanent changes in the notion of English writing that in the long term enabled the writing of an English vernacular to be more than a merely insular achievement.

From this point of view, it is revealing to note how perceptions of the French changed during the latter part of the century. In moments of strain, the term 'alien' is wielded with unabashed chauvinism: during the attacks on Richard II in the Merciless Parliament of 1388, some of his chamber knights, including two with notable interests in French writings, Sir John Salisbury and Richard's former tutor Sir Simon Burley, were accused of leading the king astray. Burley, in particular, was charged with having caused Richard 'to have many aliens, Bohemians and others in his Household'.[27] The French musicians who were engaged in Gaunt's household chapel from 1390 are also described in the accounts as 'francoys' and 'alienigenis'. However, although at first they were paid at a lower rate than their English counterparts and seemingly treated as inferior foreigners, their status changed. Gaunt employed them intensively throughout the 1390s, maintaining them at his main household in Hertford Castle with hardly a break, ensuring that in due course they were 'fully assimilated within the career structure of the household'.[28] Some of them were given additional ecclesiastical preferments. Another French musician, the composer Pycard, whose pieces are collected in the Old Hall manuscript, and who has been tentatively identified with a Picard who worked in Gaunt's chapel, is an example of a French

---

[26] Salisbury's French poetry is now lost, though other instances of French writing composed by English courtiers survive, such as Henry of Lancaster's *Livre de seyntz medecines*. For a lengthy list of English aristocratic poets and authors in the 14th and 15th cents., see Green, *Poets and Princepleasers*, 109.

[27] J. W. Sherborne, 'Aspects of English Court Culture in the Later Fourteenth Century', in Scattergood and Sherborne (eds.), *English Court Culture*, 1–27 (p. 20).

[28] A. Wathey, 'John of Gaunt, John Pycard and the Amiens Negotiations of 1392', in Barron and Saul (eds.), *England and the Low Countries*, 29–42.

artist who deliberately went native. His music shows so thorough an assimilation of English musical style that it has been described as defying 'analysis in terms of simple constructs of "influence"'.[29] The practice of French musicians, their overt attempts at cultural absorption, provides an illuminating counterpart to the French poets who sought employment alongside them in English households.

It is difficult to know precisely how many of Froissart's poems were composed in England, although it was certainly the period in which he concentrated most heavily on the genre of the love *dit*. Modern Chaucerians tend to look on him as a foreign influence upon Chaucer; 'Chaucer and the French' is seen as simply one of the principal areas of Chaucer's foreign reading, along with Italian and Latin.[30] Yet this is a misleading simplification of a complex cultural situation. Froissart's early work needs to be understood as English before it can be properly appreciated alongside Chaucer's. More broadly, several of his and Machaut's poems are Anglo-French in the sense that they were produced under the specific conditions of the Anglo-French war, whether of truce or hostage exchange or simply continuous diplomatic negotiation. A whole genre of writing arises in response to these conditions, with their subjects including the knight forced into exile, or the prisoner (Machaut's *La Fonteinne amoureuse* and the complaint 'A toi Hanri', Froissart's *L'Espinette amoureuse* and *La Prison amoureuse*).[31] Charles d'Orléans, who was taken prisoner by the English at Agincourt in 1415, and held captive in England for twenty-five years, continues this poetic tradition into the fifteenth century, along with James of Scotland, imprisoned royal author of *The Kingis Quair*.

[29] Ibid. 38.
[30] Wimsatt, for instance, describes the French reading upon which Chaucer draws in his *Book of the Duchess* as 'foreign materials' *Chaucer and his French Contemporaries*, p. x).
[31] *La Fonteinne amoureuse*, in *Guillaume de Machaut: Œuvres*, ed. E. Hoepffner, SATF, 3 vols. (Paris, 1908–21), iii. 143–244; 'A toi Hanri', in *Poésies lyriques*, ed. V. Chichmaref, 2 vols. (Paris, 1909; repr. Geneva, 1973), i. 251–3 (also quoted and tr. Wimsatt, *Chaucer and his French Contemporaries*, 78–82); *L'Espinette amoureuse*, ed. A. Fourrier, 2nd rev. ed. (Paris, 1972); *La Prison amoureuse*, ed. A. Fourrier (Paris, 1974). Jehan de Garancières composed many poems during a period of captivity at Bordeaux in 1406–7. See Y. A. Neal, *Le Chevalier poéte Jehan de Garancières (1372–1415): Sa vie et ses poésies complètes*, 2 vols. (Paris, 1953), i. 1–5.

A well-known ballade by Eustache Deschamps, written in 1384, makes perhaps the most succinct and sharply comic commentary on the convoluted relations between English and French, between French poet and French poet in English service.[32] Its context is Calais, at a time when a permanent peace treaty was being nego- tiated. Deschamps is with Graunson, but has come without an official permit ('san congié'). Two Englishmen challenge him; when Deschamps replies rudely, they threaten him ('Prinsonnier, vous estes forfais'). Instead of helping him out, Graunson pretends to abandon him, laughing loudly, and says in English that he disclaims him:

> Mais Granson s'en aloit adés
> Qui en riant faisoit la vuide:
> A eulx m'avoit trahi, ce cuide;
> En anglois dist: 'Pas ne l'adveue.'

Getting desperate, Deschamps appeals to his friend, who at the last minute vouches for him after all:

> Delez Granson fut mes retrais.
> La ne me vault treves ne pais,
> De paour la face me ride,
> De tel amour ma mort me cuide;
> Au derrain leur dist: 'Je l'adveue.'

The poem wittily contracts the notion of friendship and betrayal and the negotiations involved in turning one into the other by showing the larger political situation between France and England through a small personal incident. Deschamps darts back and forth between attack and defence; one moment he is cowering with fear, the next he is insistently repeating (by means of the refrain) the old insults against the English, that they speak in a funny way and they have tails like animals:[33]

> L'un me dist: 'dogue', l'autre: 'ride';
> Lors me devint la couleur bleue:[34]

---

[32] The poem is discussed by Piaget, *Oton de Grandson*, 167–8, and Braddy, *Chaucer and the French Poet Graunson*, 8–9. Wimsatt, *Chaucer and his French Contemporaries*, 239–40, quotes and translates the poem in full.

[33] See P. Rickard, *Britain in Medieval French Literature 1100–1500* (Cambridge, 1956), 165–6, 170–7.

[34] Deschamps seems to be playing on the traditional notion of blue as the colour of loyalty (Cf. Machaut's ballade 'Qui de couleurs saroit à droit jugier' which has

'Goday', fait l'un, l'autre 'commidre'.
Lors dis: 'Oil, je voy vo queue.'

The situation is depicted as turning nasty when Graunson, supposedly Deschamps's compatriot, speaks betrayal in the very language of the enemy. Yet unlike the speech of the English, which Deschamps renders in a kind of exaggeratedly French accent ('dogue...commidre'), Graunson's English is actually rendered as French: 'En anglois dist: Pas ne l'adveue'. Deschamps keeps up the sense of linguistic and cultural ambiguity through the timing of the refrain, which sounds increasingly as if it is being aimed at Graunson rather than the English:

'Chien,' faisoit l'un, 'vez vous vo guide?'
Lors dis: 'Oil, je voy vo queue.'

The joke here seems to be an allusion to the fact that Deschamps is riding behind Graunson, as he tells us in the first stanza: Graunson has turned tail on Deschamps in more ways than one. This is Anglo-French writing with a vengeance.

Although so far I have been stressing the points of contact and assimilation between English and French, it is also necessary to consider some of their differences. Try as hard as one might to appreciate the level of artistic patronage in the English households, a comparison with the courts of Brabant, Flanders, or Burgundy in this period reveals a quite marked disparity.[35] Philippa and Edward, Gaunt and Richard certainly employed poets and musicians in similar ways to Continental princes, and indeed often the same individuals, but the scale of their artistic transactions was much less extravagant. For example, at the court of Jeanne and Wenceslas of Brabant (to which Froissart immediately proceeded

the refrain 'Que fin azur loyauté signefie', ed. Chichmaref, no. CCLXXII, p. 235, and 'Se pour ce muir, qu'Amours ay bien servi' with the refrain: 'Qu'en lieu de bleu, dame, vous restez vert', ed. Chichmaref, no. CCXLVIII, p. 218).

[35] A. Pinchart, 'La Cour de Jeanne et de Wenceslas et les arts en Brabant', *Revue trimestrielle*, 6 (1855), 5–31, and 13 (1857), 25–67; Georges Doutrepont, *La Littéraire française à la cour des ducs de Bourgogne* (Paris 1909); André Pirro, *La Musique sous le règne de Charles VI (1380–1422)*, Sammlung musikwissenschaftlicher Abhandlungen 1 (Strasbourg, 1930); Mary D. Stanger, 'Literary Patronage at the Medieval Court of Flanders', *French Studies*, 11 (1957), 214–29. For further references, see Nigel Wilkins, 'A Pattern of Patronage: Machaut, Froissart and the Houses of Luxembourg and Bohemia in the Fourteenth Century', *French Studies*, 37 (1983), 257–84.

after Philippa's death) the number of payments recorded to musicians and poets reaches very high levels. Their court sponsored a huge number of entertainments of all kinds, hunts, feasts, *jeux*, spectacles, narrative and song recitals, as well as tournaments: Pinchart's first estimate (which he later revises upward) is of fifty-five tournaments alone between 1360 and 1389.[36] All these occasions attracted performers of both music and poetry from all over Europe, from the kings and dukes of England, France, Hungary, Prussia, Denmark, Bohemia, and Navarre to name but a few. Individuals from the English royal household, or from the Lancastrian household, are named, and others, such as the gittern player André Destrer from Bruges, are described as being in Philippa's service.

Yet perhaps the most significant impression of contrast lies not so much in sheer numbers as in the way that Continental patrons clearly gave specific and personal encouragement to the activity of poets, and in this were continuing a tradition of sponsorship which can be traced back to the twelfth century.[37] The title poet (*dictori* or, in Flemish, *spreker*) is widely applied, often with a certain kind of possessiveness, such as the way in which the town of Ghent is described as having its own poet in 1394 ('der stat spreker van Gent ghegheven'). Trouvères often wore the arms (*l'écusson*) of their master over their clothing.[38] The employment of Jehan de la Mote, Jehan le Bel, Froissart, and of the clerks in the English household chapels has much in common with these kinds of arrangements; the position of Chaucer very little. It seems as if English aristocracy, particularly if they were French by birth, cultivated the work of French artists in England in the same way as (though to a lesser extent than) their Continental counterparts

---

[36] Pinchart, 'La Cour de Jeanne et de Wenceslas', 14.

[37] The court of Flanders under Philippe d'Alsace (1170–91) and his successors actively promoted literary production: poets attached to the court during the 12th and 13th cents. included Conon de Béthune, the Châtelain de Couci, Gautier d'Arras, Jean Renart, and Adenet le Roi (Stanger, 'Literary Patronage').

[38] This does not seem to have been the case in England, even with minstrels: although minstrels were regularly given livery, there is nothing to suggest that they wore 'any kind of distinctive dress', apart, perhaps, from certain differences according to status: C. Bullock-Davies, *Menestrellorum Multitudo: Minstrels at a Royal Feast* (Cardiff, 1978), 17–18, and *A Register of Royal and Baronial Domestic Minstrels 1272–1327* (Woodbridge, 1976), 72–3.

did, but that there was no comparable indigenous tradition for poets in the English vernacular.[39]

II

We have considered some aspects of the high level of political and social exchange between England and France in the fourteenth century: do these conditions create specific instances of poetic exchange? Through the single, but richly implicated, example of the refrain 'Qui bien aimme, a tart oublie' I want to explore the ways in which cultural exchange took place through the passage of one short phrase from work to work, from poet to poet, and from one side of the Channel to the other. In order to do justice to the breadth of reference behind this phrase, we need to take account of the context for cross-cultural lyric composition in this period, and for the role of refrains both within and alongside such composition.[40]

Public poetic exchange was indeed a prominent feature of late medieval literary and musical composition. It was most widely conducted through the medium of the ballade. In a French context, the tradition of exchanging ballades developed from earlier *puy* practices involving the competitive production of *jeux-partis*. In the case of ballade exchanges two or more poets would create a sequence of ripostes and counter-ripostes, often, though not invariably, by using either the same refrain or the same poetic form as that chosen by the poet who originated the exchange. The *raison*

---

[39] Salter's nuanced yet finely emphatic account of comparable French dominance in the production, purchasing, and collecting of manuscripts among the English and French nobility in the 14th and 15th cents. has been widely followed; see Salter, 'Conditions and Status' in *English and International*; Green, *Poets and Princepleasers*; Scattergood and Sherborne (eds.), *English Court Culture*; C. A. J. Armstrong, 'L'Échange culturel entre les cours d'Angleterre et de Bourgogne à l'époque de Charles le Téméraire', in C. A. J. Armstrong (ed.), *England, France and Burgundy in the Fifteenth Century* (London, 1983), 403–17; Carole M. Meale, 'Patrons, Buyers and Owners: Book Production and Social Status' in Jeremy Griffiths and Derek Pearsall (eds.), *Book Production and Publishing in Britain 1375–1475* (Cambridge, 1989), 201–38.

[40] See also Nigel Wilkins, '"En regardant vers le païs de France": The Ballade and the Rondeau, a Cross-Channel History', in W. M. Ormrod (ed.), *England in the Fourteenth Century: Proceedings of the 1985 Harlaxton Symposium* (Woodbridge, 1986), 298–323.

d'être for these formal dialogues is thus partly a matter of display-ing technical skill by competitively matching or surpassing exter-nally imposed formal constraints. It also becomes a way of articulating other kinds of cultural competitiveness.

One example, perhaps from the middle of the century, is a set of six ballades passed between Jehan de la Mote and Philippe de Vitry.[41] Ostensibly exchanged between two compatriots, they include a stringent attack on de la Mote by de Vitry (using the old pun *amour/amer*) for his act of cultural betrayal in crossing the sea to that cursed country England:

> Là ou tu n'as d'amour fors l'amer,
> En Albion de Dieu maldicte.

This sort of topical, and highly public cross-channel exchange forms part of a larger tradition of exchange in lyric composition. The group exchanged between Machaut and Thomas de Paien in Machaut's *Le Voir Dit* illustrates the larger kind: this is the only moment in the work where another poet's work is introduced, apart from the lyrics attributed to the young Toute-Belle with whom the narrator presents himself as having an affair.[42] Other examples in narrative of formal exchanges such as these concern poetic contests: for example, the exchange of lais in the prose *Tristan* between Tristan and a female musician, and Christine de Pizan's *Dit de la pastoure*.[43]

The role of the *formes fixes* as a means by which French poets staked their claim to poetic proficiency can be particularized even further by recognizing the dominance of the refrain within these structures. The reasons for this derive from wide-ranging thir-teenth-century experimentation with forms originally associated with dance-song: by the early fourteenth century, these forms gained a new fixity in the shape of the rondeau, the ballade, and what Machaut insisted on calling the *chanson balladée* (later termed the *virelai*). The fixed element consists in the function of the refrain within each form. As the core of the lyric, the refrain encapsulates its argument or theme: much of the wit and skill of

[41] Wilkins, '"En regardant vers le païs"', 299–300.

[42] Guillaume de Machaut, *Le Voir Dit*, ed. Paulin Paris (Paris, 1875; repr. Geneva, 1969).

[43] Sidney's *Arcadia* is evidence both of the longevity of this topos and of its wholesale translation into English.

lyric poets in this period was applied to the relation between refrain and strophe.

The ballade exchanges are an extension of this principle, in that often the specific connecting element across the exchange is the refrain.[44] Machaut's collection of ballades known as *La Louange des dames* illustrates another procedure, whereby strophic lines from the ballade 'Selonc ce que j'aim chierement' are used as individual refrains for the next four ballades in the sequence.[45] Here, the refrain takes on the particular function with which it was associated throughout the thirteenth century, that is, a kind of sententious tag, formally and generically mobile, often with its own melody, and widely cited across all kinds of writing. Machaut cites one such independent refrain in his *Remede de Fortune*, a narrative *dit* which contains a single example—with music—of all the principal lyric types: *lai, complainte, chanson royale, baladelle, ballade, chanson balladée,* and *rondeau.* He does not include any music with the refrain (which is similarly absent from a twelve-stanza *priere* also set into the narrative) and so its presence has been hardly remarked.[46] Nonetheless it bears all the characteristics of the thirteenth-century type. It occurs straight after the virelai which Machaut has been asked to sing during his turn in a *carole*:

> Après ma chanson commansa
> Une dame qui la dansa,
> Qui moult me sambloit envoisie,
> Car elle estoit cointe et jolie.
> Si prist a chanter sans demeure:
> '*Dieus, quant venra li temps et l'eure*
> *Que je voie ce que j'aim si?*';
> Et sa chanson fina einsi. (3497–3504)

It is important to realize that this kind of citation is widespread among thirteenth-century romances, and rarely—if ever—implies

---

[44] See N. Wilkins, 'The Late Medieval French Lyric: With Music and Without', in Ursula Günther and Ludwig Finscher (eds.), *Musik und Text in der Mehrstimmigkeit der 14. und 15. Jahrhunderts* (Basle, 1984), 155–74 (pp. 169–70).

[45] On the history and context of such a technique, see Ardis Butterfield, 'The Refrain and the Transformation of Genre in the *Roman de Fauvel*', in Margaret Bent and Andrew Wathey (eds.), Fauvel Studies: *Allegory, Chronicle, Music and Image in Paris BN f. fr. 146* (Oxford, forthcoming).

[46] Hoepffner mentions the refrain in passing, along with the *priere*; I have not come across any other reference to it.

that a *specific* strophic song is being referred to of which the refrain is just a part. Refrains gain an autonomous role through being cited repeatedly across genres: a single refrain can occur in as many as eight separate contexts, including motets, narrative *dits*, *romans*, and different genres of chanson.[47] Nearly 2,000 have so far been identified from the thirteenth and early fourteenth centuries.[48]

The significance of refrain citation in the fourteenth century, taken over from the thirteenth, concerns this double role of a refrain, as the key formal element in a *forme fixe*, and also as a mobile piece of *sententia* on the topic of love, distinguished from a proverb by possessing a latent formal function, that is often, though not always, expressed in melodic as well as verbal terms. We misunderstand much French lyric and narrative composition if we fail to grasp how widely poets (and musicians) used refrains as a way of anchoring, structuring, and dividing their works. Machaut himself took compositional advantage of refrains across all areas of his poetic and musical repertory. However, it is only in the *Voir Dit*, his last major composition, that Machaut weaves refrains into a narrative with any consistent purpose. He does so in three major ways: by quoting common refrains as if they were proverbs; by re-quoting refrains from his inset lyrics within the narrative or the letters; and finally, by linking together pairs of lyrics with the same refrain, a practice fairly common in his *Louange des dames*.[49]

Towards the end of the *Remede de Fortune* (the last line of the *dit* before the brief epilogue), Machaut quotes in passing one of the most current refrains of the period: 'Qui bien aimme, a tart oublie' (4256). 'Qui bien aimme' seems to be a particular favourite of Machaut's: not only is it the first line of his *Lai de plour*, it occurs repeatedly in the *Voir Dit*, in two separate letters and in a narrative section late on in the work where Machaut is being warned of Toute-Belle's unfaithfulness.[50] Deschamps also uses it as the refrain

[47] See Ardis Butterfield, 'Repetition and Variation in the Thirteenth-Century Refrain', *Journal of the Royal Musical Association*, 116/1 (1991), 1–23.

[48] The standard bibliography is by Nico H. J. van den Boogaard, *Rondeaux et refrains du XIIe siècle au début du XIVe* (Paris, 1969), who gives texts only.

[49] J. Cerquiglini, *'Un engin si soutil' : Guillaume de Machaut et l'écriture au XIVe siècle* (Geneva, 1985), 34–9.

[50] Ed. Paris, Letter X, p. 67; Letter XXX, p. 238; l. 7357.

of a ballade.[51] If we trace some of the many thirteenth-century citations of this refrain, we find that it doubles (in characteristic fashion) as a proverb and as a structurally important melodic and verbal unit in a variety of songs.[52] Thus as well as occurring in a *chanson avec des refrains* (R1740); as the first line of a *chanson à refrains* by Moniot de Paris (R1188); and in two motets (M814 and M890); it also appears as a proverb in two further chansons (R518 and R36[53]) and in a collection of proverbs in Hereford MS P.3.3, fo. 164b.[54] This proverbial role is further emphasized in romance: it is scribbled onto the final flyleaf of one of the manuscripts of the *Roman de la poire*, Paris, Bibliothèque Nationale, MS fr. 2186.

From so broad a base in thirteenth- and fourteenth-century French writing and singing, 'Qui bien aimme' passes into English currency.[55] It does so in a thoroughly Anglo-French context, by being the refrain of one of Gower's ballades ('Ma dame, si ceo fust a vo plesir', *Cinquante Balades*, no. 25). Most notoriously, it occurs in place of the roundel in several manuscripts of Chaucer's *Parliament of Fowls*. Highlighted in red, it comes in Oxford, Bodleian Library, MSS Bodley 638 and Fairfax 16, Cambridge, Trinity College, MS R.3.19, and Thynne's edition after the 97th stanza introducing the final roundel. The place of 'Qui bien

---

[51] Ballade no. 1345 in *Œuvres complètes*, ed. le marquis de Queux de Saint-Hilaire and G. Raynaud, SATF, 11 vols. (Paris, 1878–1903), vii. 124–5. See the note to *The Parliament of Fowls*, 677, in *The Riverside Chaucer*, 1002.

[52] See van den Boogaard (ed.), *Rondeaux et refrains*, refr. 1585; and J. Morawski (ed.), *Proverbes français antérieurs au XVe siècle*, CFMA (Paris, 1925), no. 1835.

[53] See van den Boogaard (ed.), *Rondeaux et refrains*, 233 n.

[54] R, with a song number, refers to G. *Raynauds Bibliographie des altfranzösischen Liedes*, ed. Hans Spanke (Leiden, 1955); M refers to the numbered motets in Friedrich Gennrich, *Bibliographie der ältesten französischen und lateinischen Motetten*, Summa Musicae Medii Aevi 2 (Darmstadt, 1958). Van den Boogaard's references do not include the Hereford MS. Julia Boffey notes a further citation in an English manuscript, London, British Library, MS Harley 3362, fo. 17ᵛ, 'The Manuscripts of English Courtly Love Lyrics in the Fifteenth Century', in D. Pearsall (ed.), *Manuscripts and Readers in Fifteenth-Century England: The Literary Implications of Manuscript Study* (Cambridge, 1983), 3–14 (p. 13). There are many more.

[55] Machaut's *Lay de plour* is known to have circulated in England in the 15th cent., in Westminster Abbey MS 21. See J. Boffey, 'English Dream Poems of the Fifteenth Century and their French Connections', in Donald Maddox and Sara Sturm-Madox (eds.), *Literary Aspects of Courtly Culture* (Cambridge, 1994), 113–21 (pp. 118–19). Refrains are written onto the scrolls held by the figures in the opening miniatures introducing a copy of *Le Roman de la Rose* (London, British Library, MS Royal 19 B.xiii) owned by Sir Richard Sturry.

aimme' in the textual history of the poem has provoked much puzzlement.[56] Skeat alone among modern editors cites it directly in the text: all other editors banish 'Qui bien aimme' to the textual notes and print instead an expanded version of the eight-line song copied into Gg. Yet, as Ralph Hanna III has argued, there is no evidence that this English song pre-dates the 1440s, and hence no reason for assuming it to be Chaucerian.[57] Where, then, does this leave 'Qui bien aimme'? Since Chaucer writes, 'The note, I trowe, imaked was in Fraunce', the French refrain has often been taken rather loosely to indicate the tune of the roundel. But as Skeat, Robinson, and Brewer realized, a poem in decasyllabic lines could not easily be sung to a tune which fitted an octosyllabic line. Moreover, if we concede, as I think we should, that the surviving roundel is a later scribal addition to the *Parliament*, then there are no grounds in any case for assuming that the refrain and the roundel have any direct connection.[58]

Hanna points acutely to the 'longing' among modern editors 'for a single Chaucerian text'.[59] Perhaps one can detect a hint of nationalism here, too, in the desire to privilege a much later English addition over an earlier French citation. However, once the broader pattern of citation of 'Qui bien aimme' is appreciated, its citation at the end of the *Parliament of Fowls* is no more (and no less) puzzling than it is at the end of the *Roman de la poire*. In both cases, the reference is to a phrase which both has a simple proverbial function, and yet may also act as a melodic part of a larger whole. In this case, the presence of the refrain alerts us to the larger cultural context of the poem: whether it was Chaucer himself, or a scribe, the phrase 'Qui bien aimme, a tart oublie' was (unsurprisingly) perceived to be an appropriate comment on a

[56] Derek Brewer is the most frank in his admission of perplexity: 'These words can hardly indicate the tune since they form an octosyllabic line. Nor have they any apparent relevance to the text. I do not understand their function.' *Geoffrey Chaucer: The Parlement of Foulys* (Manchester, 1972), 127 n. 677.

[57] Ralph Hanna III, 'Presenting Chaucer as Author', in T. W. Machan (ed.), *Medieval Literature: Texts and Interpretation* (Binghamton, NY, 1991), 17–39. Hanna dates the addition in Gg to 'no earlier than circa 1460–1470 and likely later still' (p. 30); the earliest version of the roundel is in Oxford, St John's College, MS 57 ('near mid-century').

[58] Thynne, uniquely among the early witnesses, includes both the refrain and the roundel, presumably by conflating his sources.

[59] Hanna, 'Presenting Chaucer as Author', 21.

narrative of love, loyalty, and delay. Restoring the line to the poem does not necessarily give us access to 'the Chaucerian text' (although it is not impossible—given the long history of the refrain—for it to have been Chaucer's own citation). Instead it recreates a notion of the *Parliament* as a work composed within a thoroughly Anglo-French textual environment. Whoever wrote it in was participating in a long and highly developed French practice of using refrains as a form of sententious or gnomic conclusion to a statement, argument, or narrative about love.

Several fifteenth-century English works, collected by Skeat, contain French refrains and mottoes: such as 'To my soverain Lady', 'The Flower and the Leaf', 'The Assembly of Ladies', and 'A Goodly Balade'.[60] I would like to refer briefly to one further piece which contains yet another citation of 'Qui bien aimme', *A Parliament of Birds*. Evidently a fifteenth-century response to Chaucer's *Parliament of Fowls*, it is copied into Cambridge, University Library, MS Gg.4.27 in a sequence with Chaucer's *ABC*, his *Envoy to Scogan*, and two macaronic lyrics.[61] In structure it resembles an extended *chanson avec des refrains*, in that it has a different refrain at the end of each of its fifteen strophes ('Qui bien ayme' is cited after the fourth). It is interesting how much more French in style this piece is than its 'parent' narrative. Where Chaucer alludes to a possible French connection with airy (and tantalizing) vagueness ('The note, I trowe, imaked was in Fraunce'), this author incorporates French elements directly, not only by extensive quotation of French refrains but also by choosing an octosyllabic rather than decasyllabic line. The form he chooses has specific French antecedents in the strophic *saluts* and the longer narrative song *La Chastelaine de Saint-Gille*.[62]

[60] See *The Complete Works of Geoffrey Chaucer*, ed. W.W. Skeat (Oxford, 1897), vii: *Supplement: Chaucerian and Other Pieces*, 281–4, 361–79, 380–404, and 405–7, respectively. 'The Flower and the Leaf' and 'The Assembly of Ladies' have also been edited by D. A. Pearsall (1st edn. 1962; repr. Manchester, 1980).

[61] The contexts of these lyrics are discussed by Boffey, 'Manuscripts of English Courtly Love Lyrics', 12–14.

[62] For a selection of texts and discussion, see Paul Meyer, 'Le Salut d'amour dans les littératures provençale et française, Mémoire suivi de huit saluts inédits', *Bibliothèque de l'École des Chartes*, 28 (1867), 124–70, and P. Bec, 'Pour un essai de définition du salut d'amour', *Estudis romànics*, 9 (1961), 191–201. *La Chastelaine de Saint Gille* is edited by O. Schultz-Gora, *Zwei altfranzösische Dichtungen* (Halle, 1916), 37–66.

A Parliament of Birds stands in a curiously shifting cultural relation with English and French precedents. This is no doubt partly stimulated by the macaronic ending (in some manuscripts) of Chaucer's *Parliament*, which it seems the anonymous poet probably saw: Chaucer's poem (so far as we can determine from its manuscript state) thus provides not a simple English model, but itself a combined English and French one.[63] A sense of the complexity of this model is suggested by two Anglo-French moments when two of the birds (the cuckoo and the starling) rebel against the formal necessity of uttering a French refrain, and instead utter one in English. Both birds comment bitterly on their inability to speak French ('I can no french soþ for to seyne' (cuckoo) ... 'I can no skille of swich french fare | To speke in engelych I haue more deynte' (starling). The stanza in each case thus ends with an English line:

> I seye as good loue comyth as goþ (stanza 10)
> I loue hem alle alyche wel (stanza 14)[64]

Once more, the meeting-point between English and French is a locus for subtly conflicting signals. On the one hand, despite his Francophile leanings, the poet allows into his poem a comic protest against the supremacy of French in the language of love; yet he chooses birds traditionally associated with socially inferior behaviour to make the protest, and repeatedly reinforces the sense of their social undesirability. The cuckoo is described as 'þe vncurteys coukkow most vn kynde', who cannot speak *any* language without swearing (let alone French). The popinjay's piously indignant reaction speaks for the majority:

> Þe popyniay gan to pikyn mod
> And seyde coukkow lat be lat be
> I trowe þu maddyst or þu art wod
> ffor schame to speke swich dyuerste.

For three more stanzas, French order is reinstated, but the starling brings back a note of dissension. More emphatically than the cuckoo, the starling sneers at the French songs:

---

[63] The character of the 15th-cent. poem implies that its author saw Chaucer's *Parliament* in manuscript with its French refrain, even though, in the case of Gg itself, the refrain is not present. This further implies, perhaps, that the two poems were collected independently, rather than that *A Parliament of Birds* was composed specially for Gg.

[64] E. P. Hammond, 'A Parliament of Birds', *JEGP* 7 (1907–8), 105–9.

> Þe starlyng gan to sterte & stare
> And seyde þese songis ben so queynte.

Where the cuckoo found the sentiments of the songs too noble, the starling finds them too singular: his English rather than French type of refined longing for love leads him to write and paint about all women, not just one.

Again, this view is rebuffed, this time by the 'throstilcok', and the poem ends with a final French refrain that literally has the last word in the debate, sealed with 'Amen':

> En dieu maffie sanz departer   Amen

The nicely ambiguous legacy of the piece, however, is that as a whole it stands out against French precedents by its self-conscious Anglicizing: a debate about love becomes a debate about languages and cultures. In particular, the 'dyuerste' of the poem is encouraged by the poet's allowing two English refrains to usurp the most formally significant, one might say, linguistically powerful, position in the poem's structure.

Through a variety of examples, we have seen that the process of exchanging refrains took place both within and across languages: from being a means of articulating points of connection, contrast, and rivalry between poets writing in the same language, it also develops into a deeply cross-cultural exercise operating at the level of small, local units of language, proverbs, sententia, refrains. 'Qui bien aimme' is revealing of the extent to which relationships between English and French poets extended well beyond the practice of formal allusion. Instead, we can see that the two linguistic cultures shared the same clichés, a sure sign that they shared—and debated—a profoundly common currency.

III

The poetry of John Gower is supremely poised between linguistic cultures. More than this, it was clearly important to him to present himself in this way: his trilinguality is inseparable from his identity as a writer. The unique surviving manuscript of his *Cinquante Balades* (the Trentham MS, Dunrobin Castle), presented as a gift to Henry Bolingbroke towards the end of Gower's poetic career, is a careful compilation of poetry in French, Latin, and English. The purposefulness of the trilingual compliment is indicated by the first three pieces: an English poem, 'O worthi noble kyng', addressed to Henry, a Latin piece, 'Rex celi deus', revised from lines originally addressed to Richard II in Gower's *Vox clamantis*, and two French ballades, also addressed to Henry, that are interspersed with Latin verses reworked from two earlier poems in which Gower had defended the legitimacy of Henry's coronation.

The role of English in the compliment is notably slight, especially as the rest of the manuscript is made up entirely of French and a little more Latin: the *Cinquante Balades*, the *Traitié*, and two short Latin pieces. The impression given by the whole compilation is that the notion of what was pleasing to an English king at the end of the fourteenth century was still best expressed in French and Latin. The manuscript could hardly be more courtly—in the sense of being directed explicitly to the king—yet as a courtly gesture it is hard to define it as English without much qualification. Writing in English, on the showing of this manuscript, is but a small part of this English poet's courtly profile.

Given the subsequent narrowing of our linguistic history, Gower's work in English—the *Confessio Amantis*—has naturally dominated our perception of him. His writing in French and Latin has not only been largely ignored, it has also suffered from misleading comparisons with his writing in English. Perhaps the most important misconception is that his French lyrics have nothing to do with Continental French writing.[65] Yet, as I shall go on to demonstrate, and as William Calin has rightly remarked, they were 'composed in the most contemporary, Parisian court style'.[66] For this very reason, Gower's work exemplifies the cultural integration of French and English at its most profound, and yet with the curious and complex tensions in that relationship evident across his writing as a whole.

In the last part of this essay, I want to consider two aspects of Gower's 'Englishness' as a poet. Both are somewhat oblique, at least looked at from the conventional sense of 'English'. The first

[65] Fisher, *John Gower*, 74–8, repeated incautiously by Wimsatt, *Chaucer and his French Contemporaries*, 337 n. 49.

[66] W. Calin, *The French Tradition and the Literature of Medieval England* (Toronto, 1994), 371–98 (p. 380).

involves looking at some of the French lyrics in his *Cinquante Balades*: how insular are they? how Continental? in what sense are we to understand them as representing an English voice? Second, and following on from this discussion, I want to turn to the group of ballades set at the end of the *Confessio Amantis*. Their position has been remarked, but their character hardly discussed. My interest here lies in trying to decide what kind of an ending they provide for the *Confessio*; how far the *Confessio* compilation might be said to include them within its framework; and what might be implied by the shift at the last from English back into French and Latin.

Fisher's assertion that 'Chaucer... reveals a profound influence from the French court poets, whereas Gower shows little, if any, knowledge of them' is hard to understand, at least on the part of Gower.[67] In many ways, indeed, Gower's lyrics have a natural place as court collections, entirely comparable to the collections composed by Machaut and Froissart such as Machaut's *Louange des dames*, which Chaucer's sparse and more sporadic lyric survivals appear to lack. But it is not only their context which makes them comparable to contemporary French lyrics: their idiom, tightly constrained vocabulary, and argumentative structure are closely linked.

The following pair of ballades will indicate this. I begin with Gower's 'El mois de mai la plus joiouse chose | C'est fin amour':

> El mois de mai la plus joiouse chose
> C'est fin amour, mais vous, ma Dame chiere,
> Prenez à vous plutost la rouge rose
> Pour vo desport, et plus la faites chiere
> Que mon amour, o toute la priere
> Que vous ai fait maint jour y a passé:
> Vous estes franche et je sui fort lié.
>
> Je voi tout plein de flours dans vo parclose
> Privé de vous, mais je sui mis deriere:
> Ne puis entrer, que l'entree m'est forclose;
> Je prens tesmoign de vostre chamberiere,
> Qui set et voit trestoute la matiere
> De si long temps que je vous ai amé.
> Vous estes franche et je sui fort lié.

---

[67] Fisher, *John Gower*, 74.

Quant l'herbe croist et la flour se desclose,
Mai m'a osté de sa blanche baniere,
Dont pense assez plus que je dire n'ose
De vous, ma Dame, qui m'estes si fiere;
A vo merci car se je me refiere,
Vostre danger tantost m'a delaié:
Vous estes franche et je sui fort lié.

En le dous temps ma fortune est amere;
Le mois de mai s'est en hiver mué;
L'ortie truis quant je la rose quiere.
Vous estes franche et je sui fort lié.[68]

(Of all the joys of the month of May, true love is best, but you, my lady
dear, take to yourself rather the red rose for your pleasure, and hold it
dearer than my love and all the prayers that I have made you now for
many a day. You go free while I am tightly bound.

Plenty of flowers I see within your garden cherished by you while I am
thrust aside. I cannot enter there, for the gate is shut tight against me. I call
your maid to witness, who has known and seen the whole story as long as
I have loved you. You go free while I am tightly bound.

When the grass grows and the flower opens, May has rejected me from
among the followers of her white banner, and therefore I think, much
more than I dare say, of you, my lady, who are so cruel to me; for if I cast
myself once more upon your mercy, your disdain thrusts me back immediately. You go free while I am tightly bound.

In the sweet season my fate is bitter; the month of May is turned into winter;
I find the nettle when I seek the rose. You go free while I am tightly bound.)

The poem has a thoroughly conventional and highly restricted
metaphoric range: the month of May, the red rose, the enclosed
garden, grass and flowers, fortune. Two pronouns dominate: I and
you. This is cast within three rhyme-royal stanzas with a four-line
envoy. The use of an envoy, borrowed from the *chanson royale*, is
a favoured device of Gower's: in this he is entirely in line with the
late fourteenth- and early fifteenth-century French practice of
Deschamps, Christine de Pizan, Alain Chartier, and Charles d'Orléans.[69] The experience of reading through this enigmatic poem

---

[68] *The Complete Works of John Gower: The French Works*, ed. G. C. Macaulay
(Oxford, 1899), no. XXXVII, p. 367. The translation is in *The Penguin Book of French
Verse, I. To the Fifteenth Century*, ed. Brian Woledge (Harmondsworth, 1966), 230–1.

[69] This is perhaps the source of Fisher's confusion, since the envoy was of course
originally a feature of troubadour and trouvère chansons, and the *chanson royale*

confirms a sense of Gower as so deeply familiar with the medium and idiom of French lyric writing that he, like his contemporaries, is able to create disturbing systems of exchange with the apparently fixed coinage of love.

As ever, the refrain provides the key to the poem's structure of meaning. Here, it has a central metaphorical function: 'Vous estes franche et je sui fort lié' ('You are free and I am tightly bound'). This becomes clear, I think, because of the very abruptness with which it is announced at the end of each stanza as a self-enclosed statement. To take the first stanza: the speaker begins with the classic seasonal reference—May is always the month for love—but then complains that in this case there is a difference. Instead of love, his lady prefers the red rose. This is already a heavily allusive kind of language, but although the clichés are familiar, they still manage to be puzzling: is not the red rose normally a sign for love? What then does it mean to say that she amuses herself with the red rose rather than with love, and then to assert, plaintively, that she is free but he is tightly bound? One answer seems to be that she is taking the clichéd sign for the 'real' love: in other words, perversely she takes up the cliché—the rose—and refuses to translate it back into love. This, he comments ruefully, is the evidence of her freedom, and his constraint: she can play fast and loose with metaphors, he is tied to real emotion.

The second stanza brings out these concepts of constraint more explicitly, though not much less confusingly: here he talks of the barrier of the garden gate, how it is shut tightly against him, even though he can see many flowers inside with which she is intimate. What now does the flower cliché represent? In the first stanza she accepted a flower instead of his love: here he seems determined to align himself with the flowers after all, but this ruse to claim the cliché fails like the first attempt to defy it.

By the third stanza, the poet clearly feels that his relations with the whole linguistic apparatus of love are decidedly unhappy: not only does his lady reject him, so does the season of May herself. He lingers on the contrast between the liberating springtime growth of grass and newly opening flowers and his own cramped state, both as a lover and as a user of metaphor. The constant *a*

---

was the form demanded by *puys*. But in fact it was as a feature of late 14th- and 15th-century ballade composition that the envoy was resurrected.

rhymes on 'ose' mockingly underline this by harping cruelly on closure, as 'rose' is matched with 'parclose', 'forclose', and 'declose'. We hardly need reminding of the refrain, but it comes back relentlessly all the same: 'You are free and I am tightly bound.' The envoy, however, manages some kind of revenge. At first it seems he has simply succumbed. In his condition, metaphor goes out of control: for him, the sweet season is bitter, springtime is changed into winter, roses into nettles. But the constant ambiguity about the symbolic status of this rose which has dogged the entire poem now provides him with a tiny means of retaliation: no longer the rose himself, he turns the cliché back on her, only now she is no longer a rose, but a nettle. As the refrain repeats for the final time, he seems to be saying, I may be trapped by my metaphors, but try *this* for freedom, darling.

If we compare this ballade with one by Machaut—the well-known 'De toutes fleurs'—we can see how far Gower is working within the same frame of linguistic reference:

> De toutes fleurs n'avoit, et de tous fruis,
> En mon vergier fors une seule rose:
> Gasté estoit li surplus et destruis
> Par Fortune, qui durement s'opose
>   Contre ceste douce flour
> Pour amatir sa coulour et s'odour.
> Mais se cueillir la voi ou tresbuchier,
> Autre aprés li ja mais avoir de quier.
>
> Mais vraiement ymaginer ne puis
> Que la vertus, où ma rose est enclose,
> Viengne par toy et par tes faus conduis,
> Ains est drois dons naturex; si suppose
>   Que tu n'avras ja vigour
> D'amanrir son pris et sa valour.
> Lay la moy donc, qu'ailleurs n'en mon vergier
> Autre aprés li ja mais avoir de quier.
>
> Hé! Fortune, qui es gouffres et puis
> Pour engloutir tout homme qui croire ose
> Ta fausse loy, où rien de bien ne truis
> Ne de seür, trop est decevans chose;
>   Ton ris, ta joie, t'onneur
> Ne sont que plour, tristece et deshonnour.
> Se ti faus tour font ma rose sechier,
> Autre aprés li ja mais avoir de quier.

(Of all the flowers and all the fruits, there is but a single rose left in my garden: the rest has all been laid waste and destroyed by Fortune, who is now setting herself fiercely against this sweet flower, so as to spoil its colour and its scent. But if I see it plucked or broken down, after that rose I never want another.

But truly, I cannot imagine that the virtue that enwraps my rose comes from you or from your lying ways; rather it is a direct gift of Nature, and I think you will never have the strength to lessen its value and its worth. Leave it to me, then, for whether in my garden or elsewhere, after that rose I never want another.

Ah! Fortune, you who are a gulf and a pit to swallow up any man who dares to trust in your false doctrine, in which I find nothing good or certain, it is so fraudulent a thing; your smile, your joy, your honour are only tears and sadness and dishonour. If your false tricks make my rose wither, after that rose I never want another.)[70]

As in the Gower ballade we have the same tightly circumscribed metaphoric range: the rose, the garden, flowers and fruits, Fortune. As in Gower, too, the word 'rose' gathers to it rhyme words on closure: 'enclose', 's'oppose'. It would be tempting, but I think misleading, to imagine that Gower is even drawing directly on this poem: the point is rather that both poets are self-consciously working within very narrow limits of meaning, metaphor, and rhyme. Once more, we need to look to the refrain to find the argumentative nexus of the lyric. In this case, it is not a self-enclosed phrase, and indeed each stanza introduces the refrain differently: 'But if I see it plucked or broken down, after that rose I never want another.... Leave it to me, then, for whether in my garden or elsewhere, after that rose I never want another.... If your false tricks make my rose wither, after that rose I never want another.' However, despite these variations, each stanza presents the same essential message: that there is a single rose left which is under threat, but that it is the only rose he wants.

Once again, as in Gower's ballade, it is the speaker's relation to the rose which constitutes the main source of uncertainty in the poem as a whole. Two standard motifs—the rose and Fortune—are opposed in an odd and disturbing way. The extreme narrowness of the poem's metaphoric register and yet the extraordinary

---

[70] *One Hundred Ballades, Rondeaux and Virelais from the Late Middle Ages*, ed. Nigel Wilkins (Cambridge, 1969), no. 11, pp. 21–2; tr. in *French Verse*, ed. Woledge, 220–1, modified in places to accord with Wilkins's text.

density of its allusiveness—partly created also by the distribution of pronouns—is so unclear that one editor even reverses the order of the second and third stanzas.[71]

At first it seems as if the speaker is painting the rose's predicament with straightforward pathos: she is struggling for survival against a cruel enemy. When we think a little harder, however, we realize that this is an inversion of the usual lover's claim that he is the one battling against overwhelming odds. Moreover, when we contemplate the fact that the enemy turns out to be Fortune, the battle-lines now begin to seem less clearly drawn. This emerges most plainly in the third stanza where Fortune is directly addressed and described. Through the presence of this second metaphor—Fortune—which happens to be personified as a female in the same way as the rose/lady, the speaker plays a blind trick. He may seem to be addressing Fortune, but implicitly, especially when he talks of her false smiles, joy, and honour, it is hard to believe that he is not continuing to address his lady ('viengne par toy et par tes faus conduis...tu n'avras ja vigour d'amanrir son pris et sa valour ...ma rose...mon vergier'). I would describe this as the use of symbolic cliché to insinuate meaning below the surface of another cliché; in other words, since the two signs—the rose and Fortune—are both female, they can be cunningly confused, leaving the poet able to imply fickleness to his lady while in the process of declaring her single perfection. This demonstrates the potential of clichés to deliver up the kinds of meaning that cannot normally be expressed, or at least not directly: a freedom which results from their very fixity as tokens of meaning.

It would be difficult to argue from this comparison that Gower is working outside French assumptions about the language of love. He handles the stock metaphors with the ease and subtlety of a native speaker. An important point of connection between the two poets, French and English, is that both insinuate certain kinds of detachment from the terms of their subject-matter born out of the very familiarity of these terms. We must be on our guard, then, against assuming that the tone in Gower signifies anything like a cultural reaction against French writing, or at least, no more of a

---

[71] *French Verse*, ed. Woledge, 220–1; Woledge differs in this from both Wilkins and Chichmaref, no. XXXI, p. 556. It is unclear, however, on what textual authority Woledge makes this alteration.

reaction than was already contained within its own mockingly self-destructive frame of reference. Moreover, in a final envoy which acts as the epilogue to the whole work and not just to the last ballade, Gower uses French to speak to and for England:

> O gentile Engleterre, a toi j'escrits,
> Pour remembrer ta joie q'est novelle,
> Qe te survient du noble Roi Henris.[72]

The difficulty of isolating an 'English' perspective is shown by the very familiar example of Chaucer's 'Merciles Beaute'. The first example of a triple roundel in English, it represents one of the earliest moments in which a highly refined French form is articulated in English. This act of cultural translation is couched in terms that appear to give metaphorical voice to the issue of what kind of freedom a poet writing in English has in relation to a French 'fixed form'. Each rondeau presents the lover in very contrasting situations: in the first deeply wounded, apparently to death; in the second resigned to his lady's lack of pity, and in the third free from love altogether. At first sight it would seem that the poem as a whole manœuvres its way into a position of escape: from an imprisoning cluster of rhymes in the second rondeau (round 'cheyne'—'pleyne', 'feyne', 'atteyne', and 'peyne'), it suddenly seems to break loose with the striking claim:

> Sin I fro Love escaped am so fat,
> I never thenk to ben in his prison lene;
> Sin I am free, I counte him not a bene.

The confident scorn of the very English cliché 'I counte him not a bene' seems to cast off not only Love itself, but the whole respectful linguistic apparatus Love's servants are required to carry with them. It is even tempting to identify it as a larger bid for freedom in an English poet's desire to strike an independent pose against a long and domineering French tradition.

However, on closer inspection, the freedom is illusory. The line 'Sin I fro Love escaped am so fat' turns out not to be a daringly original piece of English, but is paralleled word for word in a line in *Le Livre des cent ballades* (1389) by the former English hostage the duc de Berry, 'Puis qu'a Amours suis si gras echapé'. Moreover, since it is part of the refrain, it is necessarily repeated, given the

---

[72] *French Works*, ed. Macaulay, 378.

circular repetitions of the rondeau form—and there is something hollow about a claim for victory from tradition which is forced by the rondeau form into repeated expression. And finally, as we notice from the fact that the first and third rondeaux are tied together by a repeated *b* rhyme ('kene...lene') the circularity of the whole form means that escape and servitude are not two divergent experiences but are ruthlessly inscribed on the same endless chain of love's demands.

That this is a subtle joke about the relation between love lyrics in English and a powerful French tradition is suggested by the teasing relation between 'Sin I fro Love escaped am so fat' and 'Puis qu'a Amours suis si gras echapé'. Wimsatt has argued forcefully that the duc is the borrower rather than Chaucer: but since we have no external means of dating Chaucer's poem the issue cannot be resolved.[73] Either way, there is an irony in the Anglo-French parallel. If the line *is* an English original, then its translation into French by a nobleman temporarily in English power as a hostage reabsorbs it straight back into the arena of French public poetry: if, on the other hand, the line was originally French, then we have the spectacle of an English poet ostensibly breaking free from the decorum of French lyric style yet doing so in a style that was already part of that decorum. The very existence of the parallel shows how closely the two linguistic cultures feed off each other. The refrain functions, once more, as a kind of model in miniature of cultural exchange. At once the most fixed element in a lyric structure and yet also the element which passes from work to work, the refrain gives the genre of the *forme fixe* a paradoxical openness. The genre acts not so much as a static form but as an open dialogue, inviting, through the refrain, replies and ripostes, translation and revision. Both lyric cultures (English and French) emphasize the entangled nature of their tied relationship in the way that the topic under discussion in a song so often concerns the notions of escape and constraint. That the refrains in both Gower's ballade and Chaucer's rondeau articulate such notions is thus a synecdochic feature both of the *forme fixe* genre itself and of the aggressively intimate cultural context in which it was composed.

---

[73] 'Guillaume de Machaut and Chaucer's Love Lyrics', *MÆ* 47 (1978), 68–87 (p. 83 n. 43).

The unique manuscript of the *Cinquante Balades* contains another group of eighteen ballades, known from the initial rubric as the *Traitié pour essampler les amantz marietz*. This group is placed at the end of the *Confessio Amantis* in eight out of the ten surviving copies of the *Traitié*: while, as Macaulay says, 'it is certain... that the author did not regard it as inseparable from the *Confessio Amantis*', he equally clearly regarded it as being closely associated with it. It is difficult to consider the relation of the *Traitié* to the *Confessio* without commenting in some way on the ending of the latter. It has recently been argued that the *beau retret* experienced by Amans is a profoundly moral event, that the poet repudiates not only secular love, but the whole tradition of its expression in French lyric and narrative. The same scholar, in one of the very few published discussions of the *Traitié* (to which I will return), sees it as a further moral progression from the *Confessio*, in which Gower praises married love in tones of severe implied rebuke to the frivolities of French *fin amour*.[74]

The ending of the *Confessio* is characterized by a clash of perspectives. As in a long sequence of medieval writing on secular love, by such authors as Chrétien de Troyes, Andreas Capellanus, Jean de Meun, and Chaucer, the 'conclusioun final' comes as a form of rupture. Ostensibly, the end of the work is designed to repair a break. In the words of the Confessor:

> Nou at this time that I schal
> As for conclusioun final
> Conseile upon thi nede sette:
> So thenke I finaly to knette
> This cause, where it is tobroke. (VIII. 2069–73)

Yet the process of knitting things together is itself painful and discordant. It begins with a severe disagreement ('debat and gret perplexete') between Amans and the priest, who become distanced from each other. This quarrel then precipitates a break in the narrative itself: for the first time since the beginning of the poem, the narrative couplets give way to a letter or 'bille' in twelve rhyme-royal stanzas. Genius presents the bill to Venus while the lover waits anxiously for her response. This in turn prompts the disconcerting announcement by the poet of his name.

---

[74] R. F. Yeager, *John Gower's Poetic: The Search for a New Arion* (Cambridge, 1990), 101.

The reasons for our sense of dislocation are numerous. Most immediately, they are provoked by the gentle implicit humour of Venus' question:

> And as it were halvinge a game
> Sche axeth me what is mi name. (VIII. 2319–20)

Perhaps there is a very British joke here that the formal introduction has come rather late in the day. More soberly, as John Burrow has described, the naming of the poet is part of a much larger series of questioning dichotomies, between youth and age, the author and the lover, those in love and those out of love, secular and 'honeste' love, love and marriage.[75] The shock of the ending, as John Gower is made to acknowledge his dim eyes, sunken, wrinkled cheeks, and grey hair, is a complex process of trying to decide how the various dichotomies have been superimposed, and whether this construction changes during the course of the poem: put simply, is Amans old or young? is Gower to be identified with Amans?

One of the most powerful moves in Burrow's argument occurs at its end, where he points out that the *Confessio* does not finish (as it might) with Amans's slow, contented homeward journey, armed with a rosary of black beads and the motto 'Por reposer'. Instead, 'although Gower has finished with Amans, he has not finished with himself. For he too, like Amans, has been "feigning": "fingens se auctor esse Amantem". Both old men have strenuously adopted the incongruous role of lover, but in different ways, one in (poetic) reality, the other in (real) poetry. It is therefore appropriate that *auctor* as well as *amans* should make a "beau retret" and find his own peace.'[76] Burrow goes on to say that the author 'takes his "final leve" of writing poetry about love'. Just as Amans needs to retreat from practising love, so the poet needs to stop writing about love.

Within the framework of the *Confessio*, this makes perfect sense. Not only does Gower turn away from writing on love himself, he famously counsels Chaucer to do the same. But what in that case are we to make of the eighteen French ballades that

---

[75] J. A. Burrow, 'The Portrayal of Amans in *Confessio Amantis*', in A. J. Minnis (ed.), *Gower's 'Confessio Amantis': Responses and Reassessments* (Cambridge, 1983), 5–24.
[76] Ibid. 23.

follow this repudiation, all of which are concerned with love? For that matter, it would appear that Gower wrote the *Cinquante Balades* after, rather than before, the *Confessio*. Gower does not stop writing love poetry, he simply ceases to write it in English. R. F. Yeager has argued, none the less, that the topic of the *Traitié* ballades is a further kind of repudiation. Yet the transition from the *Confessio* to the *Cinquante Balades* cannot be characterized so easily.

The tone is set by the opening rubric that stands between the *Confessio* and the first ballade:

Puisqu'il ad dit ci devant en Englois par voie d'essample la sotie de cellui qui par amours aime par especial, dirra ore apres en François a tout le monde en general un traitié selonc les auctours pour essampler les amantz marietz, au fin q'ils la foi de lour seintes espousailes pourront par fine loialté guarder, et al honour de dieu salvement tenir.

What is interesting about the rubric is the way that it makes so much of the shift from English to French. This is no ordinary continuation, but a transition between one piece of writing and another, full of the consciousness of what it means to move into a different linguistic medium. A contrast is set up between what has just been said 'en Englois' concerning 'la sotie de cellui qui par amours aime par especial', and what will be said 'en François', which will be directed 'a tout le monde en general'. The implication is that French is perceived as the language best suited to a wide audience and a larger theme; English was appropriate for 'la sotie'. At first sight, this supports a reading of the *Traitié* as designed to trump the *Confessio* morally, both through the subject-matter and in the use of the superior moral authority of French over English. Yet the claim is less straightforward than it pretends. Ironically, it is the theme of married love which is particular to Gower, whereas the foolishness of the man who loves 'par especial' is the topic of a vast body of widely circulated French writing. Gower seems to be disingenuously making use of the authority of French (note how he labours the mention of 'les auctours') to put a special case.

The envoy of the last ballade (no. 18) could yield a similar interpretation. Formally it is anomalous since it acts as a fourth stanza. From this quirkily non-conforming position, the author speaks out to the whole world, again naming himself:

Al université de tout le monde
Johan Gower ceste Balade envoie;
Et si jeo n'ai de François la faconde,
Pardonetz moi qe jeo de ceo forsvoie:
Jeo sui Englois, si quier par tiele voie
Estre excusé; mais quoique nulls en die,
L'amour parfit en dieu se justifie.

He begins here in the same third-person style as the rubric, but
then moves carefully but emphatically into a first-person voice.
Again it is tempting to take the apology for his French at face
value, but this would be to underestimate the complexities of the
statement 'Jeo sui Englois'. As in the ballade by Deschamps discussed earlier, there is a certain tension involved in asserting in the
French language that one is English, rather than French. Gower's
true confession at this post-ultimate point in the *Confessio* is that
he has led the French language astray ('forsvoie'). I take him to
mean that he has rendered—in English—a deeply French account
of a lover's experiences, and, conversely, presented—in French—a
distinctively un-French assertion of the delights of married love.
'Whatever anyone says', Gower concludes mischievously, but of
course also in perfect seriousness, 'perfect love is justified in God.'

The Latin gloss for this ballade points to the broader context of
this stanza: 'Hic in fine Gower, qui Anglicus est, sua verba Gallica,
si que incongrua fuerint, excusat.' Although the *Confessio* may end,
in English, on a note of peace ('Por reposer'), the linguistic and
cultural argument it has raised is far from resolved. Gower's continuation in French, and ultimately in Latin, indicates a certain
endemic restlessness that is a constant thread throughout his poetic
career: the *Traitié* is in this sense an important part of the *Confessio*'s complex and self-conscious layering of themes and moral
attitudes. The term *incongrua* points to the way in which Gower
uses his trilinguality to set up oblique contrasts between different
kinds of cultural perspective. We have come to see the Latin commentary to the *Confessio* as creating an 'interpretive distance'
between text and gloss:[77] the distance between English and French,
as Gower shows, is more difficult to acknowledge.

[77] A. J. Minnis, 'Authors in Love: The Exegesis of Late-Medieval Love-Poets', in
C. C. Morse, P. R. Doob, and M. J. Woods (eds.), *The Uses of Manuscripts in Literary
Studies: Essays in Memory of J. B. Allen* (Kalamazoo, Mich., 1992), 161–91 (p. 176);
cf. Minnis's earlier article '*Amor* and *Auctoritas* in the Self-Commentary of Dante
and Francesco da Barberino', *Poetica*, 32 (1990), 25–42 (p. 34).

6

Anglo-Latin in the Ricardian Age

A. G. Rigg

In the early fifteenth century, in a life of Edward the Confessor dedicated to Henry VI, the author lamented, as many have done before and since, the decline of Latin:

> Heu! decus eloquii languet moerore Latini,
> Heu! perit in tenebris veterum facundia prisca;
> Marcus abest, luget Maro, carmina Naso relegat;
> Tantaque simplicitas nostris succrevit in annis
> Quod vulgi plus sermo placet, quem dictat arator
> Vulgari lingua, quam mellica musa Maronis.
> Heu! laicus tractat victricia proelia regum,
> Heu! quod inerter erunt descripta; palatia, turres,
> Reges cum ducibus sepelit neglecta vetustas![1]

> (Now Latin eloquence, alas, lies sadly sick:
> The ancients' rhetoric grows dim and dies.
> No Tully; Virgil grieves, and Ovid's gone.
> Simplicity's the rage in recent years,
> And what the ploughman says in vulgar tongue
> Has more appeal than Virgil's honeyed muse.
> The layman treats the victories of kings
> Ineptly drawn—the palaces and towers
> And dukes and kings are buried in neglect.)

The details of the threnody are unclear: does the pristine eloquence of the ancients perish in the darkness because no one reads them or because no one writes like them any more? Cicero is absent (since there are no orators like him), but Virgil laments and Ovid banishes his own songs (since no one appreciates them). Nevertheless the gist is clear—that Latin is on the skids—and echoes the

---

[1] For all bibliographical references to Anglo-Latin authors, see the index to my *A History of Anglo-Latin Literature 1066–1422* (Cambridge, 1992).

laments of grammarians for 300 years before. What may be start-ling to certain modern readers is the hostile reference to 'simpli-city' and 'the language of the crowd that the ploughman speaks[2] in his vulgar tongue'. Is this the respect due to the language of Chaucer, Gower, the *Gawain*-poet, and (perhaps the target of the author) Langland?

Even more surprising to the modern reader is the fact that the author should be surprised. We, with perfect hindsight, know that English went on to become the natural medium of communication not only in Britain but throughout the world; we trace a literary continuity from Chaucer to T. S. Eliot and a linguistic one from the earliest Old English recipe to a computer manual. But the author's surprise is more forgivable than ours: who would have dreamed that Latin, a language with a 1500-year ancestry, would yield to one that in his day existed in dozens of scarcely mutually intelli-gible dialects, with no poetic tradition, no fine words, no grammar, and not even a fixed system of spelling? There is yet another paradox; the poet laments the decline of Latin, but, by classical standards, his own Latin is appalling: he uses -*que* for *et*, *ve* for *vel*, and *posse* for *potentia*. He could not have imagined that within a generation a breed of 'humanists' would arise who would restore true classical standards and protect the language of Cicero, Virgil, and Ovid from debasement for the next 500 years.

Many scholars have described the 'triumph of English', both as a language and as a literature. In this essay I want to examine the role and status of Anglo-Latin in the last quarter of the fourteenth century. In this period we begin to see clearly the trends that would later lead to both the demise of Latin as a medium for creative writing and its protection as a unique manifestation of classical civilization. The aim of the present book, as proposed by its editors to its contributors, was 'essays that engage the theory and definition of Ricardian literature as John Burrow presented it, essays that evaluate, modify, or indeed challenge the notion of "Ricardian Literature" in the light of work done since John Burrow's *Ricardian Poetry* was published and/or one's personal discoveries, perceptions, and insights'. The first part of this essay, therefore, sets Burrow's ideas, in many of his

---

[2] *Dictat* could also mean 'composes' or 'writes'.

writings,[3] against the background of Anglo-Latin literature in general, and later focuses particularly on its distinctive features in the Ricardian age.

BURROVIAN TOPICS

John Burrow is, as far as I know, the first person to use the epithet 'Ricardian' for literary periodization, and he discusses the advantages and drawbacks of the term.[4] In my view, there is no need to apologize for using regnal dates to characterize literary periods in the Middle Ages. I say this not only as an unrepentant monarchist, but as one who (in my *History of Anglo-Latin Literature 1066–1422*) has divided post-Conquest Anglo-Latin literature by the deaths and accessions of kings (1066, 1154, 1216, 1307, and 1422). Regnal breaks frequently mark a change of ethos (because of changes of allegiances, alliances, patronage, etc.); the fates of monarchs affect their subjects. In these terms, 'Ricardian' (marked by the end of a relatively stable era, followed by the Peasants' Revolt and twenty-two years of strife) corresponds to a shift of cultural interests and concerns.

Burrow has made many perceptive remarks on the problem of defining 'literature', particularly—but not only—in the Middle Ages.[5] His sensible remarks concern primarily Middle English, but they apply *a fortiori* to the enormous amount of Latin writing in the Middle Ages (on which I have more to say below). In selecting material for my *History* I had to make a decision at the outset, and I fell back on pragmatism, including all verse works, however dull and didactic, and giving a mention to the more literary chronicles and collections of letters, while excluding prose philosophy, theology, science, technology, documents, etc. In discussing the difficulties of ascribing homogeneity to the Ricardian poets, Burrow notes their 'unlikeness of fortune', that is, the different reception inevitably given by modern readers to

---

[3] J. A. Burrow, *A Reading of 'Sir Gawain and the Green Knight'* (London, 1965); id., *Ricardian Poetry: Chaucer, Gower, Langland and the Gawain Poet* (London, 1971); id., *Medieval Writers and their Work: Middle English Literature and its Background 1100–1500* (Oxford, 1982); id., *Langland's Fictions* (Oxford, 1993).

[4] Burrow, *Ricardian Poetry*, 2.

[5] Burrow, *Medieval Writers*, 12–23.

dialects that, like those of Langland and the *Gawain*-poet, differ from the mainstream English of Chaucer and Gower.[6] This, at least, is a problem not shared by Anglo-Latin; the general oblivion that has overtaken almost all Anglo-Latin writers means that they can all be treated equally, in a democracy of obscurity.

In many ways the writers of Latin had a different relationship to their craft and community from writers of English. Burrow notes that the diversity of English 'must have prevented contemporaries from fully understanding or appreciating work being done in dialect-areas other than their own'.[7] In contrast, Latin writers often knew each other, sometimes directly (like many of the courtiers of Henry II), sometimes by correspondence (Reginald of Canterbury) or awareness of common intellectual interests (Geoffrey of Monmouth, William of Malmesbury, Henry of Huntingdon). In any case, as they used a common language, they could know each other's writings, over any number of generations, so that there was a textual community that transgressed both geographical and temporal bounds. Participants in poetic debate contests, like Henry of Avranches and Michael of Cornwall or the pro- and anti-mendicant polemicists, may actually have collaborated to put on a good show for their audiences.

The question of professionalism must also be approached differently in the case of Latin. Burrow correctly observes that 'there is no sign in England of the specialized, professional, vernacular "writer"', and 'when applying the term "writer" to the Middle English period, one must try to avoid any suggestion of professionalism'.[8] The situation in Latin was somewhat different. Certainly no one sold books to make a living (our modern conception of a writing career), but Latin, unlike English, was a practical tool with many rewarding uses. Henry of Avranches was paid directly in both money and wine from the exchequer of Henry III. Many writers used their Latin writings as an academic now uses publications, to build up a dossier and a reputation that would earn a benefice of some kind: Geoffrey of Monmouth used the *Historia regum Britanniae* and *Vita Merlini* to obtain a bishopric. Others were attached to the court of some great figure: Robert Baston was

---

[6] Burrow, *Ricardian Poetry*, 9.   [7] Ibid. 3.   [8] Burrow, *Medieval Writers*, 29.

taken to Scotland by Edward II to celebrate his hoped-for victory over the Scots; Walter of Peterborough was in the retinue of the Black Prince at Poitiers and of John of Gaunt in Spain, apparently primarily to record their military exploits in Latin verse; John of Howden was a clerk of Queen Eleanor, mother of Edward I: although there is no sign that he was paid for his poetry, he would, like Chaucer, have had security for his writing. Above all, many Latin writers taught grammar, either at the grammar school level (Elias of Thriplow, Walter of Wimborne) or at university (John of Garland).

Writers of Latin, both prose and verse, had a greater sense than those of English that they were practising 'literature', even if they routinely disclaimed any eloquence. Burrow notes that Chaucer and Gower are the first English writers known to have spoken of their Muse;[9] Anglo-Latin writers, however, frequently invoked a Muse, often Thalia, Muse of comedy. This is not surprising: whereas the Ricardian English poets were, to all intents, initiating a literary tradition, Anglo-Latin writers were participating in one that extended back to the first century before Christ. They could draw on over 1,000 years of intertextual allusion known to all educated readers; from classical texts, the Vulgate Bible, the liturgy, philosophy, theology, science, and law they could weave a multitextured and allusive language. Walter of Wimborne casually blends a line from Horace with an allusion to the Book of Kings. Henry of Avranches tells a story of St Francis, empty-handed but happily singing as he walks through the snow; when he is set on by robbers, it is clear that Henry has simply been leading to a punchline, to refute Juvenal's saying that 'the empty-handed traveller can safely sing in the face of a thief'. Walter Map's satire on life at the court of Henry II draws effortlessly on Augustine, Porphyry, Boethius, Virgil, the Bible, classical mythology, and folklore. Between 1100 and 1300, Anglo-Latin shows great diversity of genres and forms—epigrams, verse saints' lives, classical and biblical epic, prosimetrum, lyric, verse and prose epistolography, beast-fable, satire—on all manner of topics, both religious and secular, utilizing a wide variety of metres. Interestingly, there are few tales;[10] there is at least one clear hint that these are inappropriate material for Latin, and the few examples of the

---

[9] Ibid. 18. [10] Ibid. 71–85.

genre (apart from those in collections of marvels or sermon exempla) may be parodies.

Not surprisingly, many Latin writers anticipate the Ricardian sense of awareness of themselves and their role as authors. It was a commonplace of medieval literary theory that poetry was 'lying',[11] though I have seen no sign that any Anglo-Latin poet thought that his own craft was implicated; on the other hand, Reginald of Canterbury asserts a poet's licence to create, and the author of a verse life of St Elphege attributes a taste for verse to preciosity. Another sign of literary awareness is parody, and Anglo-Latin has much of this; some is fairly simple, where a common text (the liturgy or the Bible) is used to comic effect. More interesting are cases where the nature or extent of the parody is uncertain, when the reader or listener is not quite sure of the appropriate reaction. In Middle English the most striking example is Chaucer's *Sir Thopas*, which Burrow discusses at length.[12] Among Anglo-Latin romances (*Vera historia de morte Arturi, De ortu Walwanii, Historia Meriadoci, Arthur and Gorlagon*) we are *almost* sure that the writer cannot be serious; we feel that our critical taste is being tested. Some scholars have suggested that Geoffrey of Monmouth's *Historia regum Britanniae* is a parody of contemporary historiography.

Burrow writes of the 'increasingly personal character in Middle English writing from the mid-fourteenth century'.[13] The intrusion of the author's own persona is quite common in Anglo-Latin. The Virgin Mary introduces Adam of Barking to God, to give him guidance in his writing; she places a pen in the hand of Walter of Wimborne, when he is too timid to sing her praises; similarly, Faith puts the pen in the hand of John of Garland when he is about to describe the birth of the Virgin. None of these amount to self-portrayals, but Lawrence of Durham puts himself permanently on stage in his *Dialogi*: he gives many accounts of his early life, and his two companions chaff him for his solemnity. Walter of Wimborne makes dramatic use of his fictive self, imagining himself present throughout the life of Christ. He is present at the nativity, is the donkey that takes the family to safety from Herod, appeals

[11] Cf. Burrow, *Medieval Writers*, 19.

[12] Burrow, *Ricardian Poetry*, 13–21.

[13] Burrow, *Medieval Writers*, 40; the whole question of 'autobiography' is discussed fully on 40–6.

to Christ to return to his family from his sojourn in the temple, tries to outbid Judas for Christ's price, and interferes in the crucifixion by killing the carpenter who made the cross and the smith who made the axe that made the cross.

It is now a commonplace of criticism to distinguish the author from the fictionalized narrator and to allow the author to evade responsibility for what he (as a character) or his characters say, as Chaucer does in *The Canterbury Tales*, disclaiming responsibility for the pilgrims' tales or their language. The mask of the simple reporter allows for, and encourages, an ironic stance towards the content of the narratives. Nowhere is this seen better than in Walter Map, who describes himself as a 'hunter' of tales: 'I bring you the dead animals; it is up to you to make the dishes.' What is doubly ironic in Map is that he insists that his tales have morals and that the reader must read them diligently and attentively, but the tales often defy moral analysis. Here, 200 years before Chaucer, we have a writer deliberately manipulating his audience by his ironic distance.

Anglo-Latin literature between 1100 and 1300 has no heroes comparable to those of Ricardian poetry—an Arthurian knight, a Trojan prince, Athenian nobles, a frustrated lover—and it might seem pointless to look for examples of the 'unheroic';[14] indeed, with its stress on human sinfulness, frailty, and mortality, Anglo-Latin exemplifies the view of man that gave rise to Ricardian attitudes. Nevertheless, it is worth observing that there are no heroes even where the topics might have produced them. John of Garland's rambling epic on the crusades, *De triumphis ecclesiae*, has none; nor does the nearest thing to a classical epic in Anglo-Latin, Joseph of Exeter's *Ylias*, in which the only person to come out unscathed from the Trojan War is Helen. Many protagonists in Walter Map's tales are knights and warriors, but they are usually portrayed ambiguously. The phrase 'private and quotidian'[15] is remarkably apt for the atmosphere of Lawrence of Durham's *Dialogi*, in which the sufferings of the city of Durham are seen through the eyes of three ordinary and unremarkable citizens, whose only desire is to get back to normal. A leavening of

[14] For the nature of the 14th-cent. literary hero, see Burrow, *Ricardian Poetry*, 93–110.
[15] Ibid. 101.

humour[16] is often evident. By this I mean not the deliberately comic, of which there is plenty, but the use of humour in unexpected contexts. The justifiably solemn laments of Lawrence-the-character in Lawrence's *Dialogi* are often undercut by his friend Peter's insensitive jokes. Humour is often present in religious contexts and indeed the source of religious sentiment. Lawrence ascribes the reversal of the fortunes of Joseph and his brothers to God's playfulness, and Alexander Neckam says that nature's variety is God's joke. Walter Map actually calls God *facetus* ('witty'). These writers seem to share with Chaucer's Theseus a sense that the world is an odd place and all we can do is make the best of it.

There is little to be gained by comparing Anglo-Latin with English in form and style—partly because Latin already possessed the 'eloquence' that the Ricardians were trying to emulate, partly because Latin was not normally a conversational medium and lacked the spontaneity and flexibility of English. Division of long English poems into 'books' seems to be a Ricardian innovation,[17] but was, of course, a habit fully ingrained in Latin. Allusions to an oral context, real or fictive,[18] are rare in Latin, which was always a literary medium. Even Walter Map, known to Gerald of Wales as an oral performer in the vernacular, wrote the Latin *De nugis curialium* to be read, not heard. The one exception is Reginald of Canterbury's *Vita Malchi*, which is divided into six books explicitly for oral delivery, perhaps in the monastic chapter house.

Burrow pays great attention to the Ricardian poetic technique of detailed description or 'pointing',[19] and rightly points to the Latin rhetorical tradition. Where such descriptions occur in Anglo-Latin, they usually have rhetorical sources or classical antecedents. Joseph of Exeter's account of the first meeting of Paris and Helen is striking, but may owe more to Ovid's epistle than to observation. The hunting and hawking scenes in Lawrence of Durham's *Dialogi* may also have classical analogues. One passage that appears to be original occurs in a poem on Susanna, describing her stammering when she is disturbed by the elders. A similar problem arises with what Burrow aptly calls 'drastic similes':[20] it

[16] Burrow, *Ricardian Poetry*, 111–26.
[17] Ibid. 57–62 (p. 59).
[18] Burrow, *Medieval Writers*, 50–1, 53.
[19] Burrow, *Ricardian Poetry*, 69–78; id., *Medieval Writers*, 73–4.
[20] Burrow, *Ricardian Poetry*, 135–6.

is hard to know what is 'original'. In descriptions of the Virgin Mary and Christ's passion, John of Howden and Walter of Wimborne have an amazing range of dramatic similes and metaphors; many may be original, but others come from compilations such as Richard of St Laurent's *De laudibus beatae Virginis*. As far as I know, no one has made even a partial study of Medieval Latin similes. Finally on formal matters, Anglo-Latin offers an amusing reversal of what was later to be a convention of vernacular poetry, the method of ending a dream-vision.[21] Nigel Whiteacre's *Speculum stultorum* recounts the adventures of Burnellus, an ass who wanted a longer tail. In one episode he recounts how, *en cachette*, he overheard a debate between a crow, a cock, and a hawk; finally Burnellus falls asleep and his snores disturb the birds. Here it is the dreamer that arouses the bystanders!

LATIN IN THE FOURTEENTH CENTURY

Gradually Latin was replaced by English as the medium for what we call 'literature'. The reasons for this displacement—which was shared, at different times, with all countries of western Europe—are not hard to seek: they are socio-economic and involve the rise of a literate middle class that was formally Christian but not necessarily clerical. The medieval textual community was becoming secular—not in the modern sense of 'humanist', 'rationalist', 'non-religious', but 'living in the world' (*seculum*) as opposed to the cloister. The literate class had broadened to include secular clergy of all kinds—not only parish priests and canons but many in minor orders, who might become lawyers or teachers. From the thirteenth century, friars, who were bound by vows but did not live in a cloister, also lived 'in the world'. As time goes on, we find more writers who are attached to no religious order at all. In England the language of this new literate class was English rather than French, and writers seek the widest possible audience, for both present gain and future reputation. Patronage was now possible for writers of English, and some authors (though John Gower played it safe) recognized that it was in English that the future lay.

---

[21] Burrow, *Langland's Fictions*, 12–17.

Nevertheless, it would be wrong to think of Latin as 'in decline'; the textual community still operated mainly in Latin, which was the medium for international communications, historiography, law, science, philosophy, and theology. Further, almost all the records of the past, on any topic, were in Latin; English history, for example, was known not from the *Anglo-Saxon Chronicle* but from the Latin distillations of it made by historians like Henry of Huntingdon; Chaucer knew Boethius not from King Alfred's version but directly (though aided by Jean de Meun's French translation). Vernacular writers sometimes made it clear that they were operating within a Latin context: in his *Complaint*, Thomas Hoccleve puts quotations from his source (Isidore's *Synonyma*) in the margin. Gower actually supplied his own Latin authorities for the *Confessio Amantis* by prefacing each book with a newly composed Latin verse, to which the English poem then acts as a kind of commentary.

Moreover, in the fourteenth century English scholars applied themselves to the study of books. There were many great private book collectors, and Latin books were treasured. It was also an age in which literary history began: Walter Burley wrote the *De vita et moribus philosophorum*, and Henry of Kirkstede (who died after 1378) compiled a *Catalogus scriptorum ecclesiae*, an alphabetical list of all known writers from classical times to his own day. The group described by Beryl Smalley as 'classicizing friars' wrote commentaries on theological and literary works, and some sought out texts of rare authors. A striking example of a scholar of this breadth was Thomas Walsingham (*c*.1345–1422), a younger contemporary of Chaucer; he was a historian and chronicler of St Albans. He also wrote the *Prohemia poetarum*, a collection of biographies and bibliographies of major classical and medieval poets. Other works of his were the *Arcana deorum*, a detailed analysis, with naturalistic explanations, of the myths in Ovid's *Metamorphoses*, and the *Dites ditatus*, an expansion (with literary and scientific amplifications) of Dictys Cretensis' *Ephemeris belli Troiani*, a principal source for the story of Troy. He was particularly interested in Seneca's tragedies.

Thus, while French yielded to English in the courts and parliament, Latin maintained its place as the prestige language. Ironically, it was this growing classicism that ultimately protected and purified Latin, making it less available for informal use: any renaissance, or rebirth, entails a displacement of the old. This development, however, was in the future.

RICARDIAN LATIN POETS

After this brief account of Anglo-Latin in the second half of the fourteenth century, it is time to focus specifically on the Ricardian period of 1377–99 and to ask whether there are any distinctive trends equivalent to those identified by Burrow for English poets. The Latin poems include: short poems of 1382 on the Lollards and the Peasants' Revolt ('Heu quanta desolatio', 'Praesta Jhesu', and 'Prohdolor accrevit'); Thomas Barry's poem on the battle of Otterburn (1388); Richard Maidstone's description of Richard II's return to London (1392); John Gower's *Vox clamantis* (written first after 1381 and revised after 1399), *Cronica tripertita* (after 1399), and shorter poems; the *Chronicon metricum ecclesiae Eboracensis* (between 1388 and 1396); and the final continuation (after 1399) of the *Metrical History of the Kings of England*.[22]

The first thing to note is that, apart from a few of Gower's short poems, they are all 'historical', mostly on contemporary events. Topical poems had been common since the Norman Conquest, but there was a surge of them after the accession of Edward III: from 1327 to 1377 the main themes were the Hundred Years War, Oxford university politics, controversies between friars and monks, and the Spanish campaign of the Black Prince. Thus, the historical bias of Ricardian Latin poetry fulfils a tendency already at work. In part this may be due to a new heraldic function of

---

[22] The poems discussed in this section are to be found as follows. *Political Poems and Songs Relating to English History from the Accession of Edward III to that of Richard II*, ed. T. Wright, Rolls Series, 2 vols. (London, 1859–61): 'Heu quanta desolatio', i. 253–63; 'Praesta Jhesu', i. 231–49; 'Prohdolor accrevit', i. 227–30; Maidstone, i. 282–300. Barry's poem on Otterburn is in *Johannis de Fordun Scotichronicon cum supplementis et continuatione Walteri Boweri*, ed. W. Goodall, 2 vols. (Edinburgh, 1759), ii. 406–14; a new edition of Bower is in preparation by D. E. R. Watt; on Barry, see D. E. R. Watt, *Biographical Dictionary of Scottish Graduates to* AD *1410* (Oxford, 1977), 31–2. *The Complete Works of John Gower*, ed. G. C. Macaulay, iv: *The Latin Works* (Oxford, 1902): *Vox clamantis*, 20–313 (*Visio* on 20–81), *Cronica tripertita*, 314–20. The *Chronicon metricum* is in *The Historians of the Church of York and its Archbishops*, ed. J. Raine, Rolls Series, 3 vols. (London, 1879–94), ii. 446–63. The unpublished continuation of the *Metrical History* is in London, British Library, MSS Harley 1808 and 2386.

Latin poetry. As we have mentioned, Edward II took Robert Baston to Bannockburn to celebrate his expected victory; Walter of Peterborough accompanied the Black Prince and John of Gaunt to Spain to write of the battle of Nájera (1367) and tells us that he had been at Poitiers. Richard Maidstone, a Carmelite friar, shows such detailed knowledge of the pageant for Richard II in 1392 that it seems likely that he was involved in its organization. The commemorative function of poetry is also illustrated by the *Chronicon metricum*, which was written for inclusion on a wooden *tabula*, a triptych (still extant) containing historical monuments of York. Another factor was the long tradition of poetic competition, in which two rivals squared off against each other in a demonstration of skilful and abusive poetry; this may lie behind the intra-university squabbles between monks and friars and other types of polemical Latin poetry. There are several good reasons why Latin poets would turn to political themes; what is surprising is that (unless some treasures remain buried in manuscripts, which is possible) poets wrote of nothing else, ignoring classical themes, biblical narration, and religious devotion.

Metre

A feature of many of these poems that will be less obvious to those who have not studied the history of Anglo-Latin verse is their metre.[23] Gower's *Vox clamantis*, Maidstone's pageant, and the continuation of the *Metrical History* are all in unrhymed elegiac couplets, as are some of Gower's short poems and most of those in the *Confessio Amantis*. The York *Chronicon metricum* is mainly unrhymed, in hexameters and elegiac couplets. This might at first sight seem unremarkable. Most Anglo-Latin poetry of the twelfth and early thirteenth centuries was unrhymed, often in elegiac couplets (e.g. Nigel Whiteacre's *Speculum stultorum*, a source for both Chaucer and Gower), a metre made widely popular by Ovid's epistles, etc., and used for didactic purposes by many medieval Latin poets. On the other hand, in Anglo-Latin the last use of unrhymed verse before 1367 had been by Henry of Avranches in the early thirteenth century. Between about 1240 and 1367 the predominant metres were either rhymed hexameters (mainly leon-

---

[23] For an account of metres in use in Anglo-Latin, see my *History*, 313–29.

ines) or rhythmical stanzas. In 1367 Walter of Peterborough used unrhymed elegiacs for the prologue of his poem on the battle of Nájera. This resurgence of a classical metre is paralleled by the use, in Barry's poem on Otterburn (1388), of the unrhymed lyric metre of Boethius, *De consolatione philosophiae*, Book I, metrum 2. That it may be part of a trend is suggested by the appearance, in the early fifteenth century, of a group of London schoolmasters, centred on John Seward, who experimented in unrhymed non-rhythmical lyric metres. Is this, then, an incipient 'classicism' in style, paralleled by the interests of the bibliophiles, classical friars, and Thomas Walsingham? Could the Ricardian Latin poets be following the lead of Italian poets like Petrarch and Boccaccio in their new elegance?

If so, it was only superficial. The Ricardians not only continued the usual medieval 'licences' but deviated even further from classical (and even medieval) metrical practice. Most medieval Latin poets felt free to lengthen a short vowel at the caesura of a hexameter, or to shorten final vowels (especially - ō) when necessary; these practices are common among the Ricardian poets. Moreover, there were no dictionaries to guide poets on the natural length of vowels, and it is not surprising to see some 'deviations' (e.g. Maidstone 27, *adōlescens*). Also, the metrical break after a foot (rather than at the caesura) produced a well-established form, *dactylici tripertiti*, and this is commonly used among unrhymed hexameters as well as rhymed ones. Such non-classical features, even if perfectly acceptable in a medieval context, do not suggest a thoroughgoing 'classicism'. In fact, the Ricardian poets deviate even further in their licences. A list of metrical oddities (Maidstone *sĕnties*, *nŭmĕrūm ānni*, *ŏdisse*, etc.) would be tedious, but the point can best be made by the inconsistencies: the *Metrical History* usually has *Scōt-*, *Scŏtt-*, but also *Scŏtica*, *Scŏtorum*; *prēsul*, but also *prĕsul*. The *Chronicon metricum* usually has *Brĭtŏnes*, but also *Brītōnibus* and *Brĭtŏnibus*; *mētrŏpŏlis*, but also *mētrōpŏlis*. All of them regularly use *-que* as though it were *et* (i.e. not enclitically).

Anglicization

Such metrical irregularities should not simply (or not solely) be attributed to ignorance and carelessness, since phonological developments since the thirteenth century had entirely disrupted the system of contrasting long and short vowels. In Middle English, some time after 1200, short vowels were lengthened in open syllables, so that *năme* became *nāme*, *stĕlen* became *stę̄len*, and *stŏlen* became *stōlen*. Later pronunciation of Latin, from the sixteenth to the early twentieth century, shows that Anglo-Latin had also undergone these changes, producing *cāno* 'sing'. If spoken Latin had such uncertainty in the pronunciation of its vowels— and Latin was regularly spoken, especially in university circles—it is not surprising that poets (lacking modern aids) should have diverged from classical usage and even lost interest in the whole business, making vowels long or short as their verse required.

The Anglicization of Latin is at its height in the fourteenth century; this is seen not only in pronunciation but in form, syntax, lexicon, and theme. Most forms of verse, both quantitative and rhythmical, were well established, but occasionally vernacular influences are seen. Richard Ledrede adapted English and French lyric tunes for sacred purposes (indicating the first line of the popular song). The popular 'O-and-I' refrain was used in the pro- and anti-mendicant satire of the 1360s and in 'Heu quanta desolatio'. Concatenation, in which the final words of one stanza are used in the first line of the next (as in *Pearl*), is seen in 'Ludere volentibus' (on the battle of Falkirk, 1298) and 'O miranda bonitas' (Neville's Cross, 1347). The cyclic structure of *Patience*, *Pearl*, and *Sir Gawain and the Green Knight*[24] has Anglo-Latin analogues in John of Howden's *Philomena* and Richard Rolle's *Canticum amoris*. The sustained alliteration of Richard Rolle's prose *Melos amoris* clearly owes something to vernacular alliterative verse.

Anglicisms in syntax are less easy to spot or verify, but 'Heu quanta desolatio' seems to use the imperfect subjunctive in the sense of 'ought to' (i.e. Middle English *sholde*) and *vult* as a future auxiliary. The same poem has some English vocabulary ('Quod in shopis venditur male mensuratur'); Maidstone has *aldirmanni* 'aldermen', *secta* 'suit of livery', *dextrarius* 'destrier', *phalangis* 'falding cloth', *strata* 'street', *ligii* 'liege'. (Such vocabulary is of course common in prose.) English etymologies are often used for onomastics: in 'Prohdolor accrevit', Sudbury is *de bacca dictus et austri* ('berry of the south') and Jack Straw is *duce*

---

[24] Burrow, *Ricardian Poetry*, 64–5.

stramineo ('straw leader'). Similarly, Gower's *Cronica tripertita* calls Nicholas Brembre *Tribulus* ('bramble'), Michael de la Pole *de puteo* ('of the pool'), and Robert de Vere *aper* ('boar': *Vere = verris* 'boar').

Apparent allusions to vernacular themes occasionally occur. 'Heu quanta desolatio' refers to 'blind Bayard' and 'Pers' (Plowman). Maidstone compares Richard II to Troilus and Absalom, and says that Venus would have locked him up; Richard's estrangement from London is described as the separation of a bridegroom from his bride by the actions of a *mordax* and *perfida lingua* (Malebouche). In Gower, as we will see, the paraphernalia of the dream-vision has a very English flavour.

RICARDIAN POETS AND HISTORY

The Latin poets of the Ricardian period exemplify widely different treatments of 'historical' matter. At one extreme is the very simple treatment: the continuation of the *Metrical History* is simply an updating to 1399 of the abbreviation of British history (from Brutus to Henry III) that formed, in my opinion, part of an elementary educational programme centred on York; apart from being in verse, the poem shows no 'literary' embellishments. The *Chronicon metricum* is also devoid of ornament; compiled from 'old archives' it has selected events that impinge on the history of York Minster and Christianity in the north, from Ebraucus to the York–Canterbury dispute. It is purely commemorative and is literary only by virtue of being in (very rough) verse. Maidstone's poem on the pageant of 1392 has more to do with the poetic tradition, as mentioned above. On the other hand, as the record of a day's pageantry, it has no room to manœuvre the facts; such art and design it has comes not from the poet but from the organizer of the event.

Other poems are 'historical' only from a modern point of view, in that they are witnesses to the attitudes of their time; they do not attempt to interpret, simply to persuade. Although 'Praesta Jhesu' refers to past events (such as the Donation of Constantine) it does so only to urge the value of traditional Catholic theology and its relation to the state. 'Heu quanta desolatio' reports the events of the Council of London in 1382, but from a vehemently partisan aspect; once again, there is no attempt to shape, on a large canvas, the report of history. 'Prohdolor accrevit' simply deplores the Peasants' Revolt and the part played in it by Kent. Gower's *Vox clamantis* (Books II–VII) is not really on a historical topic but is a satirical and moral treatise. Three works, however, display a thoroughgoing artistic re-presentation of events, in which 'facts' are simply elements to be manipulated into poetic form. These are Thomas Barry's poem on the battle of Otterburn, Gower's *Cronica tripertita*, and above all Gower's *Visio*.

Thomas Barry: 'Battle of Otterburn'

The Scottish victory over the English at Otterburn in 1388 has had a long literary history. Froissart gives a detailed account in French, and two later English ballads ('Chevy Chase' and 'Otterburn') romanticize it with challenges, speeches, individual combats, and death scenes. Thomas Barry (also called Varoye), canon of Glasgow and provost of Bothwell, wrote the only Latin literary treatment. He keeps close to the story as told by Froissart: the division of the Scottish army into two, the assault by one part (led by the earl of Douglas) on Newcastle, the withdrawal and English pursuit (under Henry 'Hotspur' Percy), the Scottish camp at Otterburn, the English approach from higher ground in superior numbers, the hasty Scottish preparations, the battle at dusk and through the night, the sudden defeat of the English, the slaughter and capture of prisoners, the Scots' discovery next morning of the dead (including Douglas), and their triumphant but sad return home. Nevertheless, Barry's treatment is very 'literary'. Unlike many war poets of his age, his attitude is pacific: in his address to his Muse he laments that two kingdoms cannot live at peace in one island, and at the end he prays to God, king of peace, to abolish war. He does not taunt the English; his account of the battle itself (only 32 lines of 342) is vigorous, but, like the tournament in Chaucer's Knight's Tale, is neutral and non-personal:

> Armipotentes, arcitenentes, morte ruentes hic perierunt;
> Hic meliores et probiores, arte priores, succubuerunt.

> (The men-at-arms, the archers bold, in death they fell that night;
> Though better men of greater prow, though skilled, they died in fight.)

Each of the main protagonists is given a speech, Percy at New-castle, rousing the English to pursuit, and Douglas at Otterburn rallying the troops:

> Quamvis sint multi, nil timeatis;
> Non tenet in multis gloria belli.
> Fortiter obstetis hostibus istis,
> Et sitis memores iam probitatis.
>
> (Though they be many, have no fear:
> Mere numbers bring no martial fame.
> Stand firm against our enemies,
> Your minds upon your great renown.)

Barry's main method of transforming history into literature, how-ever, is metrical. He displays a wide range of metrical forms, mainly variously rhymed hexameters (including 'run-over rhyme') but also the rare Boethian lyric metre just quoted and the unique 'octameters' (quoted above on the battle). Barry's poem, while historically accurate (as far as we know), is very much a poet's creation.

John Gower: 'Cronica Tripertita'

When Gower first wrote the *Confessio Amantis* and *Vox clamantis* he was a supporter of Richard II; it was only later that he adjusted the texts to reflect his new allegiance to Henry IV. When he wrote the *Cronica tripertita*, however, he was already extremely hostile to the memory of the deposed king, and the *Cronica* was written to gloat over Richard's fall. Its treatment of history is very selective, not only for partisan reasons but for artistic symmetry. Gower selected three periods of Richard's reign, each of which is given its own book. The first is 1387, when Richard's opponents mili-tarily defeated his supporters and (in the Merciless Parliament) had them executed or exiled; this section Gower calls the *opus huma-num*, the work of man. The second part, introduced by a prologue of lament, leaps forward ten years (though Gower simply says 'a long time') to 1397, when Richard took his revenge, executing leaders of the Merciless Parliament and exiling Archbishop Arundel (this event, although it happened earlier, is presented last for dramatic effect); Gower calls this part the *opus inferni*, the devil's work. The third and final part begins with a prologue that optimistically looks forward to its conclusion. Richard's iniquities pile up; like a mole he digs to subvert the realm:

> Sicut humum fodit euertens talpa que rodit,
> Vnde caret requie, sic alter nocte dieque,
> Vt magis euertat regnum quod demere certat,
> Sic scelus apponit et ad hoc sua robora ponit;
> Vt princeps baratri furiens regit acta theatri.

> (Like mole that chews and digs to turn the earth
> And knows no rest, so Richard night and day
> Applies his wickedness and all his might
> To overthrow this realm and bring it down,
> And rages like the Prince of Hell on stage.)

He issues blank charters, and exiles Henry, count of Derby (later duke of Lancaster). Henry invades, and Richard flees (in Gower's interpretation) to Ireland; his supporters are caught and executed. Richard returns and behaves at first like a fox, and then tries to hide like a mole again, and surrenders and is imprisoned in the Tower. Henry is proclaimed king; his triumph is nearly marred by a plot (like Discord's final intervention in Prudentius' *Psychomachia*); Richard starves himself to death, and the poem ends with a series of contrasts between Richard and Henry. This final section is the *opus Christi*, God's work.

The tripartite structure of the *Cronica*—anachronistically resembling a three-act play—reflects Richard's fall, revenge, and final fall. The passage of time is hardly mentioned, and after the initial allusion to 1387 no dates are given: the events are abstracted from real life. Richard and his allies are wholly bad (even though Richard bears the emblem of the sun, he is *tenebrosus* 'dark'), his opponents (particularly the Swan, Bear, and Horse) are wholly good. Even the Peasants' Revolt is ascribed to Richard's bad rule, and Gower avoids allusion to any other events of 1387–99 except those that impinge on his scheme. He has entirely manipulated history for his poetic and political agenda.

John Gower: the 'Visio'

I have reserved Gower's *Visio* (*Vox clamantis*, Book I, clearly composed as a separate work), written probably in 1382, to the last place, since it is the most striking example of the use of contemporary history—the Peasants' Revolt—for literary purposes. Also, of all Gower's Latin works it is the one that displays most topoi of vernacular poetry. It preserves the chronological sequence of the Revolt, from the march on London to the death of Wat Tyler, but this event is submerged in, or rather is the reason for, the personal nightmare of the dreamer. The *Visio*, more than any other dream-vision I know, mirrors the common experience of a bad dream.

The dream sequence is framed at the beginning by a prologue and preliminary scene, and at the end by the dreamer's reflections and decision to write of his experiences; these frame elements are familiar from English and French dream-visions, though not from Latin ones. The prologue begins with a proverb and a discussion in favour of the validity of dreams:

> Vox licet hoc teneat vulgaris, quod sibi nullum
>   Sompnia propositum credulitatis habent,
> Nos tamen econtra de tempore preteritorum
>   Cercius instructos littera scripta facit.
> Ex Daniele patet quid sompnia significarunt,
>   Nec fuit in sompnis visio vana Ioseph.

> (Though common gossip holds the firm belief
>   That dreams do not contain a shred of truth,
> The written word assures the opposite
>   And tells us what has happened in the past.
> From Daniel it is clear that dreams are signs;
>   What Joseph saw in sleep was not in vain.)

In a cryptogram the poet gives his name as John Gower, laments the state of the country, apologizes for his inadequacies, and asks John, author of the Book of Revelation, to aid him. The preliminary scene is in a *plesaunce* one day in June 1381; the day is described from dawn to dusk, in terms familiar from vernacular poems. At night the poet retires but, because of his anxiety, cannot at first drop off; finally he falls asleep at dawn.

The dream itself consists of four 'scenes', each succeeding the other in what, for a dream, seem like plausible transitions. The first and longest scene (165–1358) begins with the dreamer dreaming that one Tuesday (the day of Mars) he goes out to pick flowers; he sees crowds of peasants transformed into animals, and then changed from domestic animals into wild ones, under the leadership of the Jay (Wat Tyler); they attack London and the Savoy and murder the archbishop, and the trouble spreads. In the second scene (1359–592) the dreamer, terrified for his life, flees and tries to hide, and would have pressed himself under the bark of a tree if he could; days pass and he decays in body and mind, unconsoled even by Sophia (Wisdom), and laments his cruel dreams.[25] In the third scene (1593–940) he sees a ship nearby and boards it; it is assailed by a storm and a sea-monster; the ship (which stands for both the Tower of London and his troubled mind) is in danger, but God hears his prayers: Mayor William (Walworth) kills the Jay (Wat Tyler), and the storm ceases. In the fourth and final scene (1941–2058) the ship puts into land on an island; an old man tells the dreamer that this is the island of Brutus (i.e. Britain), filled with lawless men. The dreamer is frightened again: he has reached port, but now the port terrifies him and the land is more fearful than the sea. Everything vanishes, and the dreamer is utterly alone:

> Ecce nichil penitus fuerat, velut umbra set omnis
>   Turba que nauis abest, solus et ipse fui.

> (Then there was nothing there, and like a shade
>   The ship and crowd were gone; I was alone.)

A heavenly voice comforts him and tells him to write about what he has seen. The voice coincides with the crowing of the cock, and the dreamer awakes. Even after waking (2059–150) the poet is anxious, but he praises the 'wakeful sleeps' that had brought him the vision; the anxiety about writing is to replace his old care:

> Sit prior et cura cura repulsa noua

> (So let this new care drive the old away.)

In the *Visio* we see several of the themes of Ricardian vernacular poetry: the concern with the validity of dreams, the traditional garden setting, and the mechanisms of transition within the dream. Here, however, the dream is a nightmare, a psychologically convincing expression of anxiety; fear is present in both the dream and the waking moments. The writing is the poet's payment to God for

---

[25] These are not inner dreams, 'dreams-within-dreams', in the manner of *Piers Plowman*, B-text, Passus XI and XVI (see Burrow, *Langland's Fictions*, 19, 21), but the actual dream that Gower is experiencing and of which he is aware even during the dream.

his release from the nightmare, and is itself the release from anxiety. Poetry as 'expiation' is a device of Chaucer and Hoccleve,[26] but in the *Visio* it is the dream (of the Peasants' Revolt) that contains the reality.

Poetry on contemporary events is no longer fashionable. Earthquakes, revolutions, and even major conflicts such as the Second World War, Korea, the Falklands, and the Gulf have occasioned no significant body of poems, even lyrical or satirical, let alone epic. In the late fourteenth century, however, political events were the principal material for the Anglo-Latin poet. In the three works just discussed we see quite different approaches. Barry's, with its metrical variety and set scenes, is highly literary, but sticks fairly closely to the events as they are reported in other sources; the *Cronica tripertita* manipulates and disregards chronology for dramatic effect and in order to provide a very partisan account of the fall of Richard II; the *Visio* uses a frightening and calamitous event to transform the literary dream into a work of personal nightmare. The three works differ considerably in approach, but are equally innovative and imaginative in their representation of historical events.

[26] *The Legend of Good Women* is offered as expiation for Chaucer's supposedly antifeminist writings, and Hoccleve's tale of Jereslaus' wife is intended to 'purge the guilt' of his Epistle of Cupid.

7

Looking for a Sign: The Quest for Nominalism in Chaucer and Langland

A. J. MINNIS

Those who do not believe in Jesus Christ, declares Walter Hilton, are not eligible for the benefits made possible by his passion. Throughout time, no one was ever saved, nor will be saved, except through belief in Christ and his coming. Hilton proceeds to attack certain men who 'gretly & greuously erre' by saying that 'Iewes & Sareȝeins', who lack such faith, may nevertheless be saved. This erroneous view is described in terms which make it perfectly clear that Hilton is thinking of the *facere quod in se est* doctrine which has been associated with fourteenth-century Nominalism. 'Bi keping of þeir own law', convinced that their own 'trowþ is good & siker & suffisaunt to þair saluacioun', infidels may 'in that trouþ' perform many good and righteous deeds, and perhaps if they knew that the faith of Christ was better than theirs they would leave their own faith and follow it, to ensure their salvation. But this is not sufficient, Hilton retorts, because Christ is the mediator between God and man, and no one can be reconciled with God or come to heavenly bliss except through Him.[1]

This passage from the *Scale of Perfection* obviously bears comparison with Geoffrey Chaucer's praise of the pagan 'Tartre Cambyuskan', 'noble kyng' of Tzarev, for keeping the 'lay' (law) of the religion into which he was born to such a superlative extent that he

I am grateful to James Simpson and Thorlac Turville-Petre for valuable comment on earlier versions of this paper, and to Jim Binns for discussion of some rather bizarre Latin.

[1] Walter Hilton, *Scale of Perfection*, ii. 3, ed. S. S. Hussey, 'An Edition, from the Manuscripts, of Book II of Walter Hilton's *Scale of Perfection*' (Ph.D. diss., University of London, 1962), 7–9.

exemplified all the virtues which are appropriate to the ideal ruler
and knight, being 'So excellent a lord in alle thyng'. Chaucer keeps
silent, however, on his prospects for salvation.

> Hym lakked noght that longeth to a kyng.
> As of the secte of which that he was born
> He kepte his lay, to which that he was sworn;
> And therto he was hardy, wys, and riche,
> And pitous and just, alwey yliche;
> Sooth of his word, benigne, and honurable;
> Of his corage as any centre stable;
> Yong, fressh, and strong, in armes desirous
> As any bacheler of al his hous.
> A fair persone he was and fortunat,
> And kept alwey so wel roial estat
> That ther was nowher swich another man.
>   (Squire's Tale, V (F) 16–27)[2]

Hilton's terminology is also remarkably similar to the language
used by William Langland in his treatment of the salvation of that
paradigmatic virtuous pagan, the Roman Emperor Trajan, who
'took nevere Cristendom':

> 'Ac truthe that trespased nevere ne traversed ayeins his lawe,
> But lyvede as his lawe taughte and leveth ther be no bettre,
> (And if ther were, he wolde amende) and in swich wille deieth—
> Ne wolde nevere trewe God but trewe truthe were allowed'.
>   (B XII. 284–7)[3]

---

[2] For an excellent bibliography of discussions of Chaucer in relation to Nominalism see Richard J. Utz and William H. Watts, 'Nominalist Perspectives on Chaucer's Poetry: A Bibliographical Essay', *M&H* NS 20 (1993), 147–73; see further the
relevant essays in Richard J. Utz (ed.), *Literary Nominalism and the Theory of
Rereading Late Medieval Texts* (Lewiston, NY, 1995), and W. J. Courtenay's forthcoming essay, 'The Dialectic of Divine Omnipotence in the Age of Chaucer: A
Reconsideration'.

[3] The scholarly literature on Langland and Nominalism is substantial; I have
taken special note of D. Baker, 'From Plowing to Penitence: *Piers Plowman* and
Fourteenth-Century Theology', *Speculum*, 55 (1980), 715–25; Janet Coleman,
'*Piers Plowman*' and the '*Moderni*' (Rome, 1981); Gordon Whatley, '*Piers Plow-
man* B 12.277–94: Notes on Language, Text, and Theology', *MP* 82 (1984), 1–12;
Pamela Gradon, '*Trajanus Redivivus*: Another Look at Trajan in *Piers Plowman*', in
Douglas Gray and E. G. Stanley (eds.), *Middle English Studies Presented to Nor-
man Davis* (Oxford, 1983), 95–114; Robert Adams, 'Piers's Pardon and Langland's
Semi-Pelagianism', *Traditio*, 39 (1983), 367–418, also his later review, 'Langland's
Theology', in John A. Alford (ed.), *A Companion to 'Piers Plowman'* (Berkeley and
Los Angeles, 1988), 87–114 (esp. pp. 107–9).

This chapter will concentrate on the ideas in these two passages, contextualizing them within the intellectual culture of their day and with reference to the relevant scholarly literature of ours. The term 'Nominalism' is a notoriously difficult one, of course; it has been stretched in many ways, as when (for example) it is taken as overlapping substantially with 'scepticism', a move which can be both confusing and sensationalizing. As W. J. Courtenay has recently reminded us, William of Ockham would almost certainly not have thought of himself as a Nominalist; for him the term would probably have denoted a supporter of the language-theory of Peter Abelard and/or his followers.[4] Elsewhere I have argued that some of Chaucer's ideas about language have many affinities with views expressed in twelfth-century treatises on terminist logic, including the work of Peter Abelard;[5] this body of doctrine was later significantly developed by English rather than French scholars.[6] However, most if not all of the ideas in question are to be found in Jean de Meun's section of the *Roman de la Rose*, and it is this source which Chaucer seems to have been following.

So, the prospects of identifying Chaucer as some sort of Nominalist by this route are remote and unrewarding. Therefore I shall use the term 'Nominalist' here *improprie* and *secundum communem usum loquendi*, as found in much recent criticism. My concern will be with the 'Nominalist questions' as termed and identified in Russell Peck's very helpful article,[7] questions which involved the dialectic of the divine power, the economy of grace and justification, the relationship between free will and destiny, and the nature of the covenant between God and man. The vexed question of salvation outside the Christian Church served, and will serve here, as a major point of intersection for these controversial issues.

By way of focusing on the *facere quod in se est* principle, it should be said at the outset that this was neither an exclusively Nominalist nor indeed an exclusively fourteenth-century idea.

[4] W. J. Courtenay, *Schools and Scholars in Fourteenth-Century England* (Princeton, 1987), 173 n., 205.

[5] A. J. Minnis, '*A leur faiz cousines*: Words and Deeds in Jean de Meun and Chaucer' (forthcoming).

[6] W. J. Courtenay, '*Antiqui* and *Moderni* in Late-Medieval Thought', *Journal of the History of Ideas*, 48 (1987), 3–10 (p. 6).

[7] R. Peck, 'Chaucer and the Nominalist Questions', *Speculum*, 53 (1978), 745–60.

Courtenay believes that it follows a general Franciscan tradition.[8] Indeed, versions of the doctrine appear in thinkers as far apart from William of Ockham, and from each other, as Alexander of Hales, OFM, Albert the Great, OP, and the secular masters Richard FitzRalph and Jean Gerson. The doctrine was controversial, certainly, as Hilton's attack makes abundantly clear. But that does not make it specifically Nominalist. It is more accurate to say that the idea was channelled, explored, and developed by certain so-called Nominalists, a good example of which may be found in the thought of the Oxford Dominican Robert Holcot (d. 1349).

It is generally assumed that Chaucer knew Holcot's popular commentary on the Book of Wisdom, a work which enjoyed a readership that went far beyond the clerical. The main proof that Chaucer consulted this work directly was offered in Robert Pratt's 1977 article on the Nun's Priest's knowledge of dream-theory, knowledge which, Pratt argued, derived from Chaucer's consultation of Holcot.[9] Having followed up Pratt's references and compared in detail Holcot's statements with Chaucer's text, I am rather less convinced than Pratt was. But let that pass for now; in principle I see no reason why Chaucer should or could not have read Holcot's Wisdom commentary. Now, here Holcot is generally more circumspect than he is in his *Sentences* commentary and his quodlibets, works written for a more specialist and select audience. Yet the Wisdom commentary does express clearly his belief that if a man 'does what is in him' God will not ignore him, but rather ensure that he is sufficiently informed concerning those things which are necessary for his salvation.[10] But if Chaucer did read the relevant passages, he has left no record of it. What he does share with Holcot—though he certainly did not have to go to Holcot for it—is 'classicism', if that term may be used in preference to the totalizing and potentially misleading term 'humanism'.[11]

---

[8] Courtenay, *Schools and Scholars*, 213; here the debt of Ockham to Duns Scotus in particular is emphasized.

[9] R. A. Pratt, 'Some Latin Sources of the Nonnes Preest on Dreams', *Speculum*, 52 (1977), 538–70. Behind this study lies the pioneering work of K. O. Petersen, the first person to postulate Holcot's influence: *Sources of the Nonnes Preestes Tale*, Radcliffe College Monographs 10 (Boston, 1896).

[10] See further the fuller account of Holcot's doctrine on pp. 158–9 below.

[11] On this distinction see A. J. Minnis, 'From Medieval to Renaissance? Chaucer's Position on Past Gentility', *PBA* 72 (1986), 205–46.

This brings us to consider the general issue of the relationship between 'classicism' and Nominalism. As is well known, Holcot's Wisdom commentary offers an abundance of classical lore, as it draws extensively on exegesis of secular texts and mythographic treatises, and of course demonstrates his own extensive knowledge of many ancient authors. On the face of it, an interest in those Nominalist questions which bear on heathen virtue and prospects for salvation is utterly consonant with an interest in the texts and cultural traditions of pagan antiquity. It seems reasonable to suppose that such debates encouraged and stimulated the scholarly study of the relics of the past. But one did not have to be a Nominalist to be a classicist. There is not a trace of a Nominalist question in, to take two highly influential works by 'classicizing friars', Nicholas Trevet's commentary on the *Consolatio philosophiae* of Boethius and John Ridevall's *Fulgentius metaforalis*. Or in the massive *Reductorium morale* by that classicising monk Pierre Bersuire, OSB, one part of which, the *Ovidius moralizatus*, Chaucer seems to have known.[12]

To reinforce this argument, let me invite you to hear the testimony of one fourteenth-century witness who, for the moment, shall remain anonymous. There is, he claims, no substantial article of the Christian faith which God did not reveal many times before the actual advent of Christianity. A lengthy defence of the veracity of many pagan foretellings and confirmations of revealed truth follows, including reference to the sibylline prophecies, the discovery during the reign of Constantine of a tomb in which there lay a man wearing a golden medallion which bore the inscription 'Christ will be born of the Virgin Mary, and I believe in him', the insight of the three wise men from the East who understood the significance of the star of Bethlehem, and Dionysius the Areopagite's admirable reaction to the solar eclipse which occurred at Christ's crucifixion, in the middle of the lunar month when such an event could not happen naturally. Are we dealing, then, with a Nominalist? Far from it: I have been paraphrasing a passage from the *De causa Dei* of Thomas Bradwardine,[13] that most vociferous critic of

---

[12] On Chaucer and Bersuire see M. Twycross, *The Medieval Anadyomene: A Study in Chaucer's Mythography*, Medium Ævum Monographs, NS 1 (Oxford, 1972); A. J. Minnis, *Chaucer and Pagan Antiquity* (Cambridge, 1982), 20–1, 109–14 *passim*, 116–18, also *The Shorter Poems*, Oxford Guides to Chaucer: The Shorter Poems (Oxford, 1995), 99, 192–3, 195–6, 199, 203.

[13] *De causa Dei*, I. I, coroll. 32; ed. Henry Savile (London, 1618), 29–37.

the 'pestiferous Pelagians', as he termed those who dared to subvert the Augustinian explanation of the relationship between
human merit and divine reward.

Bradwardine's classicism has not received the attention it
deserves. Moreover, his much-vaunted Augustinianism is not
exclusively a matter of theological doctrine (involving the construction of a strict necessitarianism), though that is certainly
true: it also functions on the level of literary genre and strategy
as well. For the model underlying Bradwardine's *De causa Dei* is
not the *Sentences* commentary or *summa* or quodlibetal collection,
but rather Augustine's *De civitate Dei*. The initials of the fuller title
of Bradwardine's text, *De causa Dei contra Pelagium*, replicate
those of Augustine's, *De civitate Dei contra paganos*. And the
fourteenth-century text follows the style of the earlier work by
introducing extensive quotations from classical writers into technical theological discussion, juxtaposing flights of rhetoric with
rigorous logical inquiry, and strategically placing pagan virtue and
knowledge in supportive and subordinate relation to definitive
Christian doctrine, with the superiority of revealed truth regularly
being proclaimed at the expense of heathen folly and falsehood. To
some extent, then, *De causa Dei* should be seen as part and parcel
of that same cultural movement which, in fourteenth-century England, produced no less than three commentaries on *De civitate
Dei*, written by Nicholas Trevet, Thomas Waleys, and John
Baconthorpe respectively.[14] It may be added that Bradwardine
and Holcot had access to the same library, the exceptional collection amassed by the noted bibliophile Richard de Bury, which was
well-stocked with both sacred and secular texts.

But let us return to the passage from Chaucer's *Squire's Tale*
which commends King Cambyuskan for doing the best he could.
The biblical text which is most apposite here is, of course, Romans
2: 14–15: 'For when the Gentiles, who have not the law, do by
nature those things that are of the law; these, having not the law,
are a law to themselves. Who shew the work of the law written in
their hearts, their conscience bearing witness to them.' Elaborating
on this at the beginning of his *Compendiloquium de vitis illustrium
philosophorum*, John of Wales, OFM, praises the lives of pagans

[14] On these commentaries see Beryl Smalley, *English Friars and Antiquity in the
Early Fourteenth Century* (Oxford, 1960), 54, 58–65 *passim*, 88–100, 102–5, 299.

who were virtuous despite the fact that they did not have the present law: Christians promise but do not practise what they receive as precepts, while the Gentiles kept those things to which they were not bound by legal obligation.[15] This had been all said before, of course, by Gregory the Great, in his *Moralia in Job*, to which John of Wales is indebted.

Is there anything new here under the sun? Not thus far, I think. What is crucial is the argument-context in which such material may be placed, the agenda which it is supposed to further. It is when one moves from praise of pagan virtue to consideration of the fate of the souls of virtuous pagans that the situation becomes critical. Chaucer, however, refuses to be drawn. At the end of the Knight's Tale the narrator professes ignorance regarding the destination of Arcite's spirit when it 'chaunged hous'. 'I nam no divinistre' (i.e. theologian) he protests; I find nothing about souls 'in this registre', i.e. the register of table of contents of the authoritative book he is allegedly following, this being an elliptical way of saying that his source is silent on the matter. 'Arcite is coold', may Mars guide his soul: but Chaucer does not speculate as to *where* Mars will guide his soul (1(A) 2809–15). Similarly, at the end of *Troilus and Criseyde*, we are told that the soul of Troilus goes to wherever it was that 'Mercurye sorted [i.e. allotted] hym to dwelle' (V. 1826–7). These passages contrast with the narrative which is in fact a primary source for them both, Boccaccio's account (near the end of the *Teseida*) of the ascent of Arcita's soul. For the Italian text had hinted that Arcita's soul may dwell in Elysium; he is not worthy of heaven itself, but it is not appropriate that he should dwell among 'blackened souls'.[16] However, Chaucer's attitude seems to be, 'To clerkes lete I al disputison' (here I borrow a phrase from Dorigen; Franklin's Tale, V (F) 890). It is worth recalling that a similar attitude is found in one of the major repositories of classicism in the European vernaculars, the 'romances of antiquity', those 'historical novels' about pagan antiquity which

---

[15] See W. A. Pantin, 'John of Wales and Medieval Humanism', in *Medieval Studies Presented to Aubrey Gwynn* (Dublin, 1961), 309; cf. Minnis, 'From Medieval to Renaissance?', 213–14.

[16] *Teseida*, Book x, stanzas 95 and 99; tr. B. McCoy (New York, 1974), 279. In his self-commentary Boccaccio describes Elysium as the dwelling-place of 'the souls of those who had been valiant and good men, who had not, however, deserved to become gods' (tr. McCoy, 286).

constitute the basic genre to which the Knight's Tale and *Troilus and Criseyde* belong.[17] There pagans are often commended, but the issue of their salvation is left very much alone—as when, for example, the *Roman d'Énéas* quotes Dido's epitaph as saying that no better pagan would ever have lived, had not 'solitary love seized her', without speculating about her afterlife.

> Iluec gist
> Dido qui por amor s'ocist;
> onques ne fu meillor paiene,
> s'ele n'eüst amor soltaine. (2139–42)[18]

Turning now to Chaucer's interest in predestination and future contingents, which receives its fullest expression in *Troilus and Criseyde*, I would suggest that here also there is a lack of evidence which would demonstrate the specific relevance of Nominalist theology. Chaucer's knowledge of the text and gloss of the *Consolatio philosophiae* is quite sufficient to account for all the substantive statements about freedom and destiny which feature in his constructions of virtuous heathen. Here I am referring to the 'Vulgate' text of Boethius along with Jean de Meun's French translation and the extensive commentary by 'classicizing friar' Nicholas Trevet, these being the sources of Chaucer's *Boece*.[19] Moreover, Trevet seems to have been the direct source of at least one, and possibly more, passages of the *Troilus*.[20]

In short, as far as Chaucer is concerned, there seems to be no necessity to allege the influence of radical, specifically Nominalist, ideas. And such influence should not be posited without necessity. The Squire's Tale passage stands alone, tantalizing and unsupported. And even there Chaucer does not speculate on the afterlife of a man whose life on earth was exemplary.

---

[17] On this genre see especially Barbara Nolan, *Chaucer and the Tradition of the 'Roman Antique'* (Cambridge, 1992), wherein the issue of pagan virtue is discussed extensively.

[18] *Énéas: Roman du XIIe siècle*, ed. J.-J. Salverda de Grave, 2 vols. (Paris, 1925–9), i. 66.

[19] For recent discussion see A. J. Minnis (ed.), *Chaucer's 'Boece' and the Medieval Tradition of Boethius* (Woodbridge, 1993).

[20] See A. J. Minnis, 'Aspects of the Medieval French and English Traditions of the *De consolatione Philosophiae*', in M. T. Gibson (ed.), *Boethius: His Life, Thought and Influence* (Oxford, 1981), 342; Minnis, *Chaucer and Pagan Antiquity*, 100.

Moving on now to Langland, the main passages in question are B XI. 140 ff. (C XII. 73 ff.) and XII. 209 ff. (C XIII. 149 ff. and XIV. 148 ff.), together with the recuperation of many of the main issues at B XV. 384 ff. (C XVII. 117 ff.). Trajan bursts into Langland's text by interrupting (most appropriately) a discussion of baptism which the Dreamer and Scripture are having. 'Baw for bokes!' As is witnessed by a pope, St Gregory the Great, the true knight Trajan 'was ded and dampned to dwellen in pyne | For an uncristene creature' (142–3). However, 'Gregorie ... wilned' salvation to his soul, on account of the

> 'soothnesse that he seigh in my werkes.
> And after that he wepte and wilned me were graunted grace,
> Withouten any bede biddyng his boone was underfongen,
> And I saved, as ye may see, withouten syngynge of masses,
> By love and by lernyng of my lyvynge in truthe,
> Broughte me fro bitter peyne ther no biddyng myghte.
> Lo! ye lordes, what leautee did by an Emperour of Rome
> That was an uncristene creature, as clerkes fyndeth in bokes.
> Nought thorugh preiere of a pope but for his pure truthe
> Was that Sarsen saved, as Seint Gregorie bereth witnesse.'
>
> (B XI. 147–56)

Langland proceeds to indicate his source for this story. In the *Legenda sanctorum*, he explains, may be found a fuller account (160), this being a reference to the *Legenda aurea* which the Dominican Jacobus de Voragine wrote around 1260, a work so popular that it survives in over 1,000 manuscripts. The Trajan episode forms part of Jacobus' life of St Gregory, which explains why Langland is adamant that a pope witnessed to Trajan's salvation. This 'paynym of Rome' was pulled out of pain on account of 'leel love and lyvyng in truthe': blessed be the truth which broke hell's gates in this way, and saved the 'Sarsyn'[21] from Satan's power—something which 'no clergie' could (161–75). Trajan's subsequent monologue includes the citation of Christ's words at Luke 7: 50 to the prostitute (generally identified as Mary Magdalene, following John 11: 2) to the effect that *fides sua* should save her and cure her of sin (216–17). This is taken as proving that faith ('bileve') is a 'leel' (trusty, loyal) help, standing 'above logyk or lawe' (218).

---

[21] Here 'Saracen' (=Muslim) is of course used as a synonym for 'heathen' or 'pagan'.

'Of logyk ne of lawe in *Legenda Sanctorum*
Is litel alowaunce maad, but if bileve hem helpe.' (B XI. 219–20)

Similarly, in B XII, Ymaginatif argues that Trajan did not dwell 'depe' in hell, and so our Lord was able to get him out of there 'lightly', easily (209–10); a similar resolution may be offered to the problem of the penitent thief who was saved at the crucifixion—'he is in the loweste of hevene' (211). There are, in other words, degrees of punishment and reward, and that fact should be taken into account when considering such difficult matters. Whether Socrates and Solomon are saved or not, no man can tell. But, particularly in view of the fact that God gave such teachers intelligence, whereby those who have come after have been instructed, we may 'hope' that 'God for his grace' may give 'hir soules reste' (269–72). But Christian clerics, protests the Dreamer, all believe that 'neither Sarsens ne Jewes' nor any creature who lacks 'Cristendom' may be saved (274–6)—a proposition which Ymaginatif disputes. He was not alone: as we shall see, many Christian clerics would have disagreed with the Dreamer's blanket statement; Langland is setting up an extreme statement in order that it may be challenged. So, 'Contra!', exclaims Ymaginatif. The 'just man shall scarcely be saved' on the Day of Judgment (1 Peter 4: 18), which must mean that he *shall* be saved.

'Troianus was a trewe knyght and took nevere Cristendom,
And he is saaf, so seith the book, and his soule in hevene'. (280–1)

'The book' is generally assumed to be the *Legend aurea*; the statement that Trajan 'took nevere Cristendom' emphasizes the fact that he was unbaptized. Ymaginatif then explains that there are three kinds of baptism, before going on to make the apparent allusion to the *facere quod in se est* principle (284–7) which was quoted at the beginning of this chapter.

According to Janet Coleman, 'What is most significant' in Langland's exemplum of Trajan (as it appears in both the B- and C-texts of *Piers Plowman*) 'is that God can and does respond to him who does his best *ex puris naturalibus*, and this response, this acceptance, is what ultimately matters in the fact of salvation'.[22] And Robert Adams avers that Ymaginatif 'revels in the naïve Pelagianism of the story', using it to broach 'the possibility that

[22] Coleman, *'Piers Plowman' and the 'Moderni'*, 133–4.

God saves all whose lives conform to the natural law of Truth, regardless of sacramental support or explicit faith'.[23] I would like to approach such claims through, in the first instance, a consideration of what may advisedly be called the mainstream theological tradition relating to the different kinds of baptism, as alluded to at B XII. 282–3:

> 'Ac ther is fullynge of font and fullynge in blood shedyng,
> And thorugh fir is fullyng, and that is ferme bileve...'[24]

This doctrine is expounded well in that most successful of all medieval theological textbooks, the *Libri sententiarum* of Peter Lombard, who will serve as a guide along this wicked way.[25]

The Lombard firmly distinguishes between the sacrament and the thing itself (the *res* or referent as opposed to the 'sacrament' or symbol). Some people have the sacrament but not the *res*, while others have the *res* but not the sacrament. In the case of the last of these, he continues, it may be argued that martyrdom (*passio*) performs the function of baptism (*vis baptismi*). Furthermore, the Lombard quotes Augustine and Ambrose as being of the opinion that certain people can be justified and saved without baptism by water (*baptismus fluminis*). On the other hand, he continues, at John 3: 5 Christ said, 'unless a man be born again of water and the Holy Ghost, he cannot enter into the kingdom of God'. If this is true in general, then the statements cited above cannot be correct. The Master demolishes this contrary opinion with the argument that Christ's condemnation applies to those who could be baptized but are contemptuous of the sacrament. Or the words may be understood as meaning that unless a man experiences the regeneration which comes through water and the Holy Ghost, he cannot be saved, the point being that *baptismus fluminis* is not the *only*

---

[23] Adams, 'Piers's Pardon', 392.

[24] The clause 'and that is ferme bileve' has been taken as a gloss on 'fullyng' by 'fir', the idea being that here is an allusion to the relationship between steadfast faith and *baptismus flaminis* (cf. the ways in which Aquinas and Bonaventure explain this, cited on pp. 153 and 154–5 below). On the other hand, 'and that is ferme bileve' may be understood as a statement concerning the entire doctrine of the three kinds of baptism as explained in this passage; i.e. all that has been said here constitutes a 'ferme bileve' of Christianity. This suggestion is lent support by the C-text reading, 'and al is ferme bileue' (ed. Pearsall, XIV. 208).

[25] Book IV, dist. iv, cap. 4; in *Sententiae in IV Libris Distinctae*, 3rd edn., 2 vols. (Grottaferrata, 1971–81), ii. 255–9.

possible means of achieving that regeneration. Support for this view is sought in the *Glossa ordinaria* on Hebrews 6: 1–2, where it is said that baptism should be understood in several senses, 'because there is baptism by water, by blood, and by repentance'.

These statements were mulled over by generation after generation of *Sentences* commentators and compilers of *summae*. Only baptism by water is a sacrament, St Thomas Aquinas explains in his *Summa theologiae*, but a person can receive the effect of baptism through either baptism by blood (*baptismus sanguinis*) or baptism by fire (*baptismus flaminis*).[26] *Baptismus flaminis*, which is baptism by the Holy Spirit, 'takes place when the heart is moved by the Holy Spirit to believe in and love God and to repent of one's sins. For this reason it is called baptism of repentance (*baptismus penitentiae*).' In his earlier *Sentences* commentary Aquinas gave an account of how *baptismus sanguinis* confirms Christ's passion not by sacramental representation but 'in reality' (*realiter*); therefore it is not the sacrament but the *res* itself. *Baptismus penitentiae* is here discussed with reference to someone who wants to be baptized but is prevented from receiving the sacrament; in that case someone can be saved 'by faith alone and contrition'.[27] A similar view is expressed in Bonaventure's commentary on the same passage of the *Sentences*. The fact that someone can be saved by means other than *baptismus fluminis* does not render it a non-essential sacrament, for it was laid down by divine precept, and in so far as precepts are necessary for salvation therefore baptism by water is necessary. But since God is not obligated to act by the precepts he himself has instituted, if someone has the will to receive baptism but not the opportunity then *baptismus flaminis* will suffice. However, a person who is able to receive *baptismus fluminis* but does not do so is not saved.

[26] *Summa theologiae*, 3a 66. 11, responsio; Blackfriars edn., 61 vols. (London, 1964–81), lvii. 48–9. By rendering *baptismus flaminis* as 'baptism by fire' I am following Langland's translation; alternatively it may be rendered baptism of the 'wind' or 'blowing' or indeed 'of the spirit'; cf. the note by James Cunningham, *Summa theologiae*, lvii. 48. The conflation of *flamma* ('fire') and *flamen* ('a blowing') is understandable in view of the account of Pentecost in Acts 2: 2–4, 'And suddenly there came a sound from heaven, as of a mighty wind coming...And there appeared to them parted tongues, as it were of fire...And they were all filled with the Holy Ghost.'

[27] *In IV Sent.*, dist. iv, qu. 3, art. 3, questiunc. 2, in *Opera omnia*, 25 vols. (Parma, 1852–72), vii. 520.

Returning to what Peter Lombard himself says, it is important to note that he proceeds to expound the *fides sufficit* doctrine which (as we shall see) was vitally important for Langland. If baptism suffices for the salvation of very young children who are unable to believe, argues the Lombard, how much more must faith suffice for adults who desire baptism but are unable to receive it? Augustine asks the question, 'which is greater, faith or water?' and answers, 'faith'. This is supported by Christ's words, 'he that believeth in me, although he be dead, shall live' (John 11: 25). But what about those who were unable to believe in Christ specifically, because they could not possibly know of him, due to their historical circumstances?[28] Could a special dispensation be allowed to them, just as it was to those who were unable to be baptized, though they wanted to be? Peter Lombard is silent on that issue; he is not talking about virtuous heathen, though of course his words easily lend themselves to being invoked in that context. Several of the *Sentences* commentators did precisely that. St Bonaventure, for instance, considered the case of the 'good pagan' Cornelius the Centurion (as described in Acts 10), who first received the Holy Spirit and subsequently was baptized with water.[29] This does not mean that *baptismus flaminis* cannot effect salvation, Bonaventure declares, but rather that if there is nothing to prevent one from being baptized by water then one should certainly receive the sacrament. Cornelius was in the right place at the right time. The clear

---

[28]   However, as has often been noted (see e.g. Adams, 'Langland's Theology', 98), Trajan was born well after the beginning of the Christian era, and hence his historical circumstances were highly favourable. As Adams says ('Langland's Theology', 98), 'the standard opinion was that such persons could enter heaven only through baptism', given that the Christian belief system was on offer to them. However, vernacular writers often blurred together pagans from various historical periods into a single vague category. Hence Chaucer is not interested in stating that his 'Tartre Cambyuskan' was born after the advent of Christ (if we may assume that Chaucer had in mind a historical character such as Genghis Khan or Kublai Khan). Besides, none of the scholastic applications of the Trajan story which I have read specifically raises this issue in considering his salvation. And such a questioning of the emperor's acumen is, as one would expect, quite absent from 'classicizing' accounts of Trajan, such as John of Salisbury's, wherein he is presented as 'the epitome not only of benignly just and successful rulership, of government based on rational virtue and natural wisdom, but also of personal morality and justice', as Gordon Whatley puts it: 'The Uses of Hagiography: The Legend of Pope Gregory and the Emperor Trajan in the Middle Ages', *Viator*, 15 (1984), 25–63 (p. 33).

[29]   *In IV Sent.*, dist. iv, P. 2, art. 1, qu. 1, in *Opera omnia*, 10 vols. (Quaracchi, 1882–1902), iv. 106–7.

implication is, if that had not been the case then he would have been saved by *baptismus flaminis*. Earlier Bonaventure had quoted John 11: 26, 'every one that liveth and believeth in me shall not die for ever'. The *iusti* believed and were of the faith before they were baptized; therefore, had they died in such faith they would not have been eternally damned. *Gratia gratum faciens* is a disposition sufficient for salvation, as when one returns to God with one's whole heart and withdraws from error. This can occur through divine grace without baptism by water, and therefore it is possible for a person to be saved by *baptismus flaminis* alone.

In bringing the doctrine of the various types of baptism to bear on the issue of the salvation of the heathen Langland was following the tradition of the *Sentences* commentaries in general; he did not need Nominalism in particular to help him find that thread. Trajan was a tougher test-case than Cornelius, but Langland did not need to read Neopelagian theology to be aware of the depth and extent of the controversy surrounding that figure. For that was made abundantly clear by the *Legenda aurea* itself, in a passage which represents one of that text's few forays into the area of speculative theology.

On this subject some have said that Trajan was restored to life, and in this life obtained grace and merited pardon: thus he attained glory and was not finally committed to hell nor definitively sentenced to eternal punishment. There are others who have said that Trajan's soul was not simply freed from being sentenced to eternal punishment, but that his sentence was suspended for a time, namely, until the day of the Last Judgment. Others have held that Trajan's punishment was assessed to him *sub conditione* as to place and mode of torment, the condition being that sooner or later Gregory would pray that through the grace of Christ there would be some change of place or mode. Still others, among them John the Deacon who compiled this legend, say that Gregory did not pray, but wept, and often the Lord in his mercy grants what a man, however desirous he might be, would not presume to ask for, and that Trajan's soul was not delivered from hell and given a place in heaven, but was simply freed from the tortures of hell.... Then there are those who explain that eternal punishment is two-fold, consisting first in the pain of sense and second in the pain of loss, i.e. being deprived of the vision of God. Thus Trajan's punishment would have been remitted as to the first pain but retained as to the second.[30]

---

[30] *Jacobus de Voragine: The Golden Legend*, tr. W. G. Ryan, 2 vols. (Princeton, 1993), i. 179; for the Latin text see *Legenda aurea: Vulgo historia Lombardica*

Moreover, Langland's constant reference to the *Legenda* is remark-able in a text which is notorious for the way in which it covers the tracks of its sources. Why should he be so concerned to refer us to Jacobus? Because this was a safe source to cite, given its author's high reputation and unimpeachable orthodoxy, or simply because it was the main determinant of his own discussion? Or even both?

The situation is further complicated by the fact that, when a card-carrying Nominalist (still using that term according to the common *usus loquendi* of recent criticism) treats of the three types of bap-tism, the results may seem far from controversial. In a quodlibet wherein he argues that observance of the Mosaic law merited eternal life, Robert Holcot insists on the importance of grace.[31] An unnamed colleague (*socius*) had suggested that a person can be saved without baptism or grace. If one is thinking of baptism by water, Holcot argues, it may be pointed out that no catholic believes such baptism to be necessary for salvation in the sense that without it a man cannot be saved. Building on Peter Lombard, Holcot notes that two other kinds of baptism (by the shedding of blood and by fire) are equally efficacious. However, as far as grace is concerned, there is no doubt that a man who lacks it is damned. Apparently it is the *socius* who is the radical rather than Holcot. Who, then, is the Nominalist; will the pestiferous Pelagians stand up and be counted? Apparently not. At least, not here.

But Bradwardine certainly had a point. The clerics he was opposing were far from being mere rhetorical men of straw. Neo-pelagian ideas (or what were perceived as such) were certainly current, and they could worry figures like Walter Hilton and Archbishop Simon Langham, who in a 1368 mandate to the Chancellor of Oxford University labelled as an 'error' the proposi-tion that 'someone can merit eternal life *ex puris naturalibus*'.[32] It

---

dicta, ed. T. Graesse, 3rd edn. (1890, repr. Osnabrück, 1969), 196–7. The first of these theories loosely follows Aquinas's *Sentences* commentary, while the second is a verbatim quotation from it. John the Deacon's 9th-cent. *Vita sancti Gregorii* (printed in *PL* 75, 59–242) takes the line that Gregory merely wept for Trajan, whose degree of suffering in hell was thereby lessened: the emperor was not actually released from his place of torment. Cf. Whatley, 'Uses of Hagiography', 28–30.

[31] Paolo Molteni, *Roberto Holcot O.P.: Dotttrina della grazia e della giustifica-zione, con due questioni quodlibetali inedite* (Pinerolo, 1967), 174–204.

[32] *Concilia Magnae Brittaniae et Hiberniae*, ed. David Wilkins, 4 vols. (London, 1737), iii. 76; cited and discussed by James Simpson, 'The Constraints of Satire in *Piers Plowman* and *Mum and the Sothsegger*', in Helen Phillips (ed.), *Langland, the*

is also indubitable that certain aspects of Nominalist thought put great pressure on the conventional ideology of baptism. Some of them must therefore be considered at this point.

In exemplifying the subversive teaching of the alleged ringleader of the gang of 'Nominalists', William of Ockham, it is *de rigueur* to cite instances of his invocation of the absolute power of God.[33] And it is perfectly true that, according to Ockham, through the exercise of his *potentia absoluta* God can condemn the best of saints and save the worst of sinners. However, the extent to which such a claim is genuinely subversive is very debatable. Of course, some of Ockham's contemporaries did find it problematic. The masters who criticized fifty-one articles from his *Sentences* commentary at Avignon in 1326 refused to accept the excuse that God's absolute power functioned most infrequently; Ockham's argument, they declared, proceeded equally well without that condition as with it (which I take to mean that the impact of what Ockham was saying was not lessened by his appeal to *potentia absoluta*).[34] In sharp contrast, a far more positive approach has been taken by one of the most influential of Ockham's modern advocates, Philotheus Boehner, who believed that the *potentia absoluta* should be seen in terms of ultimate possibility.[35] On this interpretation, what are at issue are things

---

Mystics and the Medieval English Religious Tradition: Essays in Honour of S. S. Hussey (Woodbridge, 1990), 11–30 (p. 15).

[33] For late-medieval thought on God's absolute and ordained power see esp. H. A. Oberman, *The Harvest of Medieval Theology: Gabriel Biel and Late Medieval Nominalism*, rev. edn. (Grand Rapids, Mich. 1967), 30–56; Gordon Leff, *William of Ockham: The Metamorphosis of Scholastic Discourse* (Manchester, 1975), 14–18, 106–10, 359–60, 471–5, 477, 507–16, 513–14, etc.; W. J. Courtenay, *Covenant and Causality in Medieval Thought* (London, 1984); Marilyn McCord Adams, *William Ockham*, 2 vols. (Notre Dame, Ind., 1987), ii. 1186–207; Eugenio Randi, *Il sovrano e l'orologiaio: Due immagini di Dio nel dibattito sulla 'potentia absoluta' fra XIII e XIV secolo* (Florence, 1987); Stephen F. Brown, 'Abelard and the Medieval Origins of the Distinction between God's Absolute and Ordained Power', in M. D. Jordan and K. Emery Jr. (eds.), *Ad litteram: Authoritative Texts and their Medieval Readers* (Notre Dame, Ind., (1992), 199–215; Lawrence Moonan, *Divine Power: The Medieval Power Distinction up to its Adoption by Albert, Bonaventure, and Aquinas* (Oxford, 1994).

[34] 'Argumentum suum eque procedit absque illa condicione sicut cum illa': A. Pelzer, 'Les 51 articles de Guillaume Occam censurés en Avignon en 1326', *Revue d'histoire ecclésiastique*, 18 (1922), 240–71 (p. 252); cf. Gordon Leff, *Bradwardine and the Pelagians* (Cambridge, 1957), 191.

[35] *Ockham: Philosophical Writings*, ed. and tr. P. Boehner (London, 1957), pp. xix–xx, xlviii–xlix.

which God is able to do but might never do, and if he were to do any of them we would speak of a miracle. Miracles not being everyday occurrences, for most of the time one can be confident of the predictable and secure governance of the *potentia ordinata*; hence the somewhat sensational claims which some have made for the *potentia absoluta* are rather misleading.

Whatever the truth of this matter may be, the Ockhamist line on merit *de congruo* presented much more of a challenge to the traditional economy of grace and salvation: significantly, Bradwardine spent a lot of time attacking that particular doctrine.[36] Congruent merit involved 'half merit', 'an act performed in a state of sin, in accordance with nature or divine law' which was 'accepted by God as satisfying the requirement for the infusion of first grace'.[37] (By contrast, actions informed by grace, with established supernatural 'habits' behind them, merited *de condigno*, i.e. were fully meritorious.) Men could perform individual good deeds without a fixed supernatural *habitus* of charity behind those actions and God could accept them as meritorious *de congruo*. In this regard Ockham defended himself against the charge of Pelagianism by saying that God is not *obliged* to accept men who have rendered themselves acceptable to him (here the *potentia absoluta* came in very useful).[38] The crucial point, however, was that God had freely bound himself to reward such good deeds; under the *potentia ordinata* a righteous man living *in puris naturalibus* was inevitably rewarded with an infusion of grace: 'de potentia Dei ordinata non potest non infundere.'[39] Robert Holcot developed this aspect of Ockham's thought. In his Wisdom commentary we

[36] Cf. Leff, *Bradwardine and the Pelagians*, 74–9; id., *William of Ockham*, 493–5.

[37] Oberman, *Harvest of Medieval Theology*, 471–2; cf. Leff, *William of Ockham*, 494–5.

[38] 'Pelagius held that grace is not in fact required in order to have eternal life, but that an act elicited in a purely natural state merits eternal life condignly. I, on the other hand, claim that such an act is meritorious only through God's absolute power accepting it [as such].' *Quodlibet VI*, qu. 1, art. 1, tr. Alfred J. Freddoso, *William of Ockham: Quodlibetal Questions*, 2 vols. (New Haven, 1991), ii. 493. On Ockham's insistence on the freedom of God see further H. R. Klocker, 'Ockham and the Divine Freedom', *Franciscan Studies*, 45 (1985), 245–61; also McCord Adams, *William Ockham*, ii. 1257–347.

[39] *In Sent.*, iv, qu. 10–11, in *Guillelmi de Ockham: Opera philosophica et theologica*, Editiones Instituti Franciscani Universitatis S. Bonaventurae (St Bonaventure, NY, 1974–   ), vii. 233 (ll. 14–15).

find the argument that works done out of natural goodness are meritorious *de congruo*; they meet the standard required in order to ensure a generous divine response. If a man 'does what is in him' God will reciprocate by doing what is in Him.[40] According to God's ordained power, if a good pagan walks by the best light he has, he will merit, and receive, his eternal reward. Here, then, is the ideological context in which Holcot's insistence on grace (as noted above) may be placed. It is not so traditional after all.

All this, I believe, is far removed from the attitudes which Langland expresses at B XV. 384 ff. (C XVII. 117 ff.), which may now be discussed, after which we will consider the relationship of that passage to *Piers Plowman*'s version of the Trajan story. At B XV. 384–9 Langland's treatment of the notion that faith alone can ensure salvation makes it utterly clear that here he is thinking, at least in the first instance, of how this functions within, rather than outside, the Christian Church—in short, at this point his perspective is very similar to that of the 'Master of the Sentences' as described above. Sometimes clerics do not perform their proper functions, and fail to teach the 'folk of holy kirke' adequately. In this case, *sola fides sufficit* to save such uneducated people. However, then the speaker, Anima, proceeds to add the remark that *sola fides sufficit* can function for non-Christians also: 'And so may Sarsens be saved, scribes and Jewes' (389). Are we, then, back in the world of B XII. 284–7 (as quoted at the very beginning of this chapter), which voices the hope that genuine 'truthe' will be rewarded by God, no matter what 'lawe' is being followed? Apparently not—for Anima quickly explains exactly what is meant by this last remark. Muslims have a belief which approximates to Christianity, inasmuch as they also believe in one creator-God. Indeed, Muhammad was a Christian himself, who, having been frustrated in his ambition of becoming pope (!), set about misleading the people of Syria to whom he preached. Therefore the clear implication is that any hopes of salvation which Muslims may have are based on the extent to which their beliefs are fundamentally or residually Christian; that salvific *sola fides* is solely the faith of Christianity.[41]

[40] Cf. Oberman, *Harvest of Medieval Theology*, 235–48.

[41] Cf. the even more cautious statement of Scripture at B X. 344–55, that mere baptism (apparently *baptismus fluminis*) may suffice *in extremis* for the salvation of 'Sarsens and Jewis', but more is required of 'Cristene men'.

A little later, in the context of a discussion of the conversion of
England by St Augustine, Anima remarks that the heathen are like
'heath' or uncultivated land. This evokes a vision of a 'wilde
wildernesse' in which 'wilde beestes' spring up, 'Rude and unres-
onable', running around without keepers (458–60). So much, then,
for the restraining and civilizing force of *lex naturalis*. Likewise,
Anima declares, a newly born child is thought of as a heathen as
far as heaven is concerned, until it is baptized in Christ's name and
confirmed by the bishop. Here the importance of baptism is
affirmed. And all of these comments, I believe, serve as a contrast
with what was said about Muslims, who have, so to speak,
received some cultivation, and therefore are in a different situation
from pagans and newly born children. It is logical for Anima to go
on to say that since 'Sarsens', with 'pharisees', 'Jewes', 'scribes and
Grekes', are 'folk of oon feith' in that they honour 'the fader God',
it is relatively easy for them to add the other tenets of the Christian
creed to this the first one, 'Credo in Deum patrem omnipoten-
tem…' (B XV. 604 ff.) Once again, the necessity of believing in
specifically Christian doctrine is being hammered home. True,
'faith alone' may suffice for the salvation of those 'Sarsens' and
others (here Langland does not pursue that thought), but Christianity alone brings security, and the main advantage which such
people have is clearly defined in terms of the extent to which they
have been prepared to receive the full Christian message, because
of what they know already.

Langland makes his views even more clear in the C-text's
version of this excursus, which I see as an amplification and
elaboration of his views rather than some later shift in his
thinking in sympathy with a 'Lollard enthusiasm for conversion',
as Coleman has argued.[42] The point about *sola fides* being
sufficient for the salvation of Christians is extended with the
remark that, if priests do their job properly, we shall 'do the
bettre'. Moreover, Muslims may be saved also—but now
the condition is made fully and uncompromisingly explicit.
Within their lifespan they have to come to believe in holy
Church:

---

[42] *'Piers Plowman' and the 'Moderni'*, 141.

'Saresyns mowe be saued so yf thei so by-leyuede,
In the lengthynge of here lyf to leyue on holychurche'.
(C XVIII. 123–4; Skeat text)[43]

Thus, the necessity of conversion receives more emphasis. Jews, Gentiles, and Muslims live in accordance with law, though their specific laws are diverse, and they all love and believe in one and the same God Almighty. But our Lord 'loueth no loue' unless 'lawe be the cause' (136). The meaning of 'lawe' is rather unclear here, and Liberum Arbitrium (for he has taken over the role of Anima) proceeds to talk of law in rather a broad sense. Lechers and thieves are identified as people who love against the law, whereas those who love 'as lawe techeth' behave in a way which is in accord with charity. Seeking clarification, the Dreamer asks if Muslims know what charity is (150), to be told that they may love in a way which approximates to it, thanks to the law of nature. It is perfectly natural for a creature to honour its creator. But many men do not love him in the correct way; neither do they live in accordance with trusty belief, for they believe in a 'mene', i.e. a false mediator:

'Ac many manere men þer ben, as Sarresynes and Iewes,
Louyeth nat þat lorde aryht as by þe Legende *Sanctorum*
And lyuen oute of lele byleue for they leue on a mene'.
(C XVII. 156–8)

Muslims live after the teaching of Muhammad 'and by lawe of kynde', this being a good example of how, when nature takes its course 'and no contrarie fyndeth' (i.e. finds no belief system to restrain and cultivate it), both law and loyalty suffer: 'Thenne is lawe ylefte and leute vnknowe' (162). Clearly, Langland is here a lot less confident about the efficacy of what may be achieved *ex puris naturalibus* than Ockham and Holcot seem to be on several occasions. Followers of 'Macumeth' live in a state in which they are partly educated and partly uneducated ('as wel lered as lewed', 182), continues Liberum Arbitrium, and since our Saviour allowed such people to be deceived by a false prophet, it is up to 'holy men' to put matters right by converting them. Once again, the point is being made that clergymen should do their job properly.

---

[43] Here I cite W. W. Skeat's edition of the C-text (*The Vision of William Concerning Piers the Plowman, in Three Parallel Texts*, 2 vols. (Oxford, 1886), i. 461), which at this point I prefer to Pearsall's reading (= XVII. 123–4; p. 283). Hereafter all citations of the C-text are from Pearsall's edition.

'Holy men, as y hope, thorw helpe of the holy goste
Sholden conuerte hem to Crist and cristendoem to take'.

(C XVII. 185–6)

In the C-text's reformulation, then, Langland's excursus is concerned to affirm the superiority of Christianity over other belief systems rather than to explore the possibilities for salvation outside the Church—as were adumbrated earlier by both the B-text and the C-text. There is no trace of an appeal to the *potentia absoluta*. Indeed, so conservative here is Langland's maintenance of the standards of what some called the *potentia ordinata* that there seems to be no reason to bring the 'power distinction' to bear on the above-mentioned passages at all.

If it may be granted that in B XV. 384 ff., and more conclusively in the corresponding C-text passage, Langland's thought is at least avoiding or at most opposing certain theological doctrines which have been identified as Nominalist, the crucial question then arises, what is the structural and argumentative relationship between this material and the earlier passages in which we are offered 'naïve Pelagianism'?[44] Janet Coleman stresses the dialectical aspect of *Piers Plowman*,[45] an idea which I would wish to elaborate. When reading a scholastic *quaestio* one must not make the assumption that the initial definition of the proposition, and the arguments offered, whether pro or contra, express the personal views of the disputant. Rather those are to be sought in the ultimate *determinatio*.[46] Clear evidence of this strategy is often to be found in *Piers Plowman*, though (unfortunately for Langland's modern exegetes) what is speculative research and what is determination lacks the clear structuring and labelling which is characteristic of the formal academic *quaestio*. On this approach, then, B XI. 140 ff. (C XII. 73 ff.) and XII. 210 ff. (C XIV. 148 ff.) propose a radical solution to the problem of salvation outside holy Church, while the passages we have just discussed offer, however obliquely and imprecisely, Langland's last—and much more conservative—word on the matter.

---

[44] Adams, 'Piers's Pardon', 392.
[45] 'Piers Plowman' and the 'Moderni', 126, 134, 146, 195.
[46] Moreover, quite extraordinary opinions were sometimes expressed in the form of *dubitationes* ('doubtful statements'); thus the scholastic method could license the expressions of radical, even bizarre, thoughts, ultimately controlling them within the framework of the disputation.

I have much sympathy with this methodology, but feel obliged to enter one major caveat, namely that the difference between the supposedly 'radical' thesis and the supposedly 'conservative' resolution may not be as great as some have supposed. The role of St Gregory as mediator (at B XI. 140ff.) has, in my view, been neglected by those readers who wish to highlight those elements which may be seen in terms of the allegedly Pelagian view that Trajan has merited his salvation and that God is obliged to accept him. (Here we are talking in terms of acceptance *de potentia ordinata*. Obviously, in theory and *de potentia absoluta* God could reject Trajan.) But I believe that the passage can be read quite differently. Here Langland is fundamentally concerned with making a contrast between love and learning, and therefore Gregory's own clerical credentials are conveniently forgotten. Indeed, the saint is credited with having been fully aware of the fact that love, loyalty, and merit weigh a lot more (as it were) than the power of the entire Christian clergy:

> 'al the clergie under Crist ne myghte me cracche fro helle
> But oonliche love and leautee and my laweful domes.
> Gregorie wiste this wel...' (B XI. 144–6)

And because Gregory knew this well, he desired salvation for Trajan's soul:

> 'and wilned to my soule
> Savacion for soothnesse that he seigh in my werkes.
> And after that he wepte and wilned me were graunted grace...'
> (B XI. 146–8)

Clearly, there is a lot of 'willing' going on here, and note also the expression of the fact that St Gregory saw, and wept. The saint, in other words, was the initiator. It was *he* who made the judgement that Trajan's achievements were worthy of some reward: here is no exclusive reliance on congruent merit, no illustration of the principle that *facientibus quod in se est Deus non denegat gratiam*. For no matter to what extent Trajan had done what was in him, if Gregory had not intervened God would not have given the pagan his grace. There was nothing normative about this case, as is implied in Holcot's formulation of the general principle (cf. p. 159 above). Neither is there any evidence here of a 'baptism by fire'—once again, that would make Gregory's patronage of

Trajan quite superfluous. For in that situation Trajan would have been saved already, and certainly not in need of a rescue from hell.

Indeed, the 'love' which helped Trajan to salvation must surely be, at least in part, the saint's love rather than Trajan's. That would seem to be what is meant in the following lines, where this notion is coupled with the idea that it was Gregory who discovered (or 'learned') that this virtuous heathen had lived in truth:

> 'Withouten any bede biddyng his boone was underfongen,
> And I saved, as ye may see, withouten syngynge of masses,
> By love and by lernyng of my lyvynge in truthe,
> Broughte me fro bitter peyne ther no biddyng myghte.'
>
> (B XI. 149–52)

If Holcot's views are right, then this discovery was utterly redundant, for God would have responded to Trajan's truth within the usual order of things, *de potentia dei ordinata*. But what about the apparent emphasis on the lack of efficacy (in this case) of prayer ('bede biddyng') or the singing of masses? After all, as the text goes on to specify, it is not just anyone's prayer that is in question here, but the prayer of a pope:

> 'Lo! ye lordes, what leautee did by an Emperour of Rome
> That was an uncristene creature, as clerkes fyndeth in bokes.
> Nought thorough preiere of a pope but for his pure truthe
> Was that Sarsen saved, as Seint Gregorie bereth witnesse.'
>
> (B XI. 153–6)

These lines can easily be taken to mean that Trajan was saved not on account of Pope Gregory but because of his 'pure truthe', with Gregory playing the role of mere witness and confirmer of an event in which he was fundamentally uninvolved. But that, I believe, is to make a part-cause of Trajan's salvation into the whole. The other part-cause was not, as the text makes abundantly clear, any prayer made formally by Gregory. Rather it was the pope's other actions. He saw ('seigh'), wept ('wepte'), and desired ('wilned'), and 'his boone was underfongen',[47] 'withouten any bede biddyng' and 'nought thorough preiere'. For prayer simply did not come into

---

[47] The term 'boone' may be Englishing the Latin term *petitio* as used in Jacobus' report of what was said by the voice of God: 'I have granted your petition.' Cf. *Legenda aurea*, ed. Graesse, 196.

it—Gregory's 'boone' or request was conveyed by other means, and duly granted ('underfongen') by God. The distinction I am drawing attention to here is utterly precedented in Langland's source, the *Legenda aurea*: 'Still others, among them John the Deacon who compiled this legend, say that Gregory did not pray, but wept, and often the Lord in his mercy grants what a man, however desirous he might be, would not presume to ask for.' Jacobus also reports the opposite point of view, that Gregory was indeed 'pouring forth prayers for Trajan', and so it would seem that Langland has made a definite decision here, in face of the various options.

The originality of this recontextualizing of Trajan should be recognized. The emperor often appears in scholastic discussions of the efficacy of suffrages for the dead;[48] perhaps that (in part at least) is why, in his desire to break new ground, Langland is so emphatic that 'bede biddyng' and 'syngynge of masses' do not provide a ready answer to the problem. Trajan does not feature in the major scholastic discussions of the different types of baptism; rather it is the centurion Cornelius who tends to appear when *baptismus flaminis* is at issue. But why did Langland strike out on his own, and privilege tears over prayers?[49] Because this is utterly appropriate here, within the context of this particular discussion in its entirety. In B XI. 140 ff. feelings (particularly love) are being

---

[48] As is well brought out in Whatley's excellent article, 'Uses of Hagiography'.

[49] My argument concerning the significance of Gregory's tears has been partly anticipated by Gradon ('*Trajanus Redivivus*', 104), who however takes the text's rejection of masses as possible evidence of Langland's concern 'to point out that Trajan was saved by his own merits'. But this rejection may be explained, at least in part, by the argument that masses are being seen as an aspect of clergial learning, which here is being opposed not only to specific achievement but also to spiritual 'affection' in general, as I suggest later. Even more importantly, the rejection of masses certainly does not constitute a rejection of Gregory's role altogether. See further Whatley ('Uses of Hagiography', 53), who, whilst noting the influence of 'the old hagiographical tradition established by John the Deacon' that 'Gregory did not actually pray for Trajan but only wept for him', nevertheless regards Gregory in Langland's text as a sort of functionless fossil, an aspect of the legend which 'was impossible to dislodge...entirely'; in Whatley's view it rather gets in the way of what Langland was really interested in, the fact that 'Trajan was outside the Church's sacramental system when he was saved'. I would allow Gregory more significance than that. Moreover, Whatley argues that the rejection of the pope's prayer 'seems to contradict ll. 146–9, which describe Gregory's intercessory tears *and prayers*' (p. 53, my emphasis). In fact, ll. 146–9 do not mention prayers at all, simply the pope's desire or 'will' that the emperor should be saved, which wish was expressed (in Langland's version) through tears rather than prayers.

privileged over learning and clerical ritual, the *affectus* over intellectual *aspectus*, and actions are supposed to speak louder than written words. Law without love is not worth a bean (cf. XI. 170). Hence the remark that Trajan's salvation was something which 'no clergie ne kouthe, ne konnyng of lawes' (B XI. 165). That last phrase could be taken as implying that even the most assiduous following of the *lex naturalis*, or indeed some heathen code of behaviour which elaborates upon it, does not guarantee a spiritual reward, a thought which is utterly consonant with the views found in B XV, as summarized above. By the same token, *fides* stands 'above logyk or lawe', the *Legenda aurea* being cited as a proof-text (B XI. 219–20; quoted above, p. 151); I take that to mean that according to all logic or law Trajan should have remained in hell. Hardly consonant with fourteenth-century Neopelagianism, but utterly consonant with one of the interpretative possibilities offered by Langland's main source for the Trajan legend, the *Legenda aurea*.

Also in keeping with the *Legenda aurea* is Ymaginatif's statement that 'Troianus the trewe knyght tilde noght depe in helle', so 'Oure Lord' was able to get him out easily ('lightly'; B XII. 209–10). Jacobus, echoing Aquinas's *Sentences* commentary, had suggested that Trajan 'was not finally committed to hell or definitively sentenced to eternal punishment'. A similar suggestion is included in William of Auvergne's *Summa aurea*.[50] And in one of his disputed questions on truth, Aquinas declares that 'although Trajan was in the place of the damned, he was not damned absolutely'.[51] (The matter is complicated by the fact that in Middle English 'helle' can refer to either hell or purgatory; the Medieval Latin term *infernus* can be ambiguous in the same way.) In other words, at that point in Passus XII Langland is concerned to make relatively 'light' of the divine rescue of Trajan. Had he been concerned to emphasize the absolute power of God surely he would have placed him in the deepest pit of hell—thereby allowing the Almighty a real chance to show what He can do.

But, all due allowance having been made for these arguments, may we not still suspect that lurking behind—however far

---

[50] *Summa aurea*, lib. IV, tract. xviii, cap. 4, qu. 1, in *Summa aurea Guillelmi Altissiodorensis*, ed. Jean Ribaillier, 4 vols. in 6 (Paris, 1980–5), iv. 536.

[51] *De veritate*, qu. 6, art. 6, in *Truth: St Thomas Aquinas*, 3 vols., tr. Robert W. Mulligan (Chicago, 1952–3), i. 286.

behind—Langland's construction of Trajan is the notion of congruent merit, that being a feature of Neopelagian thought which I
have described as being more genuinely subversive than the power
distinction? The case is weak. Even if one were to isolate the
statement that 'for his pure truthe | Was that Sarsen saved' (B XI.
155–6) from its qualifying context (as described above), there is
insufficient evidence to enable its identification with a specifically
Ockhamist or Holcotian version of the theory of divine acceptability. One could equally well invoke Bonaventure's statement
that as far as the *iusti* are concerned *gratia gratum faciens* is a
disposition sufficient for salvation (p. 155 above). To be sure,
questions could be asked about what a person required to be
counted among the *iusti*: did membership entail certain *explicit*
beliefs in doctrines essential to Christianity or was *implicit* belief
sufficient on the part of the righteous who lived under the guidance of such knowledge and religious precepts as were available to
them? That was where God's helping hand, so to speak, intervened. 'It pertains to divine providence to furnish everyone with
what is necessary for salvation', declares Aquinas, providing there
is no obstruction on the human's part. Thus, if someone who had
been brought up 'in the forest or among wild beasts' followed 'the
direction of natural reason in seeking good and avoiding evil, we
must certainly hold that God would either reveal to him through
internal inspiration what had to be believed, or would send some
preacher of the faith to him as he sent Peter to Cornelius'.[52]
Ockham and Holcot pushed this sort of doctrine further by their
insistence that in the usual run of things God *had* to reward such
righteous followers of natural reason; hence their controversial line
on merit *de congruo*. So, where does Langland's Trajan stand here?
In obvious contrast with Cornelius, he lacked a St Peter figure. On
the other hand, if my view of St Gregory's definite role in Trajan's
salvation is accepted, could Gregory be regarded as a Peter who
arrived very late, 'many years after that emperor's death'?[53] But
better late than never, of course, and still (so the argument would
run) to be taken as an instance of how God is willing to provide the
crucial supplement necessary to effect the salvation of a just man.

[52] *De veritate*, qu. 14, art. 11, tr. Mulligan, ii. 262. Here Aquinas is rather more
optimistic about the spiritual development of one brought up in a 'wilde wildernesse' full of 'wilde beestes' than was Langland (cf. p. 160 above).

[53] As the *Legenda aurea* puts it; tr. Ryan, i. 178.

Then there is the issue of whether Trajan can be regarded as having received some sort of divine illumination, a veritable *baptismus flaminis*. The text is silent on that matter. However, it could be argued that Langland's statement that Trajan lived as his law taught and believed there to be no better (B XII. 285) indicates that the pagan did not receive such assistance. As does the problematic and much-emended line B XII. 288, which Kane and Donaldson give as 'wheiþer it worþ of truþe or noȝt, þe worþ of bileue is gret' and Schmidt (in his second edition) as 'wher it worth or worth noght, the bileue is gret of truth'.[54] Whatever Langland actually wrote there, he seems to have meant that, even though the truth which a pagan held was partial and incomplete by Christian standards, the fact that he had such a faith was meritorious. Now, if Trajan's world-view lacked a lot, surely he could not have experienced a divine revelation? And would that not place Langland's text well within the Neopelagian band of the ideological spectrum? The less God has to work on, so to speak, the greater the opportunity for an action *de potentia absoluta*.[55] But Langland's emphasis on the great worth of belief and the divine respect for truth seems to point rather to the dispensation of the *potentia ordinata*.[56] Yet if we apply its terms of reference to Langland's text the result is inconclusive—for the very good reason that traditionalists and radicals alike (if we may use those categories) were often imprecise about what pagans had to believe in order to be saved. Certainly they did not have to believe the whole truth and nothing but the truth, but exactly *how much* truth was needed was generally left vague. (Aquinas suggested that 'it was enough for them to have implicit faith in the Redeemer, either as part of their belief in the faith of the law and the prophets, or as part of their belief in divine providence itself'.[57]) Which meant that the extent to which they had to be divinely helped was left vague also. The following

[54] On this line see especially Whatley, '*Piers Plowman* B 12.277–94', 5–6.

[55] As when, according to Ockham, *de potentia dei absoluta* he saved certain people in antiquity without *any* kind of baptism, whether by water, blood, or fire. See Ockham's *Tractatus contra Benedictum*, iii. 3, in *Opera politica*, vol. iii, ed. H. S. Offler (Manchester, 1956), 233.

[56] *Pace* A. V. C. Schmidt ('*Piers Plowman*': *A New Translation* (Oxford, 1992), 307 n.) there is no reason to take such statements as *Quia voluit* ('Because his will was it should be!', B XII. 215a) as referring to the absolute power. Absolute power is not needed for the activities of God's helping hand as described here.

[57] *De veritate*, qu. 14, art. 11; tr. Mulligan, ii. 263.

statement by Alexander of Hales—no 'Nominalist' he—which links the principle of *facere in quod se est* to the belief in God's helping hand is quite typical: 'Si facit quod in se est, Dominus illuminabit eum per occultam inspirationem aut per angelum, aut per hominem.'[58] That sounds remarkably like what Holcot has to say on the same subject in his Wisdom commentary[59]—yet further proof that in the areas here under investigation, exclusively Nominalist doctrines are very elusive.

Finally, while it is quite correct to say that Langland uses Trajan to raise the issue of the salvation of the heathen in general, it should be recognized that he is a lot more tentative about what has happened to Socrates and Solomon than he is about the fate of Trajan's soul. Gregory, both pope and saint, witnesses to the salvation of Trajan, but as far as the rest are concerned Langland contents himself with hopeful imaginations—no more than that. It is, after all, Ymaginatif who in B XII (C XIV) argues that the just man may scarcely but definitely be saved; it is he, rather than a personification representing the highest theological authority, who adduces 1 Peter 4: 18.[60] William of Ockham and Robert Holcot were a lot more confident, as we have seen. The distance between them and Langland is quite considerable.

In order to gauge this distance more fully, and to locate Langland more precisely on the intellectual map of his day, a comparison may be made between the relevant passages of *Piers Plowman* and John Wyclif's treatment of Trajan, viewed in relation to Wyclif's unusual version of the *baptismus flaminis* doctrine. In *De ecclesia* Trajan is considered within a typical scholastic context, namely in a discussion of the value of prayers for the dead.[61] Wyclif supposes that Trajan had dwelled in purgatory rather than

[58] *Summa theologica* (Quaracchi, 1924–48), iii. 331.
[59] See esp. *Sapientiae Regis Salamonis praelectiones* (Basle, 1586), 103, 348, 521–3; cf. Holcot's *Sentences* commentary, *I Sent.*, qu. iv, art. 3, Q (Lyons, 1497), unfol. See further the discussion in Minnis, *Chaucer and Pagan Antiquity*, 56–9.
[60] I retain my view of the generally positive and powerful role played by Ymaginatif, as argued in my article 'Langland's Ymaginatif and Late-Medieval Theories of Imagination', *Comparative Criticism*, 3 (1981), 71–103; this approach has recently been reinforced by the impressive monograph of Ernest Kaulbach, *Imaginative Prophecy in the B-text of 'Piers Plowman'* (Cambridge, 1993). Such a view, however, is quite compatible with the one expressed here, namely that Langland did not choose to put the opinions in question in the mouth of an authority-figure whose status was unequivocally of the highest order.
[61] *Tractatus de ecclesia*, ed. J. Loserth (London, 1886), 531.

in hell, and that God had predestined him to glory and predestined Gregory to save him through intercession.[62] Both these resolutions have the status and power of eternal decrees, for we must believe that neither St Gregory nor a saint in heaven could change the divine judgment or alter or redirect the divine through prayers. It is evident, Wyclif declares, that Trajan died in a state of grace whereby he was predestined to glory. Moreover, Wyclif cannot believe that Trajan died in a state which would not satisfy the requirements of present justice; presumably here he means justice as understood in the contemporary Christian situation, rather than some sort of shadowy, pre-Christian justice. For in his opinion many people outside Judaism, such as Job, Nebuchadnezzar, and others like them, were catholics, and the same goes for certain people that we judge to be outside our Christian faith: they are actually within the true Church, its right and true members. Trajan and just people like him, declares Wyclif, are part of the *vera ecclesia* and have received *baptismus flaminis*, baptism by the Holy Spirit.

The version of those views found mainly in Wyclif's *Trialogus* was vociferously attacked in the vast *Doctrinale antiquitatum fidei catholicae ecclesiae* of Thomas Netter (*c.*1377–1430), Carmelite theologian and confessor of King Henry IV.[63] Wyclif, complained Netter, concealed his doctrine under ambiguous words, but there was no doubt in Netter's mind that the heretic had denied the necessity of baptism. As quoted (and somewhat simplified) by Netter, Wyclif had argued that it would detract from the divine freedom and divine power if God could not intervene to save an infant or adult within the Christian faith unless some old woman or some other person who had come in off the street should baptize them; moreover, he applied the same principle to infidels. Wyclif therefore theoretically dispensed with baptism by water, believing that all that was necessary was *baptismus flaminis* and the influx of 'material water' from the Saviour's side, an allusion to

[62] *De ecclesia*, ed. Loserth, 533–4.

[63] *Doctrinale*, v. 96–7, in *Doctrinale antiquitatum fidei catholicae ecclesiae*, 3 vols. (Venice, 1757–9), ii. 563–75; cf. ii. 611–15. Netter is responding to Wyclif, *Trialogus*, ed. G. V. Lechler (Oxford, 1869), 281–92. See further the discussion in Anne Hudson, *The Premature Reformation: Wycliffite Texts and Lollard History* (Oxford, 1988), 290–4.

the idiom of John 19: 34.[64] Romans 6: 3 claims that 'all we who are baptized in Christ Jesus are baptized in his death'; Wyclif took this to mean that Christ's merit and passion were sufficient for the baptism of the *congregatio predestinatorum*. Netter replied with a vehement reinstatement of the importance of *baptismus fluminis*. Wyclif had devalued both *baptismus fluminis* and *baptismus sanguinis*, he complains, in regarding them as mere 'antecedent signs' of *baptismus flaminis*, and arguing that unless this imperceptible (*insensibilis*) baptism is bestowed, the baptized person is not cleansed from guilt, whereas if it is lacking the other two are insufficient. This, Netter exclaims, breaks all the pronouncements of the Fathers and the Scriptures to the effect that man will perish unless he is regenerated through water. As an imperceptible form of baptism, *baptismus flaminis* would be unknown to us, and indeed be a lesser thing among Christians than that Jewish circumcision which was the figure of our own baptism.

Very similar phrasing occurs in one of Wyclif's *Responsiones ad argumenta Radulfi Strode*, Ralph Strode having been a Fellow of Merton College by 1360 and almost certainly to be identified with the 'philosophical Strode' who is one of the addressees of Chaucer's *Troilus and Criseyde* (V. 1856–7).[65] This 'friend of truth', as Wyclif terms him, had asked a question which highlighted the problems incumbent on Wyclif's theory of predestination: if a *prescitus* (a person foreknown to be damned) were to die immediately after having enjoyed the spiritual benefits of baptism, would this not interfere with his destiny? No one, replies Wyclif, should presume to deny the practice of baptism by water. Yet without it a man can be predestined to glory, providing he has experienced *baptismus flaminis*. *Baptismus fluminis* is necessary only if the water in question is understood to be the water that flows from the side of Christ.

A powerful critique of such views is mounted in Netter's *Doctrinale*, with reference to the crucial test-case of the virtuous pagan, Cornelius the Centurion appearing yet again.[66] When St Peter preached to Cornelius and certain unnamed other people,

---

[64] 'One of the soldiers with a spear opened his side: and immediately there came out blood and water.' See further 1 John 5: 6 and 8.

[65] *Responsiones ad argumenta Radulfi Strode*, in *Opera minora*, ed. J. Loserth (London, 1913), 176–8.

[66] *Doctrinale*, Venice edn., ii. 573–5.

'the Holy Ghost fell on all them that heard the word' (v. 44). But this, Netter emphasizes, was not sufficient, for subsequently Peter commanded that they should be baptized (47–8). The visible sacrament is crucial: 'quamvis bonus fuerit plena fide, dico tamen, sine visibili sacramento, vel re ipsa, salvus esse non poterat.' Cornelius had to enter into the Church, by participation in its sacraments. Membership of the Church does not come about simply by grace of predestination or by *baptismus flaminis*. When the Saviour himself said, 'unless a man be born again of water and the Holy Ghost, he cannot enter into the kingdom of God' (John 3: 5), he was speaking of 'material' water as used in *baptismus fluminis*, and not of the water which materially flowed from the side of the Saviour on the cross. As the case of Cornelius illustrates, faith is *conceived* through the influx of the Holy Spirit, but it is *born* in the reception of the visible sacrament.

Wyclif's views on baptism were quite consistent with his eucharistic theory, as Netter shrewdly observed. As an 'empty sign' (*signa vacua*) Wyclif reputed it to contain no supernatural grace, but rather to 'signify' or 'figure', and similarly he called the seven sacraments seven 'signs'.[67] And Wyclif's elevation of *baptismus flaminis* over *baptismus fluminis* was one among many manœuvres whereby the authority of the orthodox priesthood was seriously undermined. Indeed, he suggested to Strode that just as the only water utterly necessary for baptism is that which flows from the side of the crucified Christ, so the 'true sons of God' who have received the spiritual oil of predestination are best equipped to perform the priestly office, even though they may not have been anointed with material oil at a bishop's service of consecration, and lack the *character* which formal ordination imposes, along with the traditional tonsure.[68] Lollard theology elaborated upon such ideas. According to Netter, William White was the author of a tract which included the view that infant baptism was unnecessary;[69] William Swinderby was accused of the belief that baptism was of no effect if the priest or the godparents were in mortal sin.[70] Infant baptism is not required where the mother is Christian

---

[67] *Doctrinale*, Venice edn., ii.575–6.

[68] *Opera minora*, ed. Loserth, 178.

[69] *Doctrinale*, Venice edn., iii. 342.

[70] *Registrum Johannis Trefnant Episcopi Herefordensis*, ed. William W. Capes (London, 1916), 243.

because the Holy Ghost is transmitted to the child in the womb, according to Thomas Bikenmore, a clerk who was investigated by Bishop Aiscough of Salisbury in 1443.[71] And Walter Brut, a literate layman, famously posed the question, if women have the ability to baptize (allowed them in an emergency situation, when a child is near death), and if baptism is the chief sacrament, why should women not administer the other sacraments as well, and take upon themselves all the priestly duties and functions?

Even more significant for us is the curious case of Sir Lewis Clifford, one of the group of 'Lollard Knights' with which Chaucer had some association. It may be recalled that it was Clifford who brought from France to England Deschamps's poem in praise of Chaucer. Clifford is himself mentioned in it, and elsewhere Deschamps gives him the epithet 'amorous', which we may take to mean that he could speak well of love, being well versed in the fashions of *fin amor*.[72] When he allegedly renounced his Lollard views in 1402 Clifford conveyed to Archbishop Thomas Arundel a list of Lollard conclusions, which involve the devaluation of the seven sacraments as 'dead signs' (the sacrament of the altar being described as 'a morsel of dead bread').[73] Most bizarre of all is the statement that baptism is not to be performed by churchmen on a boy, because 'that boy is a second Trinity, not contaminated by sin, and it would be the worse for him if he were to pass into their hands'.[74] One can only hope that Clifford spoke better of love than he did of theology. Perhaps Langland had a point when he complained about how 'heighe' (i.e. noble) men presume to talk

---

[71] See Hudson, *Premature Reformation*, 141.

[72] See Minnis, *The Shorter Poems*, 20, 26.

[73] Thomas Walsingham, *Historia Anglicana*, ed. H. T. Riley, 2 vols. (London, 1863–4), ii. 253; John Trokelowe, Henry Blaneforde, *et al.*, *Chronica et annales* (London, 1866), 348.

[74] *Hist. Angl.*, ed. Riley, ii. 253; *Chron. et ann.* 348. K. B. McFarlane finds the whole account slightly 'fishy'—'the views Clifford is made to ascribe to the Lollards are wilder than usual': *Lancastrian Kings and Lollard Knights* (Oxford, 1972), 212. That could easily be said of the statement here quoted. However, Hudson sees some sense in it or underlying it; *Premature Reformation*, 114. My own suggestion is that here may be a version of the Lollard belief that the child of a Christian couple (perhaps more specifically of a man and woman who are members of the Wycliffite *vera ecclesia*) has been purified by the Holy Spirit and therefore is not in need of baptism. Indeed, those 'clergymen' in question could well be in a state of mortal sin (maybe even predestined to damnation), and hence less pure than he; therefore it would quite inappropriate for them to presume to minister to the boy.

'as thei clerkes were' about Christ and his powers, finding fault
with the Father who formed us all, and with 'crabbede wordes'
contradicting clerics by raising casuistical theological questions.[75]
Men who 'muse muche' about their words, Langland concludes
sadly, are brought into 'mysbileve' (B X. 103–16). A little learning
was a dangerous thing. When the heresy-hunt was on, it became
quite lethal.

The most obvious point that emerges from all this is that Chaucer's reticence about appearing as a 'divinistre', his tendency to
leave most 'disputison' to 'clerkes', was sensible and certainly safe.
Moreover, given the wide range (from the sublime to the ridicu-
lous) of the opinions canvassed above, all the major Ricardian
poets, no matter how eccentric their formulations could sometimes
be, stand out as being relatively, indeed remarkably, orthodox.
One may think particularly of the traditional views on baptism
which are given new life and vigour in *St Erkenwald* and in *Pearl*.
In the latter the Pearl-maiden is safe and sound in heaven, having
received *baptismus fluminis*. In the former the body of a pagan
judge is miraculously preserved in order that its virtuous owner
may receive the sacrament of baptism.[76] However, in this case any
suggestion of narrow legalism is brilliantly avoided by the device
of having St Erkenwald weep over the corpse—in this case a saint's
tears actually become the material water needed for *baptismus
fluminis*—and anticipate the words he will say in performing the
rite. All the conditions for the sacrament having been met, the

---

[75] On the other hand, it should be noted that certain laymen achieved impressive
levels of proficiency in theology. An excellent example is provided by Jacob Palmer,
a London bureaucrat (d. 1375), who compiled the vast *Omne bonum* and was the
scribe of a manuscript containing William of Nottingham's Gospel Harmony. See
Penn R. Szittya, *The Antifraternal Tradition in Medieval Literature* (Princeton,
1986), 67–81. Then there is the fact that in early 14th-cent. England schoolmen
produced theological books which enjoyed a popularity beyond the schools, such as
Holcot's Wisdom commentary, Thomas Ringstead's Proverbs commentary, Bradwardine's *De causa Dei*, and Richard Fitzralph's *Summa in questionibus Arme-
norum*. Such works helped prepare the ground for the vernacular theology which is
a feature of the second half of the century—and, to some extent, for Wyclif's appeal
to secular textual communities.

[76] To some extent this story derives from the version of the Trajan legend in
which the virtuous pagan is briefly restored to life in order to receive baptism; on
this see Whatley, 'Uses of Hagiography', 37–9. This specific precedent is not
considered by Clifford Peterson in the introduction to his edition of *Saint Erkenwald* (Philadelphia, 1977), who simply credits the poet with having brought
together 'the incorrupt body theme and the Trajan–Gregory legend' (p. 42).

pagan's soul ascends to partake of the heavenly banquet whilst his body blackens and corrupts. And Langland, I believe, avoided both Neopelagianism and Wycliffite predestinarianism in constructing a Trajan who is given full credit for his 'truthe' yet needs some help from a saint; here due recognition is given to both God and man (or more precisely, to both the men involved, with Gregory's role being carefully negotiated and respected). Trajan 'took nevere Cristendom'. There is no suggestion in Langland (as there is in Wyclif) that although Trajan may have seemed to be outside the Church he was actually within it, as a member of the *vera ecclesia*. Rather he 'trespased nevere ne traversed ayeins *his* lawe', the pagan code of behaviour which was the best law he had. But Langland never went so far as to assert unequivocally that that pagan in particular (and certainly not pagans in general) won salvation simply by keeping such law. St Gregory, that great willer and weeper, had his part to play.

Lewis Clifford told Arundel of a Lollard view which under-mined the efficacy of penance, 'because, as they say', faith is what matters; thus Christ assured Mary Magdalene that her faith had made her safe (cf. Luke 7: 50).[77] That is to say, faith alone suffices for the salvation of a righteous person, the traditional instruction and guidance of the Church hierarchy being dispensa-ble. In marked contrast, Langland was a great believer in penance (see especially B XX. 280–7, 305–9). Moreover, *fides sufficit* func-tions very differently in *Piers Plowman*. Though the idea initially appears in the guise of a major challenge (see p. 150 above, noting particularly Langland's allusion to the Magdalene), later it is contained within a quite unthreatening conception of educational deficiency. *Fides sufficit* in the case of those Christians who have not been properly instructed by their clergymen or in the case of heathens who possess some but not complete knowledge of the truths of Christianity. In short, special cases are being provided for here; Langland is not undermining either the Church's hierarchical apparatus or the traditional salvific process, in contrast with on the one hand the Nominalist notion of congruent merit and on the other the Wycliffite notion of the predestined *electus* who deals directly with his God. Concomitantly, Langland's Trajan is not

---

[77] *Hist. Angl.*, ed. Riley, ii. 253; *Chron. et ann.* 348; cf. MacFarlane, *Lancastrian Kings*, 212, and Hudson, *Premature Reformation*, 114.

presented as a recipient of God's *potentia absoluta* or as one who merited *de congruo* (his paganism being emphasized). Neither is the emperor seen as one of the *electi*, with the emphasis falling on his membership of the *vera ecclesia* (his paganism being minimized).[78] Therefore, as far as baptism is concerned Langland cannot be accused of being in deep sympathy with either Neopelagianism or Lollardy,[79] *pace* those who have detected the substantial influence of one or other of those ideologies in *Piers Plowman*. The fact that both influences have been alleged[80] may be taken as a visible sign that neither is very strong in the poem.

So, then, is Nominalism simply 'all in the mind' (like Ockham's universals), as far as the major Ricardian poets here discussed are concerned? I am certainly not saying that. In respect of Chaucer, my point is that there is insufficient evidence to go on. When we begin to enter those areas in which we could discover Chaucer's advocacy (or lack thereof) of some distinctively Nominalist view, the poet stops in his tracks, gesturing vaguely towards those problem regions without exploring them himself. He is content, he declares ostentatiously, to leave such matters to the experts. Whether in actuality he was or was not, we will never know, because in his texts he is just not telling. In other words, the signs run out at the crucial stage, leaving us without direction. As far as Langland is concerned, the problem regions are certainly being investigated, but the outcome is far from clear. The signs are there but they are all too ambiguous; much depends on the viewpoint of the *viator*. Are false trails being laid, trails which are meant to be recognized as false? Or are dangerous speculations being carefully ringfenced, contained within a dialectic which proceeds to affirm conclusions that offer consensus and conformity? Or is there indeed something Pelagian or at least semipelagian about aspects of Langland's thought? My own opinions may

[78] In this regard it should be noted that in the C-text Langland places extreme predestinarian views in the mouth of the figure Recklessness; see C XI. 196–311.

[79] With this statement regarding Lollardy, cf. Hudson, *Premature Reformation*, 403. This is not to question, of course, the occasional resemblances and parallels between certain passages of *Piers* and aspects of Lollard thought, on which see Hudson's full discussion, 400–8; also her article '*Piers Plowman* and the Peasants' Revolt: A Problem Revisited', *YLS* 8 (1994), 85–6.

[80] This is somewhat ironic, given Wyclif's vicious attacks on the 'doctors of signs', as he contemptuously called his Nominalist opponents. With this general discussion cf. Simpson, 'Constraints of Satire', 18–19.

be summed up as follows. It is difficult if not impossible to disentangle a sufficient number of views which would place Langland (however briefly) in the Neopelagian camp, especially in view of the complicated cross-currents of thought which characterize Ricardian England. Passages which look Nominalist on inspection turn out to be capable of less radical readings, and/or to have been placed within a dialectical framework which does not allow them the last word. Moreover, in Langland there are no Middle English terms which point to the real erogenous zones of Nominalism, the distinction between the absolute and ordained powers of God and the problematics of condign and congruent merit as found in the thought of such schoolmen as Ockham and Holcot.[81] In sum, there is no extensive 'Neopelagian Sect Vocabulary' to be identified in *Piers Plowman*.[82] True, the *facere quod in se est* principle does appear at B XII. 284–7, as it does in Chaucer's Squire's Tale and Hilton's *Scale of Perfection*.[83] But, as we noted at the very beginning of this paper, it is not exclusive to the thought of Ockham

[81] James Simpson has argued that the concepts of congruent and condign merit do shape Langland's understanding of reward; see his article 'Spirituality and Economics in Passus 1–7 of the B Text', *YLS* 1 (1987), 83–103, and also his book *'Piers Plowman': An Introduction to the B-Text* (London, 1990), 79–80, 784–5, 93, 124–7, 180. His article duly notes the fact that the distinction was in use in the 13th-cent. (pp. 93–5; Aquinas is cited on p. 95), but then seems to imply that its (alleged) subtextual presence in *Piers* supports the view of Adams 'that Langland may be described as a "semi-pelagian"' (p. 101 n. 30). No evidence from specifically 14th-cent. 'semipelagian' use of the terminology is given to support this transition in the argument. In any case, I believe that the issues in the key passages discussed by Simpson are fundamental ones in all Christian thought; as such they (1) could hardly fail to be important to Langland and (2) need not be interpreted within the distinctive terminological form proposed by Simpson, particularly since Langland himself does not adopt specific, exclusive jargon.

[82] James Simpson has suggested to me that the term 'pure' as used at B XI. 155 ('pure truthe') may echo the *ex puris naturalibus* idiom. That is certainly a possibility, though Langland may simply have thought of it as a routine intensifying adjective, as used at B VII. 11 ('pure teene'). In any case, my point about the absence in the poem of an *extensive* 'Neopelagian Sect Vocabulary' still holds.

[83] The way in which the *facere quod in se est* principle has been applied by the 'semipelagian' lobby in discussing the spiritual state of those who live in regular and ordinary Christian societies, where Christian lore and law is firmly established and basically uncontested, is in need of reconsideration. In Ockham and Holcot the definitive manifestations of the relevant terminology seem to be in discussions of either non-Christians in particular (pagans, Muslims, etc.) or of mankind in general *including* non-Christians, which means that the specific conditions appertaining in the present Christian age cannot help to solve whatever problem they are wrestling with. To put it another way, this discourse is used to push the boundaries of acceptable belief and explore the margins of merit, to formulate the tough test-

cum suis. The Nominalist questions accentuated and elaborated upon issues which had been the currency of speculative theology for generations, but their minutiae did not trouble very deeply the hearts and minds of a wider audience: that dubious privilege rather belonged to Wycliffite thought. I myself doubt if Langland was profoundly involved with Neopelagian doctrine. To me it is highly significant that when he does present ideas which were associated with it, his citations are limited to issues which had, so to speak, hit the headlines of his day;[84] thus *Piers Plowman* inscribes a few radical notions which had travelled beyond the confines of the schools, and the specialist Latin genres which they produced, to make an impact on vernacular literature. The extent of this impact is highly debatable, but it had reached as far as that learned layman Geoffrey Chaucer.

In short, it would seem that the best attitude is one of scepticism.

cases for Christian theology. Why apply it to those who are well provided for within the normal economy of grace and salvation, who live under the everyday, routine operations of the ordained power of God? Who needs a space-suit to go shopping?

[84] That such issues could arouse considerable passions may be illustrated, in addition to Hilton's attack, with reference to John Trevisa's outburst against the suggestion that Trajan was delivered from hell by St Gregory on account of the pagan's 'greet riȝtwisenesse': anyone who thinks that, Trevisa exclaims, is worse than mad and 'out of riȝt bileve'. *Polychronicon Radulphi Higden*, ed. C. Babington and J. R. Lumby, 9 vols. (London, 1865–86), v. 7.

8

Ricardian 'Trouthe': A Legal Perspective

RICHARD FIRTH GREEN

Returning to one of the major themes of his earlier *Reading of 'Sir Gawain and the Green Knight'*, John Burrow wrote in *Ricardian Poetry* that 'the pentangle on Gawain's shield is, the poet says, a "token of *trawthe*" (cf. 626); and this "truth" proves to be the common and chief issue in the tests to which the hero is submitted'.[1] By emphasizing that *Sir Gawain* is 'about *truth* in the medieval sense of the word',[2] Burrow aligns himself with other critics such as Elizabeth Salter, who called the pilgrimage to *Seynt Truþe* in *Piers Plowman* 'the great imaginative motif of the whole work',[3] and George Kane, for whom the imperfect realization of the ideal of truth becomes 'the principal formative concern of Chaucer's mature writing'.[4] Such views are now so commonplace that most modern critics would probably agree with John Alford that 'truth as a social ideal is the dominant, one might almost say the characterizing, concern of late fourteenth-century poetry'.[5] In view of the enormous significance of the word *truth* for the major Ricardian poets, it is obviously important, as Burrow himself has pointed out, 'to discover what this complex word meant to fourteenth-century writers and readers'.[6] I shall be seeking here to build on the linguistic investigations of Burrow and others, by examining some of the social, and specifically legal, contexts in which the word was used in the late Middle Ages.

[1] J. A. Burrow, *Ricardian Poetry* (London, 1971), 86.
[2] *A Reading of 'Sir Gawain and the Green Knight'* (London, 1965), p. vii.
[3] '*Piers Plowman* and the Pilgrimage to Truth', *Essays and Studies*, NS 11 (1958), 8.
[4] *The Liberating Truth: The Concept of Integrity in Chaucer's Writings*, the John Coffin Memorial Lecture, 1979 (London, 1980), 12.
[5] 'The Design of the Poem', in John Alford (ed.), *A Companion to 'Piers Plowman'* (Berkeley and Los Angeles, 1988), 33.
[6] *Reading*, 42.

Given that all the major Ricardian poets make frequent and explicit reference to the law and its processes, contemporary legal procedure might seem an obvious place to look for evidence of the cultural assumptions underlying their use of the word *trouthe*. Courts, then as now, claim to be vehicles for determining the truth (their verdicts are, etymologically speaking, 'true sayings' (Lat. *veredictum*; Fr. *voirdit*)), and they employ elaborate rules to try to ensure that those who come before them speak the truth, the whole truth and nothing but the truth. On the other hand, it is all too easy to be misled by the superficial resemblance between the form taken by trials at common law in medieval England and that of their twentieth-century counterparts into assuming that the kind of truth sought by a medieval questman was much the same as that preoccupying the members of a modern jury. In reality, however, as I hope to show, the customary processes of the medieval common law reflect traditional patterns of thought that have little place in either modern Anglo-American jurisprudence or even that of the medieval canonist and civilian. For this very reason, however, local custom offers us far richer opportunities for exploring some of the unexamined social premises implicit in much vernacular literature than the imported jurisprudence of the romanists. Customary law, for the Middle Ages in general, rested upon a concept of truth that few modern judges would have much time for. Such truth, as A. J. Gurevich describes it, 'meant something very different from the scientific "truth" on which so much reliance is placed today: to the medieval mind truth had to correspond to the ideal norms.... In a society based on the principle of fidelity to the family, kindred, lord, etc., truth could not have a value independent of the concrete interests of the group. Truth was, so to speak, "anthropomorphous".'[7]

In this chapter I want to inquire how far Gurevich's 'anthropomorphous truth' (as opposed to the 'scientific truth' we naturally regard as the proper object of forensic investigation) formed 'the common and chief issue' of the late medieval lawsuit, and to ask what importance such an inquiry might have for understanding the Ricardian poets' preoccupation with the word *trouthe* itself. Assuming with R. C. Van Caenegem that it is 'in the history

---

[7] A. J. Gurevich, *Categories of Medieval Culture*, tr. G. L. Campbell (London, 1985), 178.

of evidence [that] the interaction of general culture and legal ideas can be followed most clearly',[8] I shall be trying, in the first instance, to answer these questions by examining the modes of proof employed in medieval English lawsuits. This approach runs immediately into an obvious difficulty, however: court records were, by and large, kept in Latin or French and so can provide at best only indirect evidence for the meaning of a Middle English word like *trouthe*. How can we be sure, for instance, that something a court reporter calls *verum* or *verite* would not have been referred to in the vernacular as *sooth* rather than *trouthe*? The solution I propose is to concentrate on some literary accounts of trials, where uses of the vernacular word *trouthe* can be clearly demonstrated, while trying at the same time to minimize the obvious circularity of this approach by buttressing it with evidence from more conventional legal sources. In this way I shall hope to be able to set these trials in their larger jurisprudential context in order that the cultural significance of the Middle English word may become clearer.

In Anglo-Saxon law, the primary mode of proof had been by oath—'an oath, going not to the truth of specific fact, but to the justice of the claim or defence as a whole'.[9] In other words, litigants did not as now begin their case by swearing what lawyers call a promissory or evidentiary oath to *tell* the truth, they concluded it by swearing an assertory or judicial oath that their version of the matter at issue *was* the truth. Thus, for Roger to 'prove' that his ox is not stolen he must swear in open court that it is his own property. Cynical perjurers, so the theory went, even when they managed to avoid public opprobrium during their own lifetime, could never escape the ultimate justice of God—a legal presumption still recognized in the mid-thirteenth century: 'There is an oath tendered by one party to the other in court, or by the judge to a party, upon which no conviction follows', says Henry Bracton, 'for it is sufficient that they await the vengeance of God.'[10] From the earliest period, however, practical safeguards

---

[8] *The Birth of the English Common Law*, 2nd edn. (Cambridge, 1988), 62.

[9] Frederick Pollock and Frederick William Maitland, *The History of English Law before the Time of Edward I*, 2nd edn., rev. S. F. C. Milsom, 2 vols. (Cambridge, 1968), i. 39.

[10] *De legibus et consuetudinibus Angliae*, ed. George Woodbine and tr. S. E. Thorne, 4 vols. (Cambridge, Mass., 1968–74), iii. 342.

against cynical perjury had been attached to the judicial oath: those in good standing with the community might be asked to provide reliable witnesses (if such were available) or reliable oath-helpers (if they were not) to swear the oath alongside them; compurgation (the use of such oath-helpers) seems in fact to have been the commonest form of early proof—so common, indeed, that in England the term became synonymous with the word law itself: to 'make', 'wage', or 'be at' one's law (*facere* [*vadiare*] *suam legem*, *gager* [*estre a*] *sa ley*) meant to clear oneself with oath-helpers. Those whose reputation was more dubious could be required to support their oath by undergoing a potentially painful or humiliating ordeal. Even witness proof (which seems at first glance more closely to resemble modern 'rational' procedure) required witnesses to swear to the truth of the claim they were endorsing, not to the truth of their own account of events: 'the original judicial oath was not incidental to testimonial evidence. Rather the reverse was the case; witnesses supported the oath.'[11]

Factual evidence, it should be stressed, was far from insignificant in early law (such displays of manifest guilt as the red-handed killer still clasping her bloody knife, the hand-having thief still clutching his stolen goods, the adulterous couple still sharing their warm bed, furnished it with its simplest paradigms of proof), but where guilt was at all doubtful it tended to fall back on an appraisal of the accused rather than of the accusation. When compurgators waged their law on behalf of a neighbour they were not making a direct judgment on the facts of the case, they were saying in effect, 'Roger is a person whose word we trust and if he is ready to swear that this is his ox then we are ready to swear that his oath is sound.' By so doing, oath-helpers were putting their own reputations for honest dealing in jeopardy (which is precisely what was meant by 'waging their law'), so they would naturally have been reluctant to support anyone whose honesty was at all suspect. Whether or not the truth established by such a process conformed to the actual facts of the case was in the final analysis less important than that it should reflect 'the concrete interests of the group'—a belief that should not be too readily dismissed as either arbitrary or inequitable. The fundamental quality upon which this system of proof depended was known

---

[11] Helen Silving, 'The Oath, 1', *Yale Law Journal*, 68 (1959), 1335.

as *oathworthiness*: 'we decree', says the West Saxon King Edward (899–924), 'that those who are, by common report, perjurers, or who fail to exculpate themselves by oath, or whose oaths are sucessfully challenged in court, shall never afterwards be oathworthy (*þæt hy syðan aþwyrþe næran*); rather they shall be 'ordeal-worthy' (*ac ordales wyrþe*)'.[12] The term 'oathworthy' itself seems not to be recorded after the mid-thirteenth century (its final appearances are in Bracton, who employs such English legal terms only rarely),[13] but the concept it represented continued to be important none the less.[14] Indeed, it is one of the fundamental qualities embodied in the Ricardian keyword *trouthe*.

According to the conventional account, trial by compurgation was driven out of the judicial market by a far more rational mode of proof that began to put in an appearance in civil cases sometime after the middle of the twelfth century and in criminal ones fifty or so years later—trial by jury. Jurors, it is maintained, differ from compurgators in one crucial respect: they do not swear a judicial oath that the accused's claim is sound; their oath merely commits them to decide its soundness some time later in court. 'The oath helper', says Maitland, 'is brought in that he may swear to the truth of his principal's oath.... On the other hand, a recognitor must swear a promissory oath: he swears that he will speak the truth whatever the truth may be' (i. 140). As a consequence of this, the standard account concludes, jurors found themselves free for the first time to undertake a rational investigation of the factual basis of the accusation, where their predecessors had been forced to stop short at the public reputation of the accused. We might note that in the passage just quoted Maitland uses the word *truth* in two quite distinct senses: where the compurgator swears to 'the truth of his principal's oath' he is clearly establishing the kind of 'truth' Gurevich would recognize as anthropomorphous, whereas

---

[12] *Die Gesetze der Angelsachsen*, ed. F. Liebermann, 3 vols. (1903–16; Sindelfingen, 1960), i. 140.

[13] After explaining that 'an infamous person...one earlier convicted of perjury, because he loses his law, and is thus said to be no longer law-worthy', should be barred from jury service in an action of Novel Disseisin, Bracton adds, 'quod Anglice dicitur, "He nis nocht othesworthe the is ene gilty of othbreche"' (*De legibus*, iii. 71).

[14] The equivalent law French term *franche ley* remained in regular use well into the 14th cent. and its English calque was still known in the early 17th cent. (see *OED*, s.v. *Frank-law*).

the juror's promise to speak 'the truth whatever the truth may be' implies something far closer to our own notion of scientific truth. The first of these two senses was commonly expressed in Ricardian England by the word *trouthe* ('this . . . have I sayd', writes Thomas Usk, 'only for trouthe of my sacrament in my legiaunce'[15]), but the use of *trouthe* to express the second was still very novel in the late fourteenth century.

The *OED*'s earliest recorded instance of *truth* meaning 'a true statement or account; that which is in accordance with the fact' (s.v. 8) is taken from the A-text of *Piers Plowman*,[16] and from there it can only have been a short step to the sense 'the fact or facts; the actual state of the case; the matter or circumstance as it really is' (s.v. 11). There is a good illustration of this new sense in the courtroom scene in *The Tale of Beryn* (*c.*1430): the hero is on trial for murdering the father of a character called Machyn with a stolen knife, and his defence counsel explains to the court,

> Then were spedful for to knowe howe Beryn cam first t[h]o
> To have possessioune of the knyff þat machyn seith is his,
> To ȝewe vnknowe; I shall enfourm þe trowith as it is. (3800–2)[17]

It is important to notice, however, that a mere half-century earlier the word most likely to have been chosen in such a context would not have been *truth* at all, but *sooth*. Thus, Thomas Usk concludes his account of the events that led up to his imprisonment, 'And for comers hereafter shullen fully, out of denwere [without doubt], all the sothe knowe of these thinges in acte, but as they wern, I have put it in scripture' (*Testament*, I. vi. 193–5). For Usk, *truth* was a quality that resided not in the tale but in its teller (the personal integrity, in fact, that enables his own readers to put their faith in his testimony): 'for trewly, lady, me semeth that I ought to bere the name of trouthe, that for the love of ryghtwysnesse have thus me submitted' (I. vi. 196–8).

The very appearance of this new factual sense in the late fourteenth century attests, I believe, to a fundamental change in cul-

---

[15] *Testament of Love*, I. vi. 164–5; *Chaucerian and Other Pieces (Being a Supplement to the Complete Works of Geoffrey Chaucer)*, ed. W. W. Skeat (Oxford, 1897), 29.

[16] This example has been queried, however; see Kane, *Liberating Truth*, 24 n. 19.

[17] Ed. F. J. Furnivall, EETS ES 105 (London, 1909).

tural attitudes towards evidence and verification, and one that underlies the prominence of *trouthe* in the work of the major Ricardian poets. However, when English speakers first began to transfer a word traditionally used to describe the moral status of the actor to the epistemological status of the act, they look to have been reflecting a conceptual shift that, as I have just suggested, legal historians regard as having accompanied the introduction of jury trial some 200 years earlier. There seems in other words to be a gross temporal discrepancy between the standard legal account of this new mode of proof and the earliest signs of its effect on vernacular usage. Put crudely, a legal process that shifts its probative focus from anthropomorphic to scientific truth first makes an appearance, according to the legal historians, in the late twelfth century, yet this mode of verification makes its mark on English vernacular usage only in the late fourteenth century. In what follows I shall be trying to show that such a discrepancy is more apparent than real, that the older patterns of proof lingered on in the popular imagination long after compurgation had become peripheral in the king's courts, and that even as late as the fourteenth century many people would still have felt that the jury's job was to speak a kind of truth that promoted the concrete interests of the group, rather than one narrowly circumscribed by fact. In other words, legal historians have by and large exaggerated the rapidity with which the new modes of proof came to be accepted and underestimated the tenacity with which the popular imagination clung to its traditional notions of verification.

There are three major difficulties with the view that from the early thirteenth century onwards English law began rapidly to replace 'irrational' compurgation (irrational, that is, in its concentration on the probity of the parties) with 'rational' jury trial (rational, because it preferred to concern itself with the probative value of factual evidence). In the first place, compurgation was not rendered universally redundant: it was ousted only from the king's courts, and even there continued to maintain a significant foothold to the very end of the Middle Ages. In manorial, borough, and franchisal courts it was widely employed well into the fifteenth century, and, as T. F. T. Plucknett warns us, 'any picture of the juridical position of the bulk of the population must be taken subject to the important reservation that the extent of local custom may be larger than at present suspected';[18] such major civic jurisdictions as London and Bristol were still putting their trust in wager of law long after Chaucer's day.[19] Moreover, ecclesiastical courts, despite the far more learned and 'rational' traditions of the canon law, were similarly happy to resort to compurgation to decide criminal cases.[20] Indeed, even the common law itself continued to use compurgation to settle certain private actions (most notably, 'debt *sur contract*'),[21] as well as for resolving a number of procedural log-jams;[22] and in the chaotic aftermath of the Peasants' Revolt, when legal documents were destroyed on a massive scale, parliament returned to it as an effective way of dealing with a rash of malicious prosecutions.[23]

Secondly, there is no reason to suppose that oath-helpers had ever been indifferent to factual evidence—in Holdsworth's words, 'it would probably be difficult to get any considerable number of compurgators from the same neighbourhood and of the same rank of the accused to swear deliberately to be true that which the countryside knew to be false'.[24] No respectable oath-helper could have been expected to support a claim that he or she knew for a fact to be perjured, and where respected opinion was divided a higher premium would normally have been placed on reliable witnesses than on reliable compurgators. Moreover, except in the actual wording of the oaths, witness proof (which did claim to depend upon a knowledge of the facts) differed little, procedurally speaking, from compurgation, and it is clear that both shared the same basic jural assumptions. Thus, an Anglo-Saxon formulary gives the witness's oath in the present tense, a clear sign that its

[18] *Year Books of Richard II: 13 Richard II, 1389–1390*, ed. Theodore F. T. Plucknett (London, 1929), p. xlvii.
[19] This was particularly true of civil actions such as contract (see Robert L. Henry, *Contract in the Local Courts of Medieval England* (London, 1926), 48–90), but seems even to have extended to criminal ones (see Pollock and Maitland, *History*, ii. 635–6).
[20] See R. H. Helmholz, 'Crime, Compurgation and the Courts of the Medieval Church', *Law and History Review*, 1 (1983), 1–26.
[21] That is to say, a debt deriving from an oral agreement, as opposed to one recorded in writing; see A. W. B. Simpson, *A History of the Common Law of Contract: The Rise of the Action of Assumpsit*, 2nd edn. (Oxford, 1987), 136–44.
[22] Pollock and Maitland, *History*, ii. 634.
[23] *Statutes of the Realm (1101–1713)*, 11 vols. (London, 1810–28), ii. 31.
[24] Sir William Holdsworth, *A History of English Law*, ii, 4th edn. (London, 1936), 110.

function was assertory not promissory: 'In the name of the almighty Lord, as I stand here, a true witness for N., neither importuned nor bribed, I saw with my eyes and heard with my ears, that which I speak alongside him.'[25] For this reason, in informal accounts of early process (such as Marie de France's description of the hero's trial in *Lanval*) it is not always easy to decide which mode of proof is being employed.

Probably written for the court of the Angevin King Henry II (1133–89) at a time when the English common law was still in its formative stage, *Lanval*, as a number of commentators have pointed out, displays a remarkably detailed knowledge of legal terminology and procedure.[26] Sir Lanval, in rejecting Guinevere's sexual advances, has rashly claimed that his lady's lowliest maid is more worthy than she (297–30),[27] thereby incurring the anger not only of the queen but also of his fairy mistress (whose command not to reveal her existence he has thus foolishly broken). He immediately finds himself facing a twofold accusation before the king: a trumped-up charge of attempting to seduce the queen and a rather more credible one of slander. Of course, the first is potentially the more serious: it is, as the count of Cornwall, who acts as presiding justice in the subsequent case, points out, a *felunie*, whereas the second is only a *mesfait* (435–43). Lanval meets the king's first accusation with a word-for-word denial in the proper form (371–4), but since no one is prepared to take over the role of accuser from the king, this charge of *felunie* must inevitably lapse (443–8);[28] as a mark of respect for the king, however, the court is willing to try the lesser charge of Lanval's *mesfait*, for which the punishment is none the less dismissal and banishment (459–60). This accusation Lanval answers with what later process would

[25] Liebermann, *Gesetze*, i. 398 (the verb in the original *þæt ic him mid secge* could of course be either present or future, but an early Latin translation renders this unambiguously as *quod cum eo dico*).
[26] See, particularly, E. A. Francis, 'The Trial in *Lanval*', in *Studies in French Language and Medieval Literature Presented to Professor Mildred K. Pope* (Manchester, 1939), 115–24; and the appendix, 'Explication du jugement de Lanval', to Jean Rychner's edition of *Le Lai de Lanval* (Geneva, 1958), 78–84.
[27] Marie de France, *Lais*, ed. Alfred Ewert (Oxford, 1965), 58–74.
[28] At this date the term *felony* still covered what later law would call *treason* and it seems to have been clearly understood that, as Maitland puts it, 'it was not seemly that the king, either in his own person or by his justices, who represent his person, should be judge' where he himself was a party in the dispute (*History*, i. 410).

have called a confession and avoidance—that is to say, he admits to having boasted of his lady but pleads in his own defence that the boast was true (375–7). A panel of barons is appointed to decide the case (424–6), and though these barons may look to us more like jurors than compurgators this appearance is deceptive; oath-helpers were not always, as we might suppose, hand-picked by their principal—they might easily, as here, be assigned by the court.[29] The dilemma facing the barons, however, is of a kind that caused the old legal process particular difficulty: since Lanval has kept his fairy mistress secret, the issue sets the word of one party against that of the other, and though they are evidently inclined to put more faith in Lanval's word than Guinevere's, the relative status of the parties makes the discharge of a simple compurgation a very awkward matter.

The solution—to get Lanval to produce his mistress in court—looks to us like an obvious and familiar expedient: she is, we will naturally assume, being called as a witness for the defence so that her testimony may provide the vital evidence that Lanval's case so obviously lacks. But this is not what is going on at all. The summoning of witnesses to testify before a jury seems to have played only a very small part in medieval common law process, particularly on the civil side;[30] unlike their modern counterparts, medieval jurors were apparently expected to inform themselves in advance about the circumstances of the case they were to decide and the only evidence they would normally expect to encounter at the time of the actual trial would be written evidence. As E. A. Francis pointed out long ago,[31] the procedure adopted in *Lanval* was one known as voucher to warranty. Here is how Marie's contemporary Glanvill describes such voucher: 'if the tenant says

---

[29] In the London of Marie's day, for instance, the city aldermen (*prud'hommes*) picked the compurgators for the most serious cases (Mary Bateson, 'A London Municipal Collection of the Reign of King John', *EHR* 17 (1902), 707); see also *Leges Henrici Primi*, ed. and tr. L. J. Downer (Oxford, 1972), app. II, 430–5.

[30] The notion of the self-informing jury, a truism of medieval legal history, has recently been challenged by Edward Powell, 'Jury Trial at Gaol Delivery in the Late Middle Ages: The Midland Circuit, 1400–1429', in J. S. Cockburn and Thomas A. Green (eds.), *Twelve Good Men and True: The Criminal Trial Jury in England, 1200–1800* (Princeton, 1988), 78–116; Powell's evidence, however, is drawn entirely from the criminal side. I am grateful to James H. Landman for this reference.

[31] Francis, 'The Trial in *Lanval*', 123.

in court that the thing claimed is not his, but that he holds it as lent to him for use, or deposited to be looked after, or let to him, or given as a gage, or in any other way which implies that it is not his... but another's, then that other shall be summoned;... and thus the pleas will begin again against that other.'[32] This, by an elegant fiction, both legal and literary, is the action the count of Cornwall proposes to use in Lanval's case:

> Un serment l'engagera,
> E li reis le nus pardura,
> E s'il poet aver sun guarant
> E s'amie venist avant
> E ceo fust veir kil en deïst
> Dunt la reïne se marist
> De ceo avra bien merci,
> Quant pur vilté ne dist de li. (449–56)

(An oath shall bind him, and the king shall entrust him to us, and if he is able to procure his warrantor, and if his lady appears before us, and if what he said of her, and what upset the queen, was true, he shall be fully pardoned, since he did not speak it out of malice.)

Far from being summoned as a mere witness, then, this process will co-opt Lanval's mistress as a principal in the case.

Before the lady's actual arrival in court to defend Lanval, four of her maids precede her, and since, technically, the worthiness of her lowliest maid is what is at issue in the trial, a modern lawyer might well wish to claim that the panel of barons is now free to dispense with the evidence of the mistress. Guinevere's reaction, however, makes it quite clear that only the presence of the warrantor herself can clear Lanval, and thus that the proof she is to make must depend upon something other than simple factual verification. When she does finally arrive, the lady takes up his case just as an overlord might take up her vassal's case in a feudal court, transferring to her own shoulders the burden of proving his innocence (615–24): as E. A. Francis rightly points out, 'it is not merely her presence, and appearance, which fulfills the task set to the defendant. She makes a formal statement, asserting that Lanval's "denial" is true.'[33] The result proves decisive:

---

[32] *The Treatise on the Laws and Customs of the Realm of England Commonly Called Glanvill*, ed. G. D. G. Hall, supp. M. T. Clanchy (Oxford, 1993), 37–8.
[33] Francis, 'The Trial in *Lanval*', 123.

> Ceo qu'il en jugerunt par dreit
> Li reis otrie ke issi seit.
> N'ad un sul qui n'ait jugié
> Que Lanval ad tut desrainié.
> Delivrez est par lur esgart. (625–9)

(Whatever they shall judge of her by law, the king grants that it shall be so. There was not one who did not find that she had completely *deraigned* Lanval. He was released by their award.)

While much of the legal terminology in the poem has been examined in detail, it does not seem to have been noticed that the word *desrainié* in this passage implies exoneration by compurgation or witness proof.[34] Which of the two it is here remains a nice question, however: do the barons assume the role of oath-helpers, demonstrating their faith in the lady's oathworthiness, or of witnesses, attesting to what they have seen with their own eyes? In practice, this distinction would probably not have seemed very significant to Marie's contemporaries, for what her court is principally concerned to establish is the kind of anthropomorphous truth that makes mere factual evidence subservient to the concrete interests of the group.

When we turn to the fourteenth-century English translation of Marie's lai, *Sir Landevale*,[35] it becomes immediately clear that we have entered a new world of 'rational' jury proof. Instead of Lanval's being *deraigned* by his mistress and a panel of barons, he puts himself 'on the country' and a jury of twelve sworn knights sets out to discover the factual truth (*soth*) of the charge for themselves:

> Landavale ansuryd at hys borde
> And told hym the sothe, euery worde,

---

[34] Strictly speaking, the word *deraign* means simply 'to acquit formally', but in an age of proof by oath it came to connote compurgation. The best evidence for this use comes from the mid-13th-cent. Norman *Summa de legibus* (*Coutumiers de Normandie*, ii, ed. E.-J. Tardif (Rouen, 1896)), which explains that a 'simple personal action' is so called because 'it has to be concluded by simple law, which is popularly called *disraisnia*' (p. 198), and then goes on to make clear that by simple law it means compurgation (pp. 200–6); a later passage specifies that *disraisnia* is only to be used for denying an accusation, not for supporting one (p. 325).

[35] Printed in Thomas Chestre, *Sir Launfal*, ed. A. J. Bliss (London, 1960), 105–28. Bliss dates *Sir Landevale* to the early 14th cent. and *Sir Launfal* to the end of the same century, but his evidence is far from conclusive.

> That it was nothing so,
> And he was redy forto die tho,
> That all the countrey wold looke.
> Twelue knyghtys were dreuyn to a boke
> The soth to say and no leese,
> Altogedir as it was. (287–94)

In true medieval style, this self-informing jury acquits Landevale of the charge of treason on the basis of the queen's soiled reputation alone ('she lovyd men ondir her lorde', 300), but demands to see his lady in person before pronouncing on the slander charge:

> And sith spake they farder then,
> That yf he myght hys leman bryng,
> Of whom he maide knolishyng,
> And yef her maydenyse bryght and shyne
> Wern fairer than the quene
> Jn makyng, semblaunt and hewe,
> They wold quyte hym gode and true. (304–10)

When the lady finally appears, she makes no formal *deraignment*; she merely appeals to the evidence of the jurors' senses:

> 'And of that othir, that he saide
> That myn lothliest maide
> Was fairer þan the quene,
> Loke anone yf yt so bene.'
> The kyng beheld and sawe the southe,
> Also erlys and barons bothe;
> Euery lorde said than
> Landevale was a trew man. (485–92)

The legal procedure is much the same (though not quite so carefully delineated) in Thomas Chestre's later tail-rhyme romance *Sir Launfal*, where the only major difference is that the king withdraws his charge before the jury can formally acquit Launfal as 'a trew man' (1003–5).[36]

Though it might seem that the fundamental jural shift from anthropomorphous to scientific truth we have been discussing is

---

[36] Thomas also introduces the motif of Guinevere's rash boast, 'ʒyf he bryngeþ a fayrer þynge | Put out myn eeyn gray!' 809–10), which later justifies the lady Tryamour in blinding her (ll. 1006–8); one might note that blinding was a customary punishment for rape (Pollock and Maitland, *History*, ii. 490), so this treatment of a sexually aggressive woman may conceal a legal joke, of sorts.

clearly exemplified by the marked differences in procedure between Marie de France's late twelfth-century *Lanval* and the anonymous (early?) fourteenth-century *Landevale*, these differences are probably better characterized as points on a continuum rather than signs of a radical disjuncture. In every medieval trial the two kinds of truth were held in a kind of dynamic tension by the relationship of the litigants themselves with those who had to decide between them, and, despite the shift to jury trial, this tension was far from being resolved at the end of the fourteenth century. The issue of factual evidence had not been irrelevant in Marie de France (as we have seen), nor is anthropomorphous truth an incidental factor in *Landevale* and *Launfal* (where, after all, Guinevere's reputation becomes the basis for deciding one of the two charges). Other works suggest, moreover, that though the court procedures themselves might have changed, people had yet to come fully to terms with the new modes of evidence and proof that they implied.

This brings us to the third reason why the conventional account of the easy triumph of jury trial over compurgation is misleading. Though many legal historians assume that 'it was obvious from its inception that the jury operated very differently from an ordeal or compurgation,'[37] the distinction has undoubtedly been magnified in hindsight. There are clear signs that in its early years people saw little essential difference between jury trial and the modes of proof that had immediately preceded it; in particular, witness proof (which, as we have seen, depended, like compurgation, on an assertory oath) seems to have been easily conflated with jury proof. Thayer gives several thirteenth-century instances of confusion between an issue *en proeve* (i.e. in proof by witnesses) and *en averrement* (i.e. proof by jury), and shows that mixed panels of jurors and witnesses are still being sworn well into the fourteenth century.[38] When the citizens of Ipswich reissued their borough laws in 1291 they included procedures for merchants to secure payment for sales that had not been recorded in writing: 'provided that the sale or the delivery of the said merchandise can be proved or averred by good inquest (*prové ou averé par bone enqueste*)

---

[37] J. H. Baker, *An Introduction to English Legal History*, 2nd edn. (London, 1979), 65.

[38] James Bradley Thayer, *A Preliminary Treatise on Evidence at the Common Law* (Boston, 1898), 19–21, 102–4.

according to merchant law in the form below written [i.e. by two witnesses who were present].'[39] Those who drew up this regulation evidently regarded proof by witness and averment by inquest as much of a muchness. This conceptual confusion suggests that people in the Middle Ages may have been less impressed than are modern legal historians by the jurisprudential distinction between an assertory and a promissory oath.

A few years earlier than the Ipswich customal, the author of the Anglo-Norman *Manuel des péchés* had offered an interesting exemplum to illustrate the evils of perjury:

> Un riche & un poure cuntekerent,
> Entur vne tere pleiderent;
> Tant vnt le play auant chacé
> Qe serment al riche fu iugé.
> Bien quiderent la gent
> Qe par tant ne freit faus serement;
> Veir dire deueit, a sun ascient,
> Mes il fausa malement
> Quant le serment li fu chargé;
> E apres sun cunte out cunté,
> Pur sei dist la faucceté
> E weuchi de la verité. (2949–60)[40]

(A rich man and a poor man had a dispute and went to law over a piece of land. The proceedings had progressed so far that the oath was awarded to the rich man. People certainly did not imagine that for such a matter he would make a false oath; he should have spoken truth to the best of his knowledge, but he proved wretchedly false when the oath was administered to him. And after he had presented his case, he spoke falsehood on his own account and evaded the truth.)

Predictably enough, God is quick to punish such cynical perjury:

> Car, quant vers val se enclina,
> E le seint liure beysa,
> Vnques apres ne releua,
> Ne a prestre nul mot parla. (2965–8)

---

[39] *Borough Customs*, ed. Mary Bateson, 2 vols., Selden Society 21 (London, 1906), i. 188.

[40] The *Manuel des péchés* has never been printed in full; this passage is quoted from the parallel text in F. J. Furnivall's edition of *Robert of Brunne's 'Handlyng Synne'*, 2 vols., EETS os 119 and 123 (London, 1901–3), i. 96.

(For when he bent down and kissed the holy book, he never after arose, nor did he speak a word to the priest [i.e. he died unconfessed].)

The oath sworn by the rich man in this exemplum is clearly an assertory oath, though whether he is depicted as swearing it unsupported or with oath-helpers is less obvious.

The value of this little exemplum as a record of contemporary legal process is greatly enhanced by the fact that at least three later versions of it survive: one in Robert Mannyng of Brunne's *Handlyng Synne*, written in the early fourteenth century, another in a late fourteenth-century prose translation of the *Manuel*, called *Of Shrifte and Penance*, and a third in Peter Idley's mid-fifteenth-century *Instructions to his Son*.[41] Not even the three versions of *Lanval* can rival this series (running from *c.*1275 to *c.*1450) of four fictional accounts of the same trial for the vivid picture they give of developments in English legal process in the late Middle Ages; among the many fascinating questions they raise, however, I will deal here with two in particular: an evolving concept of truth and a remarkably stable attitude to judicial oaths.

In the early fourteenth century, Robert Mannyng was still able to imagine such a trial as amenable to a decision by compurgation or witness proof (though it may be that the very reason he chooses to set the story 'yn londoun toune' is that by his own day only a borough court could still have been imagined as capable of awarding wager of law in a real action such as this),[42] but he adds a cynical little aside suggesting his scepticism about the whole process:

> Wytnes þey alle gan hym bere
> Þat he ne wlde falsly swere,
> For ryche men are holde trewe
> Þogh here falsnes be neuer so newe. (2705–8)

---

[41] Robert Mannyng of Brunne, *Handlyng Synne*, ed. Idelle Sullens, Medieval & Renaissance Texts and Studies (Binghamton, NY, 1983), 69–70; 'Of Shrifte and Penance: A Late Middle English Prose Version of "Le Manuel des péchés"', ed. Tess S. Singer (Ph.D. diss., New York University, 1972), 82–3 (I am grateful to my colleague Nicholas Watson for bringing this edition to my attention); *Peter Idley's Instructions to his Son*, ed. Charlotte D'Evelyn (Boston, 1935), 152.

[42] The only instance of compurgation in a real action that I know of comes from the late 13th-cent. Scottish *Leges quatuor burgorum* (*Borough Customs*, i. 46), and many borough customals explicitly except proof by compurgation from such an action (e.g. Sandwich i. 171)). It seems worth pointing out, however, that the citizens of London managed to resist royal attempts to impose inquest proof on them until 1321 (Bateson, 'London Municipal Collection', 719).

On the other hand, Mannyng's version, besides including an interesting echo of the wording of an actual oath formula, shows signs
of conflating assertory and promissory oaths:

> Whan he was charged þe soþe to seye
> Þat he ne schulde for loue ne eye,
> No for lef no for loth,
> But trewly to swere hys oth,
> A nouþer þan was yn hys þoght. (2709–13)

Of Shrifte and Penance also retains the basic premiss of trial by
oath but seems inclined to nudge it in the direction of jury trial.
One passage, in particular—'He schulde sey soth at hys wytynge,
but lyud falsly. For whanne þe oth hym was charged and aftur þat
he had tolde his tale, for hym he seyde fals and þat schewod wel'—
seems to imply that he is swearing a promissory oath to give a true
account, not an assertory oath that the claim itself is true. However, by the time we come to Peter Idley (*c.*1450) the transition to
jury trial is complete.

In Idley's version it is not the principal, the rich man, who is
struck down by God's vengeance, but, far more realistically (in
terms of contemporary procedure), one of those who has been
'enpanelled in array' to serve on the 'enqueste'—in other words,
a corrupt juryman:

> A litell tale I shall reherse you therefore:
> In London it befelle, as I herde seye,
> Of a man that wilfully was forswore,
> That was enpanelled among othir in array
> And was charged þat for love, mede, or aye,
> To sey the trouthe of suche as shold be hys charge. (2729–34)

Idley's 'to sey the trouthe' here evidently corresponds to the phrase
in *Of Shrifte and Penance* 'He schulde sey soth' (p. 82), and both
render an original 'veir dire deueit' from the *Manuel des Péchés*
(2955). Robert Mannying offers only a paraphrase at this point,
but the fact that he translates 'quant le serment li fu chargé' by
'Whan he was charged þe soþe to seye' (2709) suggests that, like
the author of *Of Shrifte*, he too would have regarded *soþe*, not
trowþe, as the English equivalent of *veir* in such a context. Such a
usage is also to be found in *Sir Landevale*, as we have seen:
'Twelue knyghtys were dreuyn to a boke | The soth to say' (292–
3). Since the phrase *veir dire deueit* recalls the familiar compound

voir dit (an anachronistically literal translation might almost render it 'he should have given a verdict'), Peter Idley's version provides powerful evidence that, where fourteenth-century people had thought of a court verdict as expressing a *sooth*, by the mid-fifteenth century it had come to be regarded as an declaration of the *truth*.

In both the earlier English versions the word *truth* stands for a moral quality rather an objective state—it represents, in other words, an aspect of Gurevich's anthropomorphous truth rather than the truth of modern forensic science. The translator of *Of Shrifte*, for instance, employs *trowthe* in place of the *Manuel*'s *verité* when the subject is the truth of holy Scripture, translating 'Par tant fu mustré la verité | Qe en escripture auum troué' (2969–70) as 'By so muche the trowthe was schewed þat in holy wryt we have fonde' (pp. 82–3). While Robert Mannying does not, in fact, employ the noun *trowþe* within the story itself—though his use of the adjective ('ryche men are holde trewe') and the adverb ('trewly to swere hys oth') suggests that he associates it with honesty and integrity rather than factual accuracy—in a moralizing passage that immediately follows he makes it the antonym of perjury:

> For hys loue þat deyde on þe rode,
> Forswere 30w neuer for werldes gode,
> For 3e wete weyl & haue hyt herd
> Þat trowþe ys more þan al þe werld. (2761–4)

In the fourteenth century there had evidently been a relatively clear semantic boundary between *sooth* and *truth*, at least in legal contexts—the first applied to the factual accuracy of the thing sworn to, the second to the moral worth of the swearer. If by the mid-fifteenth century the distinction between these two categories had broken down, it can only have been because the ancient juridical, and cultural, fiction that factual truth was identical with the truth that men swore to could no longer be sustained and increasing social pressure to preserve appearances had led to the sense of the originally subordinate term *sooth* being subsumed into the more prestigious word *trouthe*.

With hindsight, it seems self-evident to us that the assertory oath of the old process and the promissory oath of the new performed quite different procedural functions and entailed radically different attitudes to evidence and proof, but the fortunes of this little exemplum from the *Manuel des péchés* suggest that such a distinction seemed far less significant to the men and women of the Middle Ages than it does to us. Perhaps the most remarkable thing about Peter Idley's version of the story is that it treats the oath of his juryman as if it were legally and morally commensurate with that of the compurgator of his source. Nowadays, we require of our jurors an honest opinion not a sworn attestation and are quite prepared to make allowances for their human fallibility should this opinion later prove to have been mistaken, but the Middle Ages seem to have made a far closer identification between the factual truth of a jury's findings and the ethical truth of the jury itself. Thus a late thirteenth-century legal tract, the *Mirror of Justices*, regards it as an abuse 'to insert into oaths the phrase, "to the best of their knowledge," so as to compel jurors to say what they opine, whereas the principal words of their oath are to the effect that they will say the truth (*qil voir dirrent*)'.[43] By implication, an erroneous verdict could still be thought of as a species of lying—a position entirely consistent with the odd view (held by both scholastics and lawyers) that to break a promise was 'a sort of retrospective act of falsification'.[44]

Of course, it would be absurd to suppose that either judges or juries were incapable of appreciating the distinction between a deliberate lie and an honest mistake,[45] but the old tradition that a lawsuit was in the final analysis a test of the defendant's personal truth seems to have taken a long time to die. It was for this reason, I believe, that juries throughout the Middle Ages showed themselves willing to make 'unacceptable rules produce acceptable results by adjusting the facts', as S. F. C. Milsom has put it, or in Thomas Green's words, 'to voice a sense of justice fundamentally at odds with the letter of the law... to say the "truth" as they knew

---

[43] *The Mirror of Justices*, ed. William J. Whittaker, Selden Society 7 (London, 1895), 173; for a jury verdict given 'super eorun intellectu' see John S. Beckerman, 'Procedural Innovation and Institutional Change in Medieval English Manorial Courts', *Law and History Review*, 10 (1992), 220 n. 109.

[44] Simpson, *History*, 386.

[45] See Morris S. Arnold, 'Law and Fact in the Medieval Jury Trial: Out of Sight, Out of Mind', *American Journal of Legal History*, 18 (1974), 277, and S. F. C. Milsom, *Historical Foundations of the Common Law*, 2nd edn. (London, 1981), 412.

it'.[46] At the same time, it helps explain why the opprobrium that attached to faulty verdicts throughout the Middle Ages should regularly have been expressed in terms of perjury:

> & þerfor ȝe questmen þat gon vp on questis,
> For eny wraþþe or wynnyng do ȝe þat best is.
> Loke þat ȝe swere truli & trewe tale telle,
> Þat ȝe dampne not ȝour soulis & wend vn to helle. (144–7)[47]

There is clearly more to such a passage than the simple feeling that dishonest jurymen had failed in their sworn undertaking to provide impartial justice; apparently people could still remember that legal verdicts had once served a rather different purpose, for this early fifteenth-century poem plainly uses the phrase 'trewe tale telle' much as the *Manuel* had used 'veir dire' or *Of Schrifte* 'sey soth'.

Such an attitude helps explain the very curious way in which jury decisions were formally challenged throughout the Middle Ages. Glanvill, writing of the Grand Assize in the late twelfth century, speaks of the penalty 'for those who swear rashly in this assize':

If the jurors are duly convicted in court of perjury, or confess to it in court, then they shall be deprived of all their chattels and moveable goods which shall pass to the king.... They shall, moreover, be cast into prison and kept there for a year at least. In addition they shall lose their law for ever and thus rightly incur the lasting mark of infamy. This penalty is justly ordained so that the fear of such punishment shall prevent all men from swearing a false oath in such a case. (*Treatise*, 36)

In the mid-thirteenth century (by which time a formal process known as attaint had been devised to deal with flawed verdicts),[48] Bracton attacks perjured jurors with similar virulence: 'they incur perpetual infamy and lose the *lex terrae*, so that they will never afterwards be admitted to an oath, for they will not henceforth be oathworthy (*quia de cetero non erunt atheswurthe*)' (*De legibus*, iii. 346). As late as the mid-fifteenth century, a strong sense of shame still attached to attaint: 'the bodies of those jurors shall be

---

[46] Milsom, *Historical Foundations*, 422, and Thomas A. Green, *Verdict According to Conscience* (Chicago, 1985), 52.

[47] Thomas J. Heffernan (ed.), 'A Middle English Poem on Lovedays', *ChauR.* 10 (1975–6), 180.

[48] See H. G. Richardson and G. O. Sayles (eds.), *Select Cases of Procedure without Writ*, Selden Society 60 (London, 1941), pp. lxxvii–lxxix.

committed to the prison of the lord king,' says Fortescue, 'their houses and buildings demolished, their woods cut down, their meadows ploughed up, and they themselves shall henceforth be infamous, and their testimony as to the truth shall nowhere be accepted.'[49]

Statutes and law reports confirm this impression that jurors were felt to be somehow deciding cases *by* oath, not merely *on* oath. Thus chapter 38 of Edward I's first statute of Westminster (1275) begins, 'Forasmuch as certain People of this Realm doubt very little to make a false Oath, which they ought not to do, whereby much People are disherited and lose their Right: It is provided that the King of his Office shall henceforth grant Attaints upon Enquests in Pleas of Land...'; and the first statute of Edward III's reign (1326) extends the action of attaint to cover 'the false Oaths of Jurors in Writs of Trepass' (i.e. in what we should call tort litigation).[50] So, too, a yearbook report of a verdict in attaint from 1341–2 begins, 'The jury [of attaint] said that the jurors of the petty jury had made a false oath, inasmuch as they said that the manor of Elledene was not given to the ancestor of John, son of Thomas de Brembleshete (uncle of Lawrence who now is plaintiff).'[51] The report concludes with a list of the punishments to be inflicted on the convicted jurors that conforms closely to those given by Glanvill, Bracton, and Fortescue, including the provision that they shall 'lose their free law for ever' (pp. 62–3).

My final literary trial, the appeal of Constance for the murder of Hermengild, also exists in several versions, though the time-span between them is not nearly as great, nor are their procedural differences nearly as marked, as in my previous examples. Unlike these, however, this trial is recorded in two major Ricardian narratives (Chaucer's *Canterbury Tales* and Gower's *Confessio Amantis*) and offers one particularly striking instance of the use of the word *trouthe*.[52] The story of Constance's trial first appears in England in an Anglo-Norman chronicle written by the Oxford

---

[49] Sir John Fortescue, *De laudibus legum Anglie*, ed. and tr. S. B. Chrimes (Cambridge, 1942), 60–3.

[50] *Statutes of the Realm*, i. 36 and 253.

[51] *Year Books of the Reign of King Edward the Third: Years XVI (First Part)*, ed. and tr. L. O. Pike, Rolls Series (London, 1896), 60–1.

[52] See the Man of Law's Tale, II (B¹) 582–693, and *Confessio Amantis*, II. 792–889.

Dominican Nicholas Trevet. Trevet describes how a knight called Sessoun, whose sexual advances have been rebuffed by Constance, murders her mistress and then hides the bloody dagger under her pillow in an attempt to incriminate her. The actual process by which she is tried is one that was known as appeal ('cist tretres...a huge crie apela la pucele de tresoun'),[53] an ancient procedure designed to enable an injured party to bring a civil action against a felon. This was a relic of a time when all law had been private law and even murderers might be sued by members of the victim's family, but by the late fourteenth century it was falling out of general use, mainly because the uncertainty of the proof involved (trial by battle) made it unattractive to most litigants. It is particularly ironic, then, that Chaucer should have included this archaic process in a tale told by the one professional representative of the king's law on his pilgrimage (though it is perhaps significant that the Man of Law's Tale is the only version in which the trial is presided over by King Alla in person).

Appeal was archaic, moreover, not only in maintaining a pocket of private procedure within an established criminal jurisdiction, but also in its reliance on the judicial oath. The appellant swore the defendant was a felon; the defendant swore that the appellant was a perjurer; and the ensuing battle proved which oath was true.[54] Of course, Constance's divine protector strikes down the knight before she can prepare her own defence, but in the normal course of things she would have been expected to provide herself with a human champion ready to counter-swear her appellant's charge. Perhaps this particular appellant has rashly assumed that Constance's manifest guilt will prevent him ever having to expose his own oath to the test; in Gower's version, indeed, he cries out: 'Lo, seth the knif al blody hiere! | What nedeth more in this matiere | To axe?' (861–3). All three versions, however, suggest that the presiding judge is unimpressed by the presumption of Constance's guilt. In Trevet, he 'ne poeit cele crueute penser de la pucele' (p. 171), and in Gower, 'no ful credence took' of the

---

[53] Ed. Margaret Schlauch, in *Sources and Analogues of Chaucer's 'Canterbury Tales'*, ed. W. F. Dempster (New York, 1941), 171.

[54] See the story in *Dives and Pauper* of the Scotsman who appeals an Englishman of treason, but loses the case because he refuses to swear a judicial oath before the battle (ed. Priscilla H. Barnum, 2 vols., EETS 275 and 280 (London, 1976–80), I. i. 255).

knight's complaint (867). It is because of similar doubts that Chaucer's Alla sets in motion a process of formal proof:

> This gentil kyng hath caught a greet motyf
> Of this witnesse, and thoghte he wolde enquere
> Depper in this, a trouthe for to lere. (628–30)

What is this *trouthe* that Alla hopes to learn here? If it is simply 'the fact or facts' of the case, why should Chaucer have prefered *truth* to the normal Ricardian word *sooth*? (Gower's knight, for instance, is urged to 'beknowe the sothe' (II. 883) after suffering divine retribution for his perjury.) And why, more to the point, does Chaucer write '*a* trouthe' rather than '*the* trouthe'?

In fact, fifteenth-century readers seem to have shared our sense of puzzlement over the line. Out of fifty-one manuscripts, only six give it in its accepted (Hengwrt/Ellesmere) form. Most of the others (forty-two in all) feel compelled to add either *caas* or *matere* after 'depper in this' (sometimes omitting *for* later in the line for the sake of metre), though, even of these, only nineteen retain the reading *a trouthe [for] to lere*. Among the others we find such variants as, 'Depper in this and trewly for to lere' (Ha¹); 'Depper in this matere trouthe to lere' (Hk); 'Depper in this caas he troweþ for to lere' (La); 'Depper in this the trouthe for to here' (Bo²); and 'Depper in this caas a trouthe to bere' (Ry¹).[55] The reason for this confusion, I suggest, is that Chaucer is using the word *trouthe* here in a sense that by the middle of the fifteenth-century was beginning to look distinctly old-fashioned, at least in such forensic contexts: the truth that Alla is seeking to discover is not, as many fifteenth-century scribes (and many subsequent readers and editors) seem to have assumed, the factual truth of the accusation against Constance, but the moral truth of the knight who is accusing her. This Chaucerian usage might, for example, be compared with the line 'to trien a trouthe be-twynne two sidis', from *Richard the Redeles* (ii. 85),[56] or the *Pricke of Conscience*'s threat of damnation for unjust judges, 'for þai wald noght til our trouthe come' (6032).[57] In Gower, as well as in Chaucer, this exemplum of

---

[55] See John M. Manly and Edith Rickert, *The Text of the Canterbury Tales*, 8 vols. (Chicago, 1940), v. 500.

[56] *Mum and the Sothsegger*, ed. Mabel Day and Robert Steele, EETS OS 199 (London, 1936), 9.

[57] Ed. Richard Morris (Berlin, 1863).

human *untrouthe* (Man of Law's Tale, II (B¹) 787; *Confessio Amantis*, II. 852) exposed by the immanent justice of the judicial oath attests to the stubborn resistance of ancient modes of proof grounded in personal oathworthiness to the challenge of more 'rational' systems of verification long after the supposed triumph of the common law jury.

Well into the next century this archaic sense can still be detected in the use of the word *trouthe* even in legal circles: '[We] offere vs', concludes an affidavit drawn up by three witnesses in 1424–5, 'when we are required of trewth, þere hit may stond in furþeryng of trewth and wirschipe of god in helthe of owre sowles, to swere and make oth vp-on a boc befor any juge Spiritual or temporal.'[58] Nevertheless, for reasons that lie far beyond the scope of this study, the old truth had evidently lost much of its cultural and legal potency during the course of the fourteenth century, and the Ricardian poets' obsession with the term may be seen in part as a conscious reaction to its attenuation. In sharp contrast to the Whiggish tone of much modern legal history, however, their nostalgia for the old law and their Saturnian suspicion of the new suggests that, far from finding in the 'rational' approach to evidence and proof entailed by jury trial the promise of a new era of justice and truth, they could see it only as another symptom of universal faithlessness and moral decay. Not for nothing does Langland characterize the father of the despair (wanhope) that paralyses the defenders of the barn of Unity in the apocalyptic final passus of *Piers Plowman* as 'a sysour that nevere swoor truthe— | Oon Tomme Two-tonge, atteynt at ech a queste' (B XX. 161–2).

---

[58] *Mittelenglische Originalurkunden von der Chaucer-zeit bis zur Mitte des XV. Jahrhunderts*, ed. Lorenz Morsbach, Alt- und Mittelenglische Texte 10 (Heidelberg, 1923), 12.

9

Ricardian Romance? Critiques and Vindications

NICOLAS JACOBS

In proposing the concept of 'Ricardian poetry', John Burrow made what was probably the first attempt to see the poetry of the last quarter of the fourteenth century—perhaps the first period of English literature in which a number of major poets can be demonstrated to have been composing more or less contemporaneously— as a coherent whole. After twenty years the time may have come to consider how the concept of a characteristic Ricardian manner has stood up. Rather than attempting to reconsider the work of Burrow's four authors in its entirety, it may be useful to focus attention on particular kinds of literature and the attitudes towards them evinced in the poetry. In this connection the case of romance is interesting for two reasons. The verse fiction classified by modern critics under that heading represents the remains of what must have been one of the most productive, if clearly heterogeneous, creative movements of the period. At the same time, the motivation of romance is to a large extent wish-fulfilment, sometimes material, sometimes moral, sometimes a mixture of the two: in consequence the ruling tone of much of it is characterized by easy optimism, by lack of complexity, and by moral certainty, all qualities which conflict with the tone of scepticism and moral inquiry which Burrow has identified as typically Ricardian.[1] The use made by the major Ricardians of the earlier romance tradition is one of the subjects addressed by him in detail. What remains to be done is to investigate their attitude to romance as such, and the

---

A version of this paper was delivered at the 6th Annual Conference of SELIM (Sociedad Española de Lengua y Literatura Inglesa Medieval) at Valladolid on 29 Sept. 1993.

[1] *Ricardian Poetry* (London, 1971), ch. 3, 'An Image of Man'.

relationship, in so far as one exists, between the major poets and the continuing tradition of verse romance.

The problems involved in such an enterprise are substantial. Romance has proved a convenient category for modern readers, but no scholar who has attempted to define it can be oblivious to the problems of doing so, and almost the only statement on the subject which would win general agreement is that no fourteenth-century author would have regarded what we call romance as a genre. On the other hand a consideration of Ricardian attitudes to different varieties of romance may give us some idea as to which, if any, were assigned anything like generic status. Next, it is by no means easy to date a mostly anonymous body of poetry with sufficient accuracy to determine what falls within our period: linguistic evidence is unreliable, literary influences and topical allusions only sporadic. As an example one need note only the recent attempt to demonstrate that *Sir Gawain and the Green Knight* is no later than 1353 and thus too early to be relevant to this inquiry.[2] Finally, there is a problem with the term 'Ricardian' itself: since the concept was originally defined in terms which have little to do, except in a contrastive sense, with popular or semi-popular romance, there is a danger that any investigation of Ricardian romance will turn into a circular argument whose predictable conclusion is that there is no such thing. In the circumstances all that can be done is to approach the material with as few preconceptions as human frailty permits and to see what emerges.

It is characteristic of romance that the central figure should endure his or her adventures or tribulations successfully and that the ending should be happy. This happy ending may, as A. V. C. Schmidt has observed,[3] be of various kinds, personal fulfilment being only one; the re-establishment of justice and good government, as in *Havelok* at the beginning of the fourteenth century or *Athelston* towards its end, or even the spiritual benefits consequent on the renunciation of worldly joys, as in the early fourteenth-century *Guy of Warwick* or the probably Ricardian *Stanzaic Morte Arthur*, are other possibilities. Romance thus has room for serious moral questions, and though the different social status of

    [2] W. G. Cooke, '*Sir Gawain and the Green Knight*: A Restored Dating', *MÆ* 58 (1989), 34–58.
    [3] A. V. C. Schmidt and Nicolas Jacobs, *Medieval English Romances* (London, 1980), i. 6–7.

the two languages earlier in the fourteenth century leaves behind it a tendency for English romances to be less sophisticated than their French counterparts, we have a fair number of them in which the happy ending is earned only by a thorough process of moral education, not all of which owe this element to French sources. On the other hand, even in some cases where the moral reformation of the hero is the main theme of a romance, the abruptness and weak motivation of his recognition of his sin and the author's apparent lack of interest either in the nature of sin or in the mentality of the sinner may give the moral lesson a curiously perfunctory air.[4] Again, those romances concerned with the sufferings of women manifest not only a comparable lack of interest in the psychology of endurance but also a curious complacency towards the sufferings themselves.

Given that a number of those romances which do address serious moral concerns, whether at a social level, as in *Havelok*, or at a personal level, as in *Ywain and Gawain* or *Sir Orfeo*, are of undoubtedly pre-Ricardian date, it seems that complacency, as well as the triviality which provides so easy a target for criticism, remains a besetting vice of romance in exactly the period when, as Burrow has demonstrated, the best poets were concerning themselves with the erosion of certainties and the undercutting of moral pretensions. Whatever debts Burrow's four poets may in their different ways owe to a more popular tradition, they appear to stand clearly apart from it in this respect. The problem is not the failure of the less sophisticated poets of the period to stand back from and question the presuppositions of their own work; one would not expect them to do so. What is more importantly lacking appears to be the kind of moral insight which would provide a stepping-stone between conventional complacency and Ricardian irony. Moral impulses, to be sure, are not entirely wanting even in the less sophisticated late fourteenth-century romances: the concern in *Sir Degrevant* for justice and good order and the interest shown in *Athelston* in the connection between private and public conduct are admirably serious, but neither, for all the vivid evocation of irrational jealousy in the latter, can be called a work of sophisticated moral analysis. The only romance which, at first

---

[4] As in *Guy of Warwick* and, most disastrously, *Sir Ysumbras*, for all the advocacy of Hanspeter Schelp, *Exemplarische Romanzen im Mittelenglischen* (Göttingen, 1967), 53–69.

sight, appears to qualify in those terms is, of course, included in Burrow's Ricardian canon; if, accordingly, we except *Sir Gawain and the Green Knight* from consideration, the distinction between polite and popular romance may, in terms of moral insight, not be great. If there is a stepping-stone at all, it may have to be sought in the less ambitious works of the major poets themselves; and few of these—perhaps only the Franklin's Tale, if that can be called unambitious, and the Wife of Bath's Tale—have much to do with romance.

That triviality and complacency could be recognized as characteristic of certain types of romance, and (it follows) that those types of romance were recognized, whatever they may have been called, as types, is clear from Chaucer's parodies. We need have no doubt of the implications of *Sir Thopas*: this is indeed, as Burrow has demonstrated in a series of brilliant studies,[5] a much subtler and more artistically constructed parody than we may have previously imagined, but a parody it remains, and however affectionate Chaucer's mockery may be of a tradition to which he owes more than he admits, there is no suggestion that he regarded the kind of romance which he is parodying as anything other than absurd. Another parody may perhaps be detected in *The House of Fame*, though the difficulty of interpreting the poem as a whole and of identifying the tone of its component parts makes the identification less secure. Nevertheless, it is hard to take the dreamer's paraphrase of the story of Aeneas altogether seriously. It is heavily larded with romance tags and clichés, among which one may note 170 'Crynge "Allas! and weylawey!"', 176 'Which that he lovede as hys lyf', 180 and again, most significantly, only nine lines later, 'That hyt was pitee for to here', 292 'Withoute drede, this ys no lye', together with other trite or platitudinous features.[6] The whole paraphrase can be read as exemplifying the reduction of

---

[5] J. A. Burrow, '*Sir Thopas*: An Agony in Three Fits', *RES* NS 22 (1971), 54–8; '"Listeth, Lordes": *Sir Thopas* 712 and 833', *N&Q* NS 15 (1968), 326–7; '"Worly under Wede" in *Sir Thopas*', *ChauR* 3 (1969), 170–3, collected, together with 'The Title "Sir"', in *Essays on Middle English Literature* (Oxford, 1984), 60–78; 'Chaucer's *Sir Thopas* and *La Prise de Nuevile*', *Yearbook of English Studies*, 14 (1984), 44–55.

[6] Many of these can be paralleled in Gower, with no detectable irony, but the heavy use of them here suggests a parodic intention. Similar effects may be intended at 139, 173, 184, 199–200, 218, 247–8, 268, 299, 313–14, 317, 404.

one of the great tragic narratives of western literature to a senti-mental tale whose emotional and aesthetic impact even on the notably undiscerning dreamer is aptly symbolized by the level plain of sand into which he emerges from the temple where he has seen the story depicted. The paraphrase may stand for the last stage of the degeneration of the romance of antiquity; we have independent confirmation, from a rather unexpected source, of the low status such matter enjoyed in the thirteenth Passus of the B-text of *Piers Plowman*, where the gluttonous Doctor of Divinity dismisses Patience's definition of Dowel as 'but a dido...a disours tale' (B XIII. 172).[7] It is worth remarking that, when Chaucer returns to the story of Dido and Aeneas in *The Legend of Good Women*, it is in an expansive and dignified manner which, as well as reflecting the poet's greater maturity, represents a return to the primary, classical sources and bears little relation to their hack-neyed derivatives as preserved in romance,[8] any more than does the comparable material, whatever its ultimate romance origins, in *Troilus and Criseyde* and the Knight's Tale.

The distinction between Chaucer's attitude to his subject-matter in these two poems and that in the *House of Fame* is significant. In the latter case the satire is at the expense of the narrative itself, with its worn-out forms and conventions, and the reader's sense of frustration at its trivialities is probably meant to be heightened by the recognition that a story of great power and significance is being demeaned by the way in which it is told. In the two later poems Chaucer has no intention of guying the manner of Boccac-cio, but he does, in a way which fits more closely with the accepted view of Ricardian irony, make fun of certain conventional attitudes carried over from romance. It is notable that the attitudes which come under criticism are predominantly those concerned with love: those which relate to war escape much more lightly. Thus, whereas an element of comic exaggeration may perhaps be detected in the account of the single combat of Palamon and

---

[7] Further light on Langland's view of romance is cast by his sardonic use of conventional imagery at B V. 158–9: 'And dame Pernele a preestes fyle—Prioresse worþ she nevere, | For she hadde child in chirie-tyme, al oure Chapitre it wiste!' The subtlety of the allusion is replaced at C VI. 136 with grotesque realism: 'For she hadde childe in þe chapun-cote she worþ chalenged at þe eleccioun.'

[8] See R. W. Frank, *The Legend of Good Women* (Cambridge, Mass., 1972), esp. 12–21, 57–78.

Arcite, the ensuing tournament seems exempt from questioning.[9] In the Knight's Tale even the conventions of love are reviewed in a vein of indulgent humour, as in Theseus' reflections on the God of Love and the absurd antics he inspires in young men; yet this too has its serious aspect, for the unruly emotions of Palamon and Arcite lead to a grave breach of the peace, and are thus a manifestation of the greater disorder which provides the tragic impetus for the whole tale.[10] Graver still, though less cosmic significance is attached to them, are the consequences of uncontrolled desire in two other tales placed in a romance setting: the rape committed by the young knight in the Wife of Bath's Tale and, I would add, the rape by false pretences plotted by Aurelius in the Franklin's Tale.[11]

Chaucer envisages, however, a much broader criticism of the amorous conventions of the Knight's Tale, though he chooses to dissociate himself from it by putting it in the mouth of a character as disreputable as Theseus is dignified. For whereas any romance material which may lie behind the *Teseida* is changed substantially there and almost out of recognition in the Boethian tragedy of the Knight's Tale, the Miller, in his vulgar parody of what he evidently sees as its absurd pretensions, disregards the whole philosophical framework of the tale and concentrates on its least important element, reducing it to a story of two men pursuing one girl. In effect, he reduces the plot of the Knight's Tale to that of a trivial romance, from which it is only a short step to his own vulgar, if in its way delightful, fabliau. Chaucer can no more be taken to present this as a serious criticism than he can in the case of the comparable opinions of the duck and goose in *The Parliament of Fowls* (554–95); but the implied warning that the high ideal of love represented in aristocratic romance can, from an unsympathetic point of view, be seen in quite another light is in keeping with the rueful sense of the fragility of human dignity noted by Burrow as characteristic of the Ricardian image of man.

---

[9] The argument to the contrary advanced by Terry Jones, *Chaucer's Knight* (London, 1980), 200–2, deserves mention. But it is to a large degree refuted by G. A. Lester, 'Chaucer's Knight and the Medieval Tournament', *Neophilologus*, 66 (1982), 460–9.

[10] Theseus' strictures provide, of course, Burrow's main illustrative example: *Ricardian Poetry*, 112–13. On the theme of order and disorder, see Charles Muscatine, *Chaucer and the French Tradition* (Berkeley and Los Angeles, 1957), 175–90.

[11] See N. Jacobs, review of *Geoffrey Chaucer: The Franklin's Tale*, ed. Gerald Morgan, *MÆ* 52 (1983), 126–31.

Less irreverent than the Miller's view, but closer to farce than that of Theseus, is the depiction of obsessive love which is the sole relic of romance in *Troilus and Criseyde*. In the first book, at least, Chaucer writes in the spirit of outright caricature; here, supremely, we are given a picture of a character who takes himself far more seriously than we, the audience, know him to have any justification for doing. It is true that he is not put in his place by a figure of authority, as Palamon and Arcite are by Theseus, Amans by Venus, Gawain by the Green Knight, or Will by the various personages with whom he imprudently argues: Pandarus is himself a rather absurd figure, and his criticism comes from below, from the world of pragmatism and good sense, not from above, from the world of philosophy and moral absolutes. In a way we are required to infer the authoritative voice from the tone of the narrative. As in the Knight's Tale, the serious aspect becomes clear in the light of the poem as a whole: the comic miseries of Troilus in the first book anticipate his tragic miseries in the fifth, and the mere silliness of a young man in love with love points forward to the dangerous imprudence of one who sets his whole heart on any worldly object. But, as with Theseus' comments, the immediate impression is that of a genial critique. Here, too, may belong those elements in the description of the Prioress in the General Prologue which suggest an ironic comparison to a romance heroine (I (A) 118–62), though it is likely that the object of the criticism here is not romance as such so much as the inappropriateness of courtly manners to a woman who is supposed to have renounced the world in general and love in particular.

Turning from Chaucer's critical allusions to romantic themes in works which are not themselves romances, and leaving aside *Thopas*, which is parody first and last, we are left with two other tales which fall into the modern category of romance: the Man of Law's and Squire's Tales. Each is in its way hard to interpret and resistant to modern critical attitudes, but neither can be left out of account. Any problems we may have with the Man of Law's Tale may well be the product of our unhistorical sense of genre, since there is no reason for Chaucer to have treated an exemplary tale, whose moral claims are different in kind from those of the more worldly courtly or chivalric romances, with the scepticism with which he approaches them. A single reference in a seemingly jocular tone to the need for wives to submit patiently to the importunity of their husbands (II (B¹) 708–14) does not amount to an attempt to ironize the tale; if we knew that Chaucer intended the Wife of Bath's Prologue to follow directly after the Man of Law's Tale it could be seen as having been inserted merely to provide a cue for that disquisition. Chaucer's purpose in couching the tale in a flat style alternating with bursts of high rhetoric remains obscure, but cannot readily be seen as stylistic parody. Though the style of such late fourteenth-century exemplary romances as the analogue *Emaré* might invite parody as much as or more than that of *Eglamour of Artois* or *Torrent of Portyngale*, Chaucer evidently refrained from mocking them, perhaps from a respect for the seriousness of their moral concerns. Gower's version of the same story is equally, and predictably, unquestioning. The romance tradition is for him a useful source of moralized stories, but no more. The Man of Law's Tale can readily be taken as an exposition of the ways of providence, as seen from a more overtly religious and less sanguine viewpoint than that of Theseus in the Knight's Tale, but the objects of Chaucer's irony are here wanting. The admirable endurance of Constance is given extra weight by contrast with a conspicuously unideal world: the moral excellence attributed elsewhere to the secular order is here superseded by the miraculous nature of divine grace, which transcends it. To ironize Constance would be inappropriate, as to ironize the divine order would be inconceivable.

The Squire's Tale is more problematic. To classify the tale of Constance as romance may appear arbitrary, and something which would not have occurred to Chaucer, but, whatever we call the Squire's Tale, it is hard to dissociate it generically from the other texts we classify as romances. Modern readers may feel that it exemplifies the vices of romance rather than its virtues, and many may be tempted to suppose that the Franklin agrees with them. The Squire's Tale, so this argument goes, is just the sort of tale that a charming but immature young man[12] would tell: it is a frothy, sentimental, and fantastical production which promises to go on at interminable length, and the Franklin, whose tone does indeed appear patronizing, does the pilgrims a service by interrupting it. And certainly, while the Squire, as a young man, has been invited

---

[12] Cf. the parody of the description in the General Prologue (I (A) 79–100) in the account of Absolon in the Miller's Tale (3314–38).

to tell a tale about love, it seems unlikely that his tale would have provided much enlightenment on the subject, whereas the middle-aged Franklin certainly has a contribution to make. But we should beware of supposing, simply because we find this kind of composition frivolous and pointless, that Chaucer must have intended the tale to exemplify these faults. Even in its truncated form it seems overlong for a parody *tout court*, and the style is in general not parodistic. In both respects it differs from *Thopas*, and we may not assume automatically that it represents Chaucer's adverse comment on another, more ambitious but equally vacuous, type of romance.

Nevertheless, some aspects of the tale suggest that Chaucer is not being altogether serious. To begin with, the fact that four main characters are named at the start and that Cambyuskan is sent in the first part four marvellous gifts suggests that we may expect at least four major episodes, an impression confirmed at the end of the second part; since that part presents us with no more than the beginning of an episode, it seems that the tale could hardly have been completed in fewer than six parts, and might indeed have been much longer, perhaps even longer than the Knight's Tale itself. Moreover, whereas the narrative progression of the Knight's Tale is straightforward, the advance summary of the plot of the Squire's Tale suggests something more complex: a framed or boxed structure, perhaps, or even an interlaced sequence. It is thus possible that Chaucer has made his Squire undertake, with the best of intentions, an enterprise which he is ill equipped to sustain, in terms both of length and of complexity.

Certain aspects of the rhetoric, too, are not quite what they seem. To disclaim rhetorical skill with the typically rhetorical device of the incapacity-topos (V (F) 35–42) is, of course, a thoroughly Chaucerian twist, but the lines 'It moste be a rethor excellent | That koude his colours longynge for that art' draw attention to the incongruity in a disconcerting way,[13] and it is odd to find the narrator using the device almost as soon as he has begun his

[13] The relation of these lines to the comparable passage in the Franklin's Prologue is not clear: in the latter, to be sure, the topos is introduced in a general context rather than for a particular rhetorical purpose, and thus the incongruity has less immediate point. Could we be certain that the composition of the Franklin's Prologue post-dates Chaucer's intention of linking the two tales, it would be tempting to read the lines as a rebuke to the Squire's supposed pretentiousness.

tale to avoid describing the beauty of his heroine. The next two incapacity-topoi are likewise suspect, if for different reasons: at 278–83 the Squire, as a 'dul man', is unable to describe the 'revel and the jolitee', yet in order to do so he would need to be one who had 'knowen love and his servyse | And been a feestlych man as fressh as May', which cannot but remind us of the Squire himself as he appears in the General Prologue, 'as fressh as is the month of May' (I (A) 92). Next, what looks to be a rhetorical question, 'who koude telle yow the forme of dances | So unkouthe, and swiche fresshe contenaunces', is, unexpectedly, given an answer, 'No man but Launcelot', whose logic is not obvious, and the statement, even more unexpected in its literal-mindedness, 'and he is deed' (283 ff.). When at 63 ff. the Squire, having declined to describe the delicacies at Cambyuskan's birthday feast, suddenly adds 'Eek in that lond, as tellen knyghtes olde, | Ther is som mete that is ful deynte holde | That in this lond men recche of it but smal', and then repeats his refusal to say anything about a detail in which he has deliberately aroused his audience's interest, someone, whether poet or narrator, is clearly playing tricks with the device of *occupatio*. The lines following 661, where the Squire lists the episodes to follow, can be read as a further variation on the device: the more usual Chaucerian practice is to give us a catalogue of what is not going to be described (as the Knight does at the beginning of his tale), and the reversal of the *occupatio* convention draws added attention to the tale's prospectively inordinate length. Finally, as an example of rhetorical exaggeration, we find at 419–21 that a tiger would have wept with pity for the lovelorn falcon: this would pass without comment in a text of the kind, except that the figure is immediately assimilated to literal reality by the qualification 'if that he wepe koude', and thus made ridiculous.

Something similar occurs with the device of anthropomorphism. The forsaken falcon says of her faithless tiercel: 'Anon this tigre, ful of doubleness, | Fil on his knees' (543–4): a bird, that is, whose courtship has been described in human terms, is suddenly compared to a tiger, and this tiger then behaves in a way appropriate only to a human. The incongruity which is exploited to humorous effect in the Nun's Priest's Tale (VII. 3160–2 ' "For whan I se the beautee of youre face, | Ye been so scarlet reed aboute youre yen, | It maketh al my drede for to dyen" '; 3179–82 'He looketh as it were a grym leoun, | And on his toos he rometh up and doon; |

Hym deigned nat to sette his foot to grounde. | He chukketh whan he hath a corn yfounde') becomes absurd here in what purports to be a serious context. With rather more subtlety, the tiercel's infidelity is described in terms of men's *newefangelnes*, which is in turn illustrated by the example—used again, we recall, in the Manciple's Tale—of a caged bird.[14] Whatever the case may be regarding the rhetoric, it is inconceivable that Chaucer could have overlooked these effects; the only possibility is that the absurdity is deliberate and meant to be appreciated.

I would suggest, indeed, that the Nun's Priest's Tale may provide the key to the understanding of the episode of the falcon. Whatever the relation between the trivial, stated moral of that tale and its deeper, implied moral, much of its point derives from the contrast between the uncompromisingly avian nature of Chauntecler and Pertelote and the learned discourses of which they deliver themselves: between the trivial nature of the events described and the inflated rhetoric with which the narrator responds to them. In the best Ricardian manner, Chaucer is here making fun of all human pretensions, with all the greater effect in that the objects of the burlesque are some of his own most cherished intellectual concerns: rhetoric, the philosophy of free will, the physiology and psychology of dreams. In a similar way, then, the episode of the falcon can be read as a gentle burlesque of a specific kind of literary pretentiousness: not, indeed, so much romance as love-vision, especially since Canacee's question at 450, 'Is this for sorwe of deeth or los of love?', is an obvious echo of the central *demande* of Guillaume de Machaut's *Jugement du roy de Behaingne*, the main source of *The Book of the Duchess*.

It would be rash to speculate on what Chaucer might have had in mind for the rest of the tale; but if we accept the argument, revived by Donald Howard,[15] that the Squire's Tale was intended to be a frame-tale, one might wonder whether the Squire is quite so naïve a narrator as has commonly been supposed, and whether the

---

[14] 610–20; cf. Manciple's Tale, IX (H) 163–74. The improbability, in the same tale, of a crow which sings 'Cokkow!' (243) is somewhat reminiscent of the passages under discussion, but it stands alone and nothing is made of it. More obviously comic in its function is the duck's hat in *The Parliament of Fowls*, 589.

[15] D. Howard, *The Idea of the 'Canterbury Tales'* (Berkeley and Los Angeles, 1976), 264–7; the idea was first mooted by Haldeen Braddy, 'The Genre of Chaucer's *Squire's Tale*', *JEGP* 41 (1942), 279–90.

several episodes might not have been planned to offer an anthology of burlesques of different poetic genres. We cannot guess
whether, if so, any of the various types of romance might have
been included. As it is, a particular type of romance appears to
have provided a frame for whatever the episodes were to have
been, and does not itself altogether escape parody: not only in the
promise or threat of extreme prolixity, but perhaps also in a
certain impatience at the conventionally marvellous. For there is
something faintly comic in the way in which the operation of the
brazen horse turns out to depend to so large an extent on the
twiddling of pins. But it is far from clear that romance as such is
the main object of the parody in the Squire's Tale: to the extent
that it is a target at all, the parody seems to have functioned at a
literary rather than a moral level, but if the chivalric episodes had
ever been written we might need to revise that conclusion.

Chaucer's attitudes to romance and its conventions may thus be
seen, as might be expected, to vary from work to work. Only in
the special and perhaps irrelevant case of exemplary romance,
which in this respect associates itself with the saints' legends and
moral exempla, does he present both form and subject-matter
without any implied criticism. Where secular romance is concerned, he sometimes parodies the form of romance, as in the
case of the romances of antiquity; sometimes queries certain
aspects of its content, as in the case of courtly and chivalric
romance; and sometimes both, as with popular romances of love
and adventure. As far as the evidence for courtly romance goes,
however, it is only the amorous excesses of romance heroes that
come in for criticism, never their martial exploits, nor do we find
any examination of the whole moral basis of chivalry. It should be
remembered, of course, that the evidence for Chaucer's attitude
towards courtly romance is scattered and somewhat equivocal. In
general we may say that, while aware of the contemporary
romance tradition and sufficiently interested in it to discriminate
between its various kinds, he shows little sign of regarding the
issues it raises as being of central importance.

The works of Chaucer thus present us with perhaps the most
varied evidence of a 'Ricardian' critique of romance. For the rest,
the testimony of *Sir Gawain and the Green Knight*, which subjects
the ideals to a much more thoroughgoing critique than Chaucer,
remains paramount. The differences between Chaucer's and the

Gawain-poet's treatment of the question are obvious enough to justify a detailed consideration of *Sir Gawain*, and in this connection it may be proper to look also at the other important Arthurian romance which can plausibly be attributed to our period: the *Stanzaic Morte Arthur*.[16] These two are, significantly enough, the two most important Middle English romances—arguably the only ones—in which the hero to some extent, in the last analysis, fails. The *Stanzaic Morte*, which is translated from a somewhat altered version of *La Mort le Roi Artu*,[17] the last part of the Vulgate Lancelot–Grail cycle, or something similar, is a sensitive, low-key, and rather elegiac rendering of the story, and it selects those elements of its source which most conform with the motifs of soiled idealism and the waste of human potential. It is in this text Lancelot's breach of loyalty, compounded by the obduracy of Gawain, rather than any structural flaw in the idea of knighthood, which brings about the ruin of the Round Table; we seldom have the sense that the ideals to which the court subscribes are themselves called in question. The nearest we ever come is perhaps in the injunction of the penitent Guinevere to Lancelot to 'thynke on thys world, how there is noght | But warre and stryffe and batayle sore' (3720–1); and the tone here is a world away from the jocular ironies of Theseus. This lack of overt questioning, however, is in part due to the lack of it in the source; and one reason why the ideals are not questioned there is not that the author saw no need to question them, but that they had already been comprehensively questioned, and found wanting, in the preceding work in the cycle, *La Queste del Saint Graal*,[18] from whose rigours the *Mort le Roi Artu* represents a substantial retreat, but in whose shadow it remains.

No allowance whatsoever is made for secular idealism in the *Queste*. Galaad has, indeed, his brief *aristeia* at the literal level of

---

[16] *Le Morte Arthur*, ed. J. D. Bruce, EETS ES 88 (London, 1903). The possibly Ricardian alliterative *Morte Arthure* cannot be classed as a romance, though it incorporates romance elements, arguably in the St Michael's Mount episode and certainly in that of Sir Priamus. *The Awntyrs of Arthur* is commonly considered to be a 15th-cent. work.

[17] *La Mort le Roi Artu*, ed. J. Frappier Textes littéraires français 58, 3rd edn. (Geneva, 1964).

[18] *La Queste del Saint Graal*, ed. A. Pauphilet, Classiques français du moyen âge 33 (Paris, 1967).

the narrative, but this serves only as a pivot for the transition to higher things. The vision of the Grail seems to involve the perception by bodily sense of the real presence of Christ in the Eucharist, something accessible only to the holiest of men, and the adventures undergone by those knights who achieve it appear to be allegorical representations of purely spiritual exercises, associated possibly with the forms of Cistercian monasticism, though the influence of the military orders should perhaps not be ruled out. The secular chivalry with which the Vulgate cycle has been up to this point concerned is superseded by this new development, and the author utterly repudiates it. Those knights who pursue the quest of the Grail as if it were just another chivalrous quest are rejected and lost. Worldly chivalry gives place to celestial: of Arthur's three Grail knights Galaad dies in ecstatic contemplation of the holy mysteries, Perceval becomes a hermit, and only Boort returns, literally to tell the tale. For the others nothing remains but the inevitable ruin of the Round Table: though on a human level that can be seen as a tragedy, and Lancelot, whose sinful attachment to the queen precipitates it, as a tragic hero, yet in the light of the Grail quest it is nothing more than the practical manifestation of what is already spiritually the case, and our regrets are wasted on it. The logic of the *Queste* is that Arthur's kingdom does not deserve to survive; on the contrary, its fall is fortunate as well as inevitable, for at least the soul of the penitent Lancelot can be saved from the wreckage.

The *Mort le Roi Artu* takes a contrastingly humane view of events. Admittedly, in the context of the whole Lancelot–Grail cycle, the calamitous end of Arthur's kingdom is an object-lesson in the dangers of building a society on secular values. But this appears not to be the primary purpose of the work: for all that the climax of the romance is the holy death of Lancelot, which implies that renunciation is in the end the only proper response to the instability and wickedness of the world, there is little overt reference to sin and less still to perfection. Boort reappears as a paragon of secular knighthood, and the author's interest is concentrated on the human tragedy of the Round Table in a way alien to the rigorist author of the *Queste*. Thus its effect, replicated in the rather world-weary elegiac tone of its English derivative, is to mitigate to a considerable degree the extreme position of the *Queste*; but the critique mounted in the latter remains the starting-point, as I believe it does with more pervasive effect for *Sir Gawain*.[19]

At first sight *Sir Gawain* promises to be a typical example of the type of romance where the hero's physical courage and fidelity are tested in a difficult trial of endurance. The trial is unusually extreme, in that there is no reason to suppose that Gawain will not lose his life when he receives the return blow from the Green Knight, and Gawain's winter journey through the wilderness is peculiarly solitary in that, unlike most quests, it involves no human contacts at all until he reaches the supposed refuge of Hautdesert. The description of the Green Knight as a figure of irrepressible natural vigour and the emphasis both on the passage of the seasons and the harshness of winter suggest strongly that we may expect a story in which the over-civilized society of Camelot is brought up against the dangerous forces of the real world outside the castle wall, and vindicated by the hero's willingness to risk death rather than dishonour. On one level this is indeed what happens, but the further we advance into the poem the less important it appears to be.

The key to the poet's concern for the ideal of knighthood is rather to be found in his account of the details of the pentangle which forms the cognizance of his shield, and specifically the fifth set of five points of excellence, the set which, superficially more heterogeneous than the other four, appears to comprise five social virtues appropriate to a knight: *fraunchyse* (liberality), *felaȝshyp* (loyal companionship), *clannesse* (purity), *cortaysye* (which needs to be defined), and *pité* (compassion). Given that all these five pentads interlace with one another, and that the knot is designed to be endless, it is clear that any conflict or inconsistency between or within the groups would render the whole incoherent. Gawain's shield in fact represents the coherence of the value system of the Round Table as the poet wished to understand it, and he is expected to exemplify in practice the compatibility of all the relevant virtues. Specifically, in connecting the five virtues of the secular code with the four groups of Christian practices and beliefs, the poet is asserting the necessary connection between spiritual ideals and earthly chivalry: in effect, he is accepting the

---

[19] The point is vigorously urged by G. V. Smithers, 'What *Sir Gawain and the Green Knight* is about', *MÆ* 33 (1963), 171–89.

pre-eminence given in the *Queste* to spiritual values but rejecting the austere polarities of that text. One could say that he is reasserting the value and dignity of worldly knighthood in the teeth of a literary orthodoxy which repudiates them. Whether the reassertion amounts to a vindication remains to be seen.

The difficulty is the rather tarnished image of secular chivalry carried over from the *Mort le Roi Artu* and the career of Lancelot in general, and this is where the details of the fifth group become important. *Fraunchyse*, *felaȝshyp*, and *pité* present few problems. *Clannesse* is a little more complicated, but since in the poem of the same title the *Gawain*-poet represents Almighty God, no less, as delivering a disquisition on the delights of married love, we may be confident that the term refers not to strict celibacy but rather abstention from fornication and adultery.[20] *Cortaysye* will thus have something like its modern sense of 'graciousness in personal relationships', though as it is also used in the *Gawain* group of the infinite generosity of divine love and the breadth of divine forbearance, it probably has spiritual dimensions here as well. What is clear is that the poet is reacting against a tendency to use the term *cortaysye* as a euphemism for sexual licence, and it seems that in order to justify a definition of knighthood in which *cortaysye* in its non-sexual sense is an essential element he is obliged to some extent to redefine the term. For if it carried its looser sense here, the fifth pentad would become internally incoherent, not to say incompatible with the other four. The hero of *Sir Gawain* thus carries on his shoulders the whole reputation of Camelot, or, what amounts to the same thing, the argument for the compatibility of secular chivalry with Christian values, rejected in the *Queste* and, it seems, reasserted here.

That this issue should prove to be important is an instance of the poet's ingenuity in confounding our expectations. Though we are given to understand that Gawain's main trial consists in the exchange of blows, it becomes clear at the end of the poem that the outcome of that trial depends on his response in the castle to the attempt by Bertilak's wife to seduce him. And that in turn rests on the definition of *cortaysye*. For Gawain, as I have suggested, this means a kind of graciousness which must nevertheless be compatible with strict purity. In context, it appears to entail mak-

[20]   *Cleanness (Purity)*, 697–708.

ing polite conversation and innocent flirtation without in any way compromising one's chastity: something which is a good deal easier in the context of a Christmas celebration than in the circumstances in which Gawain now finds himself. For the lady, *cortaysye* is indeed little more than a polite expression for adultery. It is easier for her to urge this point because in French as opposed to English romance Gawain is notorious for his susceptibility to available ladies and his willingness to oblige them. The lady (who, one suspects, has been reading too many French romances) chides Gawain for not living up to his reputation. Against her persuasive charms, his fear of giving offence by refusing her offer too brusquely and the psychologically well-judged appeal to his reputation, he has only his truth to his knightly ideals and, in his hour of need, his trust in Mary to sustain him. If the lady succeeds in imposing her definition of *cortaysye*, Gawain is lost.

And not just Gawain. A lapse into adultery would presumably lose Gawain his head, but we all have to die some time, and there are worse forms of death than decapitation. What would be still more disastrous is that a wedge would be driven between two sides of the pentangle, *cortaysye* and *clannesse*. The endless knot would disintegrate, and the ideals of the Round Table would be shown up as incoherent and hypocritical: a beautiful fabric of sophisticated elegance over a sink of sexual impropriety. Gawain, as we know, does not succeed completely in the test. But on this crucial point he does succeed, and the reputation of the Round Table is vindicated in him. The difference between his actual lapse in the Exchange of Winnings game and his threatened capitulation in the bedroom is that the first is an *incidental* fault which affects no one but Gawain himself, whereas the second would be a *structural* fault which would compromise the entire system of values which he represents.

No wonder, then, that the whole of Gawain's quest is set in motion by the desire of Morgan le Fay to deface the reputation of the Round Table, or that it should be associated with her ferocious hostility to Guinevere.[21] For Guinevere is the centre of the very intrigue which, in the fullness of time, will destroy the Round

---

[21] The parallels of detail between the account in the *Mort le Roi Artu*, 48–54, of Arthur's inadvertent sojourn in Morgan's castle, where she provides him with apparent evidence of Guinevere's infidelity, and that of Gawain's arrival at Hautdesert are suggestive and merit further investigation.

Table, and the supposition, so valiantly resisted by Gawain, that courtesy implies or even excuses adultery is the precise issue which brings about the catastrophe, as we see in the *Mort le Roi Artu* and, however hard he tries to confuse the issue, in Malory's *Morte*. Symbolically, the fact that the crucial test takes place not in the terrifying confrontation with the Green Knight in the wilderness whose menace he seems to embody but in the apparently civilized surroundings of the castle indicates that the true threat to the Round Table comes not from the boisterous world outside but from within Camelot's dangerously over-refined courtly society itself.

Thus the idea of the *Gawain*-poet as a fourteenth-century modernist subjecting the traditional ideals of chivalry and courtesy to a rigorous criticism is only half the truth. Rather, he is in part a traditionalist, redefining a set of ideals which had become notably tarnished and had, in his view, deviated from their origins, so as to defend them against a critique to which they had already been subjected a century and a half previously.[22] *Sir Gawain*, in its view of knighthood, has more in common with the rigorous yet humane theology of *Pearl* than with the ironic urbanities of Chaucer, with which perhaps *Patience* provides a closer parallel: it presents the one serious examination which has come down to us from the fourteenth century not simply of certain superficial aspects of the behaviour of romance heroes, but of the moral foundation and internal coherence of the whole system of values which underlies chivalric and courtly romance. This is not to charge Chaucer with superficiality: the truth of the matter is probably that the *Gawain*-poet's concern over the question reflects an old-fashioned concern with a code of values which for Chaucer could indeed still be put to literary use but was no longer a matter of primary interest or topical importance.

---

[22] My view thus diverges from that of A. C. Spearing, *The Gawain-Poet* (Cambridge, 1970), 191–206, who raises the possibility of a distinction (adumbrated by D. S. Brewer, 'Courtesy and the *Gawain*-Poet', in John Lawlor (ed.), *Patterns of Love and Courtesy: Essays in Memory of C. S. Lewis* (London, 1966), 54–85 (p. 75)) between 'true' and 'false' courtesy, only to reject it on the basis that there is no clear dividing line between them, and argues in consequence that a wedge is indeed driven between courtesy and Christianity. The situation described by Spearing is admittedly real enough to the poet, but I would argue that he regards it as a deformation of courtesy which needs to be corrected rather than an inherent fault which discredits it.

It could, indeed, be argued that the responses of these two poets to romance are so different that the term 'Ricardian' comes under strain if required to accommodate them both. Just as the *Gawain*-poet appears not to be sufficiently detached from the ideals of romance to be able to question them in Chaucer's genial, dispassionate, and even at times jocular way, but feels obliged to redeem them from the decadence into which he perceives them to have fallen, so there is no question of his regarding their deficiencies as a proper subject for literary parody or rhetorical funambulism. His seriousness with regard to romance is something which seems to belong to a pre-Ricardian generation, so that if an earlier dating for his work could be confirmed his disappearance from the 'Ricardian' canon would cause no great critical upset. Yet again his essentially comic view of human pomposity and self-importance seems entirely consonant with the attitudes of Chaucer and Langland. Conversely, Chaucer's concern—at once playful and obsessive—with form and style, to the extent that the rhetoric of a poem can come close to being part of its subject-matter, is so far removed from anything else in the fourteenth century that one might be tempted to regard him as the only Ricardian poet, if it were not that his recurrent use of an ironic persona associates him so firmly with Langland and Gower. But so long as we do not expect all the poets of the group to fit a single definition all the time, we shall not let such considerations obsess us.

10

The World and Heart of Thomas Usk

STEPHEN MEDCALF

Thomas Usk had a subtle, vivid, and self-questioning mind, whose besetting fault was an excess of ingenuity. For example, in his *Testament of Love*, when Love tells him that she advances not the proud and unstable but those who are meek, yet manly and enduring, she gives as examples 'David, that from keping of shepe was drawen up in-to the order of kingly governaunce; and Jupiter, from a bole, to ben Europes fere; and Julius Cesar, from the lowest degrè in Rome, to be mayster of al erthly princes; and Eneas from hel, to be king of the countrè there Rome is now stonding' (*Testament*, I. v, 126–30).[1] This at first reading is a startling list. A little thought shows that Love is for Usk not only erotic love but also the love of Troilus' hymn in *Troilus and Criseyde*, 'that of erthe and se hath governaunce', and 'with an holsome alliaunce | Halt peples joyned' (III. 1744 and 1746–7), and is therefore concerned as much with political power as with personal emotion: that Usk has in mind not only humility of starting-point, but the humiliation which a lover must expect to endure in his progress: and that Caesar and Aeneas are included presumably because of

Apart from the works cited in the notes, I owe a great deal to examining two unpublished MA theses concerned with Usk, by R. A. King and Claire Fewson, although as John Burrow genially said in connection with the former, 'The disadvantage of Stephen as an examiner is that he believes Usk makes sense.' I should also like to thank Caroline Barron, Ronald Waldron, and Alastair Minnis, whose comments on the draft were responsible for a good deal of revision.

[1] I have used the text of *The Testament of Love* provided by W. W. Skeat in *Chaucerian and Other Pieces* (Oxford, 1897), since although there are modern texts by John Leyerle and R. A. Shoaf in prospect, they are not yet to hand. Skeat's text, moreover, being very little emended, preserves the principal advantage of Thynne's print, that there is very little sophistication of the text. In dealing with a mind as wayward and subtle as Usk's, this is a real advantage.

the help which Venus gives them in the *Aeneid*. But the list still suggests a surprising capacity for lateral association.

As men with such minds are apt to be, Usk was attracted in early life by radical politics and new movements in religion, and afterwards by orthodoxy. At the end of Book II of the *Testament*, Love describes Usk, using the parable from Proverbs (7: 4–27) about a young man snared by a harlot, as 'a scoler lerninge of my lore' who went after 'love fayned' and was rescued only by being shown his true love Margaret (*Testament*, II. xiv). Part at least of what she means by 'love fayned' here is explained at the beginning of Book II, where seeds of love have been mixed with bad weeds that 'han caught the name of love' though they are in fact 'cockle', in Latin *lollia*, which Skeat, probably rightly, identifies as 'the usual spiteful fling' against the Lollards[2] (*Testament*, II. i). Usk's attraction towards Lollardy, thus described, must have been part of what he had confessed in Book I, that 'in my youth I was drawe to ben assentaunt and (in my mightes) helping to certain conjuracions and other grete maters of ruling of citizins' (*Testament*, I.vi, 53–5).

Of these 'conjuracions' Usk gave another account on 7 August 1384, in a deposition[3] which he made against John Comberton or Northampton, leader of the Drapers and mayor of London 1381–3, whose clerk he had been. Northampton was a turbulent man, whom we first hear of in 1361 as an upholder of the Drapers with 'a propensity for taking the law into his own hands', and as a disturber of the peace either in his personal interest or that of the Drapers in 1365, 1369, and 1371.[4] Of his politics there are two current interpretations. He was certainly in some way committed to breaking the power of the existing city oligarchy, in the opinion of Pamela Nightingale in so far as that was associated with those involved in the export of wool through the official wool staple, Northampton acting in the interest of the Drapers (who were adjusting to the long transition from a trade in wool to a trade in cloth): but in the opinion of Ruth Bird in so far as it was associated with the grocers and the fishmongers, in the interest

---

[2] *Chaucerian and Other Pieces*, p. xxiv.

[3] 'The Appeal of Thomas Usk', in *A Book of London English 1384–1425*, ed. R. W. Chambers and Marjorie Daunt (Oxford, 1931), 22–31.

[4] P. Nightingale, 'Capitalists, Crafts and Constitutional Change in Late Fourteenth-Century London', *Past and Present*, 1/24 (1989), 3–35.

of small masters.[5] It seems at least possible that Nightingale's view is the more just of Northampton's rise to power, and Bird's of his actions during his two years of mayoralty. During his mayoralty, he undoubtedly worked to destroy the monopolies in victualling possessed by the fishmongers and other victuallers, to the advantage of the poor, whom he also protected from clerical pressure to offer too much at baptisms, marriages, and requiems. (Nightingale points out that these actions may not have been due to simple good-heartedness: in 1392 he restored labour services at his manor in Tottenham which had not been exacted for fourteen years, and only ceased when the peasants refused to pay their rent).[6] He also took action against whores and whoremongers, apparently with overt criticism of the bishop of London and of the venality of the church courts which should have dealt with them.

In connection with these last actions, Walsingham describes Northampton's party as Lollards. Bird doubts Northampton's Lollardy, principally because in his will he founded a chantry and made bequests of property to a convent in Cheshunt and to the London Charterhouse to pray for his soul and those of his parents and others.[7] But this need mean no more than a change of opinion against Lollardy, which is common enough among the early supporters of Wyclif in the 1380s and 1390s. Walsingham and Usk seem to support each other on Northampton's partisans tending to Lollardy.

Walsingham also attributes apocalyptic motives to Northampton's party. Because of the venality of the clergy

Dicebant se utique pertimescere, ne propter talia peccata in urbe perpetrata, sed dissimulata, tota civitas, quandoque Deo ulciscente, ruinam pateretur. Quapropter, velle se purgationem civitatis ab huius modi inquinamentis, ne forte accideret eis pestis aut gladius, vel certe absorberet eos tellus.[8]

(They said that they were much afraid lest because of such sins committed in the city yet dissimulated, the whole community, whenever God should take vengeance, might be brought to ruin: and therefore that they wished to make a purgation of the community from defilements of the sort, lest

---

[5] R. Bird, *The Turbulent London of Richard II* (London, 1949), 66–81.

[6] Nightingale, 'Capitalists, Crafts', 33.

[7] Bird, *Turbulent London*, 65.

[8] Thomas Walsingham, *Historia Anglicana*, ed. H. T. Riley, 2 vols. (London, 1863–4), i. 65.

perhaps plague or the sword should fall upon them, or indeed the earth swallow them up.)

The tone is not unlike some language in the *Testament*, when Usk describes the recent troubles in London as a time when the floods rose, and in their ebbing drew away the riches in which people of his acquaintance trusted (*Testament*, II. v) and when the sun of the city failed to shine and its moon was clouded, which were the dignities of London (*Testament*, II. vi): or again, when he says that those who drew him into Northampton's party claimed that the government of London, 'left in the handes of torcencious citezins, shal bringe in pestilence and distruccion to you, good men; and therefore let us have the comune administracion to abate suche yvels' (*Testament*, I. vi).

Behind all this, were there perhaps the atmosphere and ideas of *Piers Plowman* (B), as James Simpson has hinted,[9] including Langland's thought about a commonwealth of crafts? Usk says in similar language that he at first believed that Northampton's policy was 'commen profit in cominaltee', from which would proceed 'pees and tranquilitè, with just governaunce' (*Testament*, I. vi, 65–6).

But presently, he goes on, he began to think that these 'first painted thinges' were 'of tyrannye purposed' (67–9), not without reason. Northampton was intolerant of opposition, as when in 1382 for opprobrious words against him Nicholas Exton (mayor of London later) was deprived of his aldermanry.[10] On 28 October 1383, Northampton lost the election for mayor to Nicholas Brembre, leader of the Grocers: and Usk, in his deposition against him, doubtless preserves his tone, the tone of one who identifies his supporters' minds and hearts with his own, when he said at a meeting in Goldsmiths' Hall, 'Sirs, thus be ye shape for to be over-ronne, and that I nel nought soeffre; lat us rather al be ded atones than soeffre such a vylenye.'[11]

After a series of meetings and disturbances aimed at getting a new election, Northampton was arrested by Brembre at a riot in

[9] J. Simpson, '"After Craftes Conseil clotheth you and fede": Langland and London City Politics', in N. Rogers (ed.), *England in the Fourteenth Century* (Stamford, 1993), 109–27 (pp. 120 ff.).

[10] Bird, *Turbulent London*, 34 n.

[11] 'Appeal of Thomas Usk', 28.

Fleet Street on 7 February 1384: and we hear again the tone of a leader of parties from another, though also hostile, witness, as he was being led towards Brembre's house of La Réole and saw his partisans gathered outside his own house in Cordwainer Street:

Quo vis me duceris numquid hic ibo in domum meam cui maior dixit non set ibis mecum. Et dictus Iohannes Norhampton respondit si me duxeris ultra exonero me de periculo quod inde poterit evenire.[12]

('Whither wilt thou lead me? Shall I not here go into my own home?' To whom the mayor said, 'No, but thou shalt go with me.' And the said John Northampton answered, 'If thou shalt have led me farther, I exonerate myself from the peril that could come of it.')

At that time one of his partisans, John Bere, compared him to another turbulent patron of London, St Thomas of Canterbury.[13] One thing is plain about Northampton: he had something of the charisma of which Albert Speer said, 'It is the most dangerous quality there is.'[14] It is possible therefore to understand both the devotion which Usk evidently felt for him to begin with and the traumatic conversion which now followed. Being himself arrested, Usk made the deposition of 7 August which we have already used, accusing Northampton and his associates of intending to establish absolute control over London, by force if it proved necessary, and confessing his own guilt in assisting them. In the *Testament*, apart from his change of opinion about Northampton's intentions, he gives two principal excuses for informing on him: first, the peace of London 'that is to me so dere and swete, in which I was forth growen' (*Testament*, I. vi, 98–9), and secondly, that he was charged on oath by his allegiance to the king to tell the truth. Northampton, being charged before the king at Reading on Usk's evidence, might have lost his life, though rather for his impudence in saying that he hoped the king would not proceed to judgment on him in the absence of John of Gaunt, who was in some degree his patron, than for any offences in London. In the end, he and two of the others accused by Usk, John More and Richard Norbury (the fourth principal accused man, William Essex, having fled), were sentenced to ten years' imprisonment and to exile from

---

[12] Coram Rege Roll 507, in Bird, *Turbulent London*, 139.
[13] Bird, *Turbulent London*, 83.
[14] G. Sereny, *Albert Speer: His Battle with Truth* (London, 1996), 14.

London, although they received a full pardon in December 1391 at the behest of John of Gaunt.[15]

Usk was eventually made a royal serjeant-at-arms, and, at the request of the king at some date between 2 September and 7 October 1387, under-sheriff of Middlesex—with bad timing, for it implicated him deeply on the king's side just after Richard had made the consultations with the justices about his legal position over against the magnates of the kingdom, in late August, at Shrewsbury and Nottingham, which preceded the increasingly violent counter-movements of the principal magnates, the Lords Appellant, against the king's party. At Christmas the Lords Appellant took control of London, and most probably at that time Usk was taken into the custody of the earl of Arundel. On 3 February 1388 the king's advisers were appealed of treason before the Merciless Parliament on many charges, one of which was that they had had Usk created under-sheriff, so that when they had made 'faux arestes, enditementz et atteindres' against the Lords Appellant and others, to be executed in London and Middlesex, that 'faux et malveise persone de lour couyne', Usk, should carry them out.[16] After those two of the king's advisers on whom the Lords Appellant could immediately lay hands, Robert Tresilian the chief justice of the king's bench, and Nicholas Brembre, had been unjustly executed, Usk was drawn to Tyburn along with John Blake (who was said to have formulated the king's questions to the justices about his legal position) and there hanged and beheaded, not only unjustly but inefficiently, with about thirty strokes of the axe. He met his end, says the *Westminster Chronicle*, with great contrition of heart, reciting most devoutly as he was drawn to the gallows the Placebo and Dirige, the seven penitential psalms, the Te Deum, the Nunc dimittis, the Quicunque vult and other prayers of devotion in the hour of death. To the moment of death he denied that he had done anything wrong against John Northampton, but, he said, everything he had accused him of at Reading was true. This insistence proves one thing: that he sincerely thought his accusations true, since he would scarcely go to the other side of death with a lie in his mouth, and suggests besides

[15] Bird, *Turbulent London*, 83–5.
[16] *The Westminster Chronicle 1381–1394*, ed. L. C. Hector and Barbara F. Harvey (Oxford, 1982), 258–61.

that he felt they were still held against him, or even were the real cause of his execution.[17] Probably indeed Northampton's charisma was still at work.

At some time between 1384 and 1388 he wrote *The Testament of Love*. Characteristically, he made it immensely complex, and based it on a thoroughgoingly figural and symbolic understanding of the world, working on a number of levels. In consequence, the only text we have of it, printed by Thynne in 1552, is mangled, and a number of its modern readers, who have tried to interpret it on one level only—as a political apologia, or an imitation of Chaucer's *Boece*, or a tract on courtly love, or on grace and free will—have found it incomprehensible. It is at least all four of these, and when read as Usk asks it should be, on all its levels in a way which makes each reading support each of the others, requires an intense effort, but an effort well rewarded. It is not always fully coherent, but at times both startlingly pungent and startlingly beautiful, and overall in the end deeply wise.

It is still more complex. Margaret, to whom he dedicates the book, must have at least the six meanings which he lists for her at its close, which are: a pearl (with all the properties attributed to the gem by medieval lapidaries), an actual (although perhaps fictional) woman, grace, learning, the wisdom of God, and holy Church (*Testament*, III. ix). Moreover, to explain the kinds of relation between signifier and signified which he is using, he gives four examples—first, to stress the reality of the signifier, the figural relation of manna (which nourished men's bodies, and so was itself physical) to Christ, and then three more to stress that it is nevertheless the signified that gives value and meaning to the signifier, the relations of holy flesh to the bread of the Eucharist, of the spirit to the flesh in Christ's discourse in St John's Gospel, and of the spirit to the letter in St Paul's second Epistle to the Corinthians. Of these, it is clear in the text that Margaret actually signifies Christ, when Usk expounds the natural symbolism of the formation of a pearl in a mussel as the virgin birth of Christ, and as his being given to every creature who will receive him (*Testament*, II. xii). The other terms—manna, the spirit, and so forth—also relate to her. Underlying all of them is the pearl of the parable in St Matthew's Gospel, chapter 13 (which Usk describes

[17] *Westminster Chronicle*, 314–17.

explicitly in *Testament*, I. iii), with its further meanings of the kingdom of heaven both in the heart and in eternity. For the intent of the book is to elicit what is in common between all these, most obvious perhaps in the pearl of the parable, and in Margaret the woman, as served by a courtly lover: that they all call out disinterested devotion, and the kind of service which is its own reward. And this being so, we may add two political meanings: the peace of the city of London, and King Richard as the object of loyalty. For although these two are not listed in the last chapter, it is clear that they are present in the first book of the *Testament* and implicit in the penultimate chapter (*Testament*, III. viii) when Usk gives among the lessons of love which he has learnt 'how mis-rule by fayned love bothe realmes and citees hath governed a greet throwe... how rules in love shulde ben used; how somtyme with fayned love foule I was begyled' (8–11).

Usk dedicates the book to Margaret in perhaps all these senses by the prayer formed in the initial letters of its chapters, MARGARETE OF VIRTW HAVE MERCI ON THIN VSK. From this point on I shall include in my chapter-references to the *Testament* these initials, since I have found this practice useful in recalling the book's sequence of thought, which is as follows:

Book I Prologue	M	A formal apologia for the book, and especially for writing in English.
i	A	Usk in prison laments the absence of Margaret,
ii	R	and is visited by the lady Love,
iii–iv	GA	to whom he confesses in an allegory of a ship voyage how she showed him the pearl Margaret: but two difficulties destroy his hopes of Margaret, first false slanders and secondly her preciousness compared with his unworthiness.
v	R	Love assures him of her help.
vi–vii	ET	Usk outlines the slanders against him in a fairly literal account of his dealings with Northampton.
viii	E	Love assures him that these slanders are no barrier between himself and Margaret.

	ix	O	As for his unworthiness, Love assures him of the dignity of man,
	x	F	and of the value of ill fortune in discriminating virtue and truth.
Book II	i	V	Usk outlines the book to come, and speaks of a future book in which he will praise Margaret.
	ii	I	Love sings of her (i.e. Love's) rejection in the Church and the world.
	iii	R	She and Usk together praise women and lament the faithlessness of men.
	iv–viii	TW HAV	Usk's early life is analysed as an attempt to achieve love by means of riches, dignities, power, and renown, all four of which Love shows to be external and false means.
	ix–x	EM	Love exalts the harmony of heaven as the lover's true end, and assures Usk that he is now in the true way to it,
	xi	E	which is by virtue and reason,
	xii	R	of which Margaret is the source.
	xiii	C	Through Margaret comes good, which is a participation in God, while evil is only negation.
	xiv	I	Usk's fortunes are retold in a parable (based on Proverbs) of a lover led astray by 'fayned love' but delivered.
Book III	i	O	The three books of the *Testament* are shown by Usk to correspond to the three ages of the world, Error, Grace, and Joy, and the subject of the whole book to be involved in other triads, such as Law, Philosophy, and Love.
	ii	N	Love promises Usk that he will be rewarded for his good service, which she shows to be good acts freely chosen and performed with a good heart.
	iii–iv	TH	She shows how the will is free in relation to necessity and eternity.

| v–vii | INU | In the image of a tree, the interdependence of free will, love and grace is shown, and how love is its own reward. The lady Love enters Usk's heart. |
| viii–ix | SK | Usk recapitulates in his own voice what love has taught him about the workings of grace and the will in love, truth, and righteousness. |

One's reading of this tapestry tends to be implicated with one's view of exactly when, and therefore under what circumstances, it was composed. If it was written, as it purports to be, during a second period of imprisonment some time later than the first imprisonment from which Usk escaped by testifying against Northampton, then he may have been facing death when he wrote it, and the ascetic unworldliness which it professes may be as noble as that of Boethius, on whose *De consolatione philosophiae* he partly modelled it. If the imprisonment is allegorical or fictional, then the unworldliness is probably fictional too, the *Testament* simply 'a work designed to bridge the gap between himself and his hoped-for associates by persuading them of his essential trustworthiness'[18] in some useful and well-paid situation, its apparent interest in the theology of free will and the psychology of commitment in love only a strategy 'to increase his acceptability to the Brembre faction by portraying his choices as the result not of opportunism but of free will',[19] and even its apparent love of Chaucer only 'intended to gain the good will of the poet'.[20] But the longer one studies the *Testament* the more one becomes convinced of its basic seriousness: and it is so close to the truly autobiographical, even though in the characteristic Ricardian modes of petition and confession, that if one takes it seriously one also begins to extend a certain affection to Usk, as has Paul Strohm, the author of the first two of the three caustic opinions just quoted, who has

[18] Paul Strohm, 'Politics and Poetics: Usk and Chaucer in the 1380s', in Lee Patterson (ed.), *Literary Practice and Social Change in Britain, 1380–1530* (Berkeley and Los Angeles, 1990), 83–112 (p. 100).
[19] Ibid. 102.
[20] Henry Bradley, 'Usk, Thomas', in *Dictionary of National Biography*, Compact Edition (Oxford, 1975), 2136–7.

most lately said, 'A decent and epistemologically humble stab at comprehension, rather than judgment, is what we can offer poor Usk now'.[21]

I hope, however, that I am not only moved by affection in believing that the *Testament* shows evidence of having been written under two sets of circumstances, the first in the period leading up to his under-sheriffship, the second when he was aware of the risk that his life was forfeit. The first part, from the Prologue (I. Prol. M) to well on in Book II (II. x. M) is, as Ramona Bressie and Paul Strohm hold,[22] predominantly a political apologia, for both its author's support for Northampton and his abandonment of him, laying claim, in a world where he has lost the wealth, dignity, power and renown which he had had as a member of one kind of radical faction, to a place in another kind of radical group, those who admired Chaucer and followed him in experiments in using English for high literature. The *Testament* is, among other things, the first serious attempt to write original philosophy in English, if we discount religious works like *The Cloud of Unknowing*, and its model initially is Boethius, both in the original Latin and in Chaucer's translation.[23] But Usk has conceived the further idea that his apologia could be made allegorically, as a lover's confession. Consequently, he draws a parallel between his political acts and hopes and the experiences of a lover, which rises to its most ingenious at II. iv. T. Here he renders into his love-story two of the legal conventions which were involved in making appeals of treason, such as were his models in accusing Northampton: the requirement to repeat his appeal word for word, and the offer to uphold its justice by armed combat. Love tells him how glad she was 'whan thy king and his princes by huge wordes and grete loked after variaunce in thy speche; and ever thou were redy for my sake, in plesaunce of the Margarite-perle and many mo other, thy body to oblige in-to Marces doing, if any contraried thy sawes' (113–7). Clearly, here the king is Richard II. And Love goes on, as one

---

[21] Paul Strohm, *Hochon's Arrow: The Social Imagination of Fourteenth-Century Texts* (Princeton, 1992), 160.

[22] Ramona Bressie, 'The Date of Thomas Usk's *Testament of Love'*, MP 26 (1928–9), 17–29; Strohm, 'Politics and Poetics'.

[23] Stephen Medcalf, 'Transposition: Thomas Usk's *Testament of Love'*, in Roger Ellis (ed.), *The Medieval Translator: The Theory and Practice of Translation in the Middle Ages* (Cambridge, 1989), 183–95.

would expect on the thesis so far advanced, to hint of reward from him: 'I made thou haddest grace of thy kinge, in foryevenesse of mikel misdede. To the gracious king art thou mikel holden, of whos grace and goodnesse somtyme hereafter I thinke thee enforme, whan I shew the ground where-as moral vertue groweth' (120–4).

This promise of Love's, however, is the first ground for thinking that there was a break in writing the *Testament*, and a change in the book's nature: for it is not fulfilled. She does indeed show Usk the ground where moral virtue grows (III. v. I), and even introduces it some chapters in advance by defining good service as 'resonable workinges in plesaunce and profit of thy soverayne' (III. ii. N, 45–6). But though the sovereign here may still be partly Richard II, there is no further mention of him, nor of any reward from him, nor of any sovereign but Margaret or God (except in the summary mention of the rule of Love in realms and cities in III. viii. S, which harks back to the discussions of politics at the beginning). The reward of love comes from within itself, and the 'good grace' which this may prove to be has nothing about it of worldly reward from an earthly monarch (III. vii. V).

Along with this transfiguration of plan goes a change in the story of Usk's relations with Margaret, which paradoxically suggests that he has already received an earthly reward, though one with ill consequences. At II. x. M Love had told him what is in harmony with all that we have previously heard: 'hiderto, thou hast had al her ful daunger; and so thou might amende al that is misse and al defautes that somtyme thou diddest; and that now, in al thy tyme, to that ilke Margaryte in ful service of my lore thyne herte hath continued; wherfore, she ought moche the rather enclyne fro her daungerous sete' (121–6). Thus Usk, so far, has received nothing but *daunger*, rejection, from Margaret, though he deserves better. But in the last chapter of Book II (II. xiv. I), as the climax of the parable of his going astray like the young man in Proverbs, Love asks him, 'Were thou not goodly accepted in-to grace? By my pluckinge was she to foryevenesse enclyned. And after, I her styred to drawe thee to house; and yet wendest thou utterly for ever have ben refused' (78–81). Usk is now in prison, and the knot between him and Margaret is not yet fastened: but he has, after being forgiven, been drawn to her house. Five sentences before, Love had even taken this new story a stage further: 'And so thilke Margaryte thou servest shal seen thee, by her service out of perillous tribulacion delivered, bycause of her service in-to newe disese fallen, by hope of amendement in the last ende, with joye to be gladded' (67–71).

The most natural way of fitting these passages into Usk's known life is to suppose that between II. x. M and II. xiv. I he had been taken into the king's service, understanding Margaret in these two chapters to be the king as the object of loyalty, and had fallen into new trouble as a result: which points to late 1387 and the Lords Appellant.

But there is more to be observed about the development of the *Testament*. In his Prologue Usk speaks of gleaning after 'Boece' (I. Prol. M, 110), and so he does with manifest echoes and translations up to and including the first half of II. xi. E, where Love mocks those who search for inward and heavenly goods by external and worldly means, in a list of five absurd searches ('they that sechen gold in grene trees', etc.), which closely follows *De consolatione philosophiae*, Book III, metrum 8 ('Non aurum in viridi quaeritis arbore', etc.). Thereafter, although Usk's thought is still Boethian in general character, and for one thesis, that good is defined by likeness to God, he appeals to 'Boece' by name (II. xiii. C, 49), there are no more verbal echoes. Instead, in this same chapter (II. xiii. C) he begins to draw on St Anselm's treatise on grace and free will, *De concordia praescientiae et praedestinationis necnon gratiae Dei cum libro arbitrio*,[24] of which most of Book III (ii–viii. THINUS) is a kind of transposition, following Anselm almost word for word at times, but substituting love where Anselm speaks of righteousness. He follows Anselm indeed so much more closely than he follows Boethius that one is surprised to recall that it is only Boethius whom he mentions by name in the Prologue. It seems likely that he was not acquainted with *De concordia* until about the time he wrote II. xiii. C. One wonders whether someone whom he had consulted on his philosophical and theological interest introduced him to it. Not impossibly Ralph Strode was the man. As common serjeant to the city of London from 1373 until Northampton's re-election in 1382, he must have been acquainted with Usk: as a distinguished logician (if, as is fairly certain, Strode

---

[24] Anselm, *De concordia*, in PL 158, 507–42. See further G. Sanderlin, 'Usk's *Testament of Love* and St Anselm', *Speculum*, 17 (1942), 69–73.

of London and Strode of Oxford are the same man),[25] he must have been acquainted with Anselm: and as 'the philosophical Strode' to whom Chaucer addressed *Troilus and Criseyde*, he must have shared Usk's interest in the poem (III. iv. H) as a study in issues related to those of Anselm's treatise.

To articulate and explore the thought on free will and grace for which he draws on Anselm, Usk introduces the image of a tree whose roots are in free will and whose fruit is grace. Something like this may have been in his mind as early as his mention of 'the ground where-as moral vertue groweth' in II. iv. T, 123–4, which we have already touched on. That, however, as we saw, was somehow concerned with service to the king. At the end of II. xi. E, Usk introduces the tree to full sight, but now transposed to deeper and theological meaning: for he says that he despairs of virtue, the true way to the knot which will bind him to Margaret, because 'I, as a seer tree, without burjoning or frute, alwaye welke' (104–5). From III. v to III. vii. INV it structures the whole text: and at the very end of the *Testament*, in III. ix. K, Usk tastes its fruit.

However, these four new characteristics (a loss of interest in what the king might do for Usk, a new sense that Margaret has done something for him, a change of models from Boethius to Anselm, and the introduction of the image of the tree) might all be consequences of a shift of interest from earthly and extrinsic to heavenly and intrinsic rewards, which may have been in Usk's scheme from the beginning. But there are two mechanical anomalies which support the idea of a break in the writing. Thynne, who clearly had not noticed the acrostic formed by the initial letters of the chapters, nevertheless mostly preserves it, except where pages were disordered in his exemplar or (once) when an initial was misread. But the last quotation from Boethius, which is somewhere in the middle of the area of shift, occurs in a chapter which, uniquely, he has created by running the latter half of II. x. M into the former half of II. xi. E. This looks as if in his exemplar, and perhaps therefore in Usk's original text, there were breaks which looked more like chapter breaks than did the true beginning of II. xi. E.

---

[25] A. B. Emden, *A Biographical Register of the University of Oxford to A.D. 1500*, 3 vols. (Oxford 1957–9), iii. 1807–8.

The first of these accidental breaks occurs at a natural pause, indeed at the end of the paragraph in which Love stresses for the last time that Usk has 'hiderto...had al her ful daunger' (II. x. M, 121–2), which ends with her asserting that in 'this trewe service thou art now entred' (131–2). The false chapter then begins with Usk casting back to the question occupying the conversation before a complaint of his led into the stress on Margaret's 'daunger' hitherto, saying '"Certayn", quod I, "among thinges I asked a question, whiche was the way to the knot"' (II. x. M, 133–4).

At this stage in the book, the way is said to be by reason and virtue. This is the answer of philosophy, and indeed of Boethius' *De consolatione philosophiae*: but by the light of revelation it is insufficient, since we cannot achieve virtue without grace. At the beginning of the next true chapter, II. xi. E, Usk opens up this further theme: but the way in which he does so is the second mechanical anomaly. In the full flow of Love's speech on the reasonable life, Usk intrudes two sentences in his own voice, but uniquely without any distinguishing 'quod I', which make the point: 'These olde philosophers, that hadden no knowing of divine grace, of kyndly reson alone, wenden that of pure nature, withouten any helpe of grace, me might have y-shoned th'other livinges. Resonably have I lived; and for I thinke herafter, if God wol, and I have space, thilke grace after my leude knowing declare, I leve it as at this time' (8–13). It reads like an unrevised note to himself. Love then proceeds Boethianly; shortly after comes Usk's last extended gleaning from Boethius, and then, after a praise of the sufficiency of virtue, the second false chapter break. In the second part of the true chapter, Usk objects, following Christian perception, that virtue is a kind of life which his reason has no capacity to achieve: and with this comes the image of the tree 'without burjoning or frute' (104–5), which introduces all that second part of the book drawing on Anselm to explore divine grace, in fulfilment of the note at II. xi. E.

The likelihood then is that Usk laid aside the uneasy union of Boethian aspiration with place-seeking at 'this trewe service thou art now entred' because at the worldly level he had achieved the form of service he sought, as under-sheriff of Middlesex. He then added two half-chapters which adumbrated what he needed to do to complete the book, that is to treat of grace, but lacked either the time, or the mental pressure, or perhaps simply the assistance in theology which he eventually found in Anselm, to do this. Finally, imprisoned by the Lords Appellant, when his new political motive, the king's service, had become the reason why execution for treason was close upon him, he was driven to those profound considerations of value, vocation, commitment, and the analogy between human and divine love which are the intellectual glory of the *Testament*. The joins and inconsistencies in the book are unrevised, presumably, because he suffered execution.

The deepening and intensifying of his thought, whether because of Anselm or because of his plight, are very apparent, as we shall see in a moment, if one compares his uses of his contemporaries—of Langland and of Chaucer—in the first and second halves of the book. What Anselm and his plight together brought from him can be grouped under three headings:

First, he found in Anselm an explanation of the relation of free will to God's providence, and of the nature of eternity, essentially the same as what he must have known in Boethius, but which he must have preferred as either logically or morally more cogent. This he takes over fairly unchanged, and does not seem much fired by it: but it is important in his scheme to make sense of the ideas of desert, reward, and divine justice (III. ii–iv. NTH).

Secondly, he seems to have recognized in Anselm's psychology of the will an analysis which made sense of his own shifts of loyalty. He distinguishes, after Anselm, three meanings of will: *instrument*, the soul's power freely to commit itself; *affection*, emotional depth; and *use*, willing in action. Only use is subject to external circumstance, though affection may be greater or less within individuals. In a true lover, affection that desires fervently is united to an instrument that intends to hold its troth. Such love, united to reason, cannot be destroyed, but always increases. But it remains free and, so Love assures Usk, if it is united to unreason, as it was in his loyalty to Northampton, it is right to change it.

In the analysis of will, to which he devotes III. vi. N, Usk is deeply involved. But it is in his third lesson from Anselm that he is moved to strikingly original thought. Anselm instructs him that the will cannot will righteously unless it is already righteous, and Usk transposes this to speak of love, 'wil wol not love but for it is lovinge' (III. viii. S, 21). When they come, as both do, to speak of the place of God's grace in this, it is Usk that is the more convincing because he has the model of falling in love, which Anselm does not use, to show that the beloved is the cause of love, and yet the lover freely wills it. Usk's noblest passage begins with a single sentence from Anselm, dry and cogent: 'If any man yeve to another wight, to whom that he ought not, and whiche that of him-selfe nothing may have, a garnement or a cote, though he were the cote or els thilke clothing, it is not to putte to him that was naked the cause of his clothinge, but only to him that was yever of the garnement' (III. vii. V, 130–4). But he passes at once to:

Wherfore I saye, thou that were naked of love, and of thy-selfe non have mightest, it is not to putte to thyne owne persone, sithen thy love cam thorow thy Margaryte-perle. *Ergo*, she was yever of the love, although thou it use; and there lente she thee grace, thy service to beginne. She is worthy the thank of this grace, for she was the yever. Al the thoughtes, besy doinges, and plesaunce in thy might and in thy wordes that thou canst devyse, ben but right litel in quytinge of thy dette; had she not ben, suche thing hadde not ben studyed. So al these maters kyndly drawen hom-ward to this Margaryte-perle, for from thence were they borowed; al is hoolly her to wyte, the love that thou havest; and thus quytest thou thy dette, in that thou stedfastly servest. And kepe wel that love, I thee rede, that of her thou hast borowed, and use it in her service thy dette to quyte; and than art thou able right sone to have grace; wherfore after mede in none halve mayst thou loke. Thus thy ginning and ending is but grace aloon... (III. vii. V, 135–51)

Before Usk had made the acquaintance of these doctrines, early in Book II (II. iii. R) where Love praises women and denounces men, he used Dido's lamentation in Chaucer's *House of Fame* (I. 269–85, 305–10, 332–60) to structure the sequence of emotion. Surprisingly, perhaps, although the verbal echoes are unmistakable, he took from Chaucer no particularly striking images nor picturesque words: he seems only to have wanted a starting point to imagine how a forsaken woman might denounce the fickleness of men, and, as Paul Strohm observes, 'not only catches Chaucer's sense in an economic way but goes on to embroider it sympathetically'.[26] Throughout the *Testament*, moreover, he draws on *Troilus and Criseyde* in an only slightly different way, for phrases which are certainly picturesque, but picturesque in a literally commonplace way, for they are nearly all proverbs. In fact, in only three or four cases can one be certain that it was from *Troilus* that

---

[26] Paul Strohm, *Social Chaucer* (Cambridge, Mass., 1989), 76.

he took them, because of a specific verbal twist: e.g. 'So ofte must men on the oke smyte, til the happy dent have entred, whiche with the okes owne swaye maketh it to come al at ones' (III. vii. V. 99–101), compared with Chaucer's

> whan that the stordy ook,
> On which men hakketh ofte, for the nones,
> Receyved hath the happy fallyng strook,
> The greete sweigh doth it come al at ones.
> (*Troilus and Criseyde*, II. 1380–3)

Chaucer's translation of Boethius he probably had at hand for the whole time when he was drawing on the *Consolatio*: but again with so little distinctiveness that J. A. W. Bennett actually doubted that he knew Chaucer's version at all.[27]

But the Anselmian discussion of the relation of God's foreknowledge to free will elicits a radically different use of Chaucer, to illuminate and confirm the argument at a deep level of theology. Chaucer, Love says, has in his book on Troilus fully resolved the question whether God's knowledge of things depends on their existence, in which case he cannot be their creator, or their existence depends on his knowledge of them, in which case he is the author of evil, and cannot justly judge mankind. She adds that she herself (if Usk will cast his mind back to the last two chapters of Book II) has given a 'light' answer, in saying that evil is only negation: but it is Chaucer who has dealt with the matter 'at the ful' (III. iv. H, 255). This has been understood by Skeat and others as referring to Troilus' soliloquy in the temple in Book IV of *Troilus and Criseyde*, which cannot be the case, first because as Skeat himself concedes, the soliloquy 'deals rather with predestination than with the origin of evil',[28] and secondly, because its upshot shows Troilus to be one of the 'mokel folk' whom Usk explicitly condemns at the end of the *Testament* for crying out when anything happens by free will, 'Lo, as it was destenyed of god toforn knowe, so it is thorow necessitè falle, and otherwyse might it not betyde' (III. ix. K, 32–4).

Moreover, Love's statement that Chaucer has resolved the question 'at the ful', and her general praise of Chaucer as 'the noble

---

[27] J. A. W. Bennett, *Middle English Literature* (Oxford, 1986), 348.
[28] Skeat, *Chaucerian and Other Pieces*, 482.

philosophical poete' who labours 'my name to encrese' and than whom no one is better, nor even equal, 'in scole of my rules' (III. iv. H, 248–55) suggest that it is not in the perfunctory tags of Troilus' soliloquy, but in the whole 'boke of Troilus' that the answer can be found, as a book in praise of Love herself. Usk, in that case, is arguing that *Troilus and Criseyde* should be read as proclaiming in full the answer to the problem which Love has 'lightly' given in the last two chapters of Book II of the *Testament* (II. xiii. C and xiv. I).

Usk's interpretation of *Troilus and Criseyde*, then, should be found in brief in those two chapters. And this seems to be confirmed by two small echoes from *Troilus* in the theodicy which Love expounds there. She begins (II. xiii. C, 8–10) with the first sentence borrowed from Anselm, 'Everiche qualitè and every accion, and every thing that hath any maner of beinge, it is of god; and god it made, of whom is al goodnesse and al being' ('Omnis quippe qualitas', etc.; *De concordia*, qu. 1, cap. 7). Bad is therefore simply negation. How then (as Usk asks her) can the bad which we seem to experience exist? Love answers that bad is either in evil will, or in the 'bad' as they regard it, though it is not bad, which is used to purify wrongdoers, or in the disorder of what in its first place was good. 'Our noble god, in gliterande wyse, by armony this world ordeyned, as in purtreytures storied with colours medled, in whiche blacke and other derke colours commenden the golden and the asured paynture' (II. xiii. c, 75–8). Skeat suggests an echo or a parallel here with Pandarus' words when Troilus first confessed his love for Criseyde, and Pandarus suggested he might give Troilus help even because of his own ill-success in love, since contraries set each other off:[29]

> For how myghte evere swetnesse han ben knowe
> To him that nevere tasted bitternesse?
> Ne no man may ben inly glad, I trowe,
> That nevere was in sorwe or som destresse;
> Eke whit by blak, by shame ek worthinesse,
> Ech set by other, more for other semeth.
> (*Troilus and Criseyde*, I. 638–43)

Even in this fallen world, even in the miseries of unrequited love, Usk may be feeling, if this is a real echo, God's initial harmonies may be heard. And the breaking of this harmony by evil will is

---

[29] Skeat, *Chaucerian and Other Pieces*, 477.

expounded in a similar analogy between an individual's love and the whole universe in the last chapter of Book II, where Love describes the leading astray of the innocent 'scoler lerning of my love' out of *Parables*, by 'love fayned' (xiv. I, 22). This phrase, inverted as 'fayned love', is repeated four times in this chapter (28, 31, 44, 58), and becomes so much a key phrase as to be recalled again in the summary in III. viii. S, 'how mis-rule by fayned love bothe realmes and citees hath governed a greet throwe...how somtyme with fayned love foule I was begyled' (8–12). From 'fayned love' Usk was delivered, could only have been delivered, because Love showed him Margaret (II. xiii. C). It seems a probable echo of Chaucer's resolution of the pains of Troilus, when he says of Christ:

> And syn he best to love is, and most meke,
> What nedeth feynede loves for to seke?
> (*Troilus and Criseyde*, V. 1847–8)

Characteristically, Usk, retaining 'feynede loves' to describe the contrast between a seductive woman and Margaret at the literal level of his parable, means it also of the contrast between all worldly loves and Christ, and specifically in his own life of the contrast between Northampton and the beliefs of his partisans, as we have seen, and whoever or whatever delivered him from them.

Both Usk's personal fall and recovery, and its analogues in the history of the world, are analysed in the Anselmian exploration of will in III. vi. N. At its close Love says of the lover, in whom harmoniously resolved will is united by love to reason, 'if thou voide love, than weyvest [thou] the bond that knitteth; and so nedes, or els right lightly, that other gon a-sondre; wherfore thou seest apertly that love holdeth this knot, and amaystreth hem to be bounde. These thinges, as a ring in circuit of wrethe, ben knit in thy soule without departing' (154–8). The image perhaps echoes Troilus' hymn, when he praises love that binds the elements in the universe together:

> And if that love aught lete his bridel go,
> Al that now loveth asondre sholde lepe

and prays for the grace of the creator

> That with his bond Love of his virtue liste
> To cerclen hertes alle and faste bynde,

That from his bond no wight the wey out wiste.
(*Troilus and Criseyde*, III. 1762–3, 1766–7)

After this analogue, it is perhaps reasonable to find a reminiscence of what immediately follows in *Troilus and Criseyde*, Chaucer's description of how love increases virtue in many ways in Troilus, in Love's description to Usk of the debt he owes Margaret in III. vii. V, medieval commonplace though Chaucer's picture is.

Overall, these echoes support the hypothesis that the reason for Usk's saying that Chaucer has fully resolved the question of God's relation to the existence of evil, and of the moral responsibility of mankind, is because he sees in *Troilus and Criseyde* suggestions of the original harmony of the universe, of the power of love in preserving this harmony, and of the responsibility of man for evil in following after feigned love. This is indeed perhaps not to say much more than that Usk recognizes how much there is implicit of Boethius' theodicy in *Troilus and Criseyde*, even if it is Anselm rather than Boethius who has helped him to recognize it.

Whether one could further suppose that Usk has in mind anything like Morton Bloomfield's hypothesis that Chaucer's stress in *Troilus and Criseyde* on the givenness, the long-ago fulfilment of the story, is meant as a kind of parable of God's foreknowledge of our doings,[30] I am not sure. If so, Usk must be seen as stressing more than Bloomfield appears to do that such knowledge in no way injures the actual freedom of human beings. There is one curious echo to show this, also in the last paragraph of the chapter on will, III. vi. N, where Love, assuring Usk that for all the importance of fidelity in a lover, it does not apply where love is wedded to unreason, as in his relation with Northampton, cites the proverb 'for though dronkennesse be forboden, men shul not alway ben drinklesse' (144–5). Criseyde quotes the same proverb in her first soliloquy, thinking that although she should not give Troilus her love, she does not necessarily have to flee him.

Can one say that Usk by this echo, even if it was unconscious, stresses the absolute freedom of will as instrument, in Criseyde's case in choosing to fall in love with Troilus, in his own case in choosing to turn away from Northampton, in spite of what conventional wisdom might say about loyalty in the one case, or

---

[30] Morton Bloomfield, 'Distance and Predestination in *Troilus and Criseyde*', *PMLA* 72 (1957), 14–26.

prudence in the other? There can be no doubt, at any rate, that he believed himself to have found in Anselm a reconciliation of God's foreknowledge with free will which preserves both at the full. Piling conjecture on an earlier conjecture, I fancy him discussing with Ralph Strode whether Chaucer was like Anselm in this. But it is time to turn to Langland.

The influence of Langland on Usk is a great deal less firmly established than that of Chaucer, but in so far as it can be discerned, it has the same pattern: in the Boethian *Testament* a gleaning of proverbs, in the Anselmian *Testament* an aid to deep and massive thought. Of the former sort are the many echoes alleged by Skeat[31] and others to show that Usk borrowed from *Piers Plowman*, and that the date of the C-text can be securely inferred therefrom. But of these, in my judgement, only four are more than chance, contemporaneity, common reading, and a shared taste for alliteration would easily account for. Of these only one couplet is peculiar to the C-text, in which Pride says that she is eager to show scorn to others:

> Lauhyng al aloude for lewede men sholde
> Wene y were witty and wiser then another;
> Scornare and unskilful to hem that skil shewede,
> In alle manere maneres my name to be knowe. (VI. 22–5)

Possibly Usk echoed this when he had Love tell him that she favours meek lovers, not one 'wening his owne wit more excellent than other; scorning al maner devyse but his own' (I. v. R, 117–19): the picking up of the alliterating words of three lines in succession, *wenyng, scorning, maner*, without using the second and third to alliterate, does look like an actual but involuntary reminiscence. But the other three echoes seem much more plausible, for they all come from one short speech in *Piers Plowman*, whose attraction for Usk can readily be imagined. In *Piers Plowman* Peace asserts the coming harrowing of Hell, saying of its inhabitants 'þat her wo into wele moet wende at þe laste' (C XX. 209), and argues that the suffering of both man and incarnate God is necessary so that good may be recognized—

[31] Skeat, *Chaucerian and Other Pieces*, pp. xxvii, 456–83.

For no wiht woet what wele is þat neuere wo soffrede (C XX. 211)

and,

For woet no wiht what werre is þer as pees regneth (C XX. 237).

In the Boethian *Testament* Usk uses this speech for consolation in his personal plight, saying in his own voice as an unlucky lover in I. iii. G, 'For he is worthy no welthe, that may no wo suffer' (153–4), and being assured by Love in II. ix. E, 'thy sorowe into wele mot ben chaunged' (178). In the Anselmian *Testament* the echo is part of Love's general theodicy in II. xiii. C, which also echoes Pandarus' words at *Troilus and Criseyde*, II. 638–9:[32] 'How shulde ever goodnesse of pees have ben knowe, but-if unpees somtyme reigne, and mokel yvel wrathe?' (85–6).

If these parallels are sufficient to establish that Usk was familiar with *Piers Plowman*, not only does James Simpson's conjecture about the relation of the poem to Usk's politics under Northampton seem the more plausible, but also we can accept that the image of the Tree of Love which dominates the Anselmian *Testament* owes something to Langland's Tree of Charity in B Passus XVI, C Passus XVIII.

Some direct connection between the two is commonly taken for granted. But the resemblances are not much more than are bound to exist between one allegorical orchard tree and another, and perhaps like Usk's other images of the pearl and the cloud, to which we shall presently turn, are most interesting in showing some common features of Ricardian writers. This may be seen by considering a third tree, with which neither Usk's nor Langland's can have any direct connection. This is the tree on which Martha Nussbaum bases her brilliant study of Greek thought, *The Fragility of Goodness*:[33] she adduces it from Pindar's *Eighth Nemean Ode*—'But human excellence grows like a vine tree, fed by the green dew, raised up, among wise men and just, to the liquid sky'[34] —though it seems to go back even further, to Thetis' description of the upbringing of Achilles in *Iliad*, 18. 54–60. The problem which it exemplifies, Nussbaum suggests, is, given that virtue shares with

---

[32] As quoted above, p. 240.

[33] Nussbaum, *The Fragility of Goodness: Luck and Ethics in Greek Tragedy and Philosophy* (Cambridge, 1986).

[34] Pindar, *Nemean Odes*, 8. 37–44.

a vine tree 'openness to fortune', needing a 'good stock', 'fostering weather', and 'the care of concerned and intelligent keepers',[35] how much is there in us that is (as Plato describes the soul) 'divine, immortal, intelligible, unitary, indissoluble, ever self-consistent and invariable'?[36] The tragic poets together with Aristotle, according to Nussbaum, believe that virtue is always vulnerable, that there is no final escape from luck: Plato believes in the possibility of an austere and difficult separation of the soul from circumstance, by following the good and the beautiful, which to actual undivided human nature is alien.

For what historical reason I do not know, but very fittingly, both our Ricardians use this same image to contrast their understanding of the soul and circumstance from that of 'these olde philosophers, that hadden no knowing of divine grace' (*Testament*, II. xi. E, 8). Langland, in one of his manically profound, compressed, and dreamlike meditations in the B-text, sees charity as the fruit of a tree growing in God's garden of the human heart, guarded against the fell winds of the world and the flesh, and the thefts of the Devil, by Liberum Arbitrium, Free Will, under Piers Plowman, impotently until Piers flings after the devil the stake that brings the Son of God to 'fecche that the fend claymeth, Piers fruyt the Plowman' (B XVIII. 20). Langland's treatment has more strands and a more perplexing development than I have outlined here: but this description will serve to show how, in a sense, he agrees with the tragedians and Aristotle as understood by Nussbaum over against Plato, seeing the fragility of human goodness as total. Of course, for Langland this condition is transformed by our redemption through Christ. It remains a matter of individual reading whether in Langland's view goodness was irrevocably fragile only in the history of humanity before Christ's life, and that for the baptized Christian a stable goodness is achievable though hard, or whether he thinks that Christ's historic redemption must be appropriated by the individual in some realization after baptism.

Usk's meditation is slower and more grave than Langland's. He makes more use of the tree in its actual botanical nature, to express as Pindar does with the vine-tree the problems of growth and variation in growth, and he allows more to the opinions of 'these olde philosophers'. Of Plato, like nearly all thinkers before the

---

[35] Nussbaum, *Fragility*, 1.   [36] Plato, *Phaedo*, 80B.

fifteenth-century recovery of Greek, he knows little more than comes to him through Augustine and Boethius: and yet he is instinctively more in sympathy with him than with Aristotle, at least the Aristotle described by Nussbaum who concentrates on the knottiness and fragility of empirical ethics. Usk's Aristotle, whom he appeals to by name five times, is the Aristotle who harmonizes easily with Plato, by telling us that final causes are nobler than the acts which they inspire, and that 'end' and 'good' are convertible. And Usk has in a sense resurrected the Plato of the *Symposium*, who believes that falling in love is the first step on the ladder to the Beautiful-itself, by his austere understanding of love as portrayed in such works as *Troilus and Criseyde*.

Usk, however, begins (as we have seen) at the break between the Boethian and Anselmian *Testaments* by rejecting what he has learnt, mainly through Boethius, of the opinions on salvation of the old philosophers. He has followed their prescription, living by reason, himself: and is as a result a dry tree without blossom or fruit (II. xi. E).

This Love denies, because he has not only lived by reason: he is in love with Margaret, from whom virtue proceeds, and so virtue must grow in him also. On the literal level, which Usk in this chapter carefully preserves, one might take this as an exact parallel to Plato in the *Symposium*, who also believes that the lover of wisdom begins not from reason but by falling in love. But the way in which Usk preserves Margaret's literalness is by lamenting that she is mortal, which is undoubtedly one of the reasons (in Nussbaum's scheme perhaps the principal reason) why Plato implies that the lover should pass from the mortal beloved to behold the immortal Beautiful-itself. But there is a deeper ambiguity, which I shall not pretend to resolve here, for it is in this chapter also that Usk insists that Margaret is also Christ, 'with ful vessel of grace yeven to every creature, that goodly wolde it receyve' (69–70), at once leaving Plato for Christianity yet in Nussbaum's scheme paralleling him in preferring a transcendent to an earthly love (II. xii. R).

Thereafter for a number of chapters, Love, increasingly drawing on Anselm, moves from grace to stress free will. And when she comes (at III. v. I) to develop the image of the tree, it is in order to stress the mystery of the relation of grace to free will in the mystery of the relation of a tree to the ground in which it is planted. Usk has received the grace to thrive from Margaret: but it is by free will that he has accepted it and it is by free will that he preserves his love for her, growing and enduring, again like the tree. The will now is unshakable by external circumstance, as we observed in dealing with this passage in relation to *Troilus and Criseyde*, and Usk appears in this to be siding with Boethius and therefore Plato, and incidentally against Langland. For when winds and adverse weather enter the image, which for Langland are the world, the flesh, and the devil, and a reminder that without grace the last of these will carry off the fruit, Love correspondingly insists to Usk (although not without some renewed doubt from him as interlocutor) that he can endure and even put out branches of prayer against anything that they may signify. She even encourages him to believe that because of his choice and endurance he deserves and will receive reward, calling to mind Nussbaum's critique of Plato and contrasting praise of the Greek tragic poets because they endow the spectacle of virtue with 'that love for the riskiness and openness of empirical humanity which finds its expression in recurrent stories about gods who fall in love with mortals'.[37] Plato's exaltation of virtue as invincible for her loses this.

It is only at the very end of her conversation (III. vii. V) that Love turns what she has said round by telling Usk that the reward he has deserved and already received is the grace to thrive, to endure, and to serve. Her revelation to him is also a story about a god who falls in love with a mortal and a mortal who has fallen in love with God, the Christian story which Usk shares with Langland. It admits more of the riskiness and openness of humanity than Plato does, since God unlike Plato's Beautiful-itself accepted the risks of love in accepting the 'loveday' which Love has made between him and mankind (*Testament* I. ii. R, 95), more perhaps even than the Greek tragedians, since God, unlike for example the Artemis of Euripides' *Hippolytus*, has been brought down like the pearl in the mussel 'to his lowest degree', to help mankind (*Testament* II. xii. R, 64). Unlike Langland, Usk includes the hope which is the end of his love story in the image of the tree: 'In hem shal he be, and they in god...this is the grace and the frute that I long have desyred; it doth me good the savour to smelle' (III. ix. K, 46–51). But this is only a difference of imagery: Usk follows this sentence with 'Crist, now to thee I crye of mercy and of grace'

---

[37] Nussbaum, *Fragility*, 3.

(III. ix. K, 51), paralleling the 'gradde aftur Grace' which ends *Piers Plowman*.

Given their common religion and their common culture, it must remain uncertain whether Usk took the image of the tree from Langland. They might each of them have taken it from some common classical source leading back to Pindar and Homer: or they might have taken both the image, and much of what they share in the sense they give it, from Christ's parable of the mustard-seed, or his saying 'By their fruits ye shall know them' (Matt. 13: 31–2 and 7: 16). Much the same is true of two other images which Usk shares with his contemporaries, the authors of the *Cloud* and *Pearl*.

In his first chapter, Usk says that he will be scorned 'that I, so unworthily clothed al-togider in the cloudy cloude of unconninge, wil putten me in prees to speke of love' (I. Prol. M, 95–6) and, in his last, apologizes 'for my dul wit is hindred by stepmoder of foryeting and with cloude of unconning, that stoppeth the light of my Margarite-perle, wherfore it may not shyne on me as it shulde' (III. ix. K, 85–8). Since, allegorically, he does mean in both cases that the 'cloude of unconninge' prevents him from the full knowledge and love of God, he might have derived his image from reading *The Cloud of Unknowing*. But, since the image of the cloud, apart from being naturally appropriate, is biblical, deriving from exegesis of the cloud in which Moses spoke with God on Sinai (Exod. 34: 15–18), there is no need to assign a particular source for his knowledge of it. And wherever he derived it, his use of it is more at odds with that in the *Cloud* than is his use of the tree with that in *Piers Plowman*: for he is clearly not advocating the negative way of mysticism by which the cloud is the best knowledge that we can have of God in this life. He presents the image rather as of a personal defect in his own following of the affirmative way, explicitly invoking St Paul, though not by name, by the text in Romans (1: 20) which asserts that 'the mene to bringe in knowleging and loving his creatour is the consideracion of thinges made by the creatour, wherthrough, by thilke thinges that ben made understonding here to oure wittes, arn the unsene privitees of god made to us sightful and knowing, in our contemplacion and understonding' (I. Prol. M, 54–9).

His use of the image of the pearl follows this doctrine. Given the closeness of some of his themes to those of *Pearl*—the gratuitous-ness of redemption and the mutuality of the inhabitants of heaven, such that the least of them 'shal of the gretest in glorie rejoice and ben gladded, as if he the same joye had' (III. ix. K, 44–5)—this use of its dominant image is so close to that in the *Pearl* that one must wonder if he found it there, along with some of his coinherent meanings for it: real jewel, real woman, grace, and the Christ in the heart. But all this is sufficiently understandable in terms of similar minds responding in a common tradition to the same source, Christ's parable of the pearl of great price. Both move from Christ's apparently monosemous use of the image, where only the value of the pearl is in question and any other singularly precious thing would do as well, to a polysemous use in which the qualities of the physical pearl are important. But this is a characteristically medieval move in using Christ's imagery.

However, in a bravura piece which introduces the Anselmian *Testament*, before the first actual quotation from Anselm, Usk moves much further in developing the meaning of the pearl than does the *Pearl*-poet. Such qualities as its healing power are important: its generation in a mussel, the lowest of animals, provides a symbol of the incarnation. This being so, when he speaks of the blueness of the mussel's shell (II. xii. R), Usk must be invoking the colour of the Virgin Mary, since he describes the mussel as 'moder of al vertues' in which 'by a maner of virgine engendrure' (65) pearls are formed. Curiously, however, although he thrice describes Mary in language of some beauty (here, at I. ii. R in the passage already quoted about God's loveday with mankind, in which a maid was umpire, and at II. ii. I to introduce the praise of women), he never mentions her by name. This may suggest that she is one of the meanings of Margaret, but it seems also as if Usk wants to see her as subordinate to the mystical quality of the whole created world. His anchor point for the meaning of blue is therefore not Mary, but the heavens: 'Kyndely heven, whan mery weder is a-lofte, apereth in mannes eye of coloure in blewe, stedfastnesse in pees betokening within and without' (II. xii. R, 45–7).

More explicitly than any other Ricardian writer, Usk seems to see himself in the world (as Owen Barfield has claimed more generally of medieval people) 'as if the observers were themselves *in* the picture. Compared with us, they felt themselves and the objects around them and the words that expressed those objects immersed together in something like a clear lake of—what shall we say?— of "meaning" if you choose. It seems the most appropriate word.'[38]

It is congruous with this attitude of Usk's that what he shares with his contemporaries are either phrases which (even when verbal resemblances show clearly where they come from) have an air of being drawn from a shared communal wisdom about the world, or meaningful visual images of the kind which V. A. Kolve finds structuring *The Canterbury Tales*[39] —the prison embodying a fall from good fortune in which a new kind of good is found, the pearl representing the single most valuable object in someone's experience, the tree of virtue brought out by divine grace, the cloud of ignorance of God. Perhaps one could relate to both kinds of resemblance the overall structure common to *Pearl*, *Piers Plowman*, and the *Testament*, of a confessional dialogue with a being more or less supernatural who is a spring of ancient wisdom. This dialogue is itself an image of something that Usk shares with all Ricardian writers, their habit of thinking through such images, at once picturesque and vital, and commonly drawn from a long tradition going back to Christ, to the Old Testament, or to the Greeks.

The only probable evidence of a contemporary's having read *The Testament of Love* is appropriately in the largest-scale example of such a dialogue, John Gower's *Confessio Amantis*. In the *Testament*, Love describes Chaucer as 'myne owne trewe servaunt, the noble philosophical poete in Englissh, whiche evermore him besieth and travayleth right sore my name to encrese' (III. iv. H, 248–51). In the *Confessio* Love, or rather Venus, describes Chaucer and her relation to him in very similar terms, when she tells Amans to

> gret wel Chaucer whan ye mete,
> As mi disciple and mi poete

with whose songs

> The which he for mi sake made,
> The lond fulfild is overal:
> Wherof to him in special
> Above alle othre I am most holde.

Moreover Amans is to instruct Chaucer

[38] Owen Barfield, *Saving the Appearances* (London, 1957), 95.
[39] V. A. Kolve, *Chaucer and the Imagery of Narrative* (London, 1984).

> To sette an ende of alle his werk,
> As he which is myn owne clerk,
> Do make his testament of love. (VIII. 2940–57)[40]

That this really is a reference to Usk's book becomes more apparent when one considers how odd (and therefore perhaps characteristic of Usk's style of thinking) the use of the word 'testament' was. The conflation, influenced by phonetic similarity, with 'testimony', which makes it easy for us, is ascribed by the *OED* (which sternly describes it as erroneous) only to the mid-fifteenth century: and Robert Bridges's title 'The Testament of Beauty', which makes it easier, was quite probably derived from Usk's through his friendship with Henry Bradley, who discovered Usk's acrostic and thereby identified him as the author.[41] Nor in the Prologue to Book I, where Usk introduces his title, does he seem to have in mind the nearness to death and the end of life's work which both Gower and Bridges (at 80) have in mind, and which makes the analogue with one of the two central senses, 'last will and testament'. He seems only to be setting it among the works of those 'naturel philosophers' who delighted in the study of God's goodness in creation (I. Prol. M, 64–5), though he does have in mind their destiny after death, to have their names written in 'the boke of perpetual memory' while those that hated such goodness are pressed 'in Styx, the foule pitte of helle' (80). This would be a reason thoroughly characteristic of Usk's lateral habits of mind for invoking the idea of a last will: but he may have been thinking of the other central sense, 'sacred book', derived from the original sense of 'covenant' as in Old and New 'Testament'.

Whatever the derivation, the use is thoroughly Uskian, and suggests that Gower was not only alluding to Usk's *Testament* but expected Chaucer, and perhaps Chaucer's readers, to recognize the allusion. It would be pleasant to think that at least two of his contemporaries read Usk with the attention which he gave to some of them.

---

[40] J. H. Fisher, *John Gower* (London, 1965), 62.
[41] Nowell Charles Smith, *Notes on 'The Testament of Beauty'* (London, 1931), xi.

11

The Perfection of the Pentangle and of Sir Gawain in 'Sir Gawain and the Green Knight'

GERALD MORGAN

'In god fayth, Sir Gawayn,' quoþ þe gay lady,
'þe prys and þe prowes þat plesez al oþer,
If I hit lakked oþer set at lyȝt, hit were littel daynté.' (1248–50)

The progress of the romance of *Sir Gawain and the Green Knight* is commonly taken to be a progress from absolute perfection to relative perfection. Thus John Burrow refers to 'the geometric absolutism of the pentangle passage' and subsequently observes that 'Gawain is not, as the poet claimed in the pentangle passage, "faultless" *absolutely*, like refined gold or a perfect pearl; but he is so *relatively*, in comparison with other men.'[1] Such an interpretation underlines our sense of Gawain's failure and of his decline from noble ideals. This view of Gawain's failure, linked to that of Chrétien's Yvain and Perceval, has been recently restated by Ad Putter: 'we cannot fail to be struck by the fact that the protagonists of Chrétien and the *Gawain*-poet fail.'[2] But it is a strange kind of failure that is attended by so many noble and penitential acts. It would, for example, be a long task to enumerate all the acts of generosity and courtesy that Gawain displays towards the lady in the bedroom, and without prejudice to his own chastity and to the loyalty he owes the lord. How could such conduct be improved upon? It is impossible to imagine or believe that it could be.

[1] J. A. Burrow, *A Reading of 'Sir Gawain and the Green Knight'* (London, 1965), 51, 134. For other references to this interpretation, see G. Morgan, *'Sir Gawain and the Green Knight' and the Idea of Righteousness* (Dublin, 1991), 104 n. 21.

[2] A. Putter, *'Sir Gawain and the Green Knight' and French Arthurian Romance* (Oxford, 1995), 174.

But the pentangle passage itself contains a reference to Gawain's relative and not absolute exemplification of the fifth group of five moral virtues, for 'þyse pure fyue | Were *harder* happed on þat haþel þen on any oþer' (654–5). Here we have the sense of an ideal not as impossible of fulfilment, but at its utmost point of realization, so that the narrative can be seen to exemplify rather than subvert the claim for Gawain's excellence. This is the position I adopt in my book (pp. 103–5), where I take the single reference to Gawain's relative excellence at 654–5 as a sufficient basis to establish the argument. The fact that it is not is evident from a review by Edward Wilson in which he rightly insists on the presence of both absolute and relative statements in the pentangle passage.[3]

These difficulties of interpretation arise in large measure from the lack of a context of application for the pentangle, since the pentangle as a device for Gawain is found in no other medieval romance. Putter revives the Ciceronian ideal of justice as the basis for interpreting the five moral virtues of the fifth group (p. 155 n. 13):

An excellent case for the *Gawain*-poet's familiarity with Cicero's *De Officiis* or its medieval adaptations has been made by Silverstein...who analyses the fifth set of virtues symbolized by the pentangle...in terms of the virtues that make up Cicero's ideal of justice, namely *liberalitas, amicitia, innocentia, mansuetudo*, and *pietas*.[4]

The importance of Cicero for this kind of moral analysis is evident in the fact that he is invoked by St Thomas Aquinas as a primary authority in the classification of the moral virtues in the *Summa theologiae* (hereafter referred to as *ST*). At the same time Aquinas's own discussion shows that reliance on the unmediated authority of Cicero is not in itself sufficient. Thus Cicero lists six virtues as part of justice, namely *religio, pietas, gratia, vindicatio, observantia*, and *veritas*, and yet only one of these, *pietas*, is found in the 'ideal of justice' that is attributed to him here. Aquinas observes that liberality, friendship, and humanity (or *mansuetudo*) are not mentioned by Cicero because they carry with them little of the notion

---

[3] E. Wilson, review of *'Sir Gawain and the Green Knight' and the Idea of Righteousness*, in *RES* NS 45 (1994), 408–9.

[4] Putter is here referring to T. Silverstein, 'Sir Gawain in a Dilemma, or Keeping Faith with Marcus Tullius Cicero', *MP* 75 (1977), 1–17. See also T. Silverstein, *'Sir Gawain and the Green Knight': A New Critical Edition* (Chicago, 1984), 134–5.

of debt that is the defining principle of justice (*ST* 2a 2ae 80. 1 and *ad* 2).[5] *Mansuetudo* or gentleness is the moderation of anger and hence a part of temperance, not justice. The *Gawain*-poet's *clannes* (653), in so far as it refers to chastity, as it surely must in the bedroom scenes, also belongs with temperance. The moral interest of the poem extends more widely than justice, for it is concerned with the perfecting of Gawain in himself, as well as in his relation to others.

The limited correspondence of the Ciceronian scheme of virtues to the pentangle passage may be explained by the fact that the symbol of the pentangle is nowhere used in Ciceronian moral philosophy. On the other hand it is to be found in the tradition of scholastic Aristotelianism, and is ultimately derived from Aristotle's exposition of different kinds of soul in the *De anima* (2. 3 414^{b}19–32). Here the distinction and relationship between vegetative, sensitive, and intellectual souls are clarified in terms of an analogy with geometrical figures, namely the triangle, quadrangle, and pentangle.[6] The *Gawain*-poet's insistence on the familiarity of the device of the pentangle (629–30, and 664–5) becomes readily intelligible in the light of this tradition. The *De anima* continued to be prescribed in the Faculty of Arts in the second half of the fourteenth century, and so was commented upon by all masters.[7] James of Venice's translation of the *De anima* (?1125–50) survives in 144 manuscripts, and William of Moerbeke's translation (? before 1268) in 268 manuscripts.[8] It can hardly be said that the *De anima* is a remote or unlikely source of the *Gawain*-poet's knowledge of so distinctive and complex a symbol as the pentangle. Nevertheless the relevance of scholastic Aristotelianism to *Sir Gawain and the Green Knight* continues to be doubted. Indeed Wilson concludes that the scholastic 'accounts of the three kinds of soul, or the three powers of the soul, hierarchical in structure, are wholly unlike the seamless amalgam of twenty-five penitential,

---

[5] Throughout this chapter I cite the Latin and English translation from the Blackfriars edition, *St Thomas Aquinas: Summa theologiae*, 61 vols. (London, 1964–81).

[6] For a documentation of the pentangle as a symbol of the intellectual or rational soul in scholastic Aristotelian philosophy, see '*Sir Gawain and the Green Knight*' *and the Idea of Righteousness*, 87–9.

[7] See N. Kretzmann, A. Kenny, and J. Pinborg (eds.), *The Cambridge History of Later Medieval Philosophy* (Cambridge, 1982), 628.

[8] Ibid. 76.

religious, moral, and courtly virtues which constitute the romance's pentangle and whose unhierarchical inter-relation is so emphasized' (p. 408).

When there is such a discrepancy in the interpretation of the same texts it is obviously necessary to proceed with caution. The purpose of the following discussion is to show how absolute and relative values are co-ordinated in the presentation of the pentangle and in its reference to Gawain, and how these values are derived from their original formulation by Aristotle in the text of the *De anima*. In the light of these values it will become possible to restore to the romance a more positive and sustained expression of Gawain's excellence. The romance is not darkened by failure, but is uplifted by achievement, and it is to Gawain's achievement that his fellow knights (unlike many modern readers) are so responsive. They identify with his humanity by wearing a green baldric (2516–18), and assuredly it is not a symbol of failure, but of honour and renown:

> For þat watz acorded þe renoun of þe Rounde Table,
> And he honoured þat hit hade evermore after,
> As hit is breued in þe best boke of romaunce. (2519–21)

The relationship between Gawain and the pentangle is precisely co-ordinated by the poet:

> For ay faythful in fyue and sere fyue syþez
> Gawan watz for gode knawen. (632–3)

Gawain embodies the perfection of the pentangle or is perfect in the way that the pentangle is perfect. If we are to understand the nature of Gawain it is vital that we understand Aristotle's exposition of the hierarchy of souls and the pentangle's place in a corresponding hierarchy of geometrical figures. The *Gawain*-poet has mastered these ideas, and we must follow him exactly if we are not to distort the poetic argument he has fashioned out of them.

Wilson refers to the 'unhierarchical inter-relation' (p. 408) of the constitutive parts of the pentangle. Now the pentangle certainly stands for the idea of unity in the interrelationship of parts, but not for the unhierarchical interrelationship of parts. Thus the five virtues of the fifth group are 'þyse pure fyue' (654); they have a special excellence in comparison, say, with the five senses that form the first group (640). Generosity and fidelity are practised by Gawain 'forbe al þyng' (652), and piety[9] 'passez alle poyntez' (654). In the third bedroom scene we see that chastity and fidelity are set above courtesy:

> He cared for his cortaysye, lest craþayn he were,
> And more for his meschef ȝif he schulde make synne,
> And be traytor to þat tolke þat þat telde aȝt. (1773–5)

The moral choice that is forced upon Gawain by the lady here is entirely consistent with the assumption of a hierarchy among the moral virtues that is made in the fifth group of the pentangle passage.

Wilson also refers to 'the seamless amalgam of twenty-five... virtues' (p. 408). It would be satisfying to our sense of schematic completeness if there were twenty-five virtues, but there are not. There are five senses, one bodily grace (namely, strength, if that is what is signified by the five fingers), one theological virtue (faith),

---

[9] In his revision of the Tolkien–Gordon edition, Davis glosses *pité* (654) as 'pity, compassionateness' (p. 204), and defends this reading against that of 'piety' in his notes (p. 96). Such a reading is persuasive both in itself and also in its chivalric context, and it has been adopted by most modern editors of the poem, such as Waldron (1970), Barron (1974), and Silverstein (1984). Nevertheless *MED* lends the weight of its own considerable authority to the reading 'piety' (s.v. *pite* n. 4). I think it right to do so for at least two reasons; first, because of the status of piety as the highest of the moral virtues (see *ST* 2a 2ae 81. 6), and second, because the virtue of piety is continuously relevant to the action of the poem, whereas considerations of pity are entirely absent from it. Such an emphasis on piety is characteristic of the chivalric literature of the late 14th cent. Piety is one of the outstanding virtues of the Black Prince in the Chandos Herald's *Life of the Black Prince* (1385). The Black Prince's devotion to the Holy Trinity is especially marked, both at the beginning of the poem (85–92) and at its end (4176–8), and is illustrated in the frontispiece to the University of London Library MS 1 (fo. 3ᵛ). Before the battles of Poitiers (1260–73) and Nàjera (3172–87) the Black Prince makes his prayer to God for aid, and after them he attributes the victory not to himself but to God (1427–32, and 3502–8). See the edition of D. B. Tyson, '*La Vie du Prince Noir*' *by Chandos Herald* (Tübingen, 1975). The same kind of piety is related also of Edward III at Crécy in the Chronicles of Geoffrey le Baker (1357–60) and Froissart (1369–1400). Sir Geoffroi de Charny in his *Livre de chevalerie* (c.1352) is concerned to distinguish the grades of excellence among knights, or the 'scales of honour' as M. Keen calls them: 'The good, simple and bold are *preux*: those who by their valour displayed in many places have risen to high rank are *soulverain preux*: but you may tell those who are *plus soulvereinement preux* by the wisdom with which they attribute all their glory and achievement to the grace of God and the Virgin' (M. Keen, *Chivalry* (New Haven, 1984), 13). Sir Geoffroi de Charny was faithful to his high calling as a knight when he died holding the banner of the king of France at Poitiers. And it is clear too that the piety of the Black Prince and of Gawain places them in the highest category of chivalric excellence.

and six moral virtues (courage, generosity, fidelity, chastity, courtesy, and piety). This is a list not simply of virtues, but of powers of the soul and the virtues that arise from the operation of the powers. Virtues are either intellectual or moral (Aristotle, *Ethics*, 2. 1 1103ᵃ14), so that there can be no virtue in the internal sense-powers of apprehension.[10] Human perfection or imperfection is not a matter of good or bad sight or imagination, but of the exercise of virtue or vice. The pentangle represents moral, sensitive, and bodily principles in the same way as does the intellectual soul which is the form of man and united to a body, for there are many powers of the soul.[11] Indeed the *Gawain*-poet goes beyond Aristotle to a Christian synthesis in the inclusion of the theological virtue of faith, and further underlines the religious context of virtue by references to the five wounds of Christ (642–3) and the five joys of the Virgin Mary (646–7).

The only medieval tradition that argues for the equality of the virtues and the vices is that derived from the Stoics and adopted by Cicero in the *Paradoxa Stoicorum* (3). In refuting this view, Aquinas goes so far as to say that it is heretical to believe that all suffering in hell is equal (*ST* 1a 2ae 73. 2). The orthodox opinion of the hierarchical ordering of virtues and vices is well illustrated by Dante in the *Commedia*. The structure of the *Inferno* and *Purgatorio* is founded upon the graded division of the vices, the *Paradiso* on the distinction of the virtues. The whole is a monument to the love of schematism that is so apparent on a smaller scale in the pentangle passage. Examples could be multiplied. Langland's Meed knows that lechery 'is synne of the sevene sonnest relessed' (*Piers Plowman*, B III. 58), and this corresponds with Dante's placing of the lustful in the second circle of hell (*Inferno*, v), and the seventh terrace of purgatory (*Purgatorio*, xxv–xxvii). The moral and psychological system of Aristotle is undoubtedly hierarchical. The passions are properly but not always subject to reason, and are so subject in the moral virtues of fortitude and temperance (*ST* 1a 2ae 59. 2). Justice is the most excellent of the moral virtues, as perfecting the will and governing

---

[10] See Aquinas, *ST* 1a 2ae 56. 5 *sed contra*.

[11] Wilson refers to 'the three powers of the soul' (p. 408), but this is not the opinion of Aristotle or Aquinas; see *ST* 1a 77. 2. There are eighteen powers as Aquinas enumerates them at *ST* 1a 78–82. Aquinas's exposition, apart from that on the internal senses, closely follows Aristotle's account in the *De anima*.

relations between individuals (Aristotle, *Ethics*, 5. 1 1129^{b}27), after which come fortitude and temperance, which perfect the individual in respect of the irascible and concupiscible passions (*ST* 1a 2ae 66. 4). The intellectual virtues are superior to the moral virtues, if considered absolutely, although not in relation to action (*ST* 1a 2ae 66. 3), and wisdom (*sapientia*) is the highest of the intellectual virtues (Aristotle, *Ethics*, 6.7 1141^{a}19). The theological virtues surpass the order of human reason (*ST* 1a 2ae 62. 2 and *ad* 2), and among them charity is pre-eminent (*ST* 1a 2ae 66. 6). There is nothing untoward in imputing to the *Gawain*-poet himself the claim that the virtues exist in a hierarchy. The assumption of hierarchy is compatible not only with the pentangle passage but also with the poem as a whole. Thus the knights in Camelot are seated at the Christmas feast in accordance with rank: 'þe best burne ay abof, as hit best semed' (73). The use of the adverb 'ay' suggests how precise this seating order may have been. It is the same at Hautdesert, where Gawain is welcomed in turn by the porter (807–14), the people of the castle (815–23), knights and squires (824–32), the lord (833–7), and eventually the lady (941–6). And at mealtime on Christmas Day when Gawain is seated beside the lady 'euen inmyddez' (1004), 'vche grome at his degré grayþely watz served' (1006).

At the same time as it signifies a hierarchically graded system of values, the pentangle is certainly a unified whole, and the *Gawain*-poet stresses the unity of the pentangle as a geometrical figure both at the beginning of his description (627–30) and at the end (657–61). This unity is expressed in terms proper to a pentangle, that is, of lines, points, and angles. There are 'fyue poyntez' (627, and 658), the lines (*lyne*, 628) overlap and are fastened to each other, they do not come together in any *syde* (659) or separate, and are without end 'at any noke' (660). The whole forms an 'endeles knot' (630). The poet has thus contrived to include within his description of the pentangle a realization of the geometrical figure itself. There is unity in the interrelation of parts, but it is the special kind of unity that attaches itself to a pentangle. The complex unity of a knot is very different in nature from the simplicity of a circle. Hence the focus on the five multiples of five, 'sere fyue syþez' (632) and 'alle þese fyue syþez' (656), is not only ingenious, but also emphatic in making the reader continuously aware of the distinct character of a pentangle.

Now, Aquinas is no less insistent in emphasizing the unity of the intellectual soul or form of man. Although there are many powers of the soul, there is only one formal principle or substantial form:

Sic ergo dicendum quod eadem numero est anima in homine sensitiva et intellectiva et nutritiva. (*ST* 1a 76. 3)

(We must assert, then, that the soul in man is one in number, at once sensory, intellectual, and nutritive.)

The emphasis that Aquinas places upon the unity of the soul is evident also in his rejection of the doctrine of a *forma corporeitatis*, held by such thinkers as Bonaventure and Scotus.[12] Aquinas's argument for the intellectual soul is first and foremost an argument for its unity as the form of the body, and in this respect his exposition stands out against those of his philosophical contemporaries. In order to explain this principle of unity in multiplicity he invokes Aristotle's comparison in the *De anima* of the different kinds of soul to geometrical figures. Hence Aquinas's account proceeds from the unity of the intellectual soul as the one substantial form in man (*ST* 1a 76. 3 and 4) to the multiplicity of powers (*ST* 1a 77. 2) and to the ordered relationship of powers (*ST* 1a 77. 4). The order of powers is hierarchical, but the conception of hierarchy in no way impairs or violates the conception of unity. In thus stressing the interdependence of parts and the hierarchy of powers in his account of the intellectual soul, Aquinas combines precisely those elements that are so dominant in the *Gawain*-poet's description of the pentangle.

The *Gawain*-poet stresses the familiarity of the symbol of the pentangle because he realizes that its meaning cannot always be securely established by its inherent fitness (625–6). The meaning of a text resides not merely in the text itself, but in the meanings brought to a text by those familiar with its rhetorical strategies. In the case of a rose, as in *Le Roman de la Rose*, or a sheep, as in *Piers Plowman* (B Prol. 2), the modern reader can be expected to bring to bear the relevant associations. But the case of the pentangle has proved by no means so straightforward. The most likely explanation is that modern readers are not as familiar as the poet

---

[12] The originality of Aquinas's thought in this respect may be gauged from the fact that his position was condemned by two successive archbishops of Canterbury, Robert Kilwardby in 1277 and John Peckham in 1284 and 1286.

and his original audience were with the translation of the *De anima* and hence with the analogy between geometrical figures and kinds of soul. The relevance of the tradition to the *Gawain*-poet need not be denied when it is so readily available to him and also when there is a congruity between Aristotle's account of the intellectual soul and the *Gawain*-poet's account of the pentangle. The exposition of Aquinas in the *Summa theologiae* is especially helpful in that it supplies additional detail to Aristotle's version. What is implicit in Aristotle becomes explicit in Aquinas in the identification of the relation between a pentagonal figure and the intellectual soul (*ST* ia 76. 3).

What does our familiarity with the symbol bring to our reading of the pentangle passage? The answer is that it makes us aware of that distinctive kind of perfection that a pentangle symbolizes. The use of the geometrical analogy in the first place arises from the recognition of different kinds of perfection in created things. A pentangle is neither a triangle, nor a quadrangle, and so the perfection it symbolizes is different from both, though it subsumes both. Pentangular perfection is human perfection, and this means perfectibility in accordance with the exercise of a rational principle. Every reference to the geometrical nature of the figure is designed to remind us of that fact.

The intellectual and moral virtues, unlike the theological virtues, are proportionate to human nature (*ST* ia 2ae 62. 2 *sed contra*). For Aristotle the acquisition of virtues by repeated acts is thus not an absolute process. And here Aquinas draws a distinction between the Aristotelian and the Stoic philosophy:

Non enim exigitur ad rationem virtutis quod attingat rectae rationis medium in indivisibili, sicut Stoici putabant; sed sufficit prope medium esse, ut in *Ethic.* [2. 9 1109^{b}18] dicitur. (*ST* ia 2ae 66. 1)

(For the nature of virtue does not require that a man should reach the mean of right reason as though it were an indivisible point, as the Stoics thought; it is enough that he should be close to the mean, according to the teaching of the *Ethics*.)

Mortal sin can coexist with acquired virtue, since the habit of virtue enables one to avoid sin only in most cases (*ut in pluribus, ST* ia 2ae 63. 2 *ad* 2). Christian philosophers explain this lack of completeness in terms of original sin, that is, as Aquinas understands it, the loss of the state of original justice, that gift which originally guaranteed the subjection of man to God and of the sense-powers to the intellectual powers. Original sin is a sin of nature, and so in the soul in its essence, and consequently it bears upon the powers of the soul and especially the will (*ST* 1a 2ae 83. 2 and 3). In the section on sin in the *Summa theologiae* (1a 2ae 71–89), Aquinas does not investigate the possibility of human exemption from sin, but rather the kinds, causes, and degrees of gravity of sin.

The claim for absolute perfection in any individual human being, apart, that is, from Christ and perhaps also Galahad, is irreconcilable with the thought of Aristotle and also with the symbolism of the pentangle. Nevertheless human perfection is perfect of its kind, and once its limitations have been acknowledged its degree of perfectibility deserves also to be acknowledged. Thus the poet focuses on the excellence or human perfection of Gawain in the manner of epideictic rhetoric. By the figure of *expolitio* the poet achieves the varied repetition of the same thing,[13] and in the space of eight lines there are no fewer than seven variations on Gawain's excellence: he is 'ay faythful in fyue' (632), 'for gode knawen' (633), 'as golde pured' (633), 'voyded of vche vylany' (634), 'wyth vertuez ennourned' (634), 'tulk of tale most trwe' (638), and 'gentylest kny3t of lote' (639). This is the authentic manner of romance. It is consistent with the opening description of Camelot (51–3) and also with the absoluteness of Chaucer's praise of the Knight as 'a verray, parfit gentil knyght' (*Canterbury Tales*, I (A) 72). But the assertion of Gawain's excellence is everywhere limited to and so defined by the symbol of the pentangle, just as the context of the pilgrimage defines our sense of the moral perfection of Chaucer's Knight. The pentangle is identified three times by its proper Latin name in the same stanza (620, 623, and 636), and also on one further occasion in its English form as 'þe endeles knot' (630). The excellence of the pentangle itself is also stressed. It is 'þe pure pentaungel' (664); it is painted 'of pure golde hwez' (620), and is fashioned 'ryally wyth red golde' (663). Further, it is identified as 'a syngne' (625) or symbol and as 'a figure' (627) or geometrical figure. It is not only a symbol, but it is

---

[13] See Geoffrey of Vinsauf, *Poetria nova*, ll. 1244–9, ed. E. Faral, *Les Arts poétiques du xii⁰ et du xiii⁰ siècle* (Paris, 1924), 235, and tr. M. F. Nims, *The 'Poetria nova' of Geoffrey of Vinsauf* (Toronto, 1967), 61.

also a fitting symbol, 'bi tytle þat hit habbez' (626). It is not only fitting in itself, but fitting also in reference to Gawain: 'Forþy hit acordez to þis knyȝt' (631). Just as the five points of angle of the pentangle 'fayld neuer' (658), so Gawain 'fayled neuer... in his fyue fyngres' (641). The five sides of the pentangle are matched in Gawain by his faithfulness 'in fyue' (632) and in multiples of five, 'fyue syþez' (632, and 656). Indeed the language appropriate to the one passes imperceptibly into that used of the other. Thus Gawain's chastity and courtesy 'croked were neuer' (653) and the five multiples of five were so fixed in him 'þat non ende hade' (657). The symbolism of the pentangle is the means whereby we apprehend the nature and excellence of Gawain's virtue, and the just correspondence of symbol and referent means that the argument in these stanzas is highly controlled despite the unreserved praise that is bestowed upon Gawain as a knight. The poet at no stage repudiates the symbolic value that is assigned to the pentangle, for the fitness that is asserted here is demonstrated at length throughout the course of the poem's action.

Wilson claims that the *Gawain*-poet insists on both the absolute and the relative perfection of Gawain in the pentangle passage: 'Gawain is better comparatively because he is so absolutely' (p. 409). There is a contradiction here because absoluteness and relativeness are predicated of one and the same thing, namely the relation of Gawain to other knights. If Gawain is absolutely better than other knights, then he belongs to a separate category; in other words, he is free from all imperfection, whereas they are tainted by sin. If Gawain is relatively better than other knights, then he too is sinful, but in a lesser degree. The solution to this problem seems to be that the virtues can be considered absolutely in themselves, but relatively in their exemplification in any individual human being. Aquinas argues that the virtues considered in themselves do not admit of more and less, since the nature of virtue consists in a maximum, but virtue considered on the part of the subject possessing it may be greater or less, either in relation to different persons or to the same person at different times (*ST* 1a 2ae 66. 1). The distinction is neatly summed up by him in an earlier article on the dispositions: 'justitia non dicatur magis et minus, sed justum' (*ST* 1a 2ae 52. 1). In the same way the *Gawain*-poet distinguishes between the fifth group of virtues and Gawain's possession of them. These five moral virtues are pure, that is, 'excellent, perfect, unblemished, unsullied, faultless',[14] but in the nature of things Gawain's exemplification of them is incomplete.

The distinction between the virtues considered objectively in themselves and subjectively in their human realization is one that runs throughout the pentangle passage and indeed throughout the poem as a whole. The symbol of the pentangle stands immediately for the virtues in themselves and only consequently for their realization in individuals such as Gawain. Thus the fifth group of moral virtues is 'þyse *pure* fyue' (654), and the pentangle is 'depaynt of *pure* golde hwez' (620) and is 'þe *pure* pentaungel' (664). On the other hand Gawain is 'as golde *pured*' (633).[15] The pentangle is pure, whereas Gawain is purified. In the same way Gawain is recognized and praised at Hautdesert for his '*pured* þewes' (912), whereas the lady's girdle is described as 'a *pure* token' (2398). These linguistic distinctions are well considered, and indeed vital to any coherent account of human excellence which does justice to both a standard of aspiration and a fact of realization. Thus the poet also tells us in the pentangle passage that Gawain is 'voyded of vche vylany' (634), that is, Gawain is not *voyd* or free of 'vche vylany', but *voyded* or made free.[16] Chaucer uses the adjective *voyd* in such a way as to make clear that he well understood this distinction of meanings. In *The Former Age* he writes of 'lambish peple, voyd of alle vyce' (50), but these gentle people belong to a Golden Age. In his own invented scene between Pandarus and Criseyde at the beginning of the second book of *Troilus and Criseyde* he develops the same distinctions as the *Gawain*-poet in elaborating upon the virtue of Hector and Troilus. Pandarus recommends Troilus to Criseyde as a second Hector 'In whom that alle vertu list habounde' and claims for him the 'same pris' as his brother (II. 159 and 181). Pandarus supports his declaration of the virtues of Hector and Troilus (II. 157–61 and 176–82) with a resoundingly emphatic assertion of their freedom from vice:

[14] *MED*, s.v. *pur*(e adj. 2 (a).

[15] See *MED*, s.v. *puren* v. 1 (b) 'to refine (metal); *ppl. pured*, refined, purified', and 2. (a) 'To spiritually cleanse...remove sin or guilt from (sb.); purify or free (oneself) from sin or vice'.

[16] See *OED*, s.v. *void*, a. and sb.[1] A. adj. II. 12. a. 'Devoid of, free from, not tainted with (some bad quality, fault, or defect)', and *void* v. I. 1. b. 'To rid, to make free or clear, of...some quality or condition.' This distinction is not observed in Davis's gloss of *voyded of* as 'free from' (p. 224).

> That certeynly, though that I sholde deye,
> Thei ben as voide of vices, dar I seye,
> As any men that lyven under the sonne. (II. 172–4)

But though his language of praise is emphatic, Pandarus does not go beyond the relative standards of 'men that lyven under the sonne'. The *Gawain*-poet makes us aware of such relativeness by the use of the verb, not the adjective; Gawain is 'voyded of vche vylany'.

But what is it that makes Gawain purified 'as golde' or made free of 'vche vylany'? The answer is the infusion of grace through the sacrament of the Eucharist, and that explains the placing of the description of Gawain and the pentangle immediately after his attendance at mass:

> So harnayst as he watz he herknez his masse,
> Offred and honoured at þe heȝe auter. (592–3)

The receiving of the Eucharist implies not only the absence of mortal sins, for one who receives the sacrament in a state of mortal sin adds to himself the mortal sin of sacrilege (*ST* 3a 79. 3 and 80. 4), but also the remission of venial sins (*ST* 3a 79. 4). Thus we are bound to assume that Gawain goes to mass in a state free from mortal sin, and returns from it purged of his venial sins. He is a good and noble man whose human imperfections have been supplied by grace. It is no wonder that he radiates virtue. At the same time the radiance of Gawain's virtue does not obscure the reality of his human imperfection, so that we are prepared for his inevitable lapse into sin through the withholding of the girdle. The soul's radiance is impaired by contact with sin, and this is what we understand as the stain of sin (*ST* 1a 2ae 86. 1). The mere cessation of a sinful act, as when Gawain returns the girdle to its rightful owner (2376–81), is not in itself sufficient to remove the stain of sin. What is necessary is the new infusion of grace that comes through the sacrament of penance:

Dicendum quod macula peccati remanet in anima etiam transeunte actu peccati. Cujus ratio est quia macula...importat quemdam defectum nitoris propter recessum a lumine rationis vel divinae legis. Et ideo quamdiu homo manet extra hujusmodi lumen, manet in eo macula peccati; sed postquam redit ad lumen rationis et ad lumen divinum, quod fit per gratiam, tunc macula cessat. (*ST* 1a 2ae 86. 2)

(The stain of sin continues in the soul even after the passing of the sinful act. The reason is that the stain...denotes a certain lack of radiance caused by drawing away from the light of reason or of divine law. Therefore as long as a person stays outside this light, the stain of sin remains; upon his return to the divine light and the light of reason, which is accomplished through grace, the stain passes away.)

This is explicitly acknowledged in the text in the words of the Green Knight himself, who considers Gawain as 'pured as clene | As þou hadez neuer forfeted syþen þou watz fyrst borne' (2393–4). The reference to Gawain's birth is presumably to his baptism, and is designed to cover all the actual sins that Gawain may have committed in the whole course of his life.

The relativism of the pentangle passage is taken for granted in the rest of the poem and at its end. When Gawain sets out on his quest he is mourned by his companions who think that it will not be easy to 'fynde hys fere vpon folde' (676). When he reveals his identity at Hautdesert it is acknowledged by all present that 'Byfore alle men vpon molde his mensk is þe most' (914). It is this reputation that the lady so cleverly exploits in the bedroom scenes:

> For I wene wel, iwysse, Sir Wowen 3e are,
> Þat alle þe worlde worchipez quere-so 3e ride;
> Your honour, your hendelayk is hendely praysed
> With lordez, wyth ladyes, with alle þat lyf bere. (1226–9)[17]

In playing so continuously upon Gawain's reputation for virtue, the lady is searching him out. She does so in the sure knowledge that no one can be complete in virtue, however great their reputation. The continuous testing of Gawain in this way is thus in itself a recognition of the limits of human perfection. The conclusion of the poem bears out the pentangle's representation of the relative perfection of Gawain in the Green Knight's judgement that:

> As perle bi þe quite pese is of prys more,
> So is Gawayn, in god fayth, bi oþer gay kny3tez. (2364–5)

The meaning of the pentangle is thus restated and reinforced. It is not the poet's purpose to present an absolute standard in the pentangle passage in order to subvert it, but rather a relative

---

[17] See also 1290–3, 1296–301, 1480–6, 1489–91, and 1508–34.

standard in order to exemplify it. In the process, despite the shame
and confusion that inevitably attend sin, we are given a radiant
account of how far a human being or a Christian knight can
ascend the ladder of virtue.

Although it does not overlook the reality of sin, the pentangle
passage is directed to the praise of virtue, and in the poem as a
whole the emphasis is on the excellence rather than the sinfulness
of Gawain. This is a characteristic and indeed wholesome emphasis of romance in its aspiration towards an ideal standard of
conduct, and it is misconstrued by those who think that Gawain
in some way fails his test. But a just appreciation of the balance of
virtue and of vice is difficult to achieve. Praise can mislead in
suggesting the indulgence of vice, and the representation of sin
can be taken to obscure the presence of virtue. Chaucer's portrait
of the Knight has misled some readers into assuming that it is an
unqualified or even bland expression of virtue. We need to look at
the long sequence of terms of praise used of Gawain in the pentangle passage in order to judge their fitness and so form an
appropriate image of the hero.

First of all, Gawain was 'for gode knawen' (633), that is, he was
'known as a good knight' (ed. Davis, 185 and 193). Two points are
made here. The first is that 'gode' carries a general reference to
Gawain's goodness or integrity, and this is signified also by the
comparison of him to 'golde pured' (633), yet another example of
that colour symbolism that has been so prominent in the description of his armour (568–9, 577, 591, 598, 600, 603, and 619–20).
This is the 'gode Gawan' (109) who is introduced to us seated
beside the queen at Camelot, and 'þe goode knyȝt' (381) who takes
up the Green Knight's challenge. The pentangle passage does not
tell us anything essentially different about Gawain from that which
we already know, but rather it elaborates upon Gawain's goodness
in circumstantial detail. In other words, the goodness of Gawain is
now defined in relation to the five sets of five elements signified by
the pentangle (632). This is largely, but not entirely, a matter of
moral virtue. The second point is that there is also a reference to
Gawain's reputation for virtue. Although the reputation is separate
from virtue, it is bound up with it. Here it is evident that Gawain
has a merited reputation for virtue. Reputation is prized, therefore,
in so far as it is the outward mark of virtue, and is not something
lightly to be forfeited. Again, the reputation of Gawain is clear

from the distinction accorded to him at the high table at Camelot.
The pentangle passage now proceeds to elaborate upon the kind of
distinction that Gawain possesses at court and at the same time to
convey a sense of his excellence (634–9).

Next, Gawain is 'voyded of vche vylany' (634). The *OED*
glosses *vylany* here as 'a piece of wicked conduct... a vile act',[18]
and Barron's translation, 'free from every imperfection',[19] supports
it. If such an interpretation is granted, it would mean that the poet
does indeed impute to Gawain an absolute moral perfection. But it
is not evident that the word *vylany* has here the sense of sin or
moral imperfection. It can also mean 'lack of courtesy or polite-
ness... boorishness, rusticity' (*OED*, 6), and Davis supplies the
glosses 'lack of (chivalrous) virtues, ill-breeding' (p. 223) for it
both here and also at 2374–5:

> Corsed worth cowarddyse and couetyse boþe!
> In yow is vylany and vyse þat vertue disstryez.[20]

The sense of 'ill-breeding' is supported by the use of *vylanye* by
Gawain in taking up from Arthur the Green Knight's challenge:

> þat I wythoute vylanye myȝt voyde þis table (345).

It is glossed by Davis as 'discourtesy' (p. 223), and so translated by
Barron (p. 47), and refers to the lack of courtesy that is prompted
by ill-breeding. This sense of *vylanye* is familiar to us from the
General Prologue, where it is said of Chaucer's Knight:

> He nevere yet no vileynye ne sayde
> In al his lyf unto no maner wight. (I (A) 70–1)[21]

Further confirmation of this sense in *Sir Gawain* is supplied by the
use of the related adjective *vilanous* (1497) by the lady in the
process of justifying the use of force by a knight upon a lady. It
is glossed 'boorish, ill-bred' by Davis (p. 223) and translated as 'ill-
bred' by Barron (p. 107). The very definition of *vylanye* or ill-
breeding is represented in the character of Percyvell in *Sir Percyvell
of Gales*. Percyvell is in all respects a brave man, but, despite his

---

[18] *OED*, s.v. *villainy*, sb. 1. b.
[19] *Sir Gawain and the Green Knight*, ed. W. R. J. Barron (Manchester, 1974), 61.
[20] Barron translates: 'A curse upon cowardice and avarice too! In you is ill-
breeding and vice which destroy knightly virtue' (ibid. 155).
[21] See also I (A) 725–7 and 739–40.

noble origins (5 and 15), his upbringing in the forest by his mother has not equipped him for the niceties of courtly behaviour nor for the skills expected of a knight. It had been the intention of Percyvell's father to train his son in the habits of knightly jousting (105–20; cf. *Sir Gawain*, 41–2 and 96–9), but Percyvell slays the Red Knight somewhat in the manner of David slaying Goliath (689–92), and lacks the knowledge and skill to undo the Red Knight's armour (741–64). Further, Percyvell shows his ignorance in giving orders to and threatening the king (521–32); this is the behaviour of a 'foull wyghte' (532).[22] His impatience to be dubbed a knight, which he is plainly as yet unfitted to be, gives rise to more rude and offensive language (574–80). The king perceives that he 'hadde wonnede in the wodde' and 'knewe nother evyll ne gude' (593–4).

The word *vylanye*, then, has reference to moral virtue, but is not simply identifiable with moral virtue. It has a special bearing on Gawain's birth and breeding. It reminds us that he is 'þat prynce noble' (623), and prepares us for his reception at Hautdesert as 'þat fyne fader of nurture' (919). At the same time it focuses upon his status and function as a knight. This suggests another meaning of *vylanye*, perhaps the leading sense of the word at the time the poet is writing, namely 'shame' or 'disgrace, dishonour' (*OED* 3).[23] A knight feels shame especially when he falls short of those qualities that define him as a knight. First of all that is when he shows cowardice or a lack of prowess in battle. Thus Palamon's honour is preserved in the tournament against Arcite, since, although overcome, there is no *disconfitynge* (I (A) 2719) or *disconfiture* (2721), for he is dragged to the stake without having surrendered (*unyolden*, 2642, and 2724) by twenty knights, and in the process unhorses Emetrius (2645–7); hence:

> It nas arretted hym no vileynye;
> Ther may no man clepen it cowardye. (2729–30)

And secondly there is a special shamefulness in the act of rape, as the lady is only too well aware even as she transfers the blame to the victim. Tarquinius's offence against Lucrece is an offence that gains in shamefulness by his lineage as a prince and his status as a

---

[22] The reference is to *Ywain and Gawain, Sir Percyvell of Gales, The Anturs of Arther*, ed. M. Mills (London, 1992).

[23] *OED* refers to the special frequency of its use in the 15th cent.

knight. The incomprehension of such a descent into churlishness is underlined by the narrator's pointed questions:

> Tarquinius, that art a kynges eyr,
> And sholdest, as by lynage and by ryght,
> Don as a lord and as a verray knyght,
> Whi hastow don dispit to chivalrye?
> Whi hastow don this lady vilanye?
> Allas, of the this was a vileyns dede!
> (*Legend of Good Women*, F. 1819–24)

The word *vylany* (634) has the force of shame rather than vice, so that the *Gawain*-poet is declaring of Gawain that he is free of any cause for shame, whether by his own acts or by any other kind of defect, such as humble birth or lowly status. Gawain does not feel a sense of shame because he is here untouched by anything that could cause him shame.[24] But that does not mean that he is morally perfect and is incapable of a shameful act, for the sense of shame is a laudable passion, not a virtue.[25] When Gawain discovers from the Green Knight the true significance of his act of withholding the lady's girdle, the acknowledgement of sin is at once accompanied by the impact of shame. It is Gawain's special sensitivity to shame, a mark of his nobility as a knight, that leads him to experience here such bitter humiliation:

> Þat oþer stif mon in study stod a gret whyle,
> So agreued for greme he gryed withinne;
> Alle þe blode of his brest blende in his face,
> Þat al he schrank for schome þat þe schalk talked. (2369–72)

Much of the rest of the poem concerns Gawain's courage in coming to terms with his sin by confronting and not avoiding the experience of shame. This is pre-eminently the case when he returns to Camelot and to the judgment of his peers. He is spared nothing of the shameful reality of his deed:

> He tened quen he schulde telle,
> He groned for gref and grame; (2501–4)

---

[24] Aquinas notes that the best of men lack shame because they do not expect to do anything that is worthy of shame, though they are so disposed that if they did anything dishonourable they would be ashamed of it (*ST* 2a 2ae 144. 4).

[25] Aristotle, *Ethics*, 2. 7 1108ᵃ32 and 4. 9 1128ᵇ11, and Aquinas, *ST* 2a 2ae 144. 1.

Þe blod in his face con melle,
When he hit schulde schewe, for schame. (2501–4)

Here it becomes evident that for Gawain and the poet the love of
honour and of virtue are not empty words, and their corollary is
the thoroughgoing detestation of sin. There is something inalien-
ably repellent about sin, and it fills the offender with the strongest
feelings of disgust. Indeed, the more noble the person who sins, the
greater the sense of disgust. The shame that is proper for a penitent
sinner takes on an added dimension when it is expressed by a
knight in the presence of his companions at court, for it is the
court that bestows honour upon its most distinguished represent-
atives. Thus the poet's description of Gawain as 'voyded of vche
vylany' is accompanied by 'vertuez ennourned|in mote' (634–5),
just as subsequently the experiences of 'vylany and vyse' (2375) are
united. What these chivalric or courtly virtues might be is left
unstated, for they are presumably among the virtues specified in
the following stanza. But we are to understand them in a general
sense as contributing to the honour in which he is justly held at
court.

The poet does not complete the first of the two pentangle
stanzas without adding two more superlative statements about
Gawain that round off this courtly image of him. Gawain is a
'tulk of tale most trwe' (638), that is, he is true in word and
expresses himself openly as he is inwardly. It is a noble straight-
forwardness or lack of deceit. The medieval word for this quality is
symplesse, used of the second golden arrow of the God of Love in
The Romaunt of the Rose (954). The related adjective *symple* is
used twice of Blanche in *The Book of the Duchess* (861 and 918),
and once of the Prioress in the General Prologue (I (A) 119). Such
truth or *symplesse* is the inward disposition of modesty in manners
as Aquinas expounds it (*ST* 2a 2ae 168. 1 *ad* 3), and fits the courtly
orientation of the poet's description. Finally, Gawain is the 'gentylest knyȝt of lote' (639). Davis glosses *gentyle* here as 'of gentle
birth, noble' (p. 184) and Barron translates 'in bearing the noblest
of knights' (p. 61). But *lote* is glossed as 'word, saying, speech' by
Davis (pp. 196–7), and these glosses are supported by the *MED*.[26]
The use of *lote* here suggests the more specific meaning for *gentyle*

[26] See *MED*, s.v. *lot(e* n. 3. (*b*) and 3. (*c*).

of 'courteous, polite' or 'gracious, kind, generous'.[27] Thus *gentyle* would be seen as reinforcing *trwe* in focusing upon the courtly propriety of Gawain's conduct, adding to simplicity that friendliness or affability that should also govern our conduct towards others (*ST* 2a 2ae 168. 1 *ad* 3). In the same way the friendliness of Blanche is suggested by her 'goodly, softe speche' (*Book of the Duchess*, 919). Such courtesy is always, as we may judge from the case of Percyvell, a matter of birth and breeding.

Thus the first and more general of the pentangle stanzas stresses at its end Gawain's outer manner and dignity. He is an outstanding and impressive man at court, of good repute, purified as gold, untainted by shameful acts, graced by virtues, truest of his word, and kindest or friendliest in his speech (633–9). There is an accord here between the inner and outer man, and between personal merit and public reputation. It is a convincing as well as an emphatic statement. This is clearly the best that Camelot can produce. But the *Gawain*-poet is concerned to create effects that are more subtle and detailed than these, and in the second of the pentangle stanzas he proceeds to give a more precise account of Gawain's excellence.

First, Gawain is seen to be 'fautlez in his fyue wyttez' (640). It might seem to others, as it does to Wilson (p. 408), that this is further evidence of Gawain's absolute perfection. But virtue is not to be predicated of the senses; there is no question of freedom of choice, and therefore no question of sinning. Perfect sense faculties are entirely compatible with acts of sin. But what does it mean to say that Gawain is faultless in his five senses? Surely only that he possesses these powers in their highest degree as they are found in human beings. Gawain's sense of hearing is likened implicitly to that of the deer in picking up a scent (1150 and 1182–3), but the sense of touch is finer in man than in other animals, whereas the senses of sight, hearing, and smell are inferior in man to other animals (*ST* 1a 91. 3 *ad* 1). Gawain's senses are inevitably human senses and the perfection of them a human perfection, that is, a perfection *secundum quid* not *simpliciter*. His senses function perfectly in the manner that they are intended to; for example, they are not in error in respect of their special objects, as colour of sight or sound of hearing (*De anima*, 2. 6).

[27] *MED*, s.v. *gentil* adj. 2. (*b*) and 3. (*d*).

Second, Gawain 'fayled neuer...in his fyue fyngres' (641). It is not possible to be certain in the present state of knowledge what the poet precisely intends by his reference to Gawain's five fingers. It is putting an undue strain on the line to see it as referring to five moral virtues, namely, justice, prudence, temperance, fortitude, and obedience.[28] Such a procedure would contrast unfavourably with the careful and explicit specification of the five moral virtues of the fifth group, and furthermore would introduce a degree of overlap at odds with the very nature of the pentangle. It seems likely that the reference of the five fingers is to strength, that is, one of the bodily graces along with health and beauty. Strength is a necessary requirement in a knight, and Chaucer accordingly describes his aspirant to knighthood as 'wonderly delyvere, and of greet strengthe' (I (A) 84). Gawain shows both strength and skill as well as courage in beheading the Green Knight, for he deftly wields an axe that has a head an ell (45 in.) long (208–20 and 421–6). The poet appropriately singles out Gawain's strength, but when he says that his strength never failed him we can hardly take him to mean that Gawain's strength will never decline, but that he never encountered a knight stronger than he was. The force of *neuer* (641), as commonly, is emphatic rather than simply temporal.[29] Thus in *Sir Percyvell of Gales* Percyvell acknowledges that he has never received a blow to compare with that given him by Gawain:

> And of alle that I slewe then
> Me thoghte it bot a playe,
> Agayne that dynt that I hafe tane:
> For siche one [l]aughte I never nane. (1487–90)

Third, Gawain places 'alle his afyaunce...in þe fyue woundez' (642) of Christ. Faith of its nature is first among all the virtues (*ST* 2a 2ae 4. 7), and accordingly it is the first of Gawain's virtues to be specified by the poet. Again there is an emphatic statement about the completeness of Gawain's faith, fixed as it is on Christ rather

---

[28] As proposed by R. H. Green, 'Gawain's Shield and the Quest for Perfection', *ELH* 29 (1962), 121–39, and repr. in R. J. Blanch (ed.), *'Sir Gawain' and 'Pearl': Critical Essays* (Bloomington, Ind., 1966), 176–94 (p. 188).

[29] See *MED*, s.v. *never* adv. 2. (*a*) 'As an emphatic negative...not at all, certainly not.' This emphatic use is well attested in the late 14th cent., and Davis glosses *neuer* as 'not at all' at 399, 470, and 1487 (p. 201).

than on girdles, and so reaffirmed by the knight in the fourth fitt in rejecting the temptation of the guide (2136–9 and 2156–9), in facing up to the terrifying noise of the sharpening of the axe (2205–11), and in accepting the terms of the beheading game immediately before the return blow (2250–4). It is clear that as he stands on the brink of death Gawain remains in a state of grace. Now the theological virtues of faith, hope, and charity are infused by grace (*ST* 1a 2ae 62. 1); they are not acquired by repeated acts, and so differ in kind from the moral virtues (*ST* 1a 2ae 62. 2). Only of the theological virtues can it be said that they are perfect in an absolute sense (*ST* 1a 2ae 65. 3). Thus Gawain is sustained in his various trials by his faith in God, and this faith is reaffirmed in the closing lines of the poem with their invocation of the wounded Christ on the cross (2529–30).

Fourth, Gawain derives 'alle his forsnes' from 'þe fyue joyez' (646) of the Virgin Mary. The understanding of the coexistence in human nature of theological and moral virtues is reinforced by the presentation of the moral virtue of fortitude with reference to the five joys of the Virgin Mary. Here the deeply Christian nature of the poet's thinking is very evident. Thus Gawain draws inspiration from the joy of the Virgin Mary in the nativity when he is alone in a deep and wild forest as Christmas approaches (736–9 and 748–62), and he is protected by the Virgin Mary when he is hard pressed by the lady on the third morning in the bedroom (1766–9). It becomes clear that Gawain's faith animates all that he does and accomplishes as a knight, so that it is fitting that his courage should be set in the context of his religious belief. There is a special point in placing the moral virtue of courage directly after the theological virtue of faith within the structure of the pentangle passage as a whole, for faith and courage are interconnected. Courage is firmness of mind in the face of the dangers of death, and especially of death in battle (*ST* 2a 2ae 123. 4 and 5), and a man in battle is most likely to remain firm when he is sustained by the certitude of faith. The link between faith and courage is strikingly realized by Chaucer in his portrait of the Knight:

> At mortal batailles hadde he been fiftene,
> And foughten for oure feith at Tramyssene
> In lystes thries, and ay slayn his foo. (I (A) 61–3)

What is described here is not a theoretical model of absolute perfection, but the reality of a certain kind of human experience. Many examples in the long history of human conflict could be adduced as evidence of the fact. Rowland Feilding, who became the commanding officer of the Connaught Rangers after the capture of Guillemont to the north of the Somme in September 1916, describes repeatedly the intense religious devotion of his troops.[30] It is the same profound devotion that Gawain shows to the Virgin Mary, and it is in the same way efficacious: 'quen he blusched þerto his belde neuer payred' (650). The use of the adverb *neuer* is again emphatic. It impresses on us the well-founded trust that Gawain places in the Virgin Mary, and the excellence of the courage that flows from it, not the fact that his courage has an absolute value.

Fifth is the 'fyft fyue' (651) of moral virtues that have received so much critical attention, sometimes at the expense of the other constituent parts of the pentangle. The placing of the final group of moral virtues in a climactic position points to their significance in the narrative, if not in the list of virtues. But these virtues stand high among the moral virtues, *fraunchyse* (652), *felaȝschyp* (652), and *pité* (654) being parts of justice, the most excellent of the moral virtues, and *pité* or piety being the most excellent of the parts of justice. Once again the language that the poet uses is emphatic in its praise of Gawain's virtue. Here it is his chastity and courtesy that 'croked were neuer' (653). The poet contrives to remind us again of the analogy between the pentangle and human virtue. The word *croked* is used figuratively to express the excellence of Gawain's possession of these virtues. The intended sense is 'defective',[31] but we are reminded of the proper sense of 'curved, not straight' (*MED*, 1. (*a*)). Gawain's chastity and courtesy match the straight lines of the pentangle. As such they stand for a distinctively human kind of perfection. They are after all moral virtues.

The poem contains in the person of the hero two distinct tendencies which, if not contradictory, are at least difficult to reconcile. First of all, the virtue of Gawain is elevated so that he is set apart

---

[30] R. Feilding, *War Letters to a Wife: France and Flanders, 1915–1919* (London, 1929), 138, 141, 143, 226, and 264.
[31] *MED*, s.v. *croked* ppl. 4. (*a*).

from all other men, and secondly, it is grounded in the possession of a common humanity that does not leave him unscathed by the effects of sin. But the praise of Gawain in the pentangle passage is not so indiscriminate as to rule out the presence of sin, nor the blame of him in withholding the girdle so severe as to annihilate the sense of his worth. Here the doctrine of penance, which seems so negative and disturbing a thing to many modern readers,[32] is designed to restore the radiance of virtue that has been lost and stained by sin. If Gawain has failed, then no human being has any hope of success. But, as the pentangle makes abundantly clear to us, the presence of sin can never be allowed to obscure the radiance of virtue.

[32] Thus E. Wilson, *The Gawain-Poet* (Leiden, 1976), deplores what he takes to be Gawain's 'new identity as an ascetic moralist' (p. 129).

12

The 'Pearl'-Poet in his 'Fayre Regioun'

THORLAC TURVILLE-PETRE

Of John Burrow's four Ricardians, three make claim to be national poets, two of them explicitly and the third implicitly. In the revised prologue to *Confessio Amantis*, Gower states his intention to write 'A bok for Engelondes sake', since 'fewe men endite | In oure Englissh' (*Confessio Amantis*, Prol. 22–4). Chaucer's concern at the end of *Troilus* that the variety of English dialects will prevent his little book from being understood 'wherso thow be' demonstrates his assumption that it will reach a far-flung national audience (*Troilus and Criseyde*, V. 1793–9). Langland's modification of the vocabulary typical of alliterative verse shows a concern for the comprehension of the national audience he was seeking, as John Burrow argued in one of his earliest articles.[1]

The idea of national literature that these writers invoke or to which they attach themselves is important, perhaps crucial, for any construction of a literary period, within which the critic may compare the practices and attitudes of a group of contemporaries and may analyse their affinities and the influences of one writer upon the other. It is the heterogeneity of late fourteenth-century texts that causes Burrow considerable anxiety in the introduction to *Ricardian Poetry*, and prompts him to conclude that 'The age may turn out not to have been a "period", in the full literary sense, at all.'[2] Furthermore, the term 'Ricardian', whatever qualifications may be expressed, is one that emphasizes the centrality of the metropolis and makes an association with the court in its widest sense, even if the personal involvement of Richard II is explicitly

---

[1] J. A. Burrow, 'The Audience of *Piers Plowman*', *Anglia*, 75 (1957), 373–84; repr. with a postscript in *Essays on Medieval Literature* (Oxford, 1984), 102–16.
[2] *Ricardian Poetry* (London, 1971), 9–10.

denied. And indeed London and the court formed a textual community of the greatest significance, as a centre from which texts and the interpretations of those texts were disseminated. There is no difficulty, of course, in placing Chaucer and Gower in this community, both working in London, both associated with the court, each acknowledging the work of the other. Nor, really, is there any difficulty in including Langland. In his accounts of Will's life and travels in the city, Langland is even more of a London poet than Chaucer and Gower[3] and, if some aspects of his poetic heritage are non-metropolitan, by setting *Piers Plowman* in two locations, London and the Malvern Hills, Langland announces that regional traditions are being brought into the mainstream of literary activity and transmuted in the process.

From this perspective, the *Pearl*-poet seems to stand outside the national literary scene. When we consider the differences of this poetry in terms of language and dialect, and if we accept the consequences of its lack of literary relationship to the metropolitan tradition and its failure to achieve any place in the long march of English verse, can we validly picture a national literary scene that includes the *Pearl*-poet? If a late fourteenth-century writer attaches himself to a regional culture rather than the national one, is apparently as ignorant of London writers as they are of him, directs his work to a provincial audience who alone can fully comprehend and enjoy the dialect in which he writes, can he be accounted a Ricardian in anything more than the purely chronological sense? But then, on the other hand, can we profitably talk in terms of a literary period that excludes one of the greatest writers of the age?

The significance of regionalism as a factor inhibiting the construction of a national literary scene is most easily demonstrated by proposing the term 'Edwardian' to cover the English poetry of an earlier age, the late thirteenth and early fourteenth centuries. It hardly has the ring of conviction about it, and yet there are several respects in which one could describe this as a literary period. There is, after all, a considerable body of verse sharing a number of common themes and preoccupations.[4] There are stylistic affinities

---

[3] See Caroline M. Barron, 'William Langland: A London Poet', in Barbara A. Hanawalt (ed.), *Chaucer's England: Literature in Historical Context* (Minneapolis, 1992), 91–109.

[4] See Thorlac Turville-Petre, *England the Nation* (Oxford, 1996).

and some shared metrical forms, and a quite widespread attitude towards the status of English and the sort of topics for which the language is appropriate. Nevertheless, illuminating though it can be to make comparisons between one 'Edwardian' work and another, it would be difficult to conceive of a literary period in Middle English before the late fourteenth century, and the reason for this is that 'Edwardian' poetry is essentially regional. At this time literary culture in English is fragmented, owing as much to local traditions and interests as to national trends, and a writer who wishes to be widely read will more sensibly opt for French or Latin. It is a situation reflecting a society that is comparatively settled and divided by its regional affiliations. We are not here dealing with the cosmopolitan level of society, small in numbers however dominant in cultural terms, but with the great mass of people who are comfortable only with English, those for whom Robert Mannying professes to be writing, who understand neither Latin nor French: 'þat þe Latyn no Frankys cone.'[5]

In this earlier period it can be more illuminating to trace local developments wherever this is possible. Here and there we can dimly perceive local literary traditions and relationships, even though so much of the evidence for these is lost. So the early thirteenth-century works of devotional prose composed in the south-west Midlands may properly be compared with each other in terms of their literary sources, local audience, rhetorical techniques, and even (to some degree at least) their use of a local standard language. The composition of these prose works may also be related to the evident interest in much older English literary traditions taken by scribes and annotators around Worcester at this time, and this in turn may be linked to the concerns and knowledge of Laȝamon, drawing on some notion of the patterns of Old English verse in order to capture a sense of the antiquity of his heroic matter. A path now almost entirely overgrown will lead us forward to the later thirteenth century, where the reviser of Robert of Gloucester's *Chronicle* lifted passages from Laȝamon's *Brut*, and we may then move sideways again to study the close relationship between parts of Robert of Gloucester's *Chronicle* and the *South English Legendary*, all from the same region. Even when,

---

[5] *The Story of England by Robert Manning of Brunne*, ed. Frederick J. Furnivall, Rolls Series (London, 1887), pt. 1, p. 1, l. 8.

as here rather unusually, we have evidence of interrelated texts, these provide the basis for the study of regional characteristics and developments rather than of a national culture.

These pre-Ricardians are often much concerned with local issues and sometimes specifically address a regional audience. They dwell upon local celebrities, such as St Wulfstan of Worcester, whose life is recounted in the *South English Legendary*, or Havelok with his strong Lincolnshire associations. Chronicles describing the history of the nation pay particular attention to the history of the locality, whether it be the south-west Midlands in the case of Robert of Gloucester, or the east Midlands and East Anglia in the case of Robert Mannyng of Brunne. Tales and romances are located in specific places, such as Kesteven and Lindsey in Mannyng's *Handlyng Synne*, and Grimsby and Lincoln in *Havelok*. Like Chaucer later, writers are concerned about the variety of dialects, but unlike Chaucer their concern is to use the dialect their regional audience will be comfortable with, and not at all to express themselves in a way that may invite a wider readership. So Dan Michel of Northgate is keen to advertise that his *Ayenbite of Inwyt* is written in the extraordinary 'Engliss of Kent',[6] and the author of *Cursor Mundi* explains how he has adapted for the use of his Yorkshire readers a poem on the Assumption that he attributes to St Edmund of Abingdon:

> In sotherin Englis was it draun,
> And turnd it haue I till our aun
> Langage o northrin lede
> Þat can nan oiþer Englis rede. (20061–4)[7]

This acknowledgement of the geographical limitations of English in part explains the modest pretensions of the writings of this date. Since English can make no claim to the status of the language of national culture, it makes sense for a writer to concentrate attention on a local audience, to capitalize on their interest in local places and events, their familiarity with the dialect, and their concern for issues of regional identity.

It is the implied audience that makes a poem regional, not the actual audience. This distinction will have relevance for my

---

[6] *Dan Michel's Ayenbite of Inwyt*, ed. Richard Morris, EETS 23 (London, 1866), 262.

[7] *Cursor Mundi*, ed. Richard Morris, pt. iv, EETS 66 (London, 1877), 1148.

argument later. The most explicit construction of such an audience is that created by Robert Mannyng in the prologue to his *Chronicle* completed in 1338, which quite methodically defines its own audience as 'lewed', as English, as 'simple', and also as local, living in a stable and integrated rural society. So local are they imagined to be that they have a personal relationship with the author; the work is a social performance written in response to public demand, and Manning asks for no money in return but for prayers instead. This constructed audience will be familiar with the nearby Gilbertine house at Sixhills, and indeed will know the Gilbertine who is the author's patron, Robert of Malton who 'commissioned the writing of it for the sake of his fellows':

> In þe hous of Sixille I was a throwe:
> Danz Robert of Malton þat ȝe know
> Did it wryte for felawes sake. (141–3)

This implied audience constructed by the poet may differ sharply from the actual audience that read the work in the extant manuscripts. In the prologue to *Handlyng Synne* completed after 1317, Mannyng formally gestures 'to alle crystyn men vndir sunne', but more realistically addresses the 'gode men of Brunne' and 'þe felaushepe of Symprynghame' (57–60).[8] Yet *Handlyng Synne*, complete and in extracts, became popular across the country from the late fourteenth century onwards, despite its many details directed towards a Lincolnshire audience. So, too, some of the lyrics originating in widely scattered districts of the country and copied into London, British Library, MS Harley 2253 in the 1330s by its Ludlow scribe contain allusions to places which have lost some of their point for the south-west Midland readers of this manuscript:

> Bituene Lyncolne ant Lyndeseye, Norhamptoun ant Lounde,
> Ne wot y non so fayr a may as y go fore ybounde. (17–18)[9]

It is important, then, to understand that it is not the readership the work actually reached that is at issue, but the primary audience created within the text. Yet the dispersal of such regional texts must have had two effects. One was that readers became increas-

---

[8] *Robert of Brunne's 'Handlyng Synne'*, ed. Frederick J. Furnivall, 2 vols., EETS 119 and 123 (London, 1901, 1903), i. 3.

[9] *The Harley Lyrics*, ed. G. L. Brook, 4th edn. (Manchester, 1968), no. 25, p. 63.

ingly aware of literary styles from elsewhere, and writers therefore became increasingly open to diverse influences. The other was that poets realized that they could more ambitiously reach for an audience outside their region, where references and interests that were purely local would become a handicap rather than an advantage.

The tension between region and nation is most explicitly marked by *Winner and Waster*, which stands chronologically on the brink of the Ricardian Age. The prologue marvellously evokes a sense of poetry that is newly mobile, and thus threatening to an old-fashioned regional poet with a vision of a once-settled society now everywhere assailed by change. The dreamer clings to the fragile stability invested in his description of himself as a 'westren wy' (7),[10] and aligns himself with the 'makers of myrthes' who used to serve 'lordes in londe', embodying in that last phrase the stratified rural society upon which regional poetry traditionally rested. Just as these makers have been displaced by a ghastly manifestation of newfangledness, the child without chinweeds, so the 'westren wy' has to face an uncertain future in which his son may depart for the south and abandon him to the frailty of his old age. The action of the poem itself, though, fails to endorse this conservative position; as dream-visions so often do, it takes the dreamer outside the confines of his waking mind, to the world of national issues played out by the king of England and his knights, and transports him, willy-nilly, 'southewarde' to London, to 'þe Chepe', 'Bred Strete' and 'þe Pultrie' (474–90). If I am correct in supposing that it was composed in response to financial discussions in Cheshire in 1352–3, *Winner and Waster* is a poem addressed to a regional audience, treating of those national events that have consequences for local conditions.[11]

Early fourteenth-century writers addressed the region; Chaucer, Gower, and Langland addressed the nation.[12] In that simple

---

[10] *Wynnere and Wastoure*, ed. Stephanie Trigg, EETS 297 (Oxford, 1990), 3.

[11] See Thorlac Turville-Petre, '*Wynnere and Wastoure*: When and Where?', in L. A. J. R. Houwen and A. A. MacDonald (eds.), *Loyal Letters* (Groningen, 1994), 155–66.

[12] Elizabeth Salter, in *Fourteenth-Century English Poetry* (Oxford, 1983), ch. 3, 'Mappings', emphasizes social mobility and argues that literature must have been equally mobile throughout the 14th cent. Her argument is advanced to counter earlier critics who would divide the country into distinct literary areas, and I think it needs some qualification.

distinction lies the essence of the difference between them, for it is a distinction that carries with it contrasting sets of attitudes to the value and social function of vernacular writing and the status of English as the language of poetry. It is the ambition of their claim to be national poets that is most obviously new and remarkable about these three Ricardians. If the *Pearl*-poet cannot be attached to this new movement, it leaves him standing apart from the currents of literary developments, a poor country-cousin without even a name to call his own. It seems thoroughly unsatisfactory to suppose that a writer of such remarkable gifts could have rested content within the confined world of a local audience. We, at least, want better for him.

It is the realization of the importance of making the *Pearl*-poet into a national figure that has encouraged some recent critics to bring the poet to London and even to the royal court. Since it is difficult to envisage a regional audience of sufficient sophistication, could it be, it is asked, that the *Pearl*-poet was patronized at the court of Richard II?[13] It is pointed out that Richard, as earl of Chester, relied heavily on support from Cheshire, and built up a personal bodyguard of Cheshire yeomen, 'þe which yemen and archers þe Kyng toke ynto his owne court'.[14] They were noted by contemporaries more for their rowdiness than their sophistication; but envious tongues will wag. The only physical manifestation of the poems is that strange manuscript, London, British Library, MS Cotton Nero A.x. Who might have commissioned this assembly of four north-west Midland poems with their regional language, and ordered its charmingly clumsy illustrations? It seems almost exaggeratedly provincial, the collected poems of a country poet. Is it perhaps the kind of product put together

[13] The idea was first floated by Michael J. Bennett, '*Sir Gawain and the Green Knight* and the Literary Achievement of the North-West Midlands: The Historical Background', *Journal of Medieval History*, 5 (1979), 63–88. Bennett toys with the notion again in 'The Court of Richard II and the Promotion of Literature', in Hanawalt (ed.), *Chaucer's England*, 3–20, but he rightly admits that 'the evidence for a connection between the court of Richard II and the *Gawain*-poet is highly circumstantial' (p. 14). This has not deterred John M. Bowers, who examines the connection in a full-length study, '*Pearl* in its Royal Setting: Ricardian Poetry Revisited', *SAC* 17 (1995), 111–55, arguing that the poem was written c.1395 to represent royal interests.

[14] *The Brut*, ed. F. W. D. Brie, EETS 136 (London, 1908), 353; quoted by Bowers, '*Pearl* in its Royal Setting', 116.

to appeal to some sophisticated enthusiast for rustic art? Is there any evidence to support suggestions of a London readership for the *Pearl*-poet?

Alliterative poems did indeed escape from their north-western base, and at least occasionally they reached the metropolis. 'The transmission of alliterative poems', as David Lawton observes, 'demands inter-regional communication, not always through London, both of texts and people—readers, writers, patrons, scribes—who moved between two or more milieux'.[15] London was full of immigrants from all over England, some transient members of its shifting population, some settled, and what could be more natural than for travellers from the north-west, whether Cheshire archers in the service of the king, or clerks working for St Paul's[16] or the great government offices, sometimes to carry copies of their local poetry with them, to console themselves in the loneliness of an alien environment or to show off to their southern friends. More significant, however, than the possibility of displaced northern readers is the evidence that Londoners affiliated to court circles could be persuaded to take an interest in verse that must have seemed foreign to them.

One instance is provided by the text of *Alexander and Dindimus*, copied by a scribe whose language is of the south or south Midlands into the magnificent Oxford, Bodleian Library, MS Bodley 264, in order to fill an imaginary lacuna in the text of the French *Roman d'Alexandre*.[17] Probably only a little later, early in the fifteenth century, the text of Marco Polo's *Li Livres du Graunt Caam* was added to the manuscript, with fine illuminations by

---

[15] David A. Lawton, 'The Diversity of Middle English Alliterative Poetry', *LSE* NS 20 (1989), 143–72 (p. 147).

[16] For the connection with St Paul's see R. Kennedy, 'A Bird in Bishopswood', in M. Stokes and T. L. Burton (eds.), *Medieval Literature and Antiquities* (Woodbridge, 1987), 71–87. The author of *St Erkenwald* shows interest in and good knowledge of St Paul's, and in the first line of the poem the poet covertly identifies himself and his audience as natives of Cheshire. See J. A. Burrow, '*Saint Erkenwald*, Line 1: "At London in Englond"', *N&Q* 238 (1993), 22–3.

[17] Described by A. I. Doyle, 'The Manuscripts', in David Lawton (ed.), *Middle English Alliterative Poetry and its Literary Background* (Cambridge, 1982), 88–100 (p. 93). Walter W. Skeat, in his edition, *Alexander and Dindimus*, EETS ES 31 (London, 1878), p. viii, quotes the scribe's note which contains south or south Midland forms; see J. P. Oakden, *Alliterative Poetry in Middle English: The Dialectal and Metrical Survey* (Manchester, 1930), 50.

Johannes, whose style is metropolitan.[18] The miniatures provided for *Alexander and Dindimus* are not of the same quality, and might be the work of a competent provincial artist; nevertheless the owner of this costly manuscript seems to have moved in cultured London circles. *The Siege of Jerusalem* offers an instance of a different kind. The poem is extant in several copies from the south Midlands and south-east, one of them apparently copied by Richard Frampton, a scribe active in Westminster in the first years of the fifteenth century, and working for Henry IV and prominent courtiers.[19] Together with the *Siege*, Frampton also copied into this volume, Cambridge, University Library, MS Mm. V. 14, Latin histories of Alexander and Troy.

Sadly, these two manuscripts scarcely provide evidence of a metropolitan cult for alliterative verse. Of course they may not be representative, but what they seem to show is that some Londoners might be prepared to put up with the oddities of alliterative verse for the sake of the information it provided. The texts were copied for the matter not the manner: the owner of the Bodley manuscript wanted a more complete version of the Alexander story, and Frampton was assembling a compendium of texts on ancient history for his prospective client. In both cases the alliterative poems complement works in another language, and were presumably not chosen as examples of English literary culture.

Even if there is no evidence to support the proposition that *Gawain* and *Pearl* reached London in one way or another, that does not prove that it might not have happened. If the poems had been read in London, how much difficulty would the language of Cotton Nero A.x have caused readers used to Chaucer, Gower, and Langland? Frampton's copy of the *Siege* provides some clues to this. A comparison with other texts of the poem shows that Frampton's preserves the traditional poetic diction of alliterative verse surprisingly well: for example, of the elevated words for 'man' the following are all kept by Frampton: *beern, freke, gome, leed, renke, shalk, segge,* and *wye.*[20] This is not out of

[18] See A. I. Doyle, 'English Books in and out of Court from Edward III to Henry VII', in V. J. Scattergood and J. W. Sherborne (eds.), *English Court Culture in the Later Middle Ages* (London, 1983), 163–81 (p. 167).

[19] See Doyle, 'The Manuscripts', 93–4 and n. 19.

[20] This vocabulary is discussed by Marie Borroff, *'Sir Gawain and the Green Knight': A Stylistic and Metrical Study* (New Haven, 1962), 52–90, drawing on August Brink, *Stab und Wort im Gawain* (Halle, 1920).

regard for the regularity of the alliterative pattern, for in common with most scribes of alliterative verse Frampton shows little concern for the metrical structure of what he was copying, as the presence of *freke* and *segge* in these corrupt lines neatly illustrates:

> That no freke in myght without fressh harmes
> Ne no segge vnder sonne from the toune passe.[21]

It is not the alliterative diction but the regional vocabulary that is subject to wholesale alteration; those words that Rolf Kaiser identified as northern, many of Scandinavian origin.[22]

If we take from Kaiser's lists the regional vocabulary common to northern copies of the *Siege* and to *Pearl*, we will find that many of these words are avoided in Frampton's version of the *Siege*, and some of them seem to have led to misunderstanding. In fact *Pearl* makes less extensive use of this northern vocabulary than *Gawain*, but yet the evidence of Frampton's version of the *Siege* seems to suggest that even *Pearl*'s vocabulary would have caused difficulties and that a London scribe copying *Pearl* would have felt impelled to make systematic substitutions. To cite just a few of these words that are rejected or cause trouble: *bur*, 'force, blow, wind' (ON *byrr*), is used twice in *Pearl* and also in the *Siege*, but Frampton's text alters it once to *piry*, 'blast' (290), and twice to *birth* (72 and 652), apparently indicating considerable confusion. *Lote*, 'expression' (ON *lát*), is found as *loke* (997) which makes sense in context; *mele*, 'speak' (ON *mæla*), becomes *mened* (1301), *samen* (ON *saman*) is altered to *togeder* (552), *unlappeþ* (OE) to *liftes vp* (961), and *wale* (ON *velja*) to *welde* (1276).

This implies that Frampton did not expect his readers to have patience with the regionalisms of the original text of the *Siege*, and rather suggests that unless they had been considerably modified, *Pearl*, and *Gawain* even more so, would have met with a frosty response in fashionable London circles accustomed to the work of Gower and Chaucer. Perhaps, though, such a conclusion should be treated with caution. Frampton's reader wants to get through the

---

[21] Ralph Hanna III generously gave me a copy of his transcription of Cambridge, University Library, MS Mm. V. 14. These lines correspond to ll. 679–80 in the edition by E. Kölbing and Mabel Day, EETS 188 (London, 1932), in which *myght* is followed by *fonde*, and *toune* is replaced by *cite*.

[22] Rolf Kaiser, *Zur Geographie des mittelenglischen Wortschatzes* (Leipzig, 1937).

fancy packaging to the honest meat within; but is it at least con-
ceivable that a Londoner who cultivated a taste for 'rum, ram, ruf'
(in the way that nineteenth-century Londoners took up John Clare
and William Barnes for a while) would have admired the *Pearl*-
poet because of, not despite, his regionalism? All that can be said
with certainty is that there is no trace whatsoever of such a cult of
regional verse in the Middle Ages; furthermore it is probably
anachronistic to imagine that regional varieties of English could
be valued for their difference, though that difference was perceived
and a cause of comment, and evidently led to difficulties of comprehension.

The attempt to make a Londoner out of the *Pearl*-poet seems to
me misguided, not because it is an impossibility, but because it is
never likely to be more than a hypothesis, and an unlikely one at
that. No progress can be made in that direction. We know nothing
of the poet's actual audience, and even if we did, it seems to me
that his actual audience is much less significant than his implied
audience, because the conditions of the dissemination of a text and
its later fortunes after it has left the author's hands are matters of
chance and are quite outside the author's control. What distinguishes the Ricardians is their projection of themselves as national
poets, and this has nothing necessarily to do with who in fact read
them, but everything to do with the audience inscribed in the text.

The problem for the alliterative Ricardian is how to win for a
medium associated so closely with regional traditions a position of
prestige within a national culture. Langland finds one solution,
moderating those features of his medium that might otherwise
disconcert many of the audience he intended to reach and emphasizing the metropolitan context of his poem by embedding some of
the action so firmly in London life. The *Pearl*-poet does not follow
Langland in this, and yet I would argue that he is as anxious as
Langland to gain for his work a place within the cultural life of the
nation, and to distinguish his art from that which is narrowly and
unambitiously regional.

Gawain is the Ricardian poem that gives most prominence to its
regional characteristics, using a vocabulary associated with the
north and west that combines words of Scandinavian origin with
a colloquial register that self-consciously advertises the vernacular
and local character of the medium. And yet, while *Gawain* affirms
the vitality of local literary traditions, at the same time it embraces

a national audience and claims a status within the culture as central as the work of Chaucer, Gower, and Langland. Whether or not the actual site of the Green Chapel can be identified, the critics' search through Derbyshire, Staffordshire, and Cheshire owes its impetus to the entirely accurate perception that the poet is describing with great precision a real landscape that is familiar to him. Studies of the vocabulary have shown the exactitude with which topographical terms are applied to the local hills and valleys, the 'felle' from which 'etaynez' attack Gawain (723), the 'scowtez' grazing the clouds (2167), the 'wro' out of which the Green Knight whirls (2222), and other words very restricted in their geographical spread.[23] The same vocabulary is applied to the country around Hautdesert through which Bertilak hunts:

> Bitwene a flosche in þat fryth and a foo cragge,
> In a knot bi a clyffe at þe kerre syde
> Þer as þe rogh rocher vnrydely watz fallen. (1430–2)

Readers are accustomed to imagine how this meticulous description might have appealed to the local patriotism of an audience familiar with their home territory and proud of their dialectal distinctiveness. This is surely to miss the main point by beginning at the wrong end, and we might profitably consider instead in what way these scenes imply the viewpoint of a national readership. What needs to be emphasized is that the lands beyond the Wirral are viewed not with the appreciation of a northerner, but from the perspective of an anxious southerner 'fer floten fro his frendes'. The home-base from which Gawain rides and to which he returns is Camelot, situated in some ill-defined part of the south. A northern poet had the option of setting Arthur in his northern court at Carlisle, as both the *Awntyrs of Arthur* and the *Morte Arthure* do. Gawain himself describes his home territory as 'þe londe inwyth Logres' (1055), the district that had been ruled by Brutus' eldest son Locrinus, which Geoffrey of Monmouth defines sometimes loosely as England rather than Wales and Scotland, and sometimes precisely as England south of the Humber but excluding Cornwall.[24] If the implied audience for *Gawain* is regional at

---

[23] See R. W. V. Elliott, *The Gawain Country* (Leeds, 1984), esp. ch. 6, first published as 'Hills and Valleys in the *Gawain* Country', *LSE* NS 10 (1978), 18–41.
[24] *Geoffrey of Monmouth: The History of the Kings of Britain*, tr. Lewis Thorpe (Harmondsworth, 1966), 125.

all, it is Logrian, but it is more accurate to say that it is neither northern nor southern, but national.

As Gawain rides into the Wirral, an audience situated in the north-west Midlands would have a dislocating double vision, as the familiar becomes unfamiliar, the realistic scene becomes the world of *fairie*, and the friendliness of neighbours becomes the hostility of strangers. The effect upon the non-regional audience, however, is much more straightforward as, in company with Gawain, they leave the security of home further and further behind and launch into the great adventure of 'contrayez straunge' (713). Gawain's carefully detailed journey away from Camelot through north Wales and the Wirral leads him step by step into increasingly dangerous and unfamiliar territory, attacked by terrifying beasts and wicked men; for a local audience, though, this would lead to a gradually dawning recognition of 'to quat kyth he becom' (460).

The 'castel þe comlokest þat euer kny3t a3te' (767) that suddenly appears from this threatening and isolated setting of 'misy and myre' (749) is provincial only in its geographical location. In other respects it is a second Camelot, built to the most fashionable design and inhabited by the most elegant knights and ladies. Remote from the centre of culture though these courtiers may be, there is nothing rude or unpolished about their manners, the description of which as 'Frenkysch fare' (1116) locates them within an international code of courtly behaviour. Though the inhabitants of this northern castle are a long way from Camelot, they are acutely conscious of the reputation of the Round Table and of Gawain in particular as the example of 'alle prys and prowes and pured þewes' (912). In the presence of such a model of chivalry, it is only good sense that they should take the oppor-tunity to learn from Gawain the finer points of 'talkyng noble' (917), and if they do not have a profound understanding of the ideals that motivate him, that is in the nature of courtiers every-where, including those at Camelot itself who show an equal lack of perception of the meaning of Gawain's adventure. Through this description of a 'provincial' court, the poet dispels any concept of a distinctively provincial culture of the regions. Chivalric ideals are shown to be shared by knights throughout the country, however wild and remote their habitation.

We have been made ready for this concept of cultural cohesion by the opening stanzas of the poem, which provide us with a notion of Britain and its history, its famous rulers, most notably Arthur, taken as a model of kingship by the English monarchs from Edward I on. And indeed this account of ancient Britain is set in a still wider frame, that of the noble Trojans, who subjugated the 'prouinces' of Europe and so laid the foundations for that international court-culture that Arthur most eminently exemplified and Hautdesert strove to imitate. It is just at this point of national definition that the poet addresses us as his audience, 'ȝe' who 'wyl lysten þis laye' (30). Sandwiched as we thus are between the Trojan founders and Arthur's Christmas at Camelot, our identity as readers is constructed not as members of a peripheral group but as those who share in the central ideals of knightly conduct which the poem will proceed to explore. Perhaps we live in the north-west Midlands, or perhaps we live in Logres; the matter is of no consequence because our regionality is subsumed under the international chivalric code to which we all adhere.

It may be instructive in this respect to look back once more to an 'Edwardian' poem, to consider a contrasting example. *Havelok* also begins with an account of a historical model of the nation, in this case England under the rule of good King Athelwold 'bi are-dawes' (27).[25] So, too, the poem contains precise descriptions of local settings, in this case Lincolnshire and in particular Lincoln itself with its bridge, its steep climb up to the castle, and the 'grene' south of the town 'þat þare is yet' (2830). *Havelok* also presents the region within a national setting, but in this case interest centres on the special character of the region and its people, and the design of the poem is to construct a distinct regional identity for Lincoln-shire that can relate to the national one; to find a place within the national framework for a group with a rather different ancestry and cultural tradition, represented by the marriage of Havelok the Dane to the English princess Goldeboru. In this case the audience of 'wiues, maydnes and alle men' (2) announced at the outset by the poet are the people of Lincolnshire with their particular local concerns and interests.[26]

In *Gawain*, on the other hand, the audience is a national one. The poet sets the action in the north-west in order to provide a

[25] *Havelok*, ed. G. V. Smithers (Oxford, 1987), 1.
[26] See Thorlac Turville-Petre, '*Havelok* and the History of the Nation', in Carol M. Meale (ed.), *Readings in Medieval English Romance* (Cambridge, 1994), 121–34.

convincingly realistic landscape against which the outrageous adventure can be played out, and to emphasize the unity of a society in which northerners and southerners are at one in their cultural aspirations, not in order to claim a distinctive place for the region within the nation. The detailed description of landscape is an often-noted and highly praised feature of alliterative poetry. It is with the same purpose of grounding the fantastic that the poet of *The Wars of Alexander* describes the hills and valleys of India very much in terms of his own Lancashire landscape:

> Þare was so hedous and so hoge hillis þam beforn,
> Cloȝes at was cloude-he, clyntirand torres,
> Rochis and rogh stanes, rokkis vnfaire,
> Scutis to þe scharpe schew sckerres a hundreth. (4989–92)[27]

In direct contrast to this, *Pearl* draws its landscape not from local observation but from accounts of India and other fabulous regions, based on the Alexander romances among other sources:[28]

> Dubbed wern alle þo downeȝ sydeȝ
> Wyth crystal klyffeȝ so cler of kynde.
> Holtewodeȝ bryȝt aboute hem bydeȝ
> Of bolleȝ as blwe as ble of Ynde;
> As bornyst syluer þe lef on slydeȝ,
> Þat þike con trylle on vche a tynde. (73–8)

It is important to recognize just how different *Pearl* is from *Gawain*. Our perception of *Pearl* is sometimes too much influenced by our knowledge that it is preserved in the manuscript that presumably assembles the work of one poet, and by our proper and understandable desire to look for a coherent authorial style and vision. We need at other times to consider the differences, one of which is that *Pearl* pointedly rejects those regional associations that *Gawain* exploits.

In the first place, *Pearl* is not an alliterative poem. Rather, it is a stanzaic poem with fairly regular alliteration; quite an important distinction here.[29] The form seems to have been quite widely

---

[27] *The Wars of Alexander*, ed. Hoyt N. Duggan and Thorlac Turville-Petre, EETS SS 10 (Oxford, 1989), 156.

[28] See P. M. Kean, '*The Pearl*': *An Interpretation* (London, 1967), 92.

[29] See Hoyt N. Duggan, 'Libertine Scribes and Maidenly Editors: Meditations on Textual Criticism and Metrics', in C. B. McCully and J. J. Anderson (eds.), *English Historical Metrics* (Cambridge, 1997) 219–37.

popular from the early fourteenth century. There are comparable examples in the hand of the Ludlow scribe of MS Harley 2253, but in fact the two lyrics most formally akin to *Pearl*, 'Ich herde men upon molde' and 'Weping haueþ', both in twelve-line stanzas, are likely to have been composed not in the west but in the south and east.[30] At the same date, about 1340, a London scribe copied into the Auchinleck manuscript *The Four Foes of Mankind*, a poem in sixteen-line stanzas with heavy alliteration. This is northern in origin, and the fact that it is copied without much modification to its language perhaps suggests that its scribe deliberately preserved its provincial flavour even at the loss of some comprehensibility.[31] Closer parallels to *Pearl* are found in the lyrics of the Vernon and Simeon manuscripts from Worcestershire in the 1380s, refrain poems in eight- or twelve-line stanzas with alliteration particularly in the opening verse. Despite their western preservation, these lyrics may have been composed in the east Midlands, as may also *Pety Job*, a poem copied quite widely and bearing distinct formal similarities to *Pearl*.[32] From the incomplete evidence we have, the metrical form seems to have been non-metropolitan, but it was not confined to any one region.

Secondly, the vocabulary of *Pearl* is much less markedly regional than that of the other three poems in the manuscript. Whereas *Gawain* in particular uses numerous words of quite restricted northern circulation, the vocabulary of *Pearl* is for the most part that common to the verse of the alliterative revival, rhymed and unrhymed. Gordon suggests that the differences of theme and treatment account for this: 'The Scandinavian element in ME vocabulary was rich in concrete words, such as abound in this poet's descriptive passages, but included comparatively few words useful to the theologian or the poet of spiritual experience.'[33] But of course there are notable descriptive passages in *Pearl*, including 'concrete' descriptions of river, forest, cliff, and mountain, that

---

[30] See G. L. Brook, 'The Original Dialects of the Harley Lyrics', *LSE* 2 (1933), 38–61.

[31] The original dialect and northern vocabulary is analysed by Angus McIntosh, 'The Middle English Poem *The Four Foes of Mankind*', *NM* 79 (1978), 137–44.

[32] For analysis of the dialect of the Vernon lyrics see Oakden, *Alliterative Poetry*, 128–9. On the language of *Pety Job* see *Twenty-Six Political and Other Poems*, ed. J. Kail, EETS 124 (London, 1904), p. xxiii. In his edition of *Pearl* (p. 87), E. V. Gordon notes the metrical affinities with *Pety Job*.

[33] *Pearl*, ed. Gordon, 97.

would appear to present an invitation to use the northern topo-graphical vocabulary of *Gawain* or *The Wars of Alexander* that the poet seems deliberately to shun in *Pearl*. *Gawain* calls atten-tion to the distinctiveness of its vocabulary, but the northern reader of *Pearl* would find much less in the language and diction that was regionally marked.

If the author had chosen to provide for *Pearl* the same localized setting as *Gawain*, the dream-vision form would have given him a good opportunity to do so. The conventions of the dream-vision invite such a setting, though they do not demand it. Notable Ricardian instances are Langland's portrait of Will dressed as a loller in Cornhill, living with his wife Kit and his daughter Kalote and offering prayers for those who provide for him, and the setting of the prologue to *The Legend of Good Women*, in which Chaucer offers the circumstantial detail that gives such a lively picture of the dreamer and his connections with the court 'at Eltham or at Sheene' (497). The complete absence of such localizing detail in *Pearl* is quite striking. To the frustration of those early critics who tried to piece together a life of the *Pearl*-poet from the account of the narrator, there are no specific details offered about the dreamer's circumstances. The 'spot' is an unlocalized 'erbere' in August; its flowers with their colours and scents are profusely described, but we are left to imagine for ourselves, if we choose to, the wider setting of household, landscape, and region. The dreamer must have had a wife, but she is not mentioned, and his only job-description is the metaphorical one of jeweller. Social organizations and hierarchies are described in order to provide a contrast to heavenly structures, but the dreamer himself is not located in any social position, belongs to no community, and exists in isolation from friends, relatives, and contacts of any sort.[34] Even the central relationship with his daughter is described in such a roundabout way that a number of readers have seriously doubted whether the lines refer to a family relationship at all.

There are, I think, two consequences of this refusal to ground the dream-vision in some waking reality. The first is that it encourages us to see the dreamer as a universal figure rather than a representative of some sectional or regional interest. The second

---

[34] The point is made by David Aers, 'The Self Mourning: Reflections on *Pearl*', *Speculum*, 68 (1993), 54–73.

is more specific: it is to emphasize the paradoxical solidity of the dream in contrast to the insubstantiality of the setting. There is, after all, nothing ethereal about the features of heaven. Though they have no associations with any earthly region, the heavenly landscape and its birds of flaming colours are described in terms that are glitteringly sharp:

> I welke ay forth in wely wyse,
> No bonk so byg þat did me dere3;
> Þe fyrre in þe fryth, þe feier con ryse
> Þe playn, þe plontte3, þe spyse, þe pere3,
> And rawe3 and rande3 and rych reuere3,
> As fyldor fyn her bonkes brent. (101–6)

Even more precise is the account of the heavenly Jerusalem, constructed of 'bantele3', 'foundemente3', and 'tabelment' of precious stones (992–4), and bustling with its inhabitants processing after the Lamb. This 'reme of heuenesse' (735) is the country and the city to which the dreamer belongs or wishes to belong; this is the fair region from which he is exiled to the misery of his waking life:

> Me payed ful ille to be outfleme
> So sodenly of þat fayre regioun. (1177–8)

We as readers are impelled to participate in the dreamer's sense of loss at an exile which is ours too. Together with the dreamer, we have recognized the significance of that 'courtaysye' through which we may become 'membre3 of Jesu Kryst' (457–8), inhabitants of the community that is Christendom rather than region or nation. With the dreamer we are for a short while 'kaste of kythe3 þat laste3 aye' (1198), until we and the dreamer together are taken home into the household of Christ, in the words of the final inclusive prayer:

> He gef vus to be his homly hyne
> Ande precious perle3 vnto his pay. (1211–12)

Pearl frees its readers from their provincial attachments, and although the poem is written in a language to which its northern readers are accustomed, it draws much more heavily on wider literary modes and models than on local tradition. That Chaucer knew *Pearl* itself seems to me unlikely or at least unprovable; more significantly, the parallels between Chaucer's dream-vision poems and *Pearl* demonstrate a familiarity with the same fashionable literary forms, certainly from France and probably also Italy.[35] In this way *Pearl* projects itself into the mainstream of late fourteenth-century culture, shaping a Ricardian audience who may happen to live in Chester, York, Durham, and other urban and ecclesiastical centres 'fer in the north, I kan nat telle where'. How closely the actual readership corresponded to this construction of their Ricardian interests it is impossible to say and fruitless to inquire. At any event, there is no need to bring the *Pearl*-poet to London in order to make a Ricardian of him.

---

[35] A. C. Spearing considers the connections between Chaucer and the *Pearl*-poet in *Medieval Dream-Poetry* (Cambridge, 1976), 111. That the author of *Pearl* might have known Boccaccio's *Olympia* is generally considered unlikely, but I see no good reason to doubt it.

13

'Patience' and Authority

JOHN SCATTERGOOD

There is a large measure of uniformity in the critical and interpretative approaches usually taken in relation to *Patience*, and the
structure and conduct of the poem are usually thought to raise few
problems. Like all the poems in London, British Library, MS
Cotton Nero A.x. Art. 3, the poem presents, in formal terms, a
tidy inclusiveness. The opening line, 'Pacience is a poynt, þaȝ hit
displese ofte' (1), offers a proposition which the poem's closing line
recapitulates in an almost verbatim form.[1] And the proposition
is demonstrated in the body of the poem in a fairly standard
homiletic fashion. The narrator approaches his subject indirectly
by way of the last of the beatitudes which deals with those
'qui persecutionem patiuntur' (Matt. 5: 10)[2] and presents himself
as perhaps a preacher or a teacher, but at any rate as a moral
guide:

> Wyl ȝe tary a lyttel tyne and tent me a whyle
> I schal wysse yow þer-wyth as holy wryt telles. (59–60)

He is as good as his word and delivers in a relatively short space
what he has promised: using the standard instructional method of
a *narratio* followed by a *moralitas* he retells the biblical story of
Jonah, expanding it considerably, in such a way as to stress God's
patience and the prophet's impatience. Some writers on the poem
have stressed its sacramental and penitential aspects, particularly
in relation to the conversion of the Ninevites (353–408), who are

I am grateful to my colleagues Helen Cooney and Joe Pheifer for much help in the
preparation of this essay.

[1] References are to *Patience*, ed. J. J. Anderson (Manchester, 1969), though I
have not followed Anderson's practice of dividing the text into groups of four lines.

[2] The texts of the Vulgate beatitudes and the Book of Jonah are conveniently
given in Anderson's edition of *Patience*, app. A (pp. 70–2), and I quote from this
source unless otherwise indicated.

said to have earned God's mercy through 'penaunce' (406, cf.
530).[3] Others have explored the typological relationships between
Jonah and Christ, especially in relation to the prophet's three days
inside the whale which are regularly interpreted as a prefiguration
of Christ's three days in hell (245–340).[4] But most have taken as
their starting-point the author's own description of his poem,
assumed that it is a moral homily on the virtue of patience, and
chosen to concentrate on other, presumably more interesting,
aspects of the poem—its treatment of its biblical sources, the
relationship between the narrator and his protagonist, the relationship between God and Jonah, the comedy of the poem, its verbal
texture and wit.[5] There is a high degree of consensus on what the
poem is about and how it works.

However, two features of the standard scholarly treatments of
Patience seem to me to have proved less than helpful. The first has
to do with the poet's choice of the story of Jonah as his moral
exemplum. In his fine edition of the poem, in a statement which
has become part of the conventional wisdom, J. J. Anderson
wrote: 'the poet of *Patience* takes an independent attitude
towards tradition, particularly exegetical tradition...in drawing
the lesson of patience out of the Book of Jonah, *Patience* appears
to be unique.'[6] It is true that when medieval moralists needed
examples of patience they were likely to have chosen differently.
In a chapter of his *Summa de arte praedicatoria*, which the Middle
English author may have known since it treats the topic of patience

---

[3] For an interesting account of the poem from this point of view see Anna P.
Baldwin, 'Sacramental Perfection in *Pearl*, *Patience* and *Cleanness*', in Piero Boitani
and Anna Torti (eds.), *Genres, Themes and Images in English Literature: Fourteenth and Fifteenth Centuries* (Tübingen, 1988), 125–40.

[4] See e.g. Malcolm Andrew, 'Jonah and Christ in *Patience*', MP 70 (1972–3),
230–3; and John B. Friedman, 'Figural Typology in the Middle English *Patience*', in
Bernard S. Levy and Paul E. Szarmach (eds.), *The Alliterative Tradition in the
Fourteenth Century* (Kent, Oh., 1981), 99–129.

[5] See particularly the following fine studies of the poem: David Williams, 'The
Point of *Patience*', MP 68 (1970–1), 127–36; A. C. Spearing, *The Gawain-Poet: A
Critical Study* (Cambridge, 1970), 74–95; Edward Wilson, *The Gawain-Poet* (Leiden, 1976), 46–71; W. A. Davenport, *The Art of the Gawain-Poet* (London, 1978),
103–35; Myra Stokes, 'Suffering in *Patience*', ChauR 18 (1984), 354–63.

[6] See *Patience*, ed. Anderson, 19. Compare also the comment of R. H. Bowers, in
The Legend of Jonah (The Hague, 1971), 62: 'It is the only homily that I have
encountered that extracts the theme of divine patience from the Book of Jonah.'
However, see n. 8 below.

in relation to the beatitudes, Alan of Lille advises would-be preachers:

Si quis ergo patiens desiderat, Job patientiam, Christi finem, martyrum constantiam diligenter attendat, et sic omnibus mundanis insultibus patientiae virtute illudat.[7]

(If anyone therefore desires to be patient, let him consider carefully the patience of Job, the death of Christ, the constancy of the martyrs, and so let him deride all affronts of the world in the power of patience.)

It is also true that the Book of Jonah was more often than not read typologically, and that no instance of an interpretation of it, as a whole, in relation to patience has been found. But the conduct of the poem suggests that the poet read his biblical sources closely, verse by verse, and if he used a glossed Bible it would not have been difficult for him to find individual verses which were read in relation to his moral theme. As influential an interpreter as Nicholas of Lyra, for example, comments, in relation to Jonah 4: 4, on the prophet's manifest impatience (*impatientia*) and speaks of God as 'reprehending his impatience' (*impatientiam*).[8] And, as will be shown, there are examples of exegetical uses of Jonah in relation to virtues which are closely allied to patience. The poet's relationship to the exegetical tradition is, it seems to me, rather more complex than has been supposed, and to assume that he simply ignored it or took an 'independent' line is not the case.

Second, and more serious, in my view, is the overly limited definition of the concept of patience which is sometimes taken—a definition which sees it simply as the traditional remedy for the deadly sin of anger. F. N. M. Diekstra, in an important, but often ignored, article, has reminded us that 'a too narrow conception of patience leaves us with a poem in which only some elements contribute to the theme and the rest follows a course of its own.

---

[7] See *PL* 210, 109–95. The quotation is from cols. 142–3. For a translation of this important text (which I have used for the English versions of my quotations) see Alan of Lille, *The Art of Preaching*, tr. Gillian R. Evans, Cistercian Studies Series 23 (Kalamazoo, Mich., 1981). For the argument that the author of *Patience* possibly knew this text see my article 'Alain de Lille and the Prologue of *Patience*', *MÆ* 61 (1992), 87–91. My conclusions had largely been anticipated by Francis Cairns in 'Latin Sources and Analogues of the M. E. *Patience*', *Studia neophilologica*, 59 (1987), 7–18—an article of which I was not aware when I wrote.

[8] See his *Postillae* in the edition of the Vulgate (Venice, 1481), sig. 3 E 8 r. I owe this reference to Bowers, *The Legend of Jonah*, 59–60.

It will not do to present a truncated notion of some kind of patience and note additional interests such as God's forbearance, Jonah's disobedience and the theme of the penitent sinner. The virtue of the poem is that these aspects are all related to the theme of patience.'[9] What he demonstrates in his examination of the poem is that the concept of patience is at the centre of a whole nexus of virtues and vices: not only does it relate significantly to the cardinal virtue of fortitude, but in medieval penitential schemes it is seen as a countervailing moral virtue against the sin of sloth (in both its aspects of *tristitia* and *accidia*) as well as more traditionally against anger. Referring to fortitude as a remedy against sloth Chaucer's Parson has this to say:

This vertu is so myghty and so vigerous that it dar withstonde myghtily and wisely kepen hymself fro perils that been wikked, and wrastle agayn the assautes of the devel. For it enhaunceth and enforceth the soule, right as Accidie abateth it and maketh it fieble. For this *fortitudo* may endure by long suffraunce the travailles that been covenable. (*The Canterbury Tales*, X (I) 729–30)

It is Jonah's sloth, his lack of fortitude and a capacity for 'long sufferaunce', which causes his initial fearful reluctance to undertake the journey to Nineveh to perform God's bidding (91), his somnolence as he takes refuge at the bottom of the ship while the storm rages (183–6), his instability and inconstancy as his mood swings between elation and despair (457, 480), his frequent requests for death because he is miserable (425–8, 488). In just the same way his petulance (90), his 'janglande' grumbling (433), and his easily aroused wrath (74, 411, 481) show him to be guilty of anger in a number of its traditional forms, and lacking in those virtues which enable one to resist it—in the Parson's terms, not simply 'patience' but 'mansuetude' or 'debonairetee' and 'obedience' as well.

In what follows, a reading of *Patience* is proposed which seeks to take account of these two issues. In the Parson's treatment of the

[9] 'Jonah and *Patience*: The Psychology of the Prophet', *ES* 55 (1974), 205–17. The quotation is from p. 206. Others who have appreciated that a broad definition of patience, and its related virtues, must be assumed in order to account adequately for the poem include Malcolm Andrew and Ronald Waldron, who have a brief but sound introduction to the poem in *The Poems of the Pearl Manuscript* (London, 1978), 17–21.

remedies against anger 'obedience' is the culminating quality, the highest spiritual and moral point of the virtue which has patience at its centre, and at the same time not a passive thing but the virtue translated into appropriate action:

Of pacience comth obedience, thurgh whiche a man is obedient to Criste and to alle hem to whiche he oghte to been obedient in Crist. And understond wel that obedience is parfit whan that a man dooth gladly and hastily, with good herte entierly, al that he sholde do. Obedience generally is to parfourne the doctrine of God and of his sovereyns, to which hym oghte to ben obeisaunt in alle rightwisnesse. (X (I) 674-6)

In this ideology, obedience is the duty owed to masters by servants—whether the master is God or a worldly lord ('sovereyns')—and it has both a spiritual and social dimension. Complete ('parfit') obedience, what is more, involves not only the performance of an action but the motive for doing it ('with good herte entierly') and the manner in which it is done ('gladly and hastily'). It seems to me that the poem deals principally with the theme of patience in relation to that aspect of it which is more commonly termed obedience, particularly with reference to the relationship between masters and servants, and not only does it deal with obedience but with the circumstances of that obedience—why and how an obedient action is performed. It also seems to me that the poet derived certain ideas on these matters from the exegetical tradition, which may have suggested and certainly sustained his particular reading of the story of Jonah.

Any reading of *Patience* needs to begin with the narrator, who mediates the story he tells in a particularly full and aggressive way.[10] As he describes the circumstances he claims gave rise to his poem, he creates himself, sketchily and abstractly at first but later more precisely, and he invites a reading of the poem in terms of his own, possibly fictive, experience. Having heard the beatitudes 'at a hyye masse' (9), he is prompted to think of the first which deals with 'pouerte' (13) and the last which deals with patience (33): they are similar, he thinks, in that they attract the same reward ('mede' 39), and in that they are of one 'kynde' (40). By 'kynde' he appears principally to mean 'nature', but by way of a

---

[10] On this question see the interesting, and contrasting, views of Charles Moorman, 'The Role of the Narrator in *Patience*', MP 61 (1963-4), 90-5, and J. J. Anderson, 'The Prologue of *Patience*', MP 63 (1965-6), 283-7.

pun where 'kynde' means 'kindred' or 'family' he ushers in the first of his several subtle moments of social comedy—he construes them as women ('Dame...' 31–2) and unwelcome guests, and since 'Dame Pouert' visits him and cannot be got rid of (41–2), and since she and Patience are 'play-feres' (45), he has to entertain them both.[11] On a moral and a practical level, that is, his poverty causes him to have to receive and to come to terms with patience and suffering (33–6, 41–6). Poverty makes him a disempowered underling: it 'oppresses' (43) him. And he follows this by seeing himself in relation to a larger providential scheme which limits his freedom of action:

> ȝif me be dyȝt a destyne due to haue,
> What dowes me þe dedayn oþer dispit make? (49–50)

This is framed as a question but the answer to it is clear. Resistance to overwhelming forces, he suggests, is pointless, just as it would be pointless to grumble if his 'lege lorde' were to bid him 'to ryde oþer to renne to Rome in his ernde' (52). Whether or not this is autobiographically accurate cannot be determined. But it is clear that for the purposes of the poem he presents himself in social terms as a servant, as a feudal retainer, bound to obey the commands of his lord even when what he has to do is difficult and dangerous, as the journey to Rome proverbially (and actually) was.[12] He is also a servant of not particularly high status: an 'ernde' to Rome suggests that he is a messenger of some sort, and messengers were such impecunious and insignificant figures, according to Langland, that their poverty practically ensured their safety as they travelled (*Piers Plowman*, C XIII. 32 ff.). He can be forced to do things against his will, 'maugref my chekes' (54), if his lord threatens him, and he associates his lord's ill will and good will with, presumably financial, rewards—'mede' (55) and 'hyure' (56). His insight into his situation persuades him that his options are limited by his poverty and dependent status: compliance, silent

---

[11] For some astute comments on this aspect of the poem see Jonathan Nicholls, *The Matter of Courtesy: Medieval Courtesy Books and the Gawain-Poet* (Cambridge, 1985), 81.

[12] See B. J. and H. W. Whiting, *Proverbs, Sentences and Proverbial Phrases* (Cambridge, Mass., 1968), R182 'From hence to Rome', where Rome suggests 'a long way'. To this entry should be added the instances cited in *Patience*, ed. Anderson, 52.

patience, obedience, and the like are the means by which he negotiates his way through his world, and he justifies his attitudes by telling an exemplary story to illustrate the foolishness of behaving otherwise. He makes no pretence of being an objective narrator. He intervenes frequently in the story, eliciting meanings, directing attention to moral points, and everywhere indicating the shortcomings of Jonah's behaviour. At times he is openly critical:

> Lo, þe wytles wrechche, for he wolde noght suffer,
> Now hatȝ he put hym in plyt of peril wel more. (113–14)

But usually, as will be shown, the disparagement is more subtle, depending on a telling juxtaposition or a resonantly meaningful adjective or adverb. The servant who has learnt patience tells the story of a disobedient servant whom he ushers through a sequence of educative tribulations with an amused contempt.

The exegetical tradition which saw Jonah as a disobedient servant appears to derive from Jerome's commentary on Jonah 1: 9. Here, as his lemma, Jerome quotes both the Vulgate and the Septuagint versions:

Et dixit ad eos: Hebraeus ego sum, et Dominum Deum caeli ego timeo, qui fecit mare et aridam. LXX: Et dixit ad eos: Servus Domini ego sum, et Deum caeli ego colo, qui fecit mare et aridam.[13]

(He said to them: I am a Hebrew and I fear the Lord God of heaven, who made the sea and the dry land. Septuagint—And he said to them: I am a Servant of the Lord, and I reverence the God of heaven, who made the sea and the dry land.)

And, as he comments, he uses some of the wording of the Septuagint text for his interpretation including the word *servus*, and the word *cultu* which is suggested by *colo*:

Dominum Deum caeli ego timeo, cum eius praecepta non faciat. Nisi forte respondeamus, quod et peccatores timeant Deum, servorumque sit non diligere, sed timere; quamquam in hoc loco timor pro cultu possit intelligi, juxta sensum eorum qui audiebant et adhuc ignorabant Deum.

(I fear the Lord God of heaven—because he does not perform his commands. Unless, perhaps, we may reply that sinners should also fear God, and it is not for servants to love but to fear; although in this place fear may

---

[13] PL 25, 1117–52. The quotations are from col. 1127.

be understood for reverence, following the sense of those who heard but as yet did not know God.)

The idea here that servants perform their lord's bidding because they are made to fear (*timere*) not because of reverence, esteem, or care (*diligere*), but that, in a way, *timor* may correspond to *cultus*, is an influential one and was frequently taken up by other commentators. Referring to this same passage Haymo of Halberstadt writes that Jonah 'feared God with a servile fear (*timore servili*) from whom he wished to flee'.[14] And Hugh of St Cher, in his *Postillae*, glosses the passage as follows: 'I fear as a servant (*servus*) and I do not reverence (*diligo*) as a son. Therefore he had a servile fear (*timorem servilem*), therefore he was in mortal sin.' Jonah's fearful reluctance to go to Nineveh at God's initial bidding is frequently construed as disobedience and his compliance with God's second demand that he preach is seen as a chastened return to obedience: Hugh glosses the verse 'Et surrexit Ionas et abiit in Nineven' (3: 3) with the single phrase 'Obedient (*obediens*) without delay.'[15] And, following much the same tradition of interpretation, Phillip of Harvengt, in his *De silentio clericorum*, uses Jonah as a figure for the reluctant preacher, who has to be forced into compliance with God's will.[16] Essentially, Phillip contrasts God's two commands to Jonah to go and preach to the Ninevites (1: 2; 3: 2)—which is invited because the wording of the Vulgate is so similar in each case. He interprets Jonah's initial refusal as a fear of preaching hard things (*dura*), but not so much the act of a prudent man (*prudens*) as a preference for exploring the joy of contemplation in peace and idleness, for he interprets Tharsis, following Jerome, as 'the exploration of joy' (*Tharsis quippe* 'exploratio gaudii' *interpretatur*). But Jonah was not allowed to enjoy Tharsis because of his disobedience (*inobedientia*), because he avoided obeying (*obedire*) good commands and was obedient not to God but to his own wishes. Phillip interprets the storm as resulting from the 'disobedience of the fugitive', and he draws a lengthy contrast between the whale's obedience to God's commands and Jonah's disobedience:

[14] PL 117, 127–42. The quotation is from col. 123.
[15] *Postillae* (Paris, 1533), iv, sigs. yii r. and yiii r.
[16] PL 203, 943–1206. The quotations are from cols. 1108–9.

Mira res! homo ratione preditus mandatis cœlestibus non timet contraire, et marina belua diligit obedire, et cum Propheta fallitur tutum esse aestimans remedium fugiendi, piscis ultro se offerans aures accipit audiendi. Inobedientem itaque prophetam obediens piscis detinuit, eumque poenitentem ad praeceptum Domini rursus evomuit, quia sic jubentis justitia voluit hunc punire, ut tamen nollet eum ejusdem misericordia deperire.

(A wondrous thing! A man endowed with reason is not afraid to oppose the commands of heaven, and the sea-monster takes pains to obey; and when the prophet is deceived, thinking he is safe through recourse to flight, the fish, of his own accord, offering himself, has ears to hear. And so the obedient fish makes a prisoner of the disobedient prophet, and when he was penitent vomited him out again at God's command, because the righteousness of the one who gave the command wished to punish the man in this way, even if, through his mercy, he did not wish to destroy him utterly.)

Though it is here put to another use, the contrast between fear (*timet*) and reverence (*diligit*) in the context of disobedience clearly recalls Jerome. And when Jonah, chastened by God's punishment, responds positively to the second command to preach in Nineveh, it is presented as a return to obedience:

Ad hoc verbum propheta non contendit, castigatus verbere jam non fugae praesidium apprehendit, sed eligit bona potius duce obedientia praedicare, quam laesa obedientia nocenti silentio gaudium explorare.

(At this word the prophet does not strive; restrained by punishment now he does not take the protection of flight, but chooses rather to preach good things guided by obedience, than to betray obedience by looking out for pleasure in harmful silence.)

This way of interpreting the story of Jonah as that of a disobedient servant was never a dominant one. It coexisted with other, more powerful, usually typological readings. In the Chester *Play of Barlaam*, for example, the Expositor equates Jonah with Christ because he spent three days 'in wombe of whall', but Jonah himself sees his ejection from the ship in moral terms, 'for I wrought inobedyentlie'.[17]

What seems to me to happen in *Patience* is that the poet responds to this minor tradition of interpretation of the story and puts it at the centre of his poem—though he uses other

[17] *The Chester Mystery Cycle*, ed. R. M. Lumiansky and David Mills, 2 vols., EETS ss 3 and 9 (London, 1974, 1986), i. 478.

patristic approaches as well, if they contribute in any way to his subject. It is part of the strategy of the poem—discernible in what the author adds to the biblical narrative and in his precise wording—to construe the relationship between God and Jonah as that between a master and a servant.[18] Sometimes the words 'God' and 'prophet' are used, but on other occasions the language suggests a feudal relationship. As Jonah, coming to some recognition of his subservient status, prays from the belly of the whale he calls God a 'prynce' and asks him to withhold 'thy vengaunce, thurgh vertu of routhe' (282–4), and a few lines later says:

> Haf now mercy of þy man and his mys-dedes,
> And preue the ly₃tly a lorde in londe and in water. (287–8)

Here 'lorde' suggests a worldly dimension which 'God' would not have, and 'man' has, as part of its meaning at least, the idea of 'servant'. What is more, God is sometimes invested with virtues which might properly belong to a secular lord, such as 'cortaysye', 'debonerte', 'grace', 'mercy' in lines 417–420. And equally, Jonah is elsewhere construed in terms which suggest not only that he is a servant but that he is like the narrator. Like the narrator he is sent by his lord on an 'arende' (72, 202, cf. 52) as a messenger: he bears 'typynges' (78) and a 'message' (81). And like the narrator, Jonah experiences the hardships of travel at his lord's behest: the road to Rome may have been difficult, but it is as nothing compared to Jonah's tribulations as he gets to Nineveh by an indirect route. In passages which he adds to the biblical narrative the poet stresses Jonah's travels, and modernizes them: both in the embarkation scene (97–108) and in the lines describing the storm (145–60, 217–21) there is a great deal of contemporary technical vocabulary, of the sort much favoured in some passages by alliterative poets, to do with ships and sea-voyages. Jonah is a transient, who moves from one uncomfortable lodging to another—the bottom of the storm-tossed ship, lying on a plank, 'On-helde by þe hurrok' (183–5), the woodbine-bower which is first cool and shaded and then hot (437–80), and, in between them, the belly of the whale. Significantly, his descent into the whale's belly is described as if it were the arrival of a traveller at his lodgings: he lurches in through

---

[18] On this aspect of the poem, see particularly Nicholls, *The Matter of Courtesy*, 82–4.

a gut, 'a rode þat hym þoȝt', head over heels until he fetches up in a cavern 'as brod as a halle', and there, amid the evil-smelling grease and filth 'watȝ bylded his bour þat wyl no bale suffer' (270–6).[19] The object of all this is to educate Jonah in the virtue of patient sufferance, to bring him to obedience, to make him like the narrator. And, fittingly, when he approaches this state his compliance with his lord's will echoes the narrator's as he replies to God's ironic question about his attempt to avoid undertaking the journey to Nineveh:

> Þenne a wynde of Goddeȝ worde efte þe wyȝe bruxleȝ:
> 'Nylt þou neuer to Nuniue bi no kynneȝ wayeȝ?'
> 'ȝisse, lorde', quoþ the lede, 'lene me þy grace
> For-to go at þi gre, me gayneȝ non oþer.' (345–8)

Here 'gre' recalls etymologically the second element of 'maugref' and 'bongre', the contrasted unwillingness and willingness of the introductory lines (55–6), where the narrator talks of the preferability of obedience over disobedience that experience has taught him.

The patterns of obedience and disobedience in *Patience* are also stressed by means of a series of contrasts which bring into relief the way in which various things, inanimate as well as animate, react to God's commands. Alan of Lille, in the chapter of the *Summa de arte praedicatoria* which deals with obedience, makes the point that man alone, because he is endowed with reason, resists God's commands:

Insensibilia obediunt Deo, tu qui solus praeditus es ratione, impugnas Dei voluntatem? Sol a sua semita non deviat, luna a suo tramite non aberrat, stellae suis indulgent efficiis, ad nutum Dei, campus floribus amoenatur, imbribus terra irrigatur, fronde crispatur silva, in nemore citharizat avicula, sic Deo obedieunt cuncta; tu solus impugnas ejus praecepta.[20]

(Inanimate objects obey the Lord. You, who alone are endowed with reason, do you battle against God's will? The sun does not deviate from its course; the moon does not wander from its path; the stars shine in their appointed places. At God's bidding, the field grows lovely with flowers, the earth is watered with rain, the forest rustles with leaves, the little bird

---

[19] Edward Wilson has some interesting comments on this passage: 'As Jonah was a parodic hero setting forth, so now he experiences the parodic arrival of the hero' (*The Gawain-Poet*, 65).

[20] *PL* 210, 143–5. The quotation is from col. 143.

chirps in the glade—so all things obey the Lord. You alone battle against his laws.)

And Phillip of Harvengt, it will be recalled, had made a similar point: Jonah endowed with reason (*ratione preditus*) was disobedient whereas the whale obeyed God's commands promptly. The Middle English poet, who may have taken the suggestion from either of these sources, insists on the contrast through a variety of verbal devices—mainly the liberal use of adverbs and adverbial phrases, and patterns of verbal repetition. Because God is the creator and lord of everything, says the poet, he has a right to expect obedience, and, in the Parson's terms, to expect that his commands will be obeyed 'gladly and hastily, with good herte entierly', and in general this is what he gets:

> Thenne oure fader to þe fysch ferslych biddeʒ
> Þat he hym sput spakly vpon spare drye.
> Þe whal wendeʒ at his wylle and a warþe fyndeʒ,
> And þer he brakeʒ vp þe buyrne as bede hym oure lorde. (337–40)

Here the order is given 'ferslych' (sternly) and the 'Lorde' expects it to be obeyed 'spakly' (quickly) and the whale complies precisely, 'at his wylle', 'as bede hym oure lorde'. Even more emphatically he is obeyed by the winds so as to produce the storm at sea:

> 'Ewrus and Aquiloun þat on est sittes,
> Blowes boþe at my bode vpon blo watteres.'
> Þenne watʒ no tom þer bytwene his tale and her dede,
> So bayn wer þay boþe two his bone for to wyrk.
> An-on out of þe norþ-est the noys bigynes,
> When boþe breþes con blowe vpon blo watteres. (133–8)

Not only are the winds 'bayn' (ready) to do God's command, and there is no 'tom' (delay) between his words and their actions, but the high degree of verbal similarity between lines 134 and 138— God's order and their response—also suggests that they carried out his instructions exactly. The poet uses a similar device of verbal repetition in relation to the west wind which withers Jonah's woodbine. God's instruction,

> And syþen he warneʒ þe west to waken ful softe,
> And sayeʒ unte ʒeferus that he syfle warme. (469–70)

is recalled in the action, 'þe warm wynde of þe weste wertes he swyþeʒ' (478). God is also instantly obeyed by the sun (471–6), the woodbine (443–4), and the worm (467–8)—that is to say, by the various levels of creation, except for man. Men are more problematical because they have reason and free will, but the Ninevites respond positively to Jonah's warnings about their destruction: the king reacts 'radly' (quickly) (378) and his people obey his decrees, 'Þenne al leued on his lawe and laften her synnes' (405).

All this has the effect of isolating Jonah in his initial disobedience and his eventual, reluctant, obedience—and again to help him enforce the point, the poet uses verbal repetition and recall. God's initial instruction begins as follows:

> 'Rys radly', he says, 'and rayke forth euen;
> Nym þe way to Nynyue wyth-outen oþer speche.' (65–6)

This is based on the Vulgate Jonah 1: 2, but it is significant that neither of the adverbs 'radly' (quickly) and 'euen' (directly) appears, nor does the adverbial phrase 'wyth-outen oþer speche'. Clearly, the poet, like Chaucer's Parson, was interested not only in obedience, but in the manner of that obedience. But Jonah is full of 'speche': he reacts 'wyþerly' (perversely) and, in a lengthy passage not in the Vulgate, speculates on the dangers of the mission to Nineveh and concludes by a determination to avoid it (75–88). His action, in its precise wording, recalls God's instruction but disobeys it:

> Þenne he ryses radly and raykes bilyue
> Jonas toward port Japh, ay janglande for tene. (89–90)

He goes toward Jaffa not Nineveh, 'janglande' all the time, that is, grumbling—one of the 'sins of the tongue' traditionally treated under anger. God's second order is even more peremptory than his first: 'Ris, aproche þen to prech, lo, þe place here' (349). Jonah, chastened by punishment into obedience, this time complies, but the wording of his compliance is interesting:

> Þenne þe renk radly ros as he my3t,
> And to Niniue þat na3t he ne3ed ful euen. (351–2)

Not only does 'ros' respond to the 'Ris' of this order but it recalls the 'Rys' of God's first order, as do the adverbs 'radly' and 'euen' (cf. 65): like the rest of the inanimate and animate parts of God's creation, Jonah has learnt, in his case belatedly, to obey to the letter—though his obedience is temporary—and to carry his lord's message to the right place.

The theme of obedience and disobedience is further articulated in the poem by means of allusion. In the Vulgate account Jonah's refusal to obey God's initial command to go to Nineveh is unexplained, but in *Patience* the poet has Jonah give reasons. Like any medieval messenger with something critical or unpleasant to convey he knows that he risks being harmed:

> 'If I bowe to his bode and bryng hem þis tale,
> And I be nummen in Nuniue, my nyes begynes.
> He telles me þose traytoures arn typped schrewes;
> I com wyth þose tyþynges, þay ta me bylyue,
> Pyneӡ me in a prysoun, put me in stokkes,
> Wryþe me in a warlok, wrast out myn yӡen.
> Þis is a meruayl message a man for to preche
> Amonge enmyes so mony and mansed fendes.' (75–82)

And the records are full of examples of messengers and envoys being imprisoned, tortured, maimed, and even killed.[21] But Jonah associates these dangers with the injunction to 'preche', so it looks likely that he is comparing himself with those who underwent hardship or martryrdom while preaching God's message. St Paul, in a celebrated passage, lists the various beatings he had received, frequent imprisonment, stoning, three shipwrecks, 'in journeyings often, in perils of waters, in perils of robbers, in perils by mine own countrymen, in perils by the heathen, in perils in the city, in perils in the wilderness, in perils in the sea, in perils among false heathen' (2 Cor. 11: 23–6)—but Jonah is clearly unwilling to suffer this.[22] Because the martyrs were traditionally regarded as types of

---

[21] See Norbert Ohler, *The Medieval Traveller*, tr. Caroline Hillier (Woodbridge, 1989), 64–73, for an account of the conditions under which messengers and envoys operated. I am grateful to Charlotte Morse for drawing my attention to a letter from Petrarch to Segremor de Pommiers, formerly a courier to the Emperor Charles IV and now a Cistercian monk, in which he recalls Segremor's long and difficult journeys, the dangers into which he put himself on his master's business, his frequent lack of reward, and the equally frequent criticisms received for the slightest fault (*Seniles*, X. 1).

[22] There were more recent instances of the martyrdom of Christian missionaries in gruesome circumstances, which may have been known to the poet. Compare Bede's account of the incident in 692 when two missionaries to Frisia were murdered: 'Hewald the White was killed outright with a sword, and Hewald the Black was put to lingering torture and torn agonizingly limb from limb' (*Ecclesiastical*

patience, Jonah is demonstrating here his impatience. But a few lines later, more interestingly, he complains as follows:

> 'Oure syre syttes', he says, 'on sege so hyȝe,
> In his glowande glorye, and gloumbes ful lyttel
> Þagh I be nummen in Nunniue and naked dispoyled,
> On rode rwly to-rent with rybaudes mony.' (93–6)

Here the association is clearly with Christ's passion and crucifixion ('naked dispoyled', 'rode'), and since, like the martyrs, Christ was frequently seen as a type of patience, this further highlights Jonah's impatience. But Christ is also a type of obedience. Alan of Lille quotes as one of his introductory texts in his chapter entitled 'De obedientia': 'Christus factus est pro nobis obediens usque ad mortem, mortem autem crucis' (Phil. 2: 8), which follows a verse saying that he took upon himself the form of a servant (*formam servi accipiens*).[23] And again the contrast with Jonah, who is a servant but not obedient, is clear. Jonah blames his master for the difficult 'message' he has to deliver: he is certain that he worries (*gloumbes*) very little about him, and even speculates that he intends him 'gref...þat I slayn were'. In the circumstances, Jonah feels that the message he has to take to Nineveh renders the enterprise too dangerous: '"At alle peryles", quoþ þe prophete, "I aproche hit no nerre"' (85). This may seem from his point of view like reasonable prudential wisdom, rather like the narrator's reluctance to undertake the difficult journey to Rome. But the lesson that the poem enforces is a more highly coercive one, that masters whether good or perverse, should be obeyed in all circumstances. Alan of Lille had adduced a text to this effect: 'Servi, obedite praepositis et dominis vestris, non tantum bonis et modestis, sed etiam dyscolis' (cf. 1 Pet. 2: 18). In fact much of the second half of this chapter from 1 Peter 2 is apposite to the Middle English poem. Peter urges his audience, as they go among the Gentiles, to submit themselves to every ordinance of man for the Lord's sake, whether it comes from the king or governors, if it is for the chastisement of evildoers (2: 13–14). They are to use their freedom as servants (*servi*) of God (2: 16). They are to regard it as

---

History of the English People, IV. 10, tr. Leo Shirley-Price and rev. R. E. Latham (London, 1990), 280–2.

[23] *PL* 210, 143.

worthy of thanks if they endure grief, suffering wrongfully (*patiens injuste*). And he follows this by saying that to suffer blows patiently (*patienter*) for God is deserving of grace (2: 19–20). His exemplar is Christ, who suffered patiently for us (*passus est pro nobis*, 2: 21). Whether the author of *Patience* was aware of this text is impossible to say, but his way of thinking is certainly in line with it.

To interpret the Book of Jonah as being an exemplum about a recalcitrant servant who is brought back to obedience to his master's commands through suffering—which is how, it seems to me, the author of *Patience* read it—is also consistent with its use by the Archpoet. In a sporadic way his ten surviving poems chart his relationship with Rainald von Dassel, archbishop of Cologne and chancellor of Emperor Frederick Barbarossa. The poem beginning 'Fama tuba dante sonum' is particularly interesting in this respect.[24] Rainald, who is described as the Archpoet's patron ('patronum', ll. 5), is in Vienne in the summer of 1164 with his large retinue, and various poets and other entertainers have hurried there, each one expecting a good reward: 'quisque sperat grande donum' (12). But the Archpoet, though formerly a member of the retinue—'tuus quondam adoptivus' (25)—dares not appear:

> ego caput fero pronum,
> tanquam frater sim latronum,
> reus inops racionum,
> sensus egens et sermonum. (13–16)

(I hang my head as though I were a brother of thieves, an accused person, poor in reason, without sense and speech.)

He is a 'fugitivus' from Rainald's household and he uses Jonah's flight from God as an analogy for his own situation:

> Nomen vatis vel personam
> manifeste non exponam;
> sed quem fuga fecit Ionam,
> per figuram satis bonam
> Ione nomen ei ponam. (17–21)

---

[24] See *Die Gedichte der Archipoeta*, ed. Heinrich Watenphul and Heinrich Krefeld (Heidelberg, 1958), 54–6. For the Archpoet's relationship with Rainald von Dassel and the Emperor Frederick Barbarossa see W. H. T. Jackson, 'The Politics of a Poet: The Archipoeta as Revealed by his Imagery', in Edward P. Mahoney (ed.), *Philosophy and Humanism* (Leiden, 1976), 320–38.

(Clearly, I do not openly reveal the name or the character of a poet; yet to one whom flight made a Jonah, through a good enough rhetorical figure, I may give the name of Jonah.)

Why he has absented himself from Rainald's retinue does not emerge precisely, but in the following lines he says that he feared his master's anger and compares himself to the whale in his indulgence of animal pleasures—so there may have been some sexual scandal:

> Voluptate volens frui
> comparabar brute sui
> nec cum sancto sanctus fui.
> unde timens iram tui
> sicut Ionas dei sui
> fugam petens fuga rui. (29–34)

(Wishing to enjoy pleasure I was being compared to his animal and I was not pious with the pious one. Whence, fearing your anger just like Jonah his God, seeking flight, I was ruined by flight.)

Like Jonah's, the Archpoet's attempt to flee his master has brought suffering. He is oppressed by the plague of poverty ('paupertatis premor peste', 77), and he equates this with the whale which envelops him, from which Rainald's generosity and power can free him:

> Ecce Ionas tuus plorat,
> culpam suum non ignorat,
> pro qua cetus eum vorat:
> veniam vult et implorat,
> ut a peste qua laborat
> solvas eum quem honorat
> tremit colit et adorat. (45–51)

(Look! Your Jonah weeps; he is not unaware of his fault, for which the whale devours him. He wishes and prays for your pardon, so that you may release him from the plague which afflicts him, you whom he honours, trembles at, reverences, and worships.)

The Archpoet's verses look simple, but are not: they are learned, full of allusions, and echoes, both of classical literature and of the Bible. Here *timens* (32) and *colit* (51) probably refer back, as often when the Book of Jonah is used in relation to the obedience of servants, to Jerome's *timeo* and *colo* from the Vulgate and Septuagint versions of 1:9. When Rainald has ordered the whale to release him, he says, he will resume his duties, which seem to include being sent on dangerous journeys as a messenger:

> Hunc reatum si remittas
> inter enses et sagittas
> tutus ibo quo me mittas. (66–8)

(If you forgive this offence, I shall go secure among swords and arrows where you send me.)

He also promises to write poems in Rainald's praise such as have never been heard before ('inauditas', 74) if he is rewarded. Overwhelmed by poverty he comes to heel. But what is particularly interesting about the poem is that—like Jonah—he resists, for a time at any rate.

In 1276–7 the tenants of Stoughton, a small Leicestershire village, complained to the king's court that William Schepished, abbot of Leicester, had imposed illegal labour services on them. The complaint failed, and the court, amongst other things, confirmed their unfree status. A triumphalist Latin poem, perhaps written by a canon of the abbey, derides their presumption and stresses that they are in servitude and are likely to remain so in the future:

> Quid faciet servus nisi serviet, et puer eius?
> Purus servus erit et libertate carebit.
> Judicium legis probat hoc et curia legis.[25]

(What should a servant do except serve, and his son after him? You will be a simple servant, and you will lack liberty. The judgment of the law proves this and the court of law.)

The peasants had sought redress through the law and had been defeated by means of the law, and the writer appeared confident that the verdict of the law was definitive. A hundred years or so later, when *Patience* was written, matters were not so simple: the break-up of large feudal demesnes, the increasing commutation of labour services for money, the decline in personal bondage, the shortage of labour after the Black Death, all helped to produce a freer and more confident workforce. The Statute of Labourers of 1351 complained at the outset of a new recalcitrance among

---

[25] See R. H. Hilton, 'A Thirteenth-Century Poem on Disputed Villein Services', *English Historical Review*, 56 (1941), 90–7.

servants as well as about the related problem of their expensive-
ness ('la malice de servants, queux furent preciouses et nient
voillants servir apres la pestilence'), and sought by law to curb
these tendencies.[26] The statute was assiduously applied, but with
little effect. And increasingly in literature, servants who complain
and talk back to their masters begin to appear. In the Towneley
Second Shepherds' Pageant Daw, in the traditional manner of a
shepherd, complains about his condition, but here, interestingly, he
is the servant of another shepherd, Coll, who, he says, treats him
badly, though he generalizes his personal complaint in terms of
'seruandys' and 'master-men':

> Sich seruandys as I that swettys and swynkys,
> Etys oure bred full dry and that me forthynkys;
> We ar oft weytt and wery when master-men wynkys,
> Yit commys full lately both dyners and drynkys.[27]

And even after all his work, he says, his masters are likely to
reduce his wages or pay them late. He resolves to do some
work, but not too much, and amuse himself if he can while he
does it (159–67). He justifies himself with the proverb that a
cheap bargain repays badly (170–1). Like Jonah, he is reproved
for his 'janglyng' and brought to some obedience through
threats (174–6), but not totally, because later (255) he again
complains about his circumstances. The question of how one
procured the obedience of servants was clearly not only a
problem which exercised lawmakers, but also one which
interested imaginative writers as being of some contemporary
relevance, and Langland, characteristically, confronts it in a radical
and decisive manner. Those 'wasters' who refuse to help
Piers plough his half-acre are to be disciplined, not by the law
but by the logic of their own dereliction, by 'Hunger' through
crop-failure:

> And but yf he be heyliche yhuyred elles wol he chydde
> And þat he was werkeman ywrouhte warien þe tyme.

---

[26] *Statutes of the Realm*, Record Commission, II vols. (London, 1810–20), i.
311–13. The quotation is taken from p. 311. For an authoritative account of
attempts to put this legislation into effective practice see Bertha H. Putnam, *The
Enforcement of the Statute of Labourers*, Columbia Studies in the Social Sciences 85
(New York, 1970).
[27] *The Towneley Plays*, ed. A. C. Cawley and Martin Stevens, EETS ss 12
(Oxford, 1994), xiii. 154–7.

A3enes Catones consayle comseth he to gruche:
Paupertatis onus pacienter ferre memento.
And thenne a corseth þe kyng and alle þe kynges iustices,
Suche lawes to lerne, laborers to greue.
Ac whiles Hunger was here maister ther wolde non chyde,
Ne stryue a3eynes his statuyt, a lokede so sturne. (C VIII. 335–42)

The reference here to the resistance to the king and his justices, to the laws which grieve labourers, and to the 'statuyt' make it clear that Langland has in mind the concerted attempts to give substance to the legislation of 1351, to reassert the feudal and economic force of the old relationship between masters and servants. But it is obvious that Langland feels that a political and legal solution in these terms is not possible—a view which contemporary events bore out. He also seems to feel that a solution in terms of the conventional notions of morality which sustained social and political inequalities is not possible either: the schoolbook precept from Cato's *Distichs* that one should 'remember to bear patiently the burden of poverty'—a linking of patience and poverty in relation to servants—was not sufficiently compelling in the context of late fourteenth-century actualities.

The author of *Patience*, however, seems to accept a more conservative and traditional ethos: for him it is not essentially a question of whether or not servants obey their masters because he seems to assume that obedience can always be enforced, but a question of how—whether it is done through fear or through love. His view is not a unique one. In *Jacob's Well*, preserved in a manuscript of about 1440 but possibly dating from rather earlier, the following example is given in relation to the 'frelyhede'—freedom or spontaneity—of penance:

Exaumple: Thi seruaunt or thi bondeman is fals & vnkynde to the, that wyl noght serue the, but rennyth awey to thi most enemye, & serueth him, tyl thou puttyst hym in prisoun or in stokkys, & thanne he turneth to the, & seruyth the awhyle. This is for no loue but for dreed. For whenne he is lowse, sone after he rennyth awey ayen. Thou kunnyst hym no thank, for he seruyth the noght for loue.[28]

As is often the case with exempla, the potential implications of the story far outweigh the suggested moral, but the basic meaning is,

---

[28] See *Jacob's Well: An English Treatise on the Cleansing of Man's Conscience*, ed. Arthur Brandeis, EETS 115 (London, 1900), 186.

nevertheless, important. Centrally it deals with how the obedience of servants is acquired, and it refers back to the traditional binary choice—through love or through fear. In its disabused late medieval way (and the reference to putting recalcitrant servants in prison seems to go back to one of the provisions of the Statute of Labourers)[29] this passage recognizes the intrinsic unlikelihood that service may come through love, that is, through the moral and political recognition that social inequalities are the result of divinely sanctioned institutions, that lords are 'sovereyns' as God is. Obedience is not a result of 'frelyhede', in this writer's view, but of coercion. And, it seems to me, the author of *Patience* comes to something of the same conclusion. He knows that Jonah 1:9, in Jerome's version, raises the issue of the *servus* and the question of obedience—fear or love, *timeo* or *colo*, *timeo* or *diligo*—and he knows that a whole tradition of patristic authority deals with this issue. And, despite all the modernity of his presentation of Jonah as a contemporary messenger, the poet asserts the traditional lesson of an authority which is both textual and political—that the whale and the rest of God's creation may obey him 'gladly and hastily, with good herte entierly', but that men, endowed with reason and free will, are able to choose differently, and because of their natural perverseness they often do. The Ninevites, instantly, and Jonah, reluctantly and slowly, are brought to obedience like the narrator, through fear and punishment, through suffering, or the threat of it, and it is to this extent, in what the poem sets forth as wisdom, that 'pacience is a nobel poynt, þaȝ hit displese ofte' (531). But there is a whole world of reluctance and striving implicit in that word 'displese'.

[29] 'et que mesmes les servantz refusantz servir par autiele manere fuissent punys par emprisonement de lour corps, sicome en mesme lordenance est contenuz plus au playn' (*Statutes of the Realm*, i. 311). Later clauses develop this point in more specific detail.

14

From 'Ricardian Poetry' to Ricardian Studies

CHARLOTTE C. MORSE

In publishing *Ricardian Poetry*,[1] John Burrow offered the term 'Ricardian' as a replacement for the familiar 'Age of Chaucer'. As much as any recent theorist of literature, Burrow had a political agenda within English studies. By elevating Chaucer's three major contemporaries to something like parity with him and perceiving these four major Middle English poets as constituting a period, Burrow hoped to enhance the status of medieval English literature in the larger field of English literature. He wanted to garner for Ricardian poetry the recognition and something of the affection many people had for Elizabethan, Augustan, or Victorian literature and thus secure a continuing readership for Ricardian poetry. Burrow's sense of a political need to make a strong case for Ricardian poetry within the longer tradition of English literature foreshadows, while attempting to forestall, the anxiety Lee Patterson has recently expressed over the marginalization of medieval literature.[2] Guided by René Wellek's discussion of literary periodization, Burrow recognized all periodization as an artificial, provisional construct. He offered Ricardian poetry in a heuristic spirit, as a way of *focusing attention*.

After a period of resistance to using the term 'Ricardian', critics in the 1990s aiming to contextualize late fourteenth-century Eng-

---

[1] *Ricardian Poetry* (London, 1971).
[2] See 'Historical Criticism and the Development of Chaucer Studies', and 'Historical Criticism and the Claims of Humanism', in *Negotiating the Past: The Historical Understanding of Medieval Literature* (Madison 1987), 3–39, 41–74; 'Introduction: Critical Historicism and Medieval Studies', in *Literary Practice and Social Change, 1380–1530* (Berkeley and Los Angeles, 1990), 1–14; 'On the Margin: Postmodernism, Ironic History, and Medieval Studies', *Speculum*, 65 (1990), 87–108; and *Chaucer and the Subject of History* (Madison, 1991), 3–46, 423–5.

lish literature have often adopted the term. They draw on a wider array of critical theories and practices than Burrow did in *Ricardian Poetry*, but the way in which Burrow's work has exerted its force on the field is particularly evident in American criticism.

Most important to Burrow was finding a term that did not privilege Chaucer's works over the works of his major contemporaries, the *Pearl*-poet, Gower, and Langland. That so much of the most highly valued Middle English poetry should have been written almost certainly within the reign of Richard II (1377–99) seemed to invite an exploration of the relatedness of the works of these writers.[3]

Burrow excluded from his proposal for a Ricardian poetry the necessity for discovering evidence of court patronage of literature; nevertheless, *Ricardian Poetry* has sometimes been misunderstood by being too closely associated with Gervase Mathew's *The Court of Richard II*.[4] Gaps in our knowledge of the four major poets, not only with regard to court patronage, but also extending even to the name of one of them, to gross differences in the Germanic and Romance verse traditions in which they wrote, and to our almost total ignorance of personal relationships among them—Gower and Chaucer being a partial exception—make an argument for a sharply articulated periodization difficult to mount and sustain. Nevertheless, these four wrote at the beginning of the continuing tradition of high art poetry in the English language. Alliterative poets were adapting native English verse form to sophisticated and unconventional uses, while Gower and presumably Chaucer were consciously choosing to write in English rather than French or Latin, using Romance verse forms.

In the short term, Burrow persuaded only some of the twelve reviewers of *Ricardian Poetry* to be positively interested in his idea in the terms he set out. Arguably, his case has worked most

---

[3] If, as Jill Mann suggests, the A-text of *Piers Plowman* is a revised version of the B-text for a post-1381 audience with little Latin, Langland's poetic activity was more narrowly Ricardian than Burrow took it to be; see 'The Power of the Alphabet: A Reassessment of the Relations between the A and the B Versions of *Piers Plowman*', *YLS* 8 (1994), 21–50. Steven Justice dates the B-text to 1376–7 and the C-text to probably after 1388, in *Writing and Rebellion: England in 1381* (Berkeley and Los Angeles, 1994), 232 n. 130 and 231 n. 126; he offers no date for the A-text.

[4] *The Court of Richard II* (London, 1968).

persuasively when shifted away from his own commitment to formalism and the high art tradition and toward a Ricardian studies perspective. Reviewers hostile to the idea of a Ricardian poetry, in descending order of intensity, were D. Farley-Hills, John Block Friedman, Theodore Stroud, and Albert Friedman.[5] Indifferent to the idea, but interested in the comparisons, was R. M. Wilson.[6] Sympathetically intrigued by the idea, in descending order of intensity, were Valerie Lagorio, Siegfried Wenzel, M. W. Bloomfield, M. C. Seymour, A. C. Spearing, G. C. Britton, and an anonymous reviewer.[7] Believing that lesser writers usually show most clearly the characteristics of their period, some reviewers thought that selecting only four *major* Ricardian writers was an unconventional and flawed way to establish 'Ricardian' as a literary period.[8] The reviews make a good introduction both to the virtues and problems in Burrow's approach to the four major Ricardian poets and to the issue of literary periodization.

Though setting Ricardian poetry within the long high art tradition of English poetry, Burrow conceded that the Ricardians did not consistently meet certain standards that seemed to him important qualities in the high art tradition. Ricardian poets preserved informal features of the minstrel style they took over from earlier English tradition, they left their verses unpolished, they lacked Matthew Arnold's high seriousness (a function of their persistent irony), and hardly ever achieved the sublime. R. M. Wilson summed up Burrow's reluctance to overstate the case for the Ricardians: 'By comparison with the minstrels, they are masters of ironic sophistication, though if compared with their continental contemporaries they may appear to be conservative, serious, and

[5] D. Farley-Hills, *RES* NS 23 (1972), 325–7; A. Friedman, *ELN* 11 (1973), 126–8; J. B. Friedman, *JEGP* 73 (1974), 241–4; and T. Stroud, *MP* 71 (1973), 71–3.

[6] R.M Wilson, *English*, 20 (1971), 96–8, esp. 98; Wilson slightly revises his comments in *MLR* 67 (1972), 612–13, indicating more clearly his lack of hostility to the idea of a Ricardian poetry: 'Whether the author really makes out his case for a Ricardian period of poetry is immaterial; *certainly the four poets, with all their likenesses and differences, fit together as well as do the major poets of any later period*' (italics indicate the 1972 addition).

[7] M.W. Bloomfield, *Speculum*, 48 (1973), 345–7; G. C. Britton, *N&Q* 20 (1973), 29–30; V. Lagorio, *Manuscripta*, 18 (1974), 50–1; M. C. Seymour, *ES* 54 (1973), 274–5; A. C. Spearing, *Cambridge Review*, 93 (1972), 177–9; Anon., *VQR* 48 (1972), p. liii; and S. Wenzel, *MÆ* 42 (1973), 93–5.

[8] See the reviews of Britton, Farley-Hills, A. Friedman, Spearing, and Stroud, cited in nn. 5 and 7 above.

perhaps even old-fashioned'.[9] Focusing especially on the minstrel voice and on the composition of verses, Spearing offers the most sympathetic critical assessment of Burrow's account of Ricardian style: refined readers of verse, both Spearing and Burrow respect the high art tradition and the traditional English philological view of Middle English before the Ricardians as a defective medium for high art poetry.

But Seymour and several American reviewers rejected the appropriateness of a Romantic sense of the sublime and of high seriousness, both slippery terms, for judging the Ricardians, and Bloomfield directly challenged the philological standard. The *VQR* reviewer suggests that 'a too exclusive concern for surfaces' led Burrow to 'the superficial position that all of these poets... are somehow lacking in "high seriousness"'.[10] Bloomfield objected to the use of Matthew Arnold's high seriousness as a criterion of judgement, arguing that the Ricardians, especially Chaucer, are deeply serious, and that jokes and seriousness can coinhere. Resisting Burrow's hedging in of Ricardian matter and style, Seymour attributed an emotional and imaginative grandness to the agonies the reader shares with Ricardian heroes, preferring the Ricardians to 'the dreary parochialism of "grand poetry"'.[11] Most drastically, Bloomfield challenged the view of Middle English as a defective medium, conceding only Langland's difficulty with English psychological and philosophical terminology. The Anglo-German philological tradition has relentlessly pointed out line-fillers and conventional tags, consistently regarding them as defects, making it impossible for the philologically sensitized to hear such phrases as other than defects. But Bloomfield claimed that 'If the style of Ricardian poetry is "more traditional than many people realize" ([Burrow] p. 12), it must be because its users wanted it to be so'.[12]

More than style, however, is at stake in Burrow's invocation of the sublime and high seriousness. Burrow is ultimately made uneasy by Ricardian irony, achieved through ironic framing or enclosing of Ricardian narratives, with their unheroic protagonists.[13] For all his delight in the Ricardians, Burrow is bothered

---

[9] Wilson, *MLR* 67 (1974), 612; similarly, Wilson, *English*, 20 (1971), 98.
[10] *VQR* 48 (1972), p. liii.
[11] *ES* 54 (1973), 275.
[12] *Speculum*, 48 (1973), 346.
[13] From private conversations, 1968 onward.

by the way irony occludes what values or principles Ricardian poets held inviolable, if any at all. His concern finally is ethical rather than narrowly aesthetic.

Presenting his case under three main headings—style, narrative, and anthropology, or the Ricardian image of man—Burrow distinguished the major late fourteenth-century English poets as a group from their Continental peers and predecessors in order to locate what is English about Ricardian poetry. Although Burrow is keenly aware of how much the Ricardians owe to French, Latin, and Italian literature and regrets that the relationship of English to Flemish literature is so little investigated, the more difficult task seemed to him to identify what debts the Ricardians owed to earlier writing in English and what common features their poetry shared. At least partly in reaction to Burrow's English focus and formalist analysis in *Ricardian Poetry*, which seemed to her nationalistic and artificial, Elizabeth Salter was prompted to begin reformulating the history of Middle English literature. She saw no merit in narrow periodization, nor was she aware that a shift toward Ricardian studies had already begun, especially in America.[14] Several hostile reviewers of *Ricardian Poetry*—Stroud, J. B. Friedman, and Farley-Hills—had thought Burrow should have broadened the focus of the term Ricardian. Bloomfield did just that in his review, directing the idea of the Ricardian back toward the historians from whom Burrow adopted it; back, that is, toward Ricardian studies.[15]

---

[14] Salter harshly criticized *Ricardian Poetry* while naming it only in a note; see *Fourteenth-Century English Poetry: Contexts and Readings* (Oxford, 1983), 119–23 and n. 6. For the scope of the project she was engaged upon just before her death in 1980, see the introduction by Derek Pearsall and Nicolette Zeeman to the essays by Salter collected in *English and International: Studies in the Literature, Art and Patronage of Medieval England*, ed. D. Pearsall and N. Zeeman (Cambridge, 1988), pp. xi–xiii, and the new essays in Pt. I, 'An Obsession with the Continent', 1–100, even though these new essays do not cover the 14th cent. Note that Salter and Pearsall developed the Centre for Medieval Studies at the University of York, the most influential British instance of a formal medieval studies programme, subsequently directed by Alastair Minnis and Felicity Riddy.

[15] Arguably, Burrow implied Ricardian studies when he analogized a late 14th cent. historiated initial for Psalm 68 depicting Jonah with Ricardian framed narrative and associated the particular initial with *Patience*. J. B. Friedman, *JEGP* 73 (1974), finds the 'analogy . . . superficial' and corrects Burrow's claim that Jonah is a usual figure for illustrating Psalm 68 by noting that 'David in water to knees or waist' is the usual way for 'depicting the waters of tribulation which have entered the speaker's soul' (p. 243).

Like Burrow and most of the critics sympathetic to the term 'Ricardian' as an alternative to the 'Age of Chaucer', Bloomfield was not primarily a Chaucerian. His critical and scholarly work centred on *Piers Plowman* and problems in literary theory. Bloomfield denied that a common style is requisite for constituting a literary period.[16] For Bloomfield, the looser standard of a group of works of high literary value, produced in a relatively brief span of time, was sufficient to justify attending to them within the idea of a period:

Little has indeed been done on considering the period as a whole and much of this neglect has been due to differing traditions and the apparent separateness of the writers considered. What we have in these poets is the first flowering of a literary movement since Anglo-saxon times in the vernacular. In fact, there is more to this movement than that. I should like to go further than Burrow and suggest that what we have here is the literary manifestation of a kind of proto-Renaissance (which was, alas, to be soon blighted) in England in the fourteenth century, to be seen in philosophy and logic, in an interest in classics and book collecting, in music and art, in mysticism and religious devotion, in architecture and history. In short, we have a remarkable cultural upsurge in the fourteenth century in England which has not received the attention due it. It embraced three languages and a vast variety of scholars, clergy, nobility, and creative artists. As a first step toward studying this phenomenon, as well as for its own sake, this book [*Ricardian Poetry*] is welcome.[17]

Bloomfield typifies positive response to *Ricardian Poetry* in regarding it as a 'first step' and an invitation to further inquiry.[18] Even though he slides from referring to 'the period' as defined by Burrow's Ricardians to the broader 'fourteenth century', on balance he suggests an openness to the proposition of a Ricardian poetry, indeed of a Ricardian period.

Bloomfield also suggests a broader range of investigations than Burrow implied, in effect proposing Ricardian studies. Americans

---

[16] See also Wilson's two reviews (cit. n. 6 above); for a contrasting view, see Britton, *N&Q* 20 (1973), 29–30.

[17] *Speculum*, 48 (1973), 346.

[18] Seymour and the *VQR* reviewer suggested that Burrow himself should follow up his work, while Britton, Lagorio, Spearing, and Wenzel supposed that others would take up the issues Burrow posed (cf. n. 7, above); Spearing believed that *Ricardian Poetry* would start a debate and says of it: 'fourteenth-century literature is never going to look the same again' (p. 177).

have generally responded sympathetically to the translation of Ricardian poetry into Ricardian studies.

I shall consider the effect—or lack of effect—of Burrow's idea of a Ricardian period under three categories: institutional, stylistic and narratological, and historicist. Except in the case of the institutional, I shall concentrate on responses that can be deemed positive, without limiting my discussion entirely to American critics. I am not attempting a complete history of the reception of *Ricardian Poetry* but rather sketching a history from it to recent calls for what is, implicitly, Ricardian studies. I am aware that not all the works I regard as contributing to an informed sense of the Ricardian period were presented by their authors with that aim in mind, while at least one major project—Penelope Doob's *The Idea of the Labyrinth*—began with that aim, an aim that does not seem to motivate its published form.[19]

Despite Lee Patterson's identification of medieval studies with Robertsonian allegory and conservative politics,[20] the phenomenon of 'studies' in American universities, including medieval studies, is more open than he allows.[21] Modern university disciplines

---

[19] *The Idea of the Labyrinth* (Ithaca, NY, 1990). For the term 'Ricardian' see pp. 247 and 281 n. 19, in the chapters on Virgil and Dante, respectively.

[20] See the essays cited in n. 2, esp. pp. 37–44 in *Negotiating the Past*, and also L. Patterson, 'The Return to Philology', in John Van Engen (ed.), *The Past and Future of Medieval Studies* (Notre Dame, Ind., 1994), 231–44, in which Patterson recommends an encounter with medieval studies, i.e. philology, for all graduate students in literature. Patterson rejects the principle that medieval texts can only have meanings sanctioned by other medieval texts (which he associates with exegetics and medieval studies) because it commits medieval studies to an outdated positivism and puts medievalists out of contemporary literary critical discourse. He begrudges the time students spend to master skills, often taught in medieval studies programmes, that enable work in medieval languages and in manuscript studies, for they then have less time for contemporary literary criticism. Note that Patterson is currently chair of the Medieval Studies Program at Yale University (*Directory 1996* (Medieval Academy of America, 1996), 157), and that he has encouraged Ralph Hanna III in publishing his manuscript studies *Pursuing History: Middle English Manuscripts and their Texts* (Stanford, Calif., 1996); see Hanna's account of his own career, pp. vii, 1–17.

[21] For example, in a collection of essays marked by contributions from the 'medieval clerisy' (Patterson's term) and directed to students, Paul Theiner takes an open and sanguine view of both past and present in 'Medieval English Literature', in James M. Powell (ed.), *Medieval Studies: An Introduction*, 2nd edn. (Syracuse, NY, 1992), 278–313. Patterson, however, in 'On the Margin', 102, describes the 'apprenticeship' of training in research techniques as 'servitude within a patriarchal system' and regards medieval studies as having 'traditionally policed itself with the spector Error'. For a statement on medieval studies to which Patter-

had hardly established themselves as traditional before Americans began organizing cross-disciplinary perspectives under the rubric of 'studies'—medieval studies, American studies, and the list goes on. The Medieval Academy of America, founded in the 1920s, was born of an early impulse to cross-disciplinary conversation. Nevertheless, American university teachers almost always identify first with a traditional discipline, and they research and write for that discipline, even when they also participate in cross-disciplinary configurations of teachers and courses. Relatively few institutions offer Ph.D.s in medieval studies. In many instances, students take their degrees in conventional disciplines, with a certificate in medieval studies. The effect of a 'studies' perspective is not monolithic, nor need it be innocent of theory.[22]

Generalizing about national traditions almost certainly exaggerates differences, but modest caricature, like a cartoon, may defuse irritation and intolerance if it elicits a faint shock of recognition. British critics, at least those of the generation of Burrow, Salter, and Seymour, judge literary works by criteria ultimately based on taste, while post-Second World War American critics of all but contemporary literature hardly ever judge overtly the quality of the works they study. Not surprisingly, 'studies' encourage analysis, explanation, and interpretation over judgement, an approach comfortable to many Americans. Since the Second World War,

son would take exception, see Eleanor Searle, 'Possible History', *Speculum*, 61 (1986), 779–86.

[22] Anne Middleton takes a tart view of the effects of the post-war American institutionalization of medieval studies, particularly on the writing of medieval English literary history, and challenges scholar-critics to accept the necessity of reflecting on the theory that undergirds their critical practices, in 'Medieval Studies', in Stephen Greenblatt and Giles Gunn (eds.), *Redrawing the Boundaries: The Transformation of English and American Literary Studies* (New York, 1992), 12–40. The isolation of medievalists that she describes can also be seen as part of a growing tendency of fragmentation in English studies into period-specific studies and societies. The Medieval Academy's *Directory 1996* lists 72 North American members of CARA (the Committee for Centers and Regional Associations). Of these, thirty, including Notre Dame, the Pontifical Institute, and Yale, supplied no details of their programmes. Upwards of twenty members grant only B.A. or M.A. [Bachelor's or Master's] degrees in fields connected with medieval studies. Of the forty-three programmes supplying information, some eleven sponsor faculty discussion groups, symposia, lectures or workshops, but no degree programmes; twenty-seven offer major and /or minor concentrations in medieval studies for the B.A., eleven offer minors or certificates for the Ph.D. and eight offer a Ph.D. in medieval studies. The *Directory* will be updated online; see http://www.georgetown.edu/Medieval Academy/.

American universities have fostered a sense that a struggle to convince one's peers of one's solution or position lies at the heart of research: in this general context, American literary critics have produced and preferred as interpretations and explanations fully articulated arguments, with theses and demonstrations. Americans have been bemused by a kind of British criticism that offers leisurely commentary, marked by sometimes brilliant *aperçus*, but no argument; British critics have felt assaulted by the kind of American criticism that pushes its argument too far or maintains it too rigidly or too comprehensively. Americans tend to favour grand interpretative schemes, to embrace theoretical criticism enthusiastically (even if some medievalists in English literature have been slow to do so), and to want to connect medieval criticism to wider discourses on literature and culture. 'Brilliant', 'interesting' (meaning 'intriguing' rather than 'of no interest'), 'provocative', 'convincing' are American terms of praise; 'sound', a term favoured in British circles and among historians, is rarely heard among American literary critics, except with regard to editions. While British critics have tended to find *Ricardian Poetry* valuable for particular formal analyses and for discreet comparisons among the poets, American critics, even when not admitting a debt to Burrow, have more often engaged the idea of Ricardian poetry or Ricardian studies.

That Burrow's concept of Ricardian poetry has not eventuated in a Society for Ricardian Poetry is, however, a fact, perhaps a lamentable fact. Instead, atomistically, there is a society, or something like it, for each of the four major Ricardian poets. Each one, though organized in America, has reached toward an international constituency, unlike older American societies, and most are led by British as well as American scholars. The New Chaucer Society, launched by Paul Ruggiers, held its first conference and published its first annual volume of *Studies in the Age of Chaucer* in 1979, enshrining in that title the very term, the Age of Chaucer, that Burrow had wished to replace. The New Chaucer Society is now the best established and wealthiest of the Ricardian societies. R. F. Yeager organized the Gower Society in 1982, adopting the International Congress of Medieval Studies, usually called by its meeting-place, Kalamazoo, as the venue for annual sessions and now awarding the John H. Fisher annual prize. With A. J. Minnis as British secretary, the Gower Society maintains a membership list, collects modest dues, and publishes a newsletter with information about current Gower scholarship. The *Pearl*-Poet Society, which remains a rather informal group, without newsletter, dues, or list of members, began sponsoring sessions at Kalamazoo in 1989, Kalamazoo having long served as a regular meeting-place for those interested in discussing all the works probably by this poet.[23] The Langland Conference, as I suppose it must be called, began from John Alford's decision to publish, through his own press, from 1987, the *Yearbook of Langland Studies*. The first international conference, organized by Alford and James Simpson, was held at Cambridge in 1993; there are loose plans for a second conference.

The New Chaucer Society has, both in its conference and in its publication, proved too narrowly devoted to Chaucer to absorb the scholarly and critical interests of the diverse constituency potentially invoked by the 'Age of Chaucer'.[24] How different would our academic associations be if we occasionally met, configured into a Ricardian Society, as Burrow might advocate? Were something like that to happen, it would almost certainly come from the pressure of Langlandians. For example, James Simpson, Elizabeth Robertson, and C. David Benson won sponsorship from the National Endowment for the Humanities to offer, in the summer of 1995 at the University of Colorado, a Chaucer–Langland Institute.

Langlandian Anne Middleton is one of the few medievalists who was not chary of using the term 'Ricardian'.[25] Indeed, the idea of

[23] In response to changes to the way the Kalamazoo Congress itself is run, Janet Gilligan in 1985 led the formal movement to organize, aided by the regular Kalamazoo supporters of work on the *Pearl*-poet, Robert J. Blanch, Liam O. Purdon, and Julian N. Wasserman. At first, the director of the Institute of Medieval Studies at Western Michigan University, sponsor of the congress, had created the programme by combining papers submitted to him into sessions, but by the mid-1980s responsibility for organizing sessions was shifting to societies and organizers of special projects, e.g. Festschriften. Blanch and Wasserman acknowledge the importance of Kalamazoo discussions in the development of their study *From 'Pearl' to 'Gawain': Forme to Fynisment* (Gainesville, Fla., 1995); the large Green Knight on the end-flap of the book-jacket reminds us of the largely unexplored role of Ricardian literature in popular culture.

[24] The habit of the New Chaucer Society of inviting historians (among them Caroline Barron and Eamon Duffy) to participate in its conferences gestures toward Ricardian studies; the first Langland conference also invited a historian to participate (Christopher Dyer).

[25] 'The Idea of Public Poetry in the Reign of Richard II', *Speculum*, 53 (1978), 94–114. At about the same time as Middleton accepted the term 'Ricardian' in her

Ricardian poetry authorized as well as inspired her broad stylistic investigation of the public voice of Ricardian poetry. Like Bloomfield, Middleton took the idea of 'Ricardian poetry' to be an invitation to a certain kind of medieval studies project:

The term implies a willingness to seek broad connections between social and literary history, rather than the 'influence' of one writer upon another. Unlike the earlier phrase, 'the age of Chaucer,' the notion of a 'Ricardian period' in literature enables Burrow to identify some common themes and features of style as characteristic of the era, without subordinating other writers' achievements to either the stylistic preferences or the idiosyncrasies of personal development of its crowning genius. The shift in perspective that follows this simple change of names has already been salutary for Chaucer criticism, as well as for the understanding of his major contemporaries, each of whom can be seen to have a coherent sense of his purpose, his audience and his world.[26]

In the essay that follows this introduction, Middleton sets out to identify and explore the mode of public poetry, as practised by Gower, Langland, and, with qualifications, Chaucer, a 'poetry defined by a constant relation of speaker to audience within an ideally conceived worldly community, a relation which has become the poetic subject'.[27] The voice of this poetry is a common voice, not noble or minstrel or clerical, but a middle voice, speaking (usually) in a plain style, deeply concerned with general ethical issues and with the common good, committed to peace. Because Amans and Will share a common (and unavoidable) vantage point with their audiences and articulate their common questions about life without being able to answer them, Middleton calls them implicated speakers. Theirs is 'the voice... [that] rivals the pedagogical progress, which in both cases forms the "plot," as a locus of meaning'; further, this 'voice of worldly experience and need acts as a critique of the encyclopedic mode of instruction', as the

critical vocabulary, so did Stephen Medcalf in England; see 'On Reading Books from a Half-Alien Culture', in S. Medcalf (ed.), *The Later Middle Ages, The Context of English Literature* (London, 1981), 1–55, esp. 38–41. While the term has not often been used in literary histories, Alastair Fowler speaks of 'the Ricardian effloresence' and calls the period that follows 'low pressure' in *A History of English Literature* (Cambridge, Mass., 1987), 22. More significantly, Andrew Sanders uses the term 'Ricardian' to introduce the literature of the last decades of the 14th cent., in *The Short Oxford History of English Literature* (Oxford, 1994), 47.

[26] 'The Idea of Public Poetry', 94.
[27] Ibid. 95.

instructors in both poems prove 'on the whole [to be] a remarkably inept lot and not especially well disposed to help the seeker'.[28]

Middleton's broadly stylistic analysis values the public voice of Ricardian poetry, which differentiates Ricardian from earlier medieval voices, over the plot. Penelope Doob's aesthetic of difficult poetry finds a way to conjoin something like Middleton's implicated voice with a plot at once circular and linear, i.e. labyrinthine, to account for a relationship of voice and plot that is especially characteristic of medieval dream vision poetry. Although Doob worked out the labyrinthine aesthetic to describe Ricardian poetry, she treats extensively only *The House of Fame* in *Idea of the Labyrinth*.[29] While demonstrating that the labyrinth is implied in Dante's *Commedia*, Doob suggests that it also informs 'circular' Ricardian poems, such as *Sir Gawain and the Green Knight*, *Pearl*, *Piers Plowman*, and *The Canterbury Tales*: 'Most structurally labyrinthine literature . . . is characterized by . . . a narrative pattern [that fuses circular with linear movement]: one achieves transcendent understanding *and* returns to the place from which one started, in some sense at least knowing that place for the first time'.[30] Doob implies a way of thinking about Middleton's 'public voice' that links style and narrative in the labyrinthine aesthetic.

In three other essays, one apparently written before *Ricardian Poetry*, Middleton describes Chaucer's exploitation of something like the public voice, mediated through the voices of Chaucer's 'new men', his several pilgrim narrators the Franklin, the Man of Law, the Squire, the Monk, and, above all, the Clerk, to whom Middleton devotes an extended treatment to argue his congruence with Chaucer himself.[31] The 'new men', who resemble the 'new men' of Elizabethan-Jacobean criticism in their professionalism, competitiveness, and non-noble status, tell tales that are sententious but without moral designs on the audience; they find the good of literature in its worldliness, in pleasurable free play of the

---

[28] Ibid. 110.

[29] *Idea of the Labyrinth*, 307–39.

[30] Ibid. 281 and n. 19.

[31] 'The *Physician's Tale* and Love's Martyrs: "Ensamples Mo Than Ten" as a Method in the *Canterbury Tales*', ChauR 8 (1973), 9–32; 'Chaucer's "New Men" and the Good of Literature in the *Canterbury Tales*', in Edward W. Said (ed.), *Literature and Society*, Selected Papers from the English Institute, 1978, NS 3 (Baltimore, 1980), 15–56; and 'The Clerk and his Tale: Some Literary Contexts', SAC 2 (1980), 121–50.

mind, and 'in the virtues required to derive pleasure from it: the capacity for wonder, sympathy, and thoughtful speculation'.[32] In the tales of the 'new men' Chaucer writes as a poet, 'enditing' for readers rather than 'writing' or 'making' to accommodate the social situation of the court entertainer. What began in 'Public Poetry' as a tentative association of 'new men' with 'middle class/bourgeois' becomes virtual identity in the later essays. Middleton elevates the word 'endite,' a commonplace rhyme with 'write' in Old French and Middle English (ecriter/enditer, write/endite), to the status of a critical term for the way the 'new men' write.[33] Middleton's characterization of the 'new men' has deeply influenced recent Chaucer criticism, as critics, assuming Middleton's socio-political definition of Chaucer's narrators, interpret the tales in ways consistent with such narrators or contest Middleton's view of the narrators.[34]

Middleton's arguments are responsive to Ricardian texts in imaginative ways. I doubt, however, that Chaucer was using 'endite' to distinguish sharply the writing of a poet from the writing of a maker;[35] I share with R. F. Green a sense that 'bourgeois' and 'middle class' are inadequate and misleading terms in the Ricardian period;[36] and I have considerable reservations about Middleton's interpretations of the Clerk.[37] Middleton does not use the term 'Ricardian' in her essays on Chaucer, but it seems clear that her attempt to characterize Chaucer's 'new men' is related to, if distinct from, her characterization of the public voice of Gower and Langland. She has challenged critics to think about the con-

---

[32] 'Chaucer's "New Men"', 16.

[33] Ibid. 24–7, 39, 46–7, 50–1.

[34] John M. Ganim, for example, repositions the Franklin, the Squire, and the Clerk: 'If any of the pilgrims represent the creation of a new voice, it is these pilgrims, yet that voice must articulate itself against not so much the styles of aristocratic culture, with which it may politely debate, but also and more inchoately the forms of popular and folk life.' *Chaucerian Theatricality* (Princeton, 1990), 94.

[35] Note, however, that R. F. Yeager for one, in *John Gower's Poetic: The Search for a New Arion*, Publications of the John Gower Society 2 (Cambridge, 1990), 97–8, accepts the distinction, applying it to *Confessio Amantis*, Prol. 12–24; see also David Burnley's more cautious discussion of the term, *A Guide to Chaucer's Language* (London, 1983), 161–2.

[36] *Poets and Princepleasers: Literature and the English Court in the Late Middle Ages* (Toronto, 1980), 9–10.

[37] See my 'Exemplary Griselda', SAC 7 (1985), 51–86.

stitution of Ricardian voices and the implications of our critical constructions.

In contrast to Middleton's broad sense of style as voice, Yeager invites readers of *John Gower's Poetic: The Search for the New Arion* to enter into the Ricardian situation, to imagine the momentous task Gower set for himself: to create a regular verse in English.[38] Using metrical and stylistic analysis, Yeager shows Gower able to make regular verse and, at his best, to make it effective, and able to exploit the medium of octosyllabic couplets, using his erudition and linguistic facility to thicken his verse with puns and *rime riche*. Yeager treats all of Gower's works, always sensitive to the poetry and concerned to elucidate Gower's aims as a composer. Attentive to Gower's wide use of sources, Yeager situates him with respect to the tradition of classical *auctores*, explains some of Gower's more puzzling conjunctions of materials, and finally claims Gower's *Confessio Amantis* as the product of a highly self-conscious artist. Yeager's study complements Minnis's claim for Gower as an *auctor*.[39]

In an analysis of love contained in a dream vision that is ordered by the seven deadly sins of the penitential tradition, Gower tells lurid stories to support married love and permits his guide Genius,

---

[38] *John Gower's Poetic*, 4–44. There has been intense interest in the metrics of alliterative verse as well; see Thomas Cable, *The English Alliterative Tradition* (Philadelphia, 1991), and Hoyt N. Duggan, e.g. 'The Shape of the B-Verse in Middle English Alliterative Poetry', *Speculum*, 61 (1986), 564–92; 'Alliterative Patterning as a Basis for Emendation in Middle English Alliterative Poetry', *SAC* 8 (1986), 73–105; and 'Final *-e* and the Rhythmic Structure of the B-Verse in Middle English Alliterative Poetry', *MP* 86 (1988), 119–45. These critics discover, from different beginning points, constraints on the composition of b-verses, implying, in effect, a degree of formal self-consciousness in alliterative poets which puts them closer to Gower and Chaucer than was once supposed. For discussions of Cable and Duggan, see Ralph Hanna III, 'Defining Middle English Alliterative Poetry', and Stephen A. Barney, 'Langland's Prosody: The State of Study', both in M. Teresa Tavormina and R. F. Yeager (eds.), *The Endless Knot: Essays on Old and Middle English in Honor of Marie Borroff* (Cambridge, 1995), 43–64, 65–85.

[39] 'Authors in Love: The Exegesis of Late-Medieval Love-Poets', in C. C. Morse, P. R. Doob, and M. C. Woods (eds.), *The Uses of Manuscripts in Literary Studies: Essays in Memory of Judson Boyce Allen*, Studies in Medieval Culture 31 (Kalamazoo, Mich., 1992), 161–91, esp. 171–6; '*De Vulgari Auctoritate*: Chaucer, Gower and the Men of Great Authority', in R. F. Yeager (ed.), *Chaucer and Gower: Difference, Mutuality, Exchange*, English Literary Studies, University of Victoria, 51 (Victoria, 1991), 36–74; and '"Moral Gower" and Medieval Literary Theory', in A. J. Minnis (ed.), *Gower's 'Confessio Amantis': Responses and Reassessments* (Cambridge, 1983), 50–78.

the priest of Venus, to include a mirror for princes in answer to the request of the dreamer Amans, the lover who is finally revealed as the old John Gower himself. Gower's consciousness of himself as a poet and his attitude to and complex treatment of love suggest that comparison of his work with Christine de Pizan's would be rewarding, not only for distinguishing the Ricardians but for exploring constructions of gender.[40] The only major Ricardian woman writer, Julian of Norwich, wrote in prose and in traditions of spiritual writing different from the poets. Julian ought to be included amongst the Ricardians, even if only her visions and the early version of her work fall into Richard's reign.[41] The exemplum, central to Gower and to Christine, invites comparison between them, while Julian and Christine offer some evidence of women's constructions of gender in the Ricardian era.

Burrow identified the exemplum as a major form in Ricardian narrative and characterized its mode as exemplary, thus increasing pressure for further study of the exemplum. The work of J. B. Allen and of Minnis in medieval literary theory confirms the dominance of the exemplary mode in late medieval literature, while Larry Scanlon has used Burrow's analysis of Ricardian narrative to launch his investigation into the exemplum in the Chaucerian tradition.[42] Even the best literary critical work on the exemplum before Scanlon seemed thin: formalist criticism seems to stop too short to give a satisfactory explanation for the power and appeal of medieval exempla. Making spirited use of Marxist,

---

[40] Both Gower and Christine supervised manuscript productions of their works; both claimed, and indeed Christine really had, high aristocratic patronage; both supported ethical rectitude and married love; and both were antipathetic to Jean de Meun (see Yeager, *John Gower's Poetic*, 70–6, esp. n. 73). In her *Trésor de la cité des dames* (*The Book of the Treasure of the City of Ladies, or The Book of the Three Virtues*, tr. Sarah Lawson (Harmondsworth, 1985)), Christine suggests that courtly love games were all too frequently played out in women's lives, always putting them at greater risk than the men who talked 'luf talk'. For a suggestive comparison of Christine and Gower, see Maureen Quilligan, *The Allegory of Female Authority: Christine de Pizan's 'Cité des dames'* (Ithaca, NY, 1991), 37–8.

[41] Nicholas Watson uses Julian's (early) Short Version as the basis of his essay '"Yf wommen be double naturelly": Remaking "Woman" in Julian of Norwich's *Revelation of Love*', *Exemplaria*, 8 (1996), 1–34, while Grace M. Jantzen has recently placed Julian's work in a revised interpretation of Christian mystical traditions, in *Power, Gender and Christian Mysticism*, Cambridge Studies in Ideology and Religion 8 (Cambridge, 1995).

[42] *Narrative, Authority, and Power: The Medieval Exemplum and the Chaucerian Tradition*, Cambridge Studies in Medieval Literature 20 (Cambridge, 1994).

deconstructionist, Bakhtinian, and Foucauldian theory, Scanlon shows how narrative example mediates between authority and power. He traces the double tradition of sermon and public exempla; he claims for Ricardian lay writers Chaucer and Gower and their immediate successors, especially Hoccleve and Lydgate, the appropriation of clerical authority. Indeed, Scanlon challenges conventional periodization, linking the later Middle Ages with the Renaissance as the time of a shift from clerical to lay authority. At the same time, he sharpens our view of the generational difference between the Ricardians Chaucer and Gower and the Lancastrians Hoccleve and Lydgate, showing what the younger poets did not have to do, what they could assume, and how that affects the poetry they write.

Perhaps it is inevitable that the major comparisons between one Ricardian poet and another will usually involve Chaucer. Certainly that is the case in Yeager's study as a result of his attention to Romance verse forms, while Seth Lerer's work on fifteenth-century poetry keeps the Age-of-Chaucer juggernaut rolling.[43] Chaucer and Gower are intrinsically linked by their shared project to accommodate English to Romance verse traditions, but also because these two poets evidently talked to each other, read each other's work, and shaped their poetic identities in a similar social environment. Comparisons of Langland with Chaucer are driven mostly by extrinsic circumstances: students coming fresh to Ricardian literature are likely to read Chaucer before any of the others (except perhaps *Sir Gawain and the Green Knight*), so that Chaucer's work becomes a reference point for Langland's, as it often does in James Simpson's *'Piers Plowman': An Introduction to the B-Text*.[44] Comparative study of these two poets seems to have just begun, despite the encouragement of *Ricardian Poetry*.

The most diverse of my categories is the historical, for here I propose to treat several of the issues involved in articulating a Ricardian period: first, the fifteenth-century constitution of the

---

[43] *Chaucer and his Readers: Imagining the Author in Late-Medieval England* (Princeton, 1993).

[44] (London, 1990). Simpson uses the Franklin's Tale to illustrate the high demands of 'truthe', central to Holy Church's sermon, 37–8; uses 'the fox's plan to capture the cock' in the Nun's Priest's Tale to illustrate the deliberative power of Ymaginatif, 103; uses the tavern scene at the beginning of the Pardoner's Tale to illustrate the common conjunction of the professions of waferer and minstrel, 157.

Ricardian as a literary period and the varying fates of Ricardian poets; second, the role of the court in patronage and poetry; third, the contextualizing of Ricardian poetry in contemporary anticlerical or royal and city politics; and fourth, the effect of periodization in studies of the subject. How Ricardian poets have been conceived, to what contexts—aesthetic, spiritual, political—their works responded (however indirectly), and with what concerns of their immediate audiences those works resonated, cannot be separated from the analysis of the subject in the last decades of the fourteenth-century, the current inflection of Burrow's final topic in *Ricardian Poetry*, the Ricardian 'image of man'. Localizing whenever we can the conditions that shaped the material and imaginative production of Ricardian poetry is not the only work of criticism, but it is surely important work.

The earliest case for regarding late fourteenth-century English poets, Chaucer and Gower at least, as constituting a literary period derives from fifteenth-century poets' praise and imitation of them. P. M. Kean for Chaucer and then Spearing for the Ricardians, especially Chaucer and Gower, have shown how fifteenth-century poets are indebted to the Ricardians, whose sense of themselves as poets Spearing traces to the Italian trecento, especially Dante. But for there to be a literary tradition in a language, it must be self-consciously evoked: that is what fifteenth-century poets do for the Ricardians, whom Spearing sees as the first generation of English poets (after the Anglo-Saxons) who consciously participate in the high art tradition of English (and European) poetry.[45] Making extensive use of recent work on manuscripts, much of it by British scholars, Lerer articulates several stages in the fifteenth-century reception and reaction to Chaucer, perhaps too cleverly schematizing Chaucer's earlier fifteenth-century poet-readers as, at once, subjected writers, ineffectual sons, and infantilized readers, sharply distinguishing these poets from Chaucer's 'Ricardian' generation.[46]

---

[45] P. M. Kean, *Chaucer and the Making of English Poetry* (London 1972), ii. 210–39; and A. C. Spearing, *Medieval to Renaissance in English Poetry* (Cambridge, 1985), 33–4, 59–120, 243. Spearing argues that the Ricardian poets lack self-consciousness of working in a tradition or of constituting one, and so does not endorse 'Ricardian' as a literary period. Note also Scanlon's treatment of Hoccleve and Lydgate, in *Narrative, Authority, and Power*, 298–350.

[46] *Chaucer and his Readers*, 15: 'The cultivation of a Chaucer cult, and in turn of the literary politics of Ricardian England, is a form of ... nostalgia [for a politically

Burrow himself had observed how different are the histories of reception of the four major Ricardians, with the *Pearl*-poet having had the least effect, being the least known. Gower was important in the high art tradition for two centuries, but after that his influence faded away. The direct influence of all Ricardians on the writing of poetry faded as the seventeenth century wore on (the Romantics really preferred the mostly fifteenth-century Chauceriana), though both Chaucer and Langland have influenced prose fiction. Only they have enjoyed nearly continuous readerships, usually thought of as sharply differentiated readerships, with Chaucer the choice of poets and readers in the high art tradition and Langland—admittedly with some of Chaucer's tales and apocrypha, especially in the sixteenth century—the choice of readers in radical Protestant traditions. But Linda Georgianna has destabilized this construction of dichotomous audiences for Chaucer and Langland by showing that criticism of Chaucer's work is more heavily marked by Protestant interpretations than is usually acknowledged. Some of them, cut loose from their Protestant moorings, recur in contemporary commentary on Chaucer.[47] Georgianna's work implies that the orientation of most literary history to the high art tradition has obscured an important alternative way of assessing the legacy of the Ricardians.

To many British scholars and to Burrow himself, whether the Ricardian poets could be said to have enjoyed court patronage seemed important in judging whether they were court poets and thus properly 'Ricardian' poets. Papers originally read at the Colston Research Society Symposium, Bristol, 1981, suggested that court patronage of literature, or indeed of arts other than those linked to fashion and ornament, was not much practised in Richard's court.[48] But, as Burrow ruefully noted in his introduc-

hegemonous and artistically glistening past]: a fantasy for a past world in which kings govern, courts patronize, and poets live as "laureates" under their munificent rule'; also 63, 84. Though Lerer may intend to restrict the term 'Ricardian' to the historical domain, his use of it, in the context of his argument, conveys the double sense of historical period and literary period.

[47] 'The Protestant Chaucer', in C. David Benson and Elizabeth Robertson (eds.), *Chaucer's Religious Tales* (Cambridge, 1990), 55–69.

[48] V. J. Scattergood and J. W. Sherborne (eds.), *English Court Culture in the Later Middle Ages* (London, 1983). See J. W. Sherborne, 'Aspects of English Court Culture', 1–27, esp. 15–16 on clothing and ornament; and V. J. Scattergood, 'Literary Culture at the Court of Richard II', 29–43, for a negative assessment of the effect of Richard and the magnates on courtly fashions in literature.

tion, the Colston participants had blurred the question of court patronage by clarifying the shifting constituency of the court.[49] Colston participant R. F. Green in his *Poets and Princepleasers* explains institutions of the English court and provides evidence for books and writers there during the later Middle Ages, of which there is scarcely any for the Ricardian period. But Green also notes that the chamber accounts, the most likely to contain records of payments to writers, are missing for virtually the whole period, nor are there inventories of the royal library.[50]

Records for seigneurial households are also sparse in England, but recently Ralph Hanna III has reconstructed an account of Berkeley's patronage of John Trevisa. Trevisa performed normal clerical tasks as well as translating the *Polychronicon* (1387), *De regimine principum*, and *De proprietatibus rerum* (1398) during a spell when Thomas Berkeley, securely wealthy as a result of his marriage and his policy of converting feudal obligations to money rents, had no royal appointments, i.e. governmental duties.[51] Berkeley promoted the dissemination of Trevisa's works by taking them to London for copying, and by his example stimulated others to support works of translation. While provincial magnate patronage has often been assumed in the creation of Middle English literature, it has, as Hanna says, 'resisted localization'.[52] Whether other cases can be reconstructed, Hanna's model serves as an important example of how late fourteenth-century literary patronage could operate.

Whether the Ricardian poets wrote courtly poetry and, if so, which of their works constitute courtly poetry, remains an issue. A comprehensively rhetorical criticism would treat both author and audience as well as text and would attempt to perceive the interests of both the producers and the consumers of literature. Because the most important records for discerning court patronage are lost, critics must use more indirect methods, including the poems themselves and other historical data. Minnis introduces Chaucer's shorter poems by reviewing the evidence of Chaucer's court relationships to make a strong case for a courtly poetry, which his

[49] Scattergood and Sherborne (eds.), *English Court Culture*, p. ix.
[50] *Poets and Princepleasers*, 5–6.
[51] 'Sir Thomas Berkeley and his Patronage', *Speculum*, 64 (1989), 878–916 (esp. pp. 891–2).
[52] Ibid. 878.

readings of the shorter poems support.[53] Michael J. Bennett has attempted to associate the *Gawain* manuscript with Cheshire, whence Richard II drew his most loyal retainers, and has suggested Richard's Christmas and New Year celebration at Lichfield in 1398–9 as a plausible context for a reading of *Sir Gawain and the Green Knight*.[54] Gower's claim that Richard II invited him to write the *Confessio Amantis* and Gower's dedications, first to Richard and later to Henry, earl of Derby (Henry IV), suggest that Gower conceived of himself as writing for the court, though critics continue to find the significance of both the claim and the dedications perplexing.

Such perplexity is in part a function of how court poetry is defined. Patterson, for example, does not hesitate to admit that there was a court poetry in the late Edwardian and Ricardian courts, beginning with Jean Froissart's service to Queen Philippa, 1361–*c*.1369, but defines its nature narrowly. Patterson draws upon analyses of Old French courtly lyric and Glending Olson's distinction between making and poetry to describe court poetry: it is a form of aristocratic play that transforms words into 'elegant discursive artifice', but cannot analyse or criticize court values and cannot represent the subject in history.[55] In Patterson's view, Chaucer does not move beyond court poetry until *The Canterbury Tales*, conceived after his own career was disturbed by political events of the late 1380s and written in reaction against the demands of court poetry. Both Middleton and Patterson identify

---

[53] *The Shorter Poems*, Oxford Guides to Chaucer (Oxford, 1995), 9–35.

[54] 'The Court of Richard II and the Promotion of Literature', in Barbara A. Hanawalt (ed.), *Chaucer's England: Literature in Historical Context*, Medieval Studies at Minnesota 4 (Minneapolis, 1992), 3–20, esp. 13–14. However, Hanna, citing another of Bennett's articles, has rejected his theory of a Cheshire origin for author or scribe; see 'Defining Middle English Alliterative Poetry', 56 n. 39. With special reference to *Pearl*, a more subtle argument regarding Richard II's Cheshire connections has been developed by John M. Bowers, '*Pearl* in its Royal Setting: Ricardian Poetry Revisited', *SAC* 17 (1995), 111–55, and 'The Politics of *Pearl*', *Exemplaria*, 7 (1995), 419–41.

[55] *Chaucer and the Subject of History*, 53, 58, and more generally 22–6, 32–9, 47–61. Patterson places 'Chaucer's explorations' of the 'dialectical relationship between the subject and history' in a Ricardian context, 10–12. See also L. Patterson, 'Court Politics and the Invention of Literature: The Case of Sir John Clanvowe', in David Aers (ed.), *Culture and History 1350–1600: Essays on English Communities, Identities and Writing* (New York, 1992), 7–41. On making and poetry, see Glending Olson, 'Making and Poetry in the Age of Chaucer', *CL* 31 (1979), 272–90; Olson's distinctions also inform Middleton's work, cited in n. 31 above.

Ricardian poets as bourgeois, a characterization Green and Minnis reject as virtually meaningless in the Ricardian era. Middleton explains the 'new men' as merely playing with aristocratic values, but without interest in enforcing them; Patterson argues that only outside the court is it possible to be critical of it.[56] By contrast, Scanlon recognizes a broadly defined and slightly expanding ruling class in later medieval England that would include the four poets he discusses. Evidence of courtly interest in mirrors for princes, the genre through which Scanlon focuses his investigation of the exemplum, makes him favour an inclusive conception of court poetry, while his explanation of the ideological function of exempla does not make them ineffectual.[57]

Unlike the other Ricardians, who seem to have written at least sometimes from within or for the court, whether royal, seigneurial, or clerical, Langland wrote fiction that seems to emanate from a position opposed to the court and markedly critical of the institutional Church.[58] The satire in *Piers Plowman* has long inspired historical investigation concerned with localizing its satiric thrusts, encouraging attention to the Peasant's Revolt and to anticlerical satire. The revolt links the work of Langland and Gower, though their attitudes are different, but because Chaucer mentions it only in the Nun's Priest's Tale, VII (B²) 3393–7, it has had less effect than it might in supporting a Ricardian period. Steven Justice's work on the rebels' writing may, however, change that. He shows how the rebels used Langland's work and also how their use motivated revisions in the C-text. What he discovers about the language and issues of the revolt provokes him to read the Nun's Priest's Tale as incorporating hilarious allusions to Gower and his response to the Peasants' Revolt, the *Vox clamantis*.[59]

---

[56] Patterson is influenced by Marxism but identifies himself as a liberal humanist (see 'The Claims of Humanism', 45–57, 71–4; in British terms, closer to social Fabianism). Reviewing *Chaucer and the Subject of History*, Valerie Allen and Ares Axiotis remark: 'Paradoxically, Patterson's economic motif [the emergence of a rising mercantile class] has been divested of any remnant of Marxist intention. The *oiko-nomia* ... becomes just one more code alongside others whose meanings are to be juxtaposed without explanatory ultimacy' (*RES* NS 45 (1994), 411).

[57] *Narrative, Authority, and Power*, 141–5 and *passim*.

[58] For Langland's apparent dissimilarities from Burrow's other major Ricardians, see Spearing's review, cit. in n. 7, above.

[59] Justice, *Writing and Rebellion*, 213–24; see also Scanlon, *Narrative, Authority, and Power*, 241–2. Harry Brent links Chaucer's authoritarian politics in the Clerk's Tale and the lyric 'Lak of Stedfastness' to the Peasant's Revolt through the issue of sovereignty, in 'And Gladly Teche: "Stedfastnesse" in the *Clerk's Tale* and in

Like Patterson, Justice regards *The Canterbury Tales* as a consequence of Chaucer's move away from the court, but sees the
main effect of the revolt as parallel to its effect on Langland: it
compelled them to be aware of how variously and even unpredic-
tably audiences can read. Chaucer inscribes a variety of responses
to his tales into the frame narrative, which at the least attempt to
predict, perhaps aim to control or to acknowledge with satiric
intention, the range of responses. Ricardian poetry does, often
quite openly, invite without seeming to control audience response,
a risk that, in Justice's view, Langland took with no thought of the
particular pain he would suffer as others used his words and his
Piers for their own needs. Making the audience responsible for
interpretation, as Ricardian poetry so often does, through allegory,
irony, and a resistance to closure, creates a sense of open-
endedness that is not, however, exclusively a feature of Ricardian
poetry. Rather, Thomas Reed would argue, the ubiquity of debate
in medieval institutions had long since resulted in a tradition of
debate poetry that eschews resolution.[60]

To best appreciate ironists and satirists, readers need information, and that is what recent work on Langland's anticlericalism
and on Wycliffism, both implicated in the Peasant's Revolt, supplies. Wendy Scase has now anchored the anticlerical satire in *Piers*
in late fourteenth century transformations of several earlier anticlerical discourses,[61] satire that was once explained through the
tradition of antifraternal satire in its later thirteenth-century Parisian form, when the focus of attack was clearly the friars.[62] By
the Ricardian era charges could be directed against almost bewil-
deringly various combinations of groups as well as against all
clerics; the latter, Scase says, 'was the essential strength and danger
of the new anticlericalism'.[63] Scase reads *Piers* as informed by and

the Pedagogy of Charlton Laird', in Philip C. Boardman (ed.), *The Legacy of
Language: A Tribute to Charlton Laird* (Reno, Nev., 1987), 1–19 (esp. pp. 7–8,
11–12).

[60] *Middle English Debate Poetry and the Aesthetics of Irresolution* (Columbia,
Mo., and London, 1990). Reed treats *The Parliament of Fowls* on 294–362 and *Sir
Gawain* on 385–418.

[61] *'Piers Plowman' and the New Anticlericalism*, Cambridge Studies in Medieval
Literature 4 (Cambridge, 1989).

[62] See e.g. Penn Szittya, *The Antifraternal Tradition in Medieval Literature*
(Princeton, 1986).

[63] Scase, *New Anticlericalism*, p. x.

participating in the new anticlericalism, which she divides into issues of priestly power, poverty, charity, antireligious traditions, and clerical dominion and authority. She positions *Piers* in its contemporary context, embroiled in the spiritual, institutional, theological, social, and economic contestations of the Ricardian period, and she makes us readjust our reading of *Piers*. She indicates projects that are waiting to be done, the greatest desideratum being a comprehensive study of Wyclif, other desiderata being more appropriate for literary scholars and critics. Scase and her mentor Anne Hudson make a strong case for Ricardian studies, though that was not their conscious aim.

Hudson offers a broad account of the openly controversial character of the Ricardian era in *The Premature Reformation* that implies a rationale for focusing on the Ricardian as a period. Wyclif's public preaching, 1376–9, and the condemnation of his opinions by the Blackfriars Council, 1382, mark the opening of a period when contested ideas about clerical authority, church property, and use of the vernacular were riskily but openly in play. When parliament and king in 1401 enact *De heretico comburendo*, permitting the burning of heretics, the contest is decided for those in authority.[64] Radicals advocated spiritual and ecclesiastical changes that threatened the socio-economic status quo and by implication traditional political authority, changes too risky for Henry IV, whose claim to the crown was uneasy enough: repression of Wycliffite ideas virtually coincided with the end of Richard's reign; after Oldcastle's revolt in 1414, espousing Lollard ideas was treated as open sedition.[65] Wycliffite controversies generated texts, many of which, though not especially valuable as literary art, can, as Hudson broadly suggests and Scase demonstrates for *Piers*, affect our reading of Ricardian poems. Wycliffite texts might cast light on the opening of *Cleanness*, where the speaker addresses and strongly condemns filthy or sinful priests, perhaps implying a clerical audience. Was the *Pearl*-poet attached to a clerical court of some kind?

Paul Strohm's imaginative historical criticism brings his readers into the turbulence of Ricardian London with startling immediacy.

---

[64] *The Premature Reformation: Wycliffite Texts and Lollard History* (Oxford, 1988), 1, 15, 60–119, 390–411.

[65] Ibid. 115, 394. Hudson in effect distinguishes three periods in the early reception of Wycliffite ideas.

Rather than 'privileging the literary text as the center around which all other texts are statically arrayed', Strohm has made himself sufficiently the master of London history in the Ricardian era and its aftermath that he can offer a reconstruction of 'historical events... as part of a large and unruly matrix within which new texts are constantly produced and received'.[66] Like R. F. Green, Strohm has made himself at home with historical records and with historians as well as with rhetorical conventions and literary forms. Strohm innovatively brings his readers into collision with the language of Chaucer's poems, especially his infrequently analysed short poems, and the socio-political forces contained, however stressfully, within them.[67]

Where Hudson, Justice, Strohm, and Scase make history, using archives or little-known and often unedited texts to contextualize Ricardian poetry, Patterson is most interested in historiographical paradigms, both Chaucer's and ours, though Patterson does, of course, use the work of historians in developing interpretations of the Canterbury tales in *Chaucer and the Subject of History*. Patterson uses the problem of the subject to frame his major Chaucer essays, deploying them as ammunition in his battle with the Early Modern New Historicists and with the old New Critics and the old historicists, i.e. the exegetical critics, whom he identifies with D. W. Robertson, Jr. The Chaucer essays, learned, provocative, and sometimes persuasive as they are, are not my concern here. Rather, I am interested in Patterson's configuring of the history of twentieth-century Middle English literary criticism and also in his use of the medieval subject in history to quarrel with early modernists' marginalization of the medieval.

Patterson's essays on the state of medieval literary studies have grown out of his presentation at the centennial Modern Language Association convention, 1983, of exegetics and New Criticism as sibling rivals.[68] He further pursued the history of Middle English literary studies in the two learned and stimulating essays that open *Negotiating the Past* (1987). There he links exegetics with medieval studies; with Robertson's extreme political conservatism; with

---

[66] *Social Chaucer* (Cambridge, Mass., 1989), 8.
[67] Burrow, *Ricardian Poetry*, 43–4, is critical of the short poems, arguing that they are not suited to the loose-woven Ricardian style; Strohm does not directly address this problem.
[68] See *Negotiating the Past*, p. xiii.

responsibility for perpetuating a monolithic, serenely hierarchical, and idealized Middle Ages first dreamed by nineteenth-century conservatives; and links medieval studies with excessive emphasis on the special skills of the 'medieval clerisy', e.g. palaeography, philology. In 'The Claims of Humanism', Patterson treats rather gently the modernist ahistoricity of New Criticism, with its endless reworking of G. L. Kittredge's drama, and almost represses the tendency it shared with exegetical criticism to write 'unified'—now often called 'totalizing'—critical interpretations.[69] Patterson opposes the positivism he associates with medieval studies to the theorizing favoured by descendants of the New Critics, from deconstructionists to critical historicists, as if needing to reproduce the sibling rivalry of exegetics and New Critics. However impatient he may be with those who wish to recuperate how medieval folks could have understood, which need not be the limit of how we understand them, one might hope that his desire to engage history would lead to a more charitable attitude to projects differently conceived from those he would undertake.

In 'On the Margin' (1990) Patterson expresses harsher views of New Criticism for its alliance with modernism and of American New Historicism for its conservative drift. His animus derives from what William D. Paden calls 'his perception of a hegemonic Renaissance' that defines the Middle Ages as premodern, as Other, as—Patterson fears—irrelevant. In 'Scholars at a Perilous Ford', Paden regards both Patterson and Stephen Nichols as gloomy and

---

[69] Middleton shares some of Patterson's concerns; see n. 22 above. David Aers sets his critique of deconstruction applied to Chaucer within the frame of Patterson's essays; see 'Medievalists and Deconstruction: "An Exemplum"', in John Simons (ed.), *From Medieval to Medievalism* (New York, 1992), 24–40. For a restatement of Patterson's characterization of medieval English literary studies and an illuminating discussion of modernism, see Scanlon (Patterson's student), *Narrative, Authority, and Power*, esp. 3–9, 45–54. The exchanges between William McClellan and Lars Engle in *Exemplaria*, 1/2 (1989) are helpful in bringing into focus Kittredge's tremendous influence, especially on American critics; see Engle, 'Chaucer, Bakhtin, and Griselda', 429–59, and 'Bakhtin, Chaucer, and Anti-essentialist Humanism', 489–97; and McClellan, 'Bakhtin's Theory of Dialogic Discourse, Medieval Rhetorical Theory, and the Multi-Voiced Structure of the *Clerk's Tale*', 461–88, and 'Lars Engle—"Chaucer, Bakhtin, and Griselda": A Response', 499–506. Engle suggests a correspondence between Derek Brewer's Gothic Chaucer and Bakhtinian dialogism and describes Kittredge as 'a pioneer of a kind of limited dialogic in interpretation' (p. 490).

suspects them of being overwrought, 'talking [more] of academic politics' than of the state of medieval studies.[70] Paden's optimism and tolerant acceptance of 'Otherness' are attractive, but Patterson does have a point: it is quite remarkable, if one reads books like Charles Taylor's *Sources of the Self* or Lawrence Stone's books on the family and divorce, how thin their knowledge of the Middle Ages seems to be.[71] They are justified, one might argue, by Jacob Burckhardt's view of Renaissance individuality, to whom the New Historicists owe a huge and, as one of my Renaissance colleagues remarks, a largely unacknowledged debt; Patterson exposes that debt.

Given the American university system that sets teachers competing with one another for students in the cafeteria of higher education, a system where departments of literature and history are reluctant to require much or any work in early periods and where low enrolments justify reallocation of resources (circumstances in the UK are better but bear some resemblance to the USA as do Australian and Canadian circumstances), Patterson's alarm for medieval literature, and even medieval studies, is not altogether beside the point and not unrelated to Burrow's motivation in writing *Ricardian Poetry*. Patterson's stridency and antagonism toward perceived enemies to the liberal humanism he espouses and his irritation with the disciplines necessary for many kinds of medieval scholarship put off even his potential allies. He admits that feminists are already successfully engaged in talking beyond the boundaries of medieval studies; correspondingly, the issue of *Speculum* devoted to gender studies conveys a more positive attitude to the future than does the issue on the new medievalism to which Patterson and Nichols contributed.[72] The

---

[70] William D. Paden, 'Scholars at a Perilous Ford' in William D. Paden (ed.), *The Future of the Middle Ages: Medieval Literature in the 1990s* (Gainesville, Fla., 1994), 3–31 (pp. 22, 24).

[71] C. Taylor, *Sources of the Self: The Making of Modern Identity* (Cambridge, Mass., 1989); L. Stone, *Road to Divorce: England 1530–1987* (Oxford, 1990). By contrast, Louis Dupré, *Passage to Modernity: An Essay in the Hermeneutics of Nature and Culture* (New Haven, 1993), is well informed about the Middle Ages.

[72] *Speculum*, 68/2 (1993), 305–471, a special issue entitled 'Studying Medieval Women: Sex, Gender, Feminism', ed. Nancy F. Partner; and *Speculum*, 65/1 (1990), 1–108, a special issue entitled 'The New Philology', ed. Stephen G. Nichols, including Patterson's 'On the Margin'. Dismayed by hostile responses, Nichols responds in 'Philology and its Discontents', in Paden (ed.), *The Future of the Middle Ages*, 113–41. See also the related volume, concerned with Romance languages,

subject in history, the focus of Patterson's recent study, answers to his need to talk to Renaissance—or early modern—scholars. If their agenda sets his, the subject is nevertheless engaging, thorny, and broadly attractive.

Patterson's several general essays have inspired David Aers to reformulate the quarrel with early modernists, turning it into an invitation to Ricardian studies and into a challenge to find ways to honour the role of Christianity in the lives of late medieval people. In 'A Whisper in the Ear of the Early Modernists' Aers echoes Patterson's attack on idealizing exegetical critics for providing New Historicists with a conventional view of the Middle Ages as a homogeneous, stable, hierarchical culture which did not produce individual selves or consciousnesses.[73] This view of the Middle Ages, Aers explains, whether celebrated or deplored, did not originate with the nostalgia of exegetical critics[74] but with the antagonism of Renaissance humanists. Major western thinkers have concurred with this view, e.g. Burckhardt, Marx, Weber, and Foucault, all of whom use the Middle Ages as an idealized 'Other', describing it as a culture lacking those conditions that would produce individual subjectivity or alienated consciousness. For example, Marx and Weber were mainly interested in using the Middle Ages to critique capitalist, industrial society. By demonstrating through late medieval penitential practices that late medieval people experienced and represented interiority, or self-consciousness, long before *Hamlet*, Aers believes that he can thwart the early modernist plot to marginalize the medieval, challenge the nostalgia of Marxist theory, and thus raise large and urgent issues about history. Long sympathetically engaged with Marxism, Aers has a serious commitment to history and a generous respect for the skills of the medieval clerisy and for good scholarship with perspectives different from his own. He asks a

edited by Marina S. Brownlee, Kevin Brownlee, and Stephen G. Nichols, *The New Medievalism* (Baltimore, 1991).

[73] 'A Whisper in the Ear of Early Modernists; or, Reflections on Literary Critics Writing the "History of the Subject"', in Aers (ed.), *Culture and History 1350–1600*, 177–202.

[74] See ibid. 199 n. 15 (for p. 181), where Aers suggests that critics who deny subjectivity to Criseyde exemplify the kind of 'unified medieval world' he and Patterson hold the exegetical critics responsible for. In listing such critics, Aers includes several who would not have associated themselves with exegetics, e.g. A. David, R. O. Payne, and Robert Jordan.

splendid series of questions at the end of 'A Whisper', concluding that 'we need to suspend the master narrative of Dark Ages to Renaissance or of feudalism to capitalism'. And then he asks, 'What if subjectivity is more bound into a microhistory that is less linear than the master narrative determining the story told by Burckhardt...and...suggested...by Foucault? What if, in England, there was a greater preoccupation with "interiority", and with the divided self in the 1380s than in 1415–20? If this turned out to be so, why?'[75] Aers proposes, I take it, to engage in Ricardian studies, in microhistory, using medieval penitential practice as the site for testing several common features of master narratives by which western intellectuals have understood past and present in the last 100 or 200 years. Such a microhistory centred on the human subject takes us back to Ricardian poetry and to Burrow's discussion of the Ricardian image of man—with a difference.

Burrow aimed at a more modest goal and conceived the project in more distinctly literary terms than Patterson or Aers. And yet the position Burrow took in *Ricardian Poetry* resembles theirs. Burrow's characterization of the mode of Ricardian narrative as literal and its intention as exemplary was greeted on both sides of the Atlantic as a welcome challenge to exegetical criticism. Unacknowledged then was Burrow's implicit challenge, in the use of the term 'exemplary', to the strictures of New Critical formalism, for the exemplary has designs on the audience, suggesting authorial intention, and solicits responses, suggesting not fixed but varying interpretations, conditioned by a broad range of social factors. The exemplary thus requires a more fully realized rhetoric than New Criticism permitted, as Scanlon's work on the exemplum shows.

The translation of Ricardian poetry into Ricardian studies may not seem wholly desirable to Burrow, or indeed to other contributors to this volume, though to me it has always seemed inevitable and invigorating. Burrow invited us to *focus attention* on the Ricardian poets as a group and implied that we might extend our gaze beyond the major poets to test and where necessary recast his observations. Indeed, we must look before, after, and all around the Ricardians *and* at ourselves and our context. We need manuscript studies, textual scholarship, linguistic studies, formal

[75] Ibid. 197.

analysis of rhetoric and narrative, and cultural criticism. We need scholars and critics oriented to the articulation of medieval differences and others oriented to the contemporaneity of the medieval, and we need to maintain a conversation between the two. 'The lyf so short, the craft so long to lerne' makes it impossible for any critic or scholar to master all texts, all discourses, all practices. At least occasionally convening medievalists concerned with Ricardian England under the rubric of 'Ricardian Studies' might produce a stimulating and informative conversation across the disciplines and across divides within disciplines. Such a conversation needs to be respectful of the many different kinds of projects necessary if we are to accomplish something like Aers's goal of using microlevel Ricardian studies to challenge macrolevel cultural interpretation.

Keeping Ricardian poetry, not just Chaucer's poetry, on the reading lists of students in the twenty-first century was already an implicit goal of Burrow's *Ricardian Poetry*. Broadening Burrow's perspective to Ricardian studies, embracing the issues he addressed, and expanding beyond them gives us the flexibility to keep the aesthetic, rhetorical, political, ethical, spiritual, and intellectual dimensions of Ricardian writing alive in and to the culture we inhabit.

J. A. Burrow: A Bibliography

C. J. Burrow

1957

'Keats and Edward Thomas', *Essays in Criticism*, 7: 404–15.
'Irony in the *Merchant's Tale*', *Anglia*, 75: 199–208; repr. in Burrow, *Essays in Medieval Literature*, 49–59.
'The Audience of *Piers Plowman*', *Anglia*, 75: 373–84; repr. and rev. in Burrow, *Essays on Medieval Literature*, 102–16.

1959

'An Approach to the *Dream of the Rood*', *Neophilologus*, 43: 123–33; repr. in Martin Stevens and Jerome Mandel (eds.), *Old English Literature: Twenty-Two Analytical Essays* (Lincoln, Nebr., 1968), 253–67.
'The Two Confession Scenes in *Sir Gawain and the Green Knight*', MP 57: 73–9; repr. in Robert J. Blanch (ed.), *'Sir Gawain and the Green Knight' and 'Pearl': Critical Essays* (Bloomington, Ind., 1966), 123–34.

1961

'"A Maner Latyn Corrupt"', *MÆ* 30: 33–7.

1964

'*Cupiditas* in *Sir Gawain and the Green Knight*', RES NS 15: 56; repr. in D. R. Howard (ed.), *Critical Studies of 'Sir Gawain and the Green Knight'* (Notre Dame, Ind., 1968), 325–6.

1965

A Reading of 'Sir Gawain and the Green Knight' (London; pbk., 1977).
'The Action of Langland's Second Vision', *Essays in Criticism*, 15: 247–68; repr. in R. J. Blanch (ed.), *Style and Symbolism in 'Piers Plowman': A Modern Critical Anthology* (Knoxville, Tenn., 1969), 209–27; also in Burrow, *Essays on Medieval Literature*, 79–101.

'*The Wanderer*: Lines 73–87', *N&Q* 210, NS 12: 166–8.

1968

'"Listeth, Lordes": *Sir Thopas*, 712 and 833', *N&Q* 213, NS 15: 326–7; repr. in Burrow, *Essays in Medieval Literature*, 66–9.

1969

(Ed.), *Geoffrey Chaucer: A Critical Anthology*, Penguin Critical Anthologies (Harmondsworth; 2nd edn., 1982).

'Words, Works and Will: Theme and Structure in *Piers Plowman*', in S. S. Hussey (ed.), '*Piers Plowman*': *Critical Approaches* (London), 111–24.

'"Worly under Wede" in *Sir Thopas*', *ChauR* 3: 170–3; repr. in Burrow, *Essays on Medieval Literature*, 74–8.

1971

Ricardian Poetry: Chaucer, Gower, Langland and the 'Gawain' Poet (London and New Haven; repr. Harmondsworth, 1992).

'*Sir Thopas*: An Agony in Three Fits', *RES* NS 22: 54–8; repr. in Burrow, *Essays on Medieval Literature*, 61–5.

'Chaucer, *c*.1343–1400', in A. E. Dyson (ed.), *English Poetry: Select Bibliographical Guides* (London and New York), 1–14.

1972

(Ed.), *Sir Gawain and the Green Knight* (Harmondsworth; repr. New Haven, 1982).

'Two Notes on *Sir Gawain and the Green Knight*', *N&Q* 217, NS 19: 43–5.

1973

'Bards, Minstrels and Men of Letters', in David Daiches and Anthony Thorlby (eds.), *Literature and Western Civilization: The Medieval World* (London), 347–70.

1975

'Henryson: *The Preaching of the Swallow*', *Essays in Criticism*, 25: 25–37, repr. in Burrow, *Essays on Medieval Literature*, 148–60.

1977

(Ed.), *English Verse 1300–1500*, Longman Annotated Anthologies of English Verse 1 (London).
'Fantasy and Language in *The Cloud of Unknowing*', *Essays in Criticism*, 27: 283–98; repr. in Burrow, *Essays on Medieval Literature*, 132–47.

1978

'A Further Note on Dunbar', *Forum for Modern Language Studies*, 14: 85–6.

1979

'Poems without Contexts: The Rawlinson Lyrics', *Essays in Criticism*, 29: 6–32; repr. in Burrow, *Essays on Medieval Literature*, 1–26.
'"Young Saint, Old Devil": Reflections on a Medieval Proverb', *RES* NS 30: 385–96; repr. in Burrow, *Essays on Medieval Literature*, 177–91.
'The Alterity of Medieval Literature', *New Literary History*, 10: 385–90.

1980

'Laȝamon's *Brut* 10,642: "Wleoteð "', *N&Q* 225, NS 27: 2–3.

1981

'Langland *Nel Mezzo del Cammin*', in P. L. Heyworth (ed.), *Medieval Studies for J. A. W. Bennett, Ætatis Suæ LXX* (Oxford), 21–41.
'The Poet as Petitioner', *SAC* 3: 61–75; repr. in Burrow, *Essays in Medieval Literature*, 161–76.

1982

Medieval Writers and their Work: Middle English Literature and its Background 1100–1500 (Oxford).
'*Sir Gawain and the Green Knight*', in Boris Ford (ed.), *The New Pelican Guide to English Literature*, i: *Medieval Literature*, part 1: *Chaucer and the Alliterative Tradition* (Harmondsworth), 208–23.
'Autobiographical Poetry in the Middle Ages: The Case of Thomas Hoccleve', *PBA* 68: 389–412; repr. in J. A. Burrow (ed.), *Middle English Literature: British Academy Gollancz Lectures* (Oxford, 1989), 223–46.

1983

'*Sir Thopas* in the Sixteenth Century', in Douglas Gray and E. G. Stanley
(eds.), *Middle English Studies Presented to Norman Davis in Honour of
his Seventieth Birthday* (Oxford), 69–91.
'The Portrayal of Amans in *Confessio Amantis*', in A. J. Minnis (ed.),
Gower's 'Confessio Amantis': Responses and Reassessments (Cam-
bridge), 5–24.
Introd. to V. J. Scattergood and J. W. Sherborne (eds.), *English Court
Culture in the Later Middle Ages* (London), pp. ix–x.

1984

Essays on Medieval Literature (Oxford).
'Chaucer's *Knight's Tale* and the Three Ages of Man', in *Essays on
Medieval Literature*, 27–48; repr. in Piero Boitani and Anna Torti
(eds.), *Medieval and Pseudo-Medieval Literature: The J. A. W. Bennett
Memorial Lectures, Perugia, 1982–3* (Tübingen and Cambridge), 91–
108.
'The Title "Sir"', in Burrow, *Essays on Medieval Literature*, 69–74.
'Honour and Shame in *Sir Gawain and the Green Knight*', in Burrow,
Essays on Medieval Literature, 117–31.
'Allegory: The Literal Level', in Burrow, *Essays on Medieval Literature*,
192–212.
'Hoccleve's *Series*: Experience and Books', in R. F. Yeager (ed.), *Fifteenth-
Century Studies: Recent Essays* (Hamden), 259–73.
'Chaucer's *Sir Thopas* and *La Prise de Nuevile*', in Claude Rawson (ed.),
English Satire and the Satiric Tradition (Oxford), 44–55; also *Yearbook
of English Studies*, 14: 44–55.

1986

The Ages of Man: A Study in Medieval Writing and Thought (Oxford;
pbk., 1988).
'The Canterbury Tales I: Romance', in Piero Boitani and Jill Mann (eds.),
The Cambridge Chaucer Companion (Cambridge), 109–24.
'Chaucer's Canterbury Pilgrimage', the F. W. Bateson Memorial Lecture,
Essays in Criticism, 36: 97–119.

1987

'Old and Middle English (*c*.700–1485)', in Pat Rogers (ed.), *The Oxford
Illustrated History of English Literature* (Oxford; pbk., 1990), 1–58.

'*The Avowing of King Arthur*', in Myra Stokes and T. L. Burton (eds.), *Medieval Literature and Antiquities: Essays in Honour of Basil Cottle* (Cambridge), 99–109.

Annotations to *Sir Thopas*, in Larry D. Benson (ed.), *The Riverside Chaucer*, 3rd edn. (New York), 917–23.

1988

'The Poet and the Book', in P. Boitani and A. Torti (eds.), *Genres, Themes, and Images in English Literature from the Fourteenth to the Fifteenth Century: The J. A. W. Bennett Memorial Lectures, Perugia, 1986* (Tübingen), 230–45.

'Problems in Punctuation: *Sir Gawain and the Green Knight*, Lines 1–7', in D. M. Reeks (ed.), *Sentences: Essays Presented to Alan Ward on the Occasion of his Retirement from Wadham College, Oxford* (Southampton), 75–88.

1989

Ed. and introd. to *Middle English Literature: British Academy Gollancz Lectures* (Oxford).

'Two Notes on the Middle English *Patience*, Lines 56 and 329', *N&Q* 234, NS 36: 300–3.

'A Note on *The Owl and the Nightingale*, Line 376', *N&Q* 234, NS 36: 427.

1990

'The Sinking Island and the Dying Author: R. W. Chambers Fifty Years On', *Essays in Criticism*, 40: 1–23.

'Hoccleve and Chaucer', in Ruth Morse and Barry Windeatt (eds.), *Chaucer Traditions: Studies in Honour of Derek Brewer* (Cambridge), 54–61.

'Chaucer, Geoffrey', in A. C. Hamilton (ed.), *The Spenser Encyclopaedia* (Toronto, Buffalo, and London), 144–8.

'*Piers Plowman* C. V. 86–7', *N&Q* 235, NS 37: 10–11.

'Reason's Horse', *YLS* 4: 139–44.

'The Shape of the Vernon Refrain Lyrics', in Derek Pearsall (ed.), *Studies in the Vernon Manuscript* (Cambridge), 187–99.

1991

The Problem of Autobiography in Langland's 'Piers Plowman', University of Nottingham Byron Foundation Lecture for 1991 (Nottingham).

'Poems without Endings', *SAC* 13: 17–37.

'The Future of Old English: The case for its Continuing Importance', *Times Literary Supplement* 4613 (30 Aug. 1991), 11–12.

1992

(Ed., with Thorlac Turville-Petre), *A Book of Middle English* (Oxford; 2nd edn. 1996).

'Old and Middle English (*c.*700–1485)', in Pat Rogers (ed.), *An Outline of English Literature* (Oxford), 1–57.

'The Griffin's Egg: Gower's *Confessio Amantis* I 2545', in Toshiyuki Takamiya and Richard Beadle (eds.), *Chaucer to Shakespeare: Essays in Honour of Shinsuke Ando* (Cambridge), 81–5.

1993

Langland's Fictions (Oxford).

Thinking in Poetry: Three Medieval Examples, the William Matthews Lectures 1993, delivered at Birkbeck College, London, 17 and 18 May 1993 (London).

'*Saint Erkenwald*, Line 1: "At London in Englond"', *N&Q* 238, NS 40: 22–3.

1994

Thomas Hoccleve, Authors of the Middle Ages 4: English Writers of the Late Middle Ages (Aldershot).

'The Uses of Incognito: *Ipomadon A*', in Carol M. Meale (ed.), *Readings in Medieval English Romance* (Cambridge), 25–34.

1995

'Elvish Chaucer', in M. Teresa Tavormina and R. F. Yeager (eds.), *The Endless Knot: Essays on Old and Middle English in Honor of Marie Borroff* (Cambridge), 105–111.

'Thomas Hoccleve: Some Redatings', *RES* NS 46: 366–72.

1997

'Redundancy in Alliterative Verse: *St Erkenwald*', in o.s. Pickering (ed.), *Individuality and Achievement in Middle English Poetry* (Cambridge), 119–28.

Index